Beginning POJOs

From Novice to Professional

Brian Sam-Bodden

David Chan

Apress®

Beginning POJOs: From Novice to Professional

Copyright © 2006 by Brian Sam-Bodden

ISBN-13 (pbk): 978-159059-596-1

ISBN-10 (pbk): 1-59059-596-3

Printed and bound in the United States of America 9 8 7 6 5 4 3 2 1

Lead Editor: Steve Anglin
Technical Reviewer: Dilip Thomas
Editorial Board: Steve Anglin, Dan Appleman, Ewan Buckingham, Gary Cornell, Jason Gilmore, Jonathan Hassell, James Huddleston, Chris Mills, Matthew Moodie, Dominic Shakeshaft, Jim Sumser, Matt Wade
Project Manager: Kylie Johnston
Copy Edit Manager: Nicole LeClerc
Copy Editor: Hastings Hart
Assistant Production Director: Kari Brooks-Copony
Production Editor: Katie Stence
Compositor: Susan Glinert
Proofreader: Lori Bring
Indexer: Michael Brinkman
Artist: April Milne
Cover Designer: Kurt Krames
Manufacturing Director: Tom Debolski

Distributed to the book trade worldwide by Springer-Verlag New York, Inc., 233 Spring Street, 6th Floor, New York, NY 10013. Phone 1-800-SPRINGER, fax 201-348-4505, e-mail orders-ny@springer-sbm.com, or visit www.springeronline.com.

For information on translations, please contact Apress directly at 2560 Ninth Street, Suite 219, Berkeley, CA 94710. Phone 510-549-5930, fax 510-549-5939, e-mail info@apress.com, or visit www.apress.com.

The source code for this book is available to readers at www.apress.com in the Source Code section.

I dedicate this book to my wife Anne for her unwavering love and support and to my two-year-old son Michael for putting a smile on my face every time I felt like quitting.

Contents at a Glance

Contents

About the Author

BRIAN SAM-BODDEN has spent over ten years working with object technologies, with an emphasis on the Java platform. He holds dual bachelor degrees from Ohio Wesleyan University in computer science and physics and is the president and chief software architect for Integrallis Software (www.integrallis.com), where he focuses on object modeling and Java, particularly Java EE. He has worked as an architect, developer, mentor, trainer, and code monkey for several Fortune 500 companies in various industries including taxation, insurance, retail sciences, telecommunications, banking, finance, distribution and scientific data management. As an independent consultant, he has promoted the use of open source in the industry by educating his clients on the cost benefits and productivity gains they can achieve. He is a frequent speaker at user groups at both national and international conferences. He is a Sun Certified Java Programmer, Developer, and Enterprise Architect. Brian also co-authored the Apress Java title *Enterprise Java Development on a Budget: Leveraging Java Open Source Technologies* (2004). Aside from spending time with his wife and son, Brian spends most of his time writing code or on the mat practicing Brazilian jiujitsu.

Acknowledgments

Regardless of how many names appear on the cover, writing a book is a team effort. First of all I would like to extend my gratitude to my editor Steve Anglin for pushing me to write and finish the work you're holding. Along with Steve, I would like to send a million thanks to the tireless team at Apress, including project manager Kylie Johnston, production editor Katie Stence, copy editor Hastings Hart, and fellow author and technical reviewer Dilip Thomas.

I'd also like to thank Joseph Nusairat for his contributions to the Tapestry chapter and for helping me develop the companion application to the book.

I'd like to thank my wife for proofreading the entire manuscript and not killing me during the long process of writing this book.

As with my first book, I've benefited from the work of many in the open source community. Hopefully by showcasing their works in this book I can begin to repay the enormous contributions that they have made.

Finally, I want to thank you, the reader, for taking the time to explore what this book has to offer.

Introduction

Java's history is a thorny and convoluted one. From its origins at Sun, better known for its hardware than its software, Java was born as a stealth project targeting consumer devices. Along came the Web, and Java provided the only way to do anything remotely close to rich animation. Applets running on the HotJava Browser showcasing a dancing Duke was my "oh, now that's cool" moment of 1995. So we set out to write enormously large applets that were slow to run and then the browser wars began and you could only guess whether it was going to run or your user would see a big gray box on their browsers. Today applets still have their niche, mostly in the least-expected places, like the computer in an oil lube bay or a conveyor-controlling application in a distribution center.

But Java was still the new kid on the block. In the late '90s, Web applications were being built on the CGI platform and a trove of scripting languages. At that point Java came into its own with the servlet API and what was viewed as the golden hammer of its time, the EJB specification. At that point I was already tainted by the complexity of the Distributed Component Object Model (DCOM) and Common Object Request Broker Architecture (CORBA), so to paraphrase Bruce Tate, I ate the elephant and it was good! Well, guess what? By the time we entered the 21st century the elephant already was the animal of choice in large corporate IT departments, it started to face fierce competition in the wild. It had to run on Pearls, fight Pythons and lately tried to avoid the red light at the end of the tunnel (is that a Ruby on Rails?).

Fortunately for us the elephant went on a diet by staying away from the Sun ;-). Today we can build Java applications with a similar level of agility as that showcased by the scripting language camps. POJOs are not a new technology or technique but are a "going back to the basis" philosophy in which we concentrate more on the business functionality and less on the plumbing required to build robust applications. This movement to simplify and rethink our development practices has been driven primarily by the open source community, which has produced a variety of agile, lightweight frameworks. Without open source, Java would be the beast that you use only at work because your boss tells you it's your only choice. In this book you'll learn about the lightweight frameworks and tools that I use in my day-to-day work and that I only not need but enjoy using.

Who This Book Is For

This book targets beginning to intermediate Java developers looking to build enterprise Web applications with the latest offerings from the open source Java community. In this book you'll explore different approaches to building a Java Web application using a step-by-step approach.

How This Book Is Structured

The chapters in this book are centered on the concept of an application tier and the tools or frameworks used to build that tier. You can read each chapter independently of the others, since I provide a simple introductory example in most chapters, which is followed by a more involved use of the tool in the context of the example application used throughout the book.

- **Chapter 1, Introduction:** This chapter will set the stage for the application that we will build and rebuild during the course of the book. You'll learn some of the design and architecture decisions that culminated in the creation of the sample application.

- **Chapter 2, Eclipse:** This chapter introduces my development environment of choice, the Eclipse IDE, and a few plug-ins that will make your development easier and more enjoyable.

- **Chapter 3, Building with Ant:** This chapter sets out to create a solid Ant-based build system that will be used in the rest of the book. This chapter offers "best practices" and a collection of Ant-based tools that can improve your builds.

- **Chapter 4, Object Relational Mapping with Hibernate:** This chapter gives you an introduction to the sometimes frustrating art of mapping objects to relational databases. You'll learn how to use Hibernate, the most popular and powerful ORM tool.

- **Chapter 5, Business Services with JBoss:** This chapter sets out to build the business tier of the example application using EJB3 technologies on the JBoss application server. This chapter sets the stage for subsequent chapters by showing alternative ways to tackle different tiers of the application.

- **Chapter 6, The Spring Framework:** This chapter showcases the Spring Framework agile approach by building the same set of services built in Chapter 5 using Spring Bean Services.

- **Chapter 7, Tapestry:** This chapter shows the hidden gem of the Java Web application frameworks. You'll use Tapestry to build the user interface of the sample application.

- **Chapter 8, Testing:** This chapter offers a concise and pragmatic look at testing Java EE applications by revisiting JUnit and introducing TestNG, DbUnit, and EasyMock.

- **Chapter 9, Continuous Integration:** This chapter delves into the practice of Continuous Integration using the CruiseControl build scheduler.

- **Chapter 10, Additional Topics:** This chapter serves as an introduction of some of the tools that complete the features of a real-world application, such as AOP with AspectJ and adding RSS feeds with the Informa library.

Prerequisites

The code in this book uses Java 5 features such as annotations and some of the newer syntax and constructs.

Downloading the Code

The code for the book's application has been released as an open source project under the Java.net community. You can download prepackaged EAR and WAR files, or you can use CVS to obtain the source and build the application on your own machine. There are also CVS source snapshots in ZIP form available from the project site and the Apress website.

The project website is located at http://techconf.dev.java.net, and the book website is hosted under the Integrallis website at www.integrallis.com.

Contacting the Author

I encourage you to contact me at bsbodden@integrallis.com. To discuss the application, use the application discussion forum at http://techconf.dev.java.net.

CHAPTER 1

Introduction

Whether you are new to the Java Platform, Enterprise Edition (Java EE) or have been at it for a few years now, your experience may be like mine— working with the platform with just what the specifications provide will quickly drive you insane! The Java EE specification did not foresee that with the power that it was unleashing unto developers it was also adding a plethora of problems. These problems are more related to the process of designing, building, and maintaining a distributed application than with the actual APIs. That's where open source comes into play. The projects showcased in this book have been created to ease, support, speed up, and enhance the building of Java EE applications.

This book is primarily about tapping into the large set of open source resources available to you, the developer. Particularly when it comes to the Java EE platform, open source is leading the pack and going beyond the confines of the specifications by providing technical innovations not seen in commercial products, as well as a solid and stable infrastructure for enterprise-level applications. In recent years parts of the Java EE specification have come under fire from many industry experts, and this has resulted in the emergence of many lightweight frameworks and containers as well as an abundance of supporting tools that fill in the gaps in the specifications. The question that most developers are stuck with nowadays is whether they need a Java EE application server altogether. The reality is that most of the lightweight frameworks available do not attempt to replace every function that an application server provides, but they provide alternative ways to tap into the application server resources. Most experts complain about applications using an Enterprise JavaBeans (EJB) container when they simply need a Web container, and I fully agree with them on this point, until the EJB3 specification has been finalized. As you'll see in Chapter 5, the EJB3 specification will enable the building of truly POJO-based distributed, multitier applications that can easily grow based on demand.

We will also explore the world of lightweight frameworks, and compare and contrast how the different approaches can fit different application needs and different development teams.

The Java EE Market

To fully understand some of the forces behind the changes in the Java EE world, a quick look at the market evolution is needed. The Java EE market has evolved swiftly, first by going through a phase of consolidation and now by entering a phase of commoditization. This second phase has been driven largely by the fact that in order to show value, application server vendors can no longer rely on their core application server. This has created a market of value-added offerings, particularly in the area of development tools and development productivity. Many of the open source tools and frameworks showcased in this book are in this category.

Open source is also changing the way programming is being studied in universities around the world; new generations of programmers leaving academia and entering the workplace have either used or contributed to open source. Students nowadays can learn by examining enterprise-level software that displays contributions from many sources from around the world.

At corporate IT departments worldwide, programmers are rallying behind open source projects like Ant, JUnit, Apache Tomcat, Spring Framework, and JBoss. The battle for the acceptance of open source has been largely fought at the level of the programmer and middle management. However, upper management, given the recent impact of Linux on corporations, is beginning to see the many advantages of open source, especially in the area of enterprise Java. Organizations seeking to reduce software development expenses have found that open source software (OSS) provides a lower cost of ownership when compared to commercial offerings, primarily because open source software is free, both in price and restrictions.

One of the reasons the open source community is so prolific is because all but the most trivial software is difficult and expensive to produce, and the canned solutions provided by commercial products often fail to provide a complete solution. The complexity of building software systems is a direct consequence of the nature of real-world business problems, which are driven by changing requirements, rapidly evolving technologies, multiple data sources, service-level agreements, interoperability, time to market, return on investment, and many other factors. The inability to cope with and balance all these forces results in projects that go over budget, are late, and in most cases fail to meet functionality expectations. These projects quickly spiral out of control due to their inability to cope with complexity and change.

Even if such systems deliver in a specific area of business functionality, their overall business value is diminished by their maintenance costs. These horror stories aren't rare; on the contrary, they're the norm. One survey found that 84 percent[1] of all enterprise software systems are considered failures. This failure rate is a characteristic signature of the "software crisis" that's plaguing the industry. Projects fail due to a combination of poor engineering and management choices. A 2002 study by the Carnegie Mellon Software Engineering Institute (SEI) lists the following top 10 reasons why software projects fail:

- Inexperienced staff

- Lack of team cohesion and experience

- Lack of emphasis in using modern software-engineering practices

- Lack of a process or incorrect emphasis in the application of a process

- Inadequate project management methodology

- Unclear, misunderstood, and undiscovered requirements

- Size (the larger the projects the more likely they are to fail)

- Lack of planning and estimating

- System-specific and technology-related issues being considered too late in the process

- New technologies and unforeseen problems

---

1. According to a Standish Group survey, which studied about 8,000 software projects in the US in 1995.

The IT industry has championed several approaches for dealing with the inherent complexity of designing, building, and maintaining software-intensive enterprise systems. Object-oriented, component-based, distributed systems represent state-of-the-art, enterprise-level systems technology. This book deals with some of the issues of building enterprise applications at a practical level when the "silver bullet" that has been handed to the information technologist is Java, specifically Java EE. Java EE is promising, especially for the inexperienced technologist because it makes a perfect technological silver bullet. The real-world experiences are far from software utopia, as a recent study by the Seybold Group suggests that there is a gap between management's expectations of Java EE and the achieved results. One of the reasons for this is the lack of tools that cover the many aspects of Java EE development. It is in this area that open source enterprise Java tools and frameworks are emerging to help bridge the gap.

Learning how to build enterprise applications with a combination of open source frameworks and tools provides a low-cost, low-risk, ideal prototyping environment in which to master distributed computing technologies. Open source lowers the entry barrier into the Java and Java EE worlds by providing choices besides the traditional proprietary offerings.

The rest of this chapter introduces a real-world example that puts the application of Java EE technologies into clearer perspective. It introduces a realistic business problem to be used as the backdrop for the learning process of designing, building, and deploying an enterprise Java system using open source technologies. We will start with the requirements which will set the stage for design, architectural, and implementation approaches explored in the rest of the book.

Case Study: The TechConf Website

The TechConf website case study presented in this chapter is a technology-conference management system encompassing a collection of systems and utilities used to advertise, prepare, and support one or more technology conferences. A technology conference is an event that spans a predetermined period of time and consists of one or more sessions (presentations, keynotes, and so on).

As a frequent speaker and attendee of technology conferences, I thought the domain was well-suited for the purposes of this book. The main stakeholders, that is, the people who have a vested interest in the system, are technologists, just like you and me, which makes it easier to relate to the needs of the user, and consequently, make the gathering of requirements, analysis, and design processes clearer.

Technically, a technology conference presents some unique challenges in the fields of distributed computing and enterprise development due to the dynamic nature of the information requirements and the logistics involved in running such an event.

If you are like me and most other programmers, you'll want to jump right into the code, and you might think that the sooner you start coding the sooner you'll finish your project. Well, for all but the most trivial of applications this is not true; a certain amount of planning has to happen before you write a single line of code. Feel free to prototype to your heart's content, but without design, a stable, correct and maintainable solution is rarely achieved. So bear with me for the next few pages. They might help you in your next project.

Defining the Stakeholders

To understand the dynamics of the system, it's important to determine who the stakeholders are and how their individual information needs to change over time. The main stakeholders to be considered in the context of a technology conference are as follows:

- **Attendees:** individuals attending the conference
- **Presenters:** individuals presenting one or more sessions at a conference
- **Sponsors:** organizations sponsoring and promoting the conference
- **Administrators:** the person or persons organizing and running the conference

To create a clear picture of the changing needs of the stakeholders, it's useful to view the conference as three separate periods of time: the preconference, the conference, and the post-conference periods. After all, event management is all about timelines. Figure 1-1 illustrates the three stages of the conference.

Preconference

During the preconference period, data is collected, evaluated, and created. Collected data includes documents such as calls for papers, abstracts, and outlines for the different presentations. From the collected documents, content must be created and also maintained as the source documents change. Aside from the document management needs, facilities must be provided for attendees to register and manage the schedule of events they plan to attend. At this time it's also crucial to provide information in a timely manner to make the process of registering and getting to the conference easier. Among the experience-enhancing utilities are items that allow you to obtain driving directions or information about special conference rates for travel and hotel accommodations.

Conference

The information needs at conference time are crucial to the success of the conference. Satisfied attendees are more likely to return the following year. Being able to cut through the noise, pinpoint areas of interest, and choose sessions to attend are factors of great importance to improving an attendee's experience. Providing interactivity and constant feedback ensures that attendees are always in tune with the heartbeat of the conference. At the beginning of the conference, attendees need to be checked in and given conference badges. Changes or updates to any sessions or presentations need to be communicated effectively in order for attendees to manage their schedules.

Postconference

Once the conference has closed its doors, a large amount of work remains to be performed. Attendees are now alumni, and as such they're a prime target audience for future conferences. Providing a sense of continuity is important to alumni and future attendees of a technology conference. There should be a bridge from the topics and content of previous conferences to ongoing and future conferences.

In the realm of document management, these requirements translate to the management of the transition of dynamic documents into static documents or archives. The numerous documents such as presentation slides, notes, follow-up discussions, and supporting materials related to different presentations or sessions must now be made available to the conference alumni and possibly to the general public. For the organizers of the conference, information such as the number of attendees, the popularity of topics and other statistical information is a crucial business indicator that will determine the future changes and enhancements made to the conference.

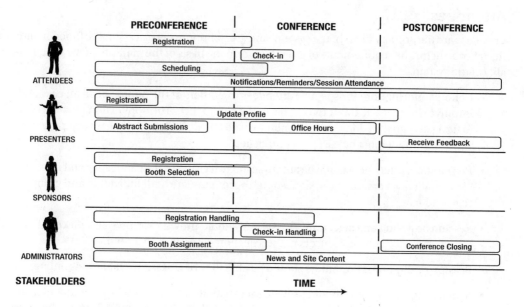

Figure 1-1. *Stakeholders' requirements timeline*

The Business Problem

To manage the information needs of a technology conference, a software system is needed that will provide an interactive information channel that manages the needs of the different stakeholders. There is a business drive mandating the creation of the systems to serve as the basis for a new line of products tailored to the organization, execution, and maintenance of technology conferences. These products are to be sold as a collection of components or subsystems that can be adapted to the particular needs of a customer.

The separation of roles and functionality needs to be clear in order to have a system that can be easily customized and enhanced. It's important for the system to account for the fact that attendees and presenters are geographically dispersed. There should be no need (or as little need as possible) for users to install or configure any software.

General Application Requirements

This section outlines the general business requirements that the system must meet. Based on the general software distribution and configuration requirements, the primary medium chosen for the application is the Internet, in particular the Web. The Web provides the advantage of nearly zero cost for distribution and configuration. As the design process gets under way, refinements based on real-world constraints will be factored in. The following requirements have been organized by stakeholders to facilitate the separation of functionality at the design stages.

Attendees

Attendees are the primary focus of the system, and greater priority is placed on the functionality that affects them. The requirements of attendees form the basis of the majority of the functionality of the system.

- **General information:** Prospective attendees (members of the public) need an easy and intuitive way to learn about the details of the conference. The application must be easy to navigate, and the addition of common website functionality such as news and printable views of content must be easily accomplished.

- **Registration:** Attendees should be able to securely register for the conference and receive confirmation via email. The system should accommodate both individual and group registrations.

- **Session browsing and selection:** The system should provide intuitive and powerful search capabilities to assist users in the selection of sessions to attend.

- **Session evaluations:** Presenters should be able to review session evaluations online.

- **Scheduling:** The system should provide users with the ability to easily view and manage their schedules. The scheduled data should be available in a variety of formats that target different mediums and devices (for example, the Web, personal digital assistants [PDAs], and emails on demand).

- **Notification and reminders:** The system should provide users with the ability to subscribe to a conference notification service. These notices can include mailing lists, schedule-related reminders, and session-related news.

- **Accommodation assistance:** The system should provide a way for attendees to find area maps, venue maps, hotel directions, locations of interest, restaurants, and other information to enhance their experience at the conference.

Presenters

Properly assisting and serving presenters will result in a higher quality of content for the conference. This in turn benefits the primary stakeholders, the attendees.

- **Registration:** Presenters should be able to securely register for the conference and receive confirmation via email.

- **Profile information:** Presenters should be able to enter contact information and biographical information, upload a picture, and provide other information of interest.

- **Call for papers:** Potential presenters should be able to submit abstracts for a session. The system should allow the presenter to select the target audience, the session track (session category), and the room requirements for a session.

- **Speaker availability:** Presenters should be able to schedule the "office" hours during which they can be available to assist attendees with questions or problems related to a session.

- **Books by a presenter:** Presenters who are published authors can select one or more books from a list of their published books and associate them with a session. The list of books will be presented as part of the session information. The list of books and the detailed information for each book is obtained from an external provider at runtime.

Sponsors

Sponsors make a financial investment in a conference. Their interest is based on the rewards of public exposure and an improved industry image. It gives them an opportunity to connect with the community and provides them with a forum to present their products and services. The presence of high-profile industry players as sponsors legitimizes a technology conference. Ensuring that it's easy for sponsors to participate in the conference is of the utmost importance to the success of the event.

- **Registration:** The system should allow sponsors to register and select a level of sponsorship.

- **Booth selection:** The system should allow sponsors to select a conference booth. Booths are allocated based on sponsorship level.

Administrators

Managing the complex interactions of a conference is a challenging process. One of the goals of the system is to ease the tasks of management and reduce the amount of personnel needed.

- **Check-in and registration:** Administrators need to check in attendees as they arrive at the conference and provide them with badges and other materials.

- **Speaker evaluations:** The system should provide administrators with the ability to create and view the results of speaker evaluations.

- **News:** Administrators should have an easy interface to update conference-related news.

- **Booth assignment:** Administrators should have the ability to select a booth for a sponsor based on sponsorship level and physical requirements.

- **Conference closing:** An interface must be provided for conference administrators to easily transition the selected content into a static site. Specific data now becomes legacy data and must be relocated or archived appropriately.

- **Dashboard:** Utilities must be provided for conference administrators to gather statistics and performance indicators for the conference. These tools should be able to provide a snapshot view of the overall health and success indicators of the conference.

Architectural Requirements

Architectural requirements refer to the infrastructure needs that must be present for the system to achieve the desired business goal. A multitude of factors are involved in determining these requirements, such as the technologists' experience with similar systems, operational constraints, existing physical infrastructure, and application services needed across multiple systems (cross-cutting concerns). These requirements are useful in performing a gap analysis of infrastructure features when selecting a product or set of products on which to build enterprise applications. It's the architect's job to then make the build vs. buy decisions.

A set of general architectural requirements can be listed from the general application requirements previously outlined and the experience gained while building similar systems.

- **Data management and persistence:** Data must be easy to store, retrieve, search, and modify. Data integrity shouldn't be compromised in the face of multiple sources attempting to modify the same data.

- **Maintainability and extensibility:** The system must be easy to maintain and extend. Pieces of functionality should be easily added or removed, or turned on or off, depending on the operational characteristics applicable to a specific deployment.

- **Security:** Data must be stored and retrieved in a secure and efficient fashion. Users of the system must have access to functionality according to their roles or security levels.

- **Scalability and reliability:** Multiple users should be able to interact with the system. The performance characteristics of the system shouldn't change dramatically with an increase in the concurrent user base.

- **Personalization and customization:** The user interface should have a customizable look and feel, allowing for branding and dynamic changes based on the identity of the user.

- **Document and content management:** The system should provide the ability to manage the variety of documents used and also allow for the manipulation, classification, editing, and transformation of document-based information.

- **Administration:** The system should provide a framework to easily add management capabilities to individual components. Administrative functions should be relatively easy to create and customize.

- **Messaging:** Asynchronous communication facilities are expected to be required between certain subsystems. The architecture must provide a messaging framework or the ability to seamlessly integrate one.

- **Integration with legacy and external resources:** The system should facilitate the acquisition of data from external and legacy sources, as well as the ability to publish data to external entities in an industry-standard fashion.

Figure 1-2 diagrams the architectural requirements.

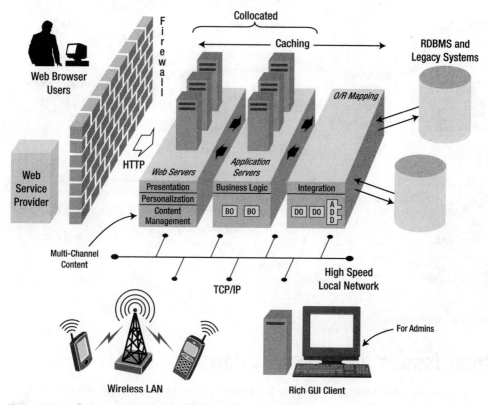

Figure 1-2. *Architectural requirements diagram*

Based on the architectural requirements outlined in the previous section, you should begin to see a clearer vision of the system's architecture. It should accommodate both the functional requirements (business and application requirements) and nonfunctional requirements (architectural requirements). The architecture diagram for the TechConf website is divided into tiers of functionality, which can represent a logical or physical partitioning of the system.

The architecture consists of the following tiers (following the well-known partitioning of the Java EE platform):

- **Client tier:** represents client-facing portions of the system

- **Presentation tier:** represents subsystems responsible for the generation of the user interface presentation-handling logic

- **Business tier:** represents subsystems responsible for the handling of business logic

- **Integration tier:** represents subsystems responsible for integrating external sources and destinations of information, including any legacy systems

Figure 1-3 shows the application tiers and how messages are exchanged between them.

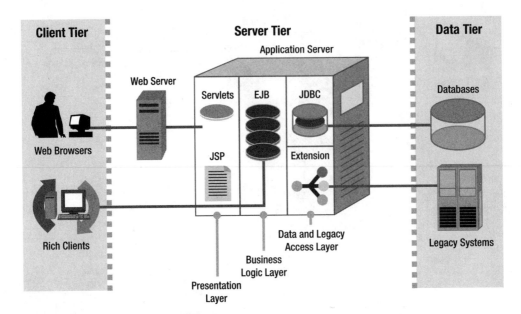

Figure 1-3. *Application tiers*

Open Issues and Assumptions

The dynamic nature of enterprise development forces you to make assumptions based on previous experiences and to delay dealing with certain aspects of the system until later in the development stages.

Assumptions

Some of the assumptions made are the result of implied requirements gathered from stakeholders' meetings and projections about the future usage of the system. Some of these assumptions include the following:

- Concurrency requirements are expected to increase over time.

- A large percentage of attendees are technologically savvy.

- Applications will be accessed remotely via the Internet using a browser-based interface.

- The conference internal network will be protected with an HTTP firewall.

- A large percentage of attendees carry network-ready PDAs or other mobile computing devices.

Open Issues

It's expected that as the system is designed and developed, your understanding about the dynamics governing its behavior will coalesce. New relationships and interfaces will be discovered, and previously unidentified usage scenarios will appear. Preparing for such discoveries by infusing flexibility in your designs is key for any system that will evolve in a controlled fashion. Some expected open issues are as follows:

- Unidentified stakeholders

- With multiple channels being serviced by the application, the need to find a way to produce channel-specific content

- The need to create several system-level components for authentication, registration, and the handling of payments

- The large number of implementation choices available

- Unidentified alternate usage scenarios

- Unidentified requirements

Design Road Map

To tackle the ongoing design process of the TechConf system, you should follow a simple design road map that will guide you through the creation of the models and the subsequent production of the code that will materialize those models into a working software system. The road map consists of several steps or activities, many of which can be accomplished in parallel as follows:

- **Creation of an analysis object model (domain model):** An understanding of the domain is documented in the form of a static model (class model) that will serve as guidance during the requirements analysis and creation of the design models. This step gives a high-level foundation from which it's easier to see subsystems of related objects and components emerge. A domain model also serves as a way to validate any assumptions or preconceived notions about the domain and solidifies and centralizes the knowledge about a problem domain.

- **Requirement analysis:** Actors are defined from the analysis and architectural documents. User use cases are created for high-level interactions of the primary actors with the system. User use cases are then broken up into system-level use cases if necessary. System-level use cases depict actions taken by specific components in the system to accomplish a task needed for the fulfillment of a user use case. Quick assessment of the reuse of system-level use cases is performed. High-priority use cases are written in detail to curtail major risks (detail doesn't mean implementation-specific details). Analysis of requirements continues iteratively for as long as the project or product is alive.

- **Iteration planning:** Iterations are planned based on a group of use cases. Integration planning is performed to determine points of integration, and modifications or enhancements to the overall automation of the integration process are made. In this book, each chapter is set as an iteration that sets out to fulfill a certain number of use cases.

- **Iteration execution:** Detail is added to use cases, both user and system use cases. Tests are written for each feature, and integration code or scripts are created or enhanced. Detailed, dynamic models are created (detailed enough to be implemented and detailed enough to utilize any forward-engineering features of the CASE tools available to the maximum). Class diagrams for any subsystems created are defined, and the overall model diagram is updated to reflect the results of the iteration. Whenever necessary, component diagrams and subsystem diagrams are created, thereby displaying the component interfaces and their relationships to the object models.

The activities described provide a baseline for the development plan. As the system evolves, the choices of the models and diagrams created have a strong impact on how a specific problem is solved. Experience is the best guide as to how to pick the number and types of diagrams needed. Again, always remember that the code is the final product and that no amount of diagrams will make a customer happy. Figure 1-4 shows a diagram depicting the activities followed for the TechConf system.

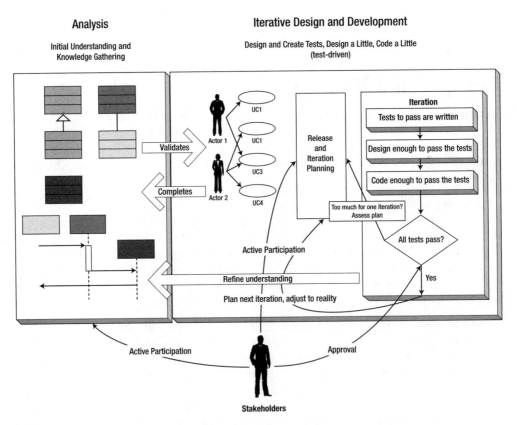

Figure 1-4. *TechConf system design road map*

Finding and Refining Candidate Domain Model Elements

Based on the TechConf requirements discussion and high-level architectural blueprints introduced earlier, you can compile a list of candidate domain models. For this one you could use Class-Responsibility-Collaboration (CRC) cards or simply (as performed here) create a list of nouns and verbs by manually scanning the source documents. This process isn't merely a manual process, because it entails analyzing the understanding of the system and eliminating and discovering new candidate classes and new operations that weren't present in the source documents. This newly discovered domain knowledge can then be added to the source documents to ensure that it isn't lost.

The resulting filtered list of nouns is obtained by deleting synonyms and nonentities (candidates that might be properties or modifiers, or may represent a state of an object). After analysis, the resulting list shrinks in size. Now the structural relationships between the candidate objects can be modeled. This process will further refine the candidate objects and will resolve many ambiguities about the understanding of the problem domain that haven't been previously encountered. After this initial analysis of the problem we arrive at the list of nouns representing candidate entities as shown in Table 1-1.

Table 1-1. *TechConf Candidate Entities (Nouns)*

Noun	Description
Sponsor	An individual or company sponsoring a conference
Conference administrator	An individual with privileged access to conference-related functions
Presenter	An individual who presents one or more sessions
Attendee	A registered user who is attending a conference
Organization	A non-individual legal entity
Conference	An event that consists of one or more sessions
Conference Track	A high-level classification of the topics covered in a conference
Presentation	A collection of materials and information to be conveyed to an audience in a predetermined amount of time
Session	A scheduled presentation
Schedule	A list of events that an attendee or a presenter will attend during a conference
Venue	A physical location where a conference takes place
Booth	A temporary structure where sponsors can showcase their products during a conference
Room	A room that is part of a venue
Abstract	A document that briefly explains the intent of a given presentation

Of course as we develop the application we will find more candidate classes and possibly remove or merge some of the previously discovered classes. The model shown in Figure 1-5 is the result of an iterative process following Peter Coad's Domain Neutral Component (DNC) technique. In the intermediate models, I chose to model the actions embodied in the verbs (or action phrases) gathered as objects in the domain model. Later these objects become the basis for the service classes in the system. Based on research into parallel object-oriented programming languages conducted at Stanford University[2] it was concluded that real-time tasks such as making a reservation or purchasing an airplane ticket should be modeled as objects that encapsulate (façade) the complexity of the task and simplify the associations between participating objects.

The question of whether to model the structure or behavior first is one that many beginning and intermediate modelers deal with during every new project. We recommend doing both simultaneously because modeling behavior validates the structural integrity of the model, and well-defined entities that reflect a domain naturally fall into place when modeling behavior.

■**Tip** Don't overanalyze with the noun and verb exploration. Concentrate on finding the principal candidates; others will emerge as you refine the analysis and design.

With this preliminary list of nouns, you'll begin to construct a static model, and the behavioral part of the domain model will begin to emerge. I want to emphasize that this is an iterative process and that the models produced will evolve as the system is constructed. In addition, certain assumptions made are validated while others are refuted. Remember, the analysis of the system helps you gain a deeper understanding of it, but it doesn't prevent you from deducing knowledge that might be erroneous and based on naive, preconceived notions.

After repeating this discovery and refinement process (and after further discovery during development), you should end up with a domain model that should resemble that shown in Figure 1-5.

---

2. R. Chandra, A. Gupta, and J. L. Hennessy, *Integrating concurrency and data abstraction in the COOL parallel programming language* Technical Report CSL-TR-92-511, Computer Systems Lab, Stanford University, February 1992.

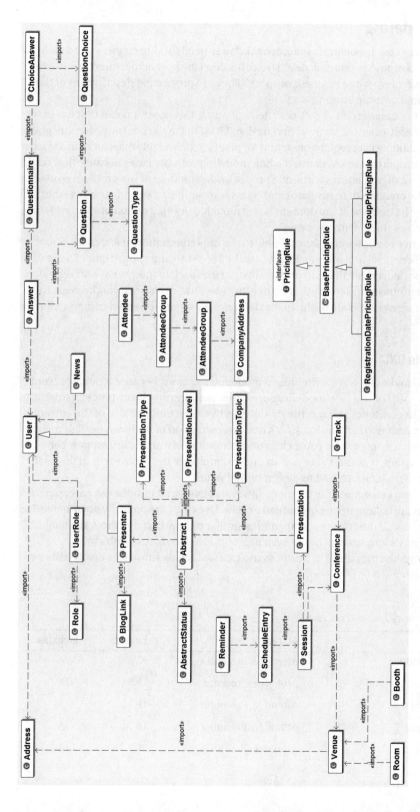

Figure 1-5. *The TechConf domain model class diagram*

Use Case Modeling

The main goal of use case modeling is to understand user needs and to enable you to view a system from the customer's point of view. Use cases describe how actors interact with the system in order to achieve some business purpose. They are procedural descriptions of the process of functional decomposition.

Even though use cases aren't object-oriented in nature, this doesn't mean that use cases have no value in object-oriented analysis and design (OOAD). On the contrary, they are good vehicles for understanding user requirements and for planning deliverable milestones in a system.

Of course, it's important to use caution when modeling with use cases because they could lead to the definition of procedures without a proper understanding of the problem domain. This can lead to the creation of many "artificial" classes to support a specific use case that taints and distorts the essence of the domain being modeled. As long as you understand this, you should have no problem with use cases.

In my experience use cases are of great value to the implementation of test cases, and they promote a test-driven (test-first approach) process. In this sense, the completion of a use case becomes a tangible deliverable that can provide instant feedback to the system's stakeholders. With the current emphasis on service-driven architectures, use cases are a good vehicle to define the goals of services and are useful in the definition of service-oriented components like session façades.

Use Cases and the DNC

Applying the DNC makes for a great prelude to modeling use cases because it helps prevent one of the cardinal sins of use case modeling: use cases dictating an object-model's structure. When use cases drive a model's shape, the model effectively becomes a slave of the current functionality being addressed and no longer is a true representation of the business. This means that although a use case might give you a clear understanding of a single interaction between an actor and the system, it doesn't give you an understanding of the problem domain (as the domain model does), which can lead to design tunnel vision.

To an extent, you can equate the moment-interval classes with either a use case, part of a use case, or an encapsulation of one or more use cases. Use cases are typically documented as short but concise textual descriptions or scenarios similar to how Extreme Programming (XP) creates user stories, descriptions of how a system is supposed to solve a problem.

Table 1-2 shows the partial list of business use cases, showing the actors involved as well as any use cases extended or included.

Table 1-2. *TechConf Preliminary List of Use Cases*

Use Case ID	Name	Actors	Extends	Includes
UC-1	Browse Schedule	Attendee, Presenter	N/A	N/A
UC-2	Add Schedule Reminder	Attendee, Presenter	UC-1	N/A
UC-3	Remove Schedule Entry	Attendee, Presenter	UC-1	N/A
UC-4	Mail Schedule	Attendee, Presenter	UC-1	N/A
UC-5	Browse Sessions	Attendee, Presenter	N/A	N/A

Table 1-2. *TechConf Preliminary List of Use Cases*

Use Case ID	Name	Actors	Extends	Includes
UC-6	Add Session To Schedule	Attendee, Presenter	UC-5	N/A
UC-7	Browse Presenter Session	Presenter	N/A	N/A
UC-8	Log In	Attendee, Presenter	N/A	N/A
UC-9	Register	Attendee, Presenter	N/A	N/A
UC-10	View Profile	Attendee, Presenter	N/A	N/A
UC-11	Edit Profile	Attendee, Presenter	UC-10	N/A
UC-12	Submit Abstract	Presenter	N/A	N/A
UC-13	Browse Abstracts	Presenter	N/A	N/A
UC-14	Edit Abtract	Presenter	UC-13	N/A
UC-15	Evaluate Abstract	Administrator	N/A	UC-15
UC-16	View News	Anyone	N/A	N/A
UC-17	Edit News	Administrator	UC-16	N/A
UC-18	Process Registration at Venue	Administrator	N/A	N/A
UC-19	View Statistics	Administrator	N/A	N/A
UC-20	Process Booth Request	Administrator	N/A	N/A
UC-21	Browse Booths	Sponsor	N/A	N/A
UC-22	Request Booth	Sponsor	UC-21	N/A

Refining Use Cases with Sequence Diagrams

The UML sequence diagram models the dynamic behavior of a system by depicting object interactions over time. These interactions are expressed as a series of messages between objects. UML sequence diagrams are ideal for elaborating a use case execution in terms of objects from your domain model. One sequence diagram is typically used to represent a single use case scenario or flow of events. The message flow of a sequence diagram matches the narrative of the corresponding use case.

Sequence diagrams are an excellent way to document use case scenarios and refine and synchronize a use case diagram with respect to a domain model. A sequence diagram typically shows a user or actor and the object and components they interact with in the context of a use case execution.

Whenever necessary, I use sequence diagrams in the book to refine and validate a use case against the application's domain model.

■**Tip** Don't assign operations to a class without first refining complex use cases with sequence or interaction diagrams.

Modeling Best Practices

Model-driven development is a practice that takes time to master, but the results are well worth the effort. I've compiled a list of best practices taken from the literature and from my experiences to help you get started.

- Keep models simple. Don't overmodel.

- Use color in your models. Color greatly enhances your ability to quickly grasp both the static and dynamic elements of a model.

- Choose model element names carefully. A model name can greatly influence the person who has to turn it into code.

- Avoid design or implementation-specific constructs in the analysis model.

- Keep models and source code synchronized. Incremental changes are easier to incorporate.

- In modeling, no single view is sufficient. Approach a complex system with a small set of independent views.

- The best models are connected to reality, and reality is all about trade-offs. Flexibility and performance are sometimes at odds when modeling a system.

- There will be a point in a model's life when the level of detail can be expressed only in code. Make sure that you don't get stuck trying to graphically model something that can be easily coded. UML notes are a great way to address some of these issues at the model level.

The Open Source Tools

The choice of tools used to build the TechConf project comes from my experience building Java EE applications and the collective knowledge of many colleagues, readers, speakers, and authors in the Java community. The choices presented here are not a one-size-fits-all collection of projects (although some are a must for most Java applications, like Ant) but they are what I have found to cover the current requirements and inject a level of agility that I haven't been able to achieve with a purely commercial solution. I'm not advocating that you take a one-sided approach and try to build everything solely on open source. In most of my professional engagements my clients have already settled on a commercial solution but are looking to open source to complement their commercial purchase. In general I find that the mix of open source projects I used in each assignment is built around:

- Filling a gap in a commercial solution

- Standardizing on a known, proven approach

- Avoiding vendor lock-in

- Improving the productivity of a team

- Easing the maintenance of the product

Figure 1-6 shows a map of the projects and tools used to build TechConf and how they relate to each other and to the different tiers and functional concerns of the application.

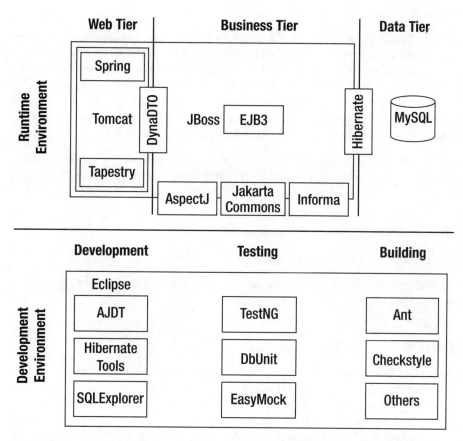

Figure 1-6. *Some of the open source tools used in TechConf*

Useful Open Source Resources

There are many sites on the Internet dedicated to managing open source projects and providing news concerning open source.

- apache.org:

  - jakarta.apache.org: The Jakarta project (jakarta.apache.org) is a collection of Java projects referred to as subprojects. Many of the subprojects are frameworks that can be incorporated into applications. For example, regular expressions are covered by the Jakarta Commons project. Other subprojects are intended for web development, and some are development tools. As projects mature and become mainstream, they might be promoted to top-level projects such as Ant, which is at ant.apache.org.

  - xml.apache.org: The XML projects are a collection of subprojects for creating, parsing, and transforming XML documents.

- `sourceforge.net`: SourceForge.net is the world's largest repository of open source projects. Many but not all of the projects are Java-based. Many of the hosted projects are stable, production-quality projects, but even more of them are still in the planning or early development stage.

- `java.net`: This site is the realization of a vision of a diverse group of engineers, researchers, technologists, and evangelists at Sun Microsystems to provide a common area for interesting conversations and innovative development projects related to Java technology. The community continues to grow, with industry associations, software vendors, universities, and individual developers and hobbyists joining every day. As they meet, share ideas, and use the site's collaboration tools, the communities they form will uncover synergies and create new solutions that render Java technology even more valuable.

- `codehaus.org`: Codehaus is an open source community that caters to projects which are not under the "GPL or other business-hostile licenses." Projects such as Middlegen, XDoclet2 and Drools are making Codehaus their home.

- `tigris.org`: This site is a mid-sized open source community focused on building better tools for collaborative software development.

- `gjt.org`: Giant Java Tree is a collection of unrelated Java packages.

- `objectweb.org`: ObjectWeb.org hosts open source middleware projects and adaptable components.

Summary

Java has emerged as the number one language and environment for enterprise computing, and it has also become one of the most widely used languages in the open source community. At the time of this writing there are upward of 10,000 Java open source projects on SourceForge—second only to C++. Though not every Java open source project is applicable to the creation of enterprise applications, you'll nevertheless find a largely untapped set of resources for Java EE. This chapter also introduced the Technology Conference Management System, which presents a fairly complex and representative problem that encompasses several areas of enterprise development.

The rest of the book will guide you through the process of designing and developing the applications that make up the case study. The case study weaves together the knowledge gained in the individual chapters. By tackling the software development process one layer at a time in an incremental and iterative fashion, this book will provide you with insight about the planning involved at various stages of the software-development life cycle. By using open source Java EE offerings and supporting tools, you'll be able to build a basic yet complete enterprise system. Each subsequent chapter is devoted to a tier of the application and to one or more stages (or activities) of the software-development process. Wherever necessary, multiple solutions to a particular problem will be demonstrated to provide you with some insight into the typical decisions encountered while developing an enterprise Java application.

As you prepare for a journey into the Java EE world, it's important to remember that sound design practices—not technology—should drive the development of enterprise applications. Although at specific points you might have to make an implementation decision that's driven by the shortcomings of a particular technology, you should always keep in mind the greater picture of a solid design based on the problem space rather than the solution space. In this era of agile methodologies and techniques, many are quick to dismiss software modeling. But as Scott Ambler (www.agilemodeling.com) and others have demonstrated, software modeling can be just another weapon in your arsenal of agile methods.

In this chapter you've learned a solid set of techniques and with the help of open source modeling tools you can make your models more robust and resilient to requirements and technology changes.

CHAPTER 2

■ ■ ■

Eclipse

When the JavaBeans specification surfaced, the idea of a component marketplace was on everyone's mind, akin to the rich component ecosystem for technologies like ActiveX. Well, that pipe dream never came to be a reality, and by now it is obvious that the same mistakes occurred with the EJB technologies. Some blame the specifications (and that might be partially true), but by far the largest set of responses I've gotten point to one obvious area—it's the tools, stupid!

Early successful Java development environments were mostly commercial and proprietary closed systems in which only a selected few commercial partners could extend and build the environment. Some tools like Borland JBuilder provided a semblance of a plug-in framework, but none of them ever attained mass adoption (regardless of what the vendors' marketing literature would tell you). Even though a lot of Java developers work effectively with a smorgasbord of tools and command-line utilities, many developers like to work in a cohesive integrated development environment (IDE).

The Java open source IDE market was really weak before the emergence of Sun's NetBeans IDE, which although successful, failed to gain widespread support from many commercial vendors or the open source community. The second major open source effort to create a Java IDE followed in late 2001. The Eclipse IDE (www.eclipse.org), amazingly, was a fairly full-featured product that was (even at version 1.0) ready to help the masses of new and old Java developers be more productive. Eclipse represented a new way for a commercial vendor to do business, in that IBM, the parent company behind the Eclipse project, donated an estimated $40 million for its development.

Eclipse came from IBM's acquisition of renowned tools maker Object Technologies International (OTI), creator of the VisualAge line of products and well-known for its Smalltalk tools. The Eclipse project is more than just an open source Java IDE; Eclipse is a tool integration platform and, more importantly, a community of projects and ideas.

This chapter is about introducing Eclipse into your development environment and complementing Eclipse with a variety of open source plug-ins that can make development more enjoyable and agile. This chapter by no means provides an exhaustive coverage of Eclipse, but it should help you get started with this powerful and popular IDE.

Installing Eclipse

Eclipse is distributed as a single compressed archive that is available for the Windows platform, Solaris, AIX, HP-UX, Mac OS X and for several of the existing Linux architectures. Eclipse requires that you have Java Runtime Environment (JRE) 1.4 or higher. For the purpose of the book exercises (and for technologies like EJB3 which depend on Java annotations) you will need JRE 1.5 or higher as shown in the output of the command java -version.

```
java version "1.5.0_05"
Java(TM) 2 Runtime Environment, Standard Edition (build 1.5.0_05-b05)
Java HotSpot(TM) Client VM (build 1.5.0_05-b05, mixed mode, sharing)
```

Eclipse doesn't provide a fancy wizardlike installer. Instead, first uncompress the archive to a suitable location such as c:\eclipse. I'll refer to this as the ECLIPSE_HOME directory. In the ECLIPSE_HOME directory you'll find the executable eclipse.exe. To run Eclipse for the first time simply execute the eclipse.exe file. I recommend that you create a shortcut on the Desktop, Start menu or Quick Launch bar on the Windows taskbar. On the initial run, Eclipse will prompt you to select a directory for all your user files, which is referred to as the workspace, as shown in Figure 2-1. If you're using a shared computer, I recommend that you choose a location under your user directory.

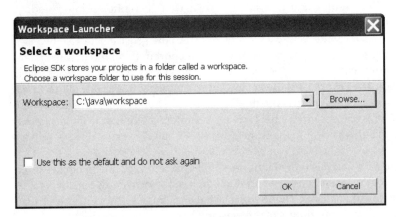

Figure 2-1. *Eclipse Workspace Launcher dialog*

When Eclipse starts for the first time, you'll be greeted by the Welcome view running on the Workbench as shown in Figure 2-2. The Welcome view provides a nicely structured way to get started with using Eclipse by providing easy access to tutorials and samples. Also, help is always available by selecting Help ➤ Help Contents.

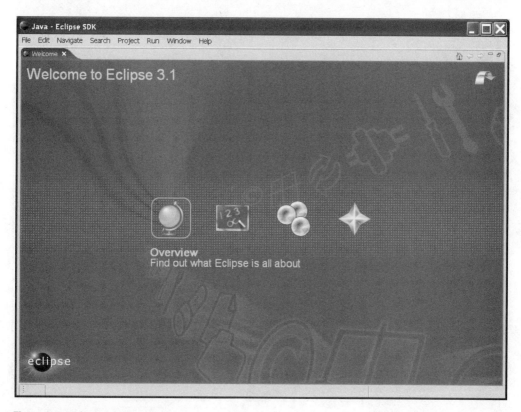

Figure 2-2. *Eclipse Welcome view*

Using Eclipse

Once you close the Welcome view, you'll be presented with the Workbench showing the default Java perspective as shown in Figure 2-3. The Workbench is the top-level component of Eclipse; it is the main window and shows one perspective at a time. A perspective is a window divided into several sections used for viewing and editing a resource in your workspace.

The Eclipse Java perspective is where we will spend most of your time as a Java developer. Eclipse provides several built-in perspectives tailored for Java development, debugging, version control with CVS, resource management and plug-in development among others. Based on certain operations (like running a Java class in debug mode) Eclipse will automatically switch perspectives for you. You can also switch perspectives by selecting Window ➤ Open Perspective and selecting a perspective. As you can see from Figure 2-3, a perspective is composed of one or more views and an editor pane. In Figure 2-3 we have the Package Explorer view on the left side, which gives you a Java Package-centric view of your projects; to the right we have the empty editor pane, and on the far right there's the Outline view. On the lower half of the right side, the Problems view is displayed.

The views in an Eclipse perspective reflect the needs of a related set of tasks. In the case of the Java perspective, the task is to create, test, and execute Java classes. Central to any perspective is the editor or editors associated with it.

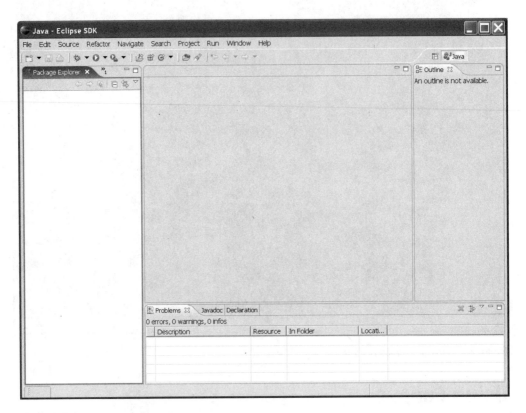

Figure 2-3. *Java perspective*

Creating an Eclipse Project

Let's start by creating a simple Eclipse Java project. Select File ➤ New ➤ Project, which will bring up the New Project wizard as shown in Figure 2-4.

The default selection is "Java Project". Click Next, which starts the New Java Project wizard. The wizard's initial dialog provides an input field for the project name, and the rest of the dialog is divided into three sections to configure the new project's contents, JDK compliance level, and directory structure. As it is shown in Figure 2-5, the name of the sample project is "helloworld-j2se".

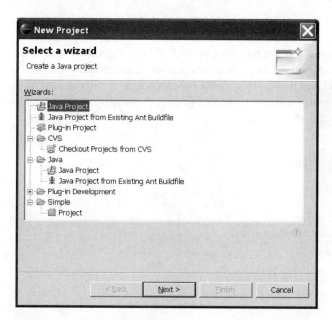

Figure 2-4. *Creating a new project*

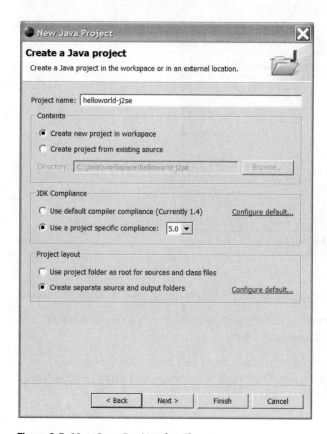

Figure 2-5. *New Java Project details*

In the Contents section, select "Create new project in workspace", which will create a directory for the project in the Eclipse workspace directory you selected during the installation. As mentioned before, we will be using JDK 1.5; therefore in the JDK Compliance section select "Use a project specific compliance" and select 5.0 from the pop-up menu. Finally, in the "Project layout" section, it is a good practice to separate the Java source files from the compiled class files by selecting "Create separate source and output folders". Clicking Next will bring up the Java Settings tabbed dialog as shown in Figure 2-6.

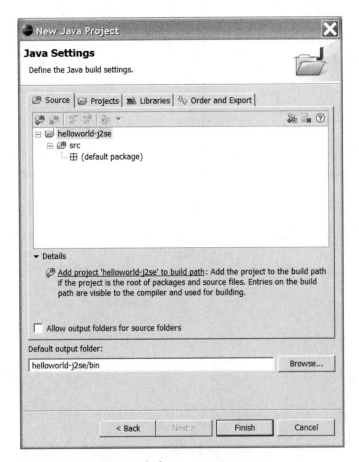

Figure 2-6. *Java Settings dialog*

The four tabs in this dialog allow you to customize several build-path settings, including

- **Source:** In this tab you can specify which resources in a source folder will be available to the compiler via inclusion and exclusion filters.

- **Projects:** In Eclipse you can create project dependencies by making the classes in another project available to the current project. See the Order and Export item below to determine what is visible to other projects linked to a project.

- **Libraries:** In this tab you can make items available to a project's classpath by adding JAR files relative to the project directory or external JARs located in the file system. Internal Eclipse JARs are also available as well as predefined libraries which can contain one or more JARs grouped under a library name like JRE System Library. Another way to add JARs to a project is indirectly as a classpath variable.

- **Order and Export:** In this tab you can determine the order in which elements are made available to the project's classpath. Entries checked are exported, which means that they will become available to any other projects that list the current project as a dependency.

To complete the project setup click Finish, closing the dialog. The Package Explorer view should look like that shown in Figure 2-7.

Figure 2-7. *Package Explorer showing newly created project*

Creating a Java Interface

Like any modern IDE, Eclipse provides many wizards to guide you through the development of a Java application. Let's start by creating a simple Java interface. We will call this interface the Greeter interface and place it in the package com.integrallis.j2se, and extend the java.io. Serializable interface. We can create a new Java class by right-clicking on the project node in the Package Explorer and selecting New ➤ Interface, which will invoke the New Java Interface wizard as shown in Figure 2-8.

To make the Greeter interface extend the Serializable interface, click the Add button to the right of the "Extended interfaces" section. As you type the name of any interface, the dialog will show you the matching interfaces in the project's classpath, so begin to type "serializable". In the list that appears, select "Serializable - java.io" and click OK. Back in the New Java Interface dialog, complete the information for the new interface as shown in Figure 2-8 and click Finish. The new Java interface should now appear in the Java editor in the center of the Workbench. Complete the Greeter interface source code as shown in Figure 2-9.

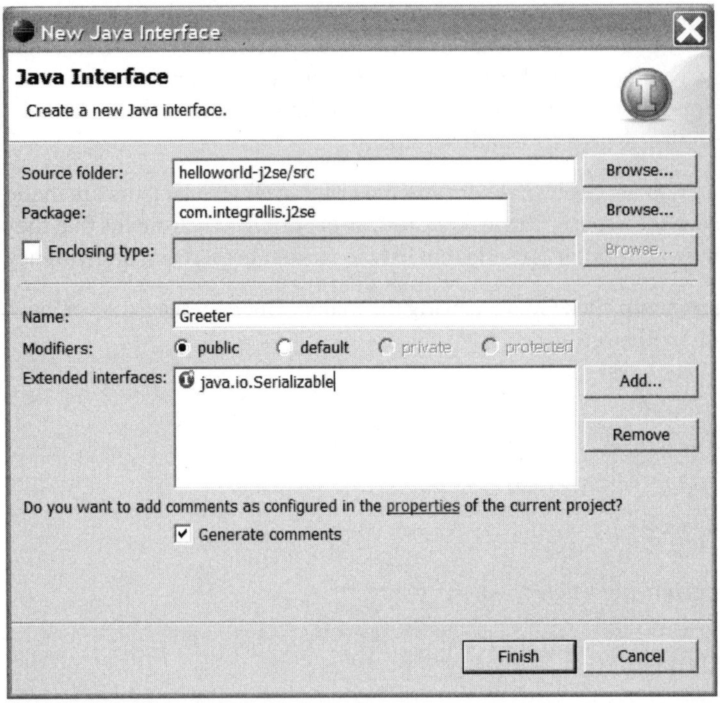

Figure 2-8. *New Java Interface wizard*

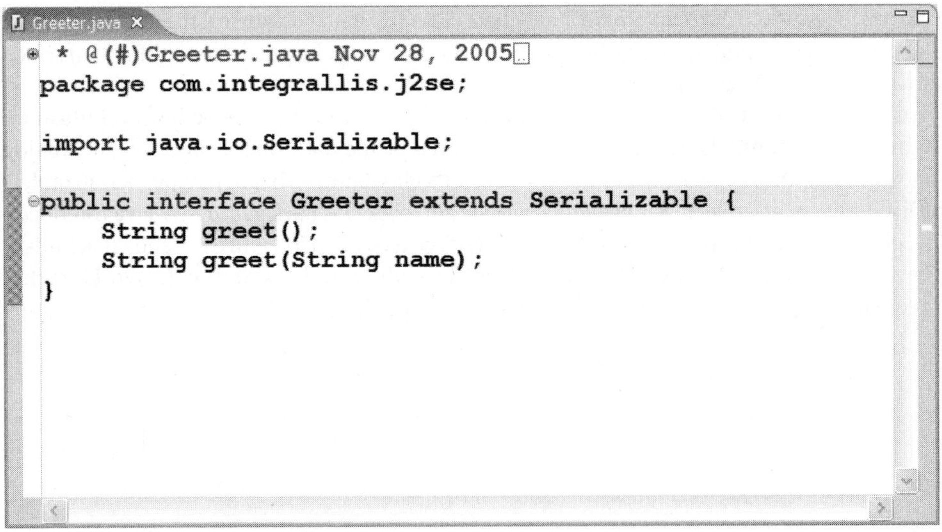

Figure 2-9. *Eclipse Java editor*

Some of the noticeable features of the Java code editor are described in the following sections.

Code Folding

As shown in Figure 2-9, the top comment on the class is folded (denoted by the plus symbol in the gutter). Clicking the plus symbol will expand the folded section, and the symbol will change to a minus sign.

Javadoc Pop-up Help

Hovering the cursor over a class for which Javadoc is available in the classpath makes a small pop-up appear with the name of the element you are hovering over. Pressing F2 will bring up a window containing help text about the class, as shown in Figure 2-10.

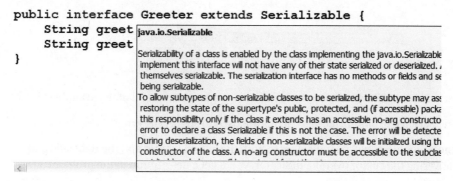

Figure 2-10. *Javadoc pop-up help text*

View Synchronization

Figure 2-11 shows the Outline view. The power of the Java perspective also lies in the synchronization between the editor and the supporting views. If you select an item on the Outline view, it is highlighted on the editor and vice versa.

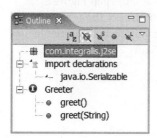

Figure 2-11. *Outline view*

Keeping your code healthy is easy with Eclipse. For example, in Figure 2-12 we show the introduction of an error in the code for the Greeter interface.

Figure 2-12. *Synchronization between editor and view*

Eclipse will immediately display the location of the error in several of the available views:

- In the Package Explorer tree view, icons are used to signify the error.

- In the editor, there will be indicators in both the left side gutter and the right side gutter. By hovering the cursor over the indicator, you'll get a description of the problem.

- In the Problems view, you'll see a description of the problem with resource, line number, and folder location.

Creating a Java Class

Let's expand the sample application by creating an implementation of the Greeter interface. In the Package Explorer, select the com.integrallis.j2se package, right-click the node, and select New ➤ Class, which will bring up the New Java Class wizard as shown in Figure 2-13.

Name the class GreeterImpl. To the right of the Interfaces section, click the Add button and type "greeter" in the "Choose interfaces" input box. The auto-complete feature should find the Greeter interface after you type just a few letters as shown in Figure 2-14. Click OK, and back in the New Java Class wizard, click Finish.

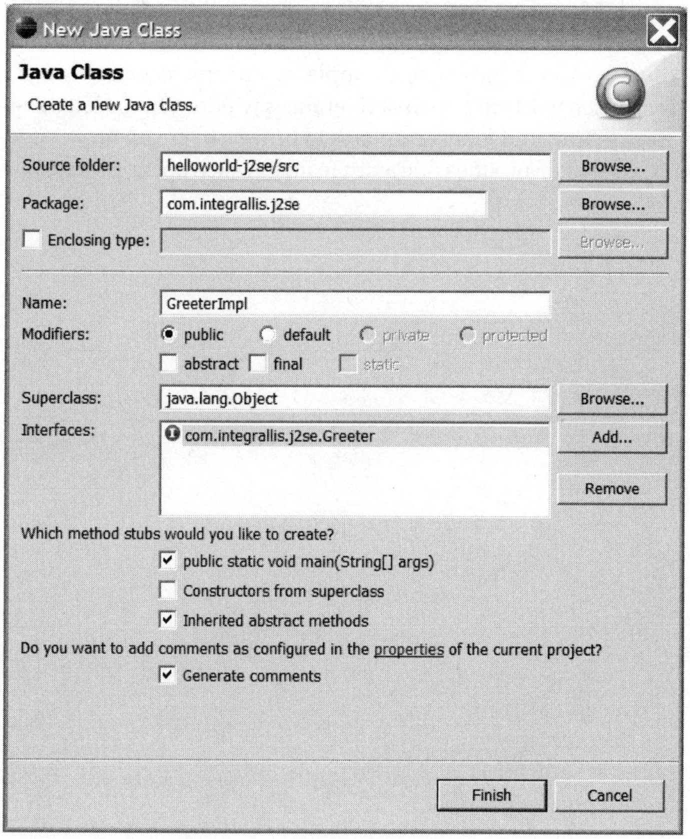

Figure 2-13. *New Java Class wizard*

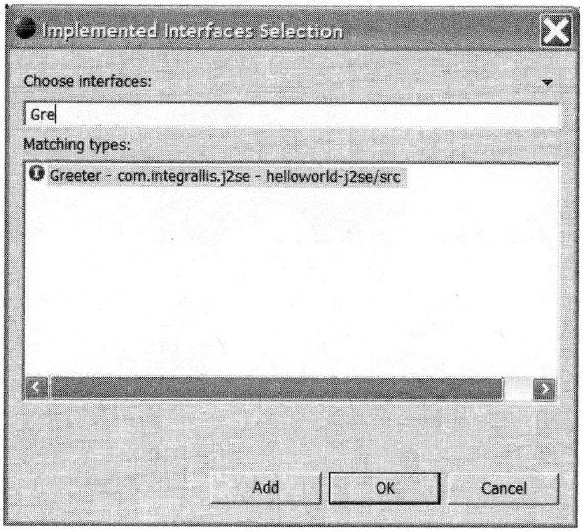

Figure 2-14. *Interface selection in New Java Class wizard*

Complete the code as shown in Listing 2-1. Let's test the template abilities of the Eclipse Java editor by typing "sysout" and Ctrl+Space. The string "sysout" is the identifier of one of the many predefined templates. You can explore the existing templates and create your own by selecting Window ➤ Preferences, which will bring up the Preferences window. In the left pane, expand the items under Java, then Editor, and then Templates to browse or create new templates. Ctrl+Space can also be used to invoke the code assist feature, which opens a scrollable list of possible code completions.

Listing 2-1. *A Simple Java Class*

```java
package com.integrallis.j2se;

public class GreeterImpl implements Greeter {

    public String greet() {
        return "Hello World";
    }

    public String greet(String name) {
        return "Hello " + name;
    }

    public static void main(String[] args) {
        Greeter greeter = new GreeterImpl();
        System.out.println(greeter.greet());
        System.out.println(greeter.greet("Michael"));
    }
}
```

Running a Java Class

To run the GreeterImpl class from the Package Explorer, right-click on the GreeterImpl.java node and select Run As ➤ Java Application. This should result in output similar to that shown in Figure 2-15 depicting the Console view.

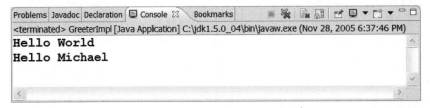

Figure 2-15. *Console view showing the results of running the* GreeterImpl *class*

A side effect of running the `GreeterImpl` class is that now a run configuration has been created for that class. If you select Run ➤ Run from the main menu, you'll see the details about the run configuration as shown in Figure 2-16.

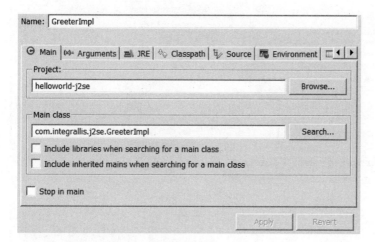

Figure 2-16. *Run configuration for the `GreeterImpl` class*

Debugging a Java Class

To debug a Java class in Eclipse is as simple as running a Java class. First, let's add a breakpoint to the `GreeterImpl` class `String greet(String)` method by right-clicking on the left hand-side gutter and selecting Toggle Breakpoint, which will result in a small blue circle on the gutter representing the breakpoint as shown in Figure 2-17.

```
/* (non-Javadoc)
 * @see com.integrallis.j2se.Gre
 */
public String greet(String name)
                        + name;
Toggle Breakpoint
Toggle Breakpoint Enabled
Breakpoint Properties...
```

```
/* (non-Javadoc)
 * @see com.integrallis.j2se.Gre
 */
public String greet(String name)
    return "Hello " + name;
}
```

Figure 2-17. *Breakpoint toggling*

Like most elements in the Eclipse UI, you can right-click on the breakpoint icon and inspect the breakpoint properties. To run the class in debug mode, in the Package Explorer right-click on the GreeterImpl.java node and select Debug As ➤ Java Application. Eclipse will automatically switch to the Debug perspective as shown in Figure 2-18. Pressing F6 will step over code and reveal the values of the parameter name as shown in the Variables view.

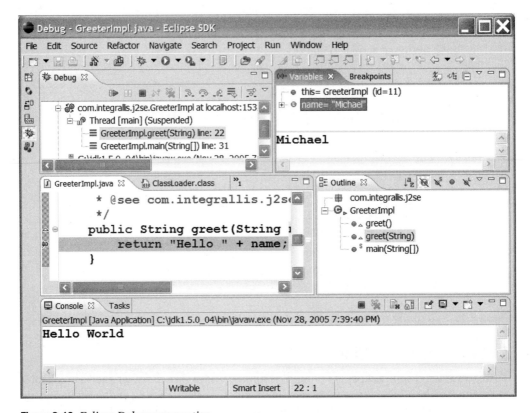

Figure 2-18. *Eclipse Debug perspective*

Eclipse Plug-ins

What makes Eclipse very appealing to a Java developer is the wealth of plug-ins, both commercial and open source, that exist to make every aspect of development more agile and enjoyable. The rest of the chapter will concentrate on showing some of the plug-ins that I've found to be the most useful when trying to develop an enterprise Java application. Many of the open source tools used in this book to develop the TechConf sample application provide for integration with the Eclipse platform via plug-ins.

■**Note** The TechConf project discussed in this book was developed mainly using Eclipse (although you should be able to work with the code with your favorite IDE or with simple stand-alone tools such as VI, Emacs and the command line). As you'll see in Chapter 3 when we learn about the Ant build tool, it is important that your applications be completely independent of your choice of IDE.

Concurrent Versions System

Projects with multiple developers require a shared source-code repository. Because open source projects have many contributors, they definitely require a central repository. Typically, these contributors are distributed throughout the world and connected only via the Internet. The de facto standard for open source version control is the Concurrent Versions System (CVS). CVS, an open source project itself, provides secure, multiuser version-control access over TCP/IP networks, including the Internet. This section isn't intended to be a comprehensive introduction to CVS and its features; instead the intention is to provide an overview of CVS for the purpose of gaining access to the current source code of open source Java projects. A lot of times this is needed because the latest version of the source code is only in CVS and isn't released in any other form. Some well-managed projects release the latest source code every night as ZIP files.

Understanding CVS

The CVS server is a TCP/IP-based application that provides access over the Internet to a CVS repository. The repository is a directory on the server machine. Contained within the repository are multiple modules. Each module is often a separate application or project.

Connecting to a CVS repository requires a properly formatted CVSROOT connection string. The format is as follows:

```
:pserver:[[user][:password]@]host[:[port]]/pathToRepository
```

The :pserver: part of the string indicates that the pserver protocol is being used for the connection. The pserver protocol is used for remote connections via the password-authenticating server, and it's the most commonly used way to remotely access a CVS repository. Another way to connect is via the ext protocol, which can be useful for running CVS through secure shell (SSH) for secure access to sources over the open Internet. The CVSROOT can optionally contain user and password information. If they aren't provided, the CVS client will prompt you to enter them. The host is the domain name or IP address of the server. If the CVS server isn't listening on the standard 2401 port, an optional port can be included. The CVSROOT is completed with the directory of the CVS repository on the server.

In the developer's local workspace, CVS directories are used to keep track of version-controlled files and the repository. The CVS directory contains the following three files:

- **Entries:** Contains a list of version-controlled files, their version, date, and type

- **Repository:** Contains the corresponding directory in the repository

- **Root:** Contains CVSROOT

CVS Concepts

CVS attempts to foster collaboration by providing developers access to all files in the repository. Each developer checks out a copy of the repository to a local workspace. All changes are made and unit-tested in the workspace. When changes are applied to the repository, the file version is incremented. A version history is maintained.

CVS doesn't require files to be locked in order to change them. It allows multiple developers to work on the same file in their local workspace. When multiple developers make changes to the same file, CVS handles the merging of those files.

CVS Commands

Understanding the basic CVS commands for authentication, checking out, committing, updating, and comparing is fundamental to the basic usage of any CVS client application.

A CVS repository is a collection of intellectual property that requires restricted access. In the case of open source projects, the repository is available for anyone to view. However, security is used to determine who is authorized to make changes directly to the repository. The CVS login command is used to authenticate users through username and password verification.

■**Note** CVS authentication doesn't protect files from being viewed during file transfers over the Internet. SSH should be used to protect file transfers in sensitive repositories.

The checkout command may be the most confusing of all CVS commands because it doesn't have the same meaning as it does in other version-control software (VCS) applications. In CVS, the checkout command is used to get an initial local copy of the module from the CVS repository Some other VCS programs require files to be locked and refer to this process as "checking out," which causes the confusion.

After the local copy of the source has been modified and unit-tested, it must be submitted back to the repository. The commit command is used to apply the local changes or new files to the repository. The commit command should also be accompanied by a short explanation of the change. The explanation becomes associated with the version change for auditing and communication purposes.

The update command is used to synchronize the local copy with the current version in the repository. This means that files committed to CVS by other members of the development team will replace the local files. Files that have been modified locally will be noted as modified and may require merging. It's a good idea to update on a daily basis and prior to running a final unit test and commit. Some clients have a query update that identifies the differences between the local copy and the remote server version.

CVS provides the diff command to compare files. You can use the diff command to compare local files with those in the repository. You can also use it to identify differences between versions of the same file.

CVS in Eclipse

Like many of the Eclipse features, CVS integration is implemented as a perspective. To display the CVS perspective, select Window ➤ Open Perspective ➤ Other, which will bring up the Select Perspective dialog from where you can select the CVS Repository Exploring perspective as shown in Figure 2-19.

Figure 2-19. *Switching perspectives*

The companion project to the book, the TechConf application, is hosted in the java.net community site under `http://techconf.dev.java.net`. To gain guest access to the code we first need to add the java.net CVS repository. Instructions on how to connect are available at `http://techconf.dev.java.net/servlets/ProjectSource`. To add a CVS repository, right-click on the CVS Repositories view and select New ➤ Repository Location, which will bring up the Add CVS Repository dialog as shown in Figure 2-20.

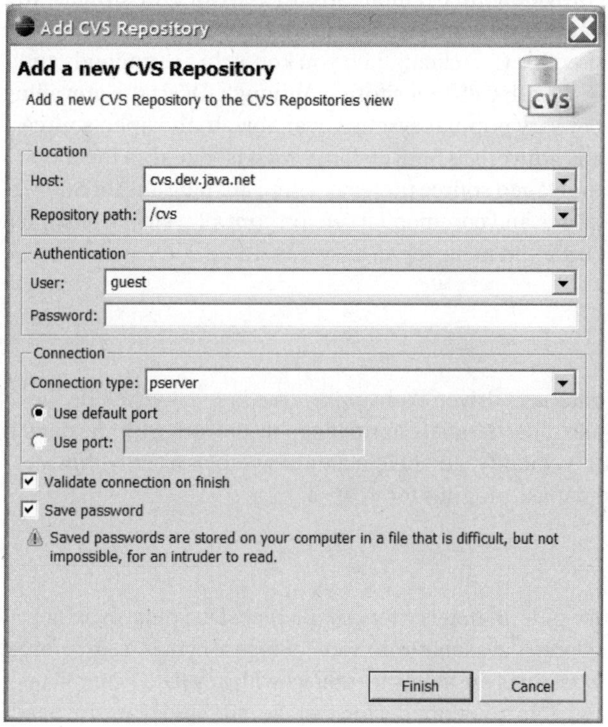

Figure 2-20. *Adding a CVS repository*

The CVS server or host for java.net is cvs.dev.java.net, the repository path is /cvs. For anonymous access, the user is "guest" with a blank password. Like most CVS servers, the connection type is pserver using the default port.

After entering all the required connection information as shown in Figure 2-20, click Finish. The new CVS repository should now be available under the CVS Repositories view. Expanding the new repository node reveals Branches, HEAD, and Versions nodes. Next, expand the HEAD node and locate the techconf module.

You can use the HEAD node to check out and create a new Eclipse project. After you expand the HEAD node and locate the desired module from the list of available modules, right-clicking the module reveals the Check Out as Project and the Check Out As options. The Check Out as Project option automatically checks the module out to the Eclipse workspace. If an alternative location is required, use the Check Out As option. Either option will copy the files from the CVS repository, create a project, and add the project to the Navigator.

To check out the module as a project in the Eclipse workspace, right-click on the node and select Check Out As, which will bring up the Check Out As dialog. Select "Check out as a project in the workspace" and click Finish. Once the project is added to the Navigator, the CVS commands are available as a submenu on the Team context menu. You can update the project by right-clicking the project in the Navigator and choosing Team ➤ Update.

After all the files in the repository have been retrieved, you should have your own local copy of the TechConf project. To gain read/write access to the project, as with most projects, it is expected that you submit patches first, and based on merit the project's leads will grant you a developer role.

Having access to a project's source code is one of the most compelling reasons for using open source. Although most projects provide source bundles in either ZIP or TAR formats, you can gain insight into the project's direction and allow for contribution if you have access to the current source code. If you're familiar with a CVS client, then you know that commands and architecture are necessary for interacting with CVS repositories. Although CVS is the prevailing version control system, there are other very popular systems available. In the open source category, a system that's winning many converts is Subversion, which is touted as the most likely replacement for CVS on most large open source projects. There are plug-ins for Subversion, and for most of the other open source and commercial version control systems, and most are modeled after CVS plug-ins, which should make for an easy transition.

Database Plug-ins

A great portion of the time testing a database-driven Web application is spent checking the contents of a relational database. While most databases provide tools to work with the data, it is convenient to be able to create, query, modify, and delete database tables from within an IDE. There are several open source database plug-ins for Eclipse.

SQL Explorer

SQL Explorer is an open source Eclipse plug-in that is a fork of the JFaceDbc plug-in, which became a commercial product. SQLExplorer is available from SourceForge at http://sourceforge.net/projects/eclipsesql. SQLExplorer features the ability to interact with any JDBC-compliant database and provides support for pluggable functionality for specific database platform needs and tools like Hibernate.

SQLExplorer requires Eclipse version 3.0X to 3.1 and the Graphical Editing Framework version 3.X (GEF). GEF can be found at http://www.eclipse.org/gef/. Like most Eclipse plug-ins, SQLExplorer consists of a single perspective that provides a collection of views and editors. To install the plug-in, follow these simple steps:

- Download the SQLExplorer file net.sourceforge.sqlexplorer_2.2.4.zip.

- Extract the SQLExplorer.zip file into the Eclipse installation directory.

- Restart Eclipse.

Once it's installed, you can access the SQLExplorer perspective from the menu by selecting Window ➤ Open Perspective ➤ Other and selecting the SQLExplorer option. Figure 2-21 shows the SQLExplorer perspective loaded in Eclipse.

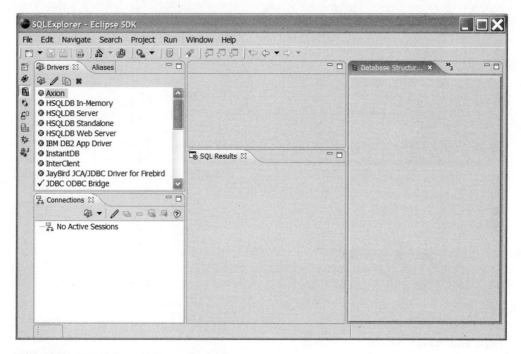

Figure 2-21. *SQLExplorer Eclipse perspective*

To get started using the plug-in, you need to first configure a driver. For the TechConf application we are using the MySQL database; therefore we will configure the MySQL JDBC driver called MySQL Connector/J available from the MySQL website at http://dev.mysql.com/downloads. The driver is distributed as a JAR file packed in a ZIP file. For this book I used the 3.0.14 production version of the driver. Download and uncompress the archive to a suitable location.

To create a new driver, right-click on the Drivers view and select "Create new Driver" as shown in Figure 2-22.

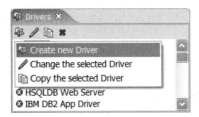

Figure 2-22. *Creating a new driver*

In the "Create new Driver!" dialog enter the information for the MySQL driver, including the Name and the Example URL as shown in Figure 2-23.

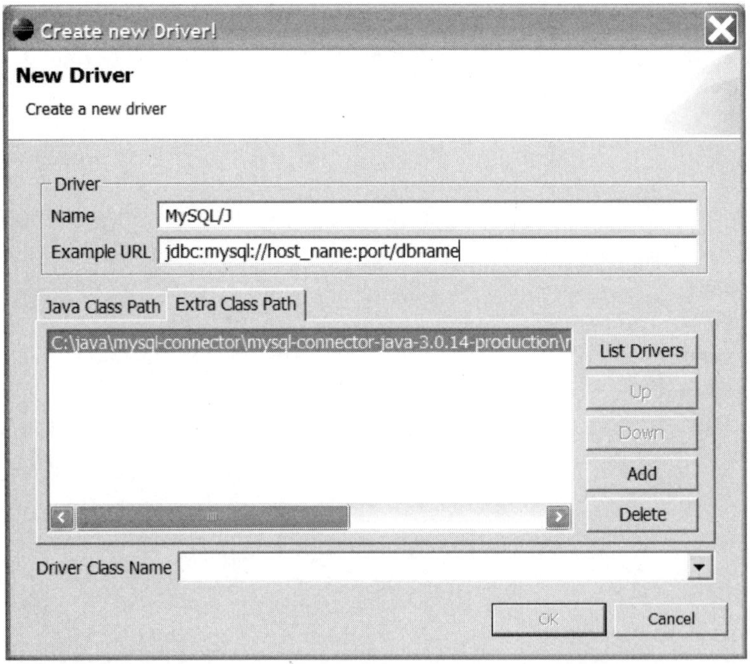

Figure 2-23. *"Create new Driver!" dialog*

On the Extra Class Path tab click the Add button and navigate to the location where the MySQL driver JAR file is located. The file name follows the pattern mysql-connector-java-VERSION.jar. Select this file and click the List Drivers button, which should populate the Driver Class Name drop-down. Select the org.gjt.mm.mysql.Driver class as shown in Figure 2-24.

Figure 2-24. *Driver Class Name selection*

With the database installed and configured as explained in Chapter 4, we can now configure a SQLExplorer alias. Select the Aliases view, right-click and select "Create new Alias". Complete the "Create new Alias" dialog as shown in Figure 2-25 and click OK.

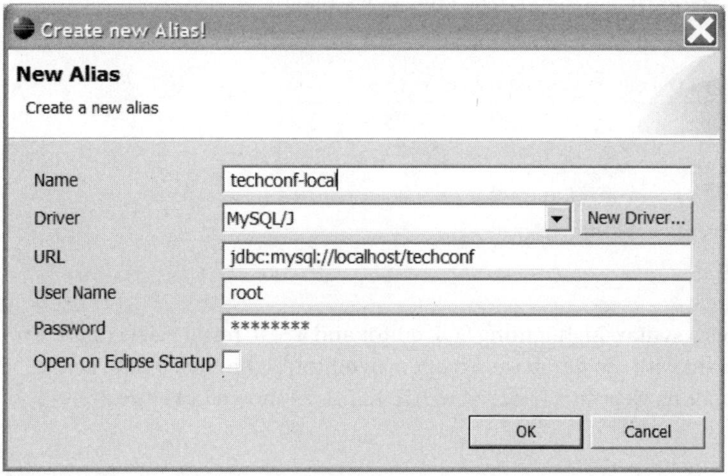

Figure 2-25. *"Create new Alias" dialog*

To connect to the newly created alias, right-click on the alias node in the Aliases view and select Open. The Connection dialog should appear; click OK, and the connection should now be established. The Database Structure View provides a hierarchical view of your database, displaying tables, views, and other database artifacts as shown in Figure 2-26.

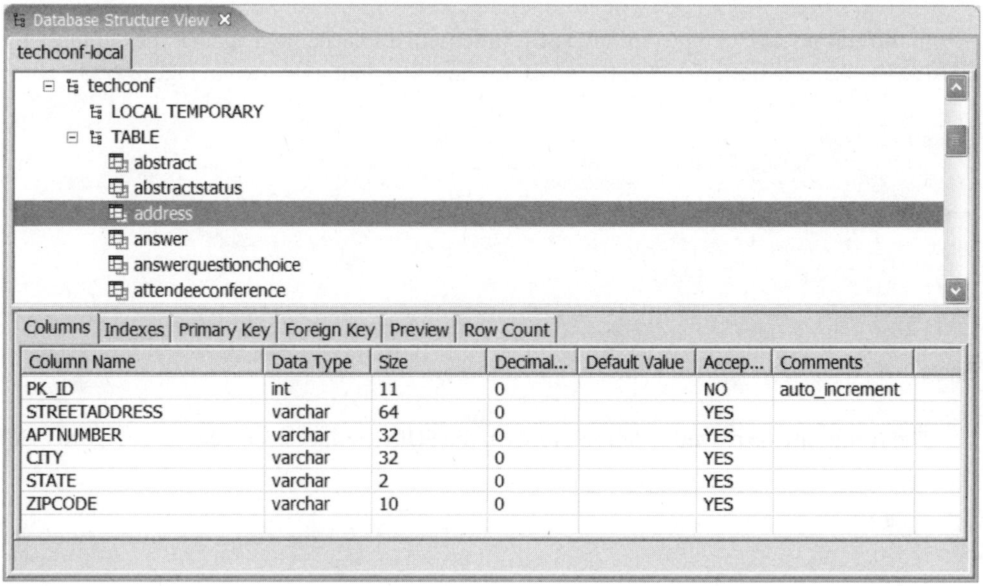

Figure 2-26. *Database Structure View*

The Database Structure View provides a pane at the bottom that shows details about the node selected in the tree view. If you select a particular table you can see information about the columns, indexes, primary and foreign keys, number of rows, and a preview of the contents. Figure 2-27 shows the Database Structure View with the Preview tab selected. This tab is particularly useful while testing if you have a few items in a table.

Columns	Indexes	Primary Key	Foreign Key	Preview	Row Count		
PK_ID	STREETADDRESS	APTNUMBER	CITY		STATE	ZIPCODE	
1	747 Howard Street	<NULL>	San Francisco		CA	94103	
2	204 Bluestone Ct.	<NULL>	Westerville		OH	43081	
3	123 Main Street	123	Boobaloo		OH	43076	

Figure 2-27. *Table preview*

SQLExplorer provides a syntax-highlighting SQL editor and a SQL results view that are a convenient way to interact with the database. To open an editor, right-click on the active session under the Connections view and select New SQL Editor as shown in Figure 2-28.

Figure 2-28. *Opening a SQL editor*

In the editor you can type any valid SQL statement and execute it against the database by clicking the Execute button on the far left of the view's toolbar as shown in Figure 2-29.

Figure 2-29. *Entering a SQL statement in the editor*

The results are displayed in tabular form in the SQL Results view as shown in Figure 2-30.

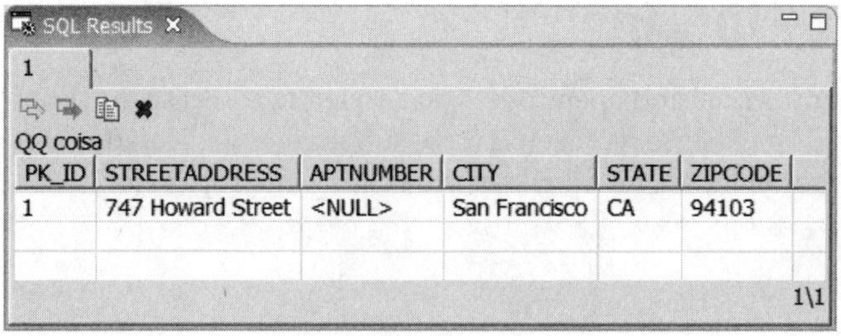

Figure 2-30. *Results of executing a SQL statement*

Other convenient features provided by SQLExplorer are available via the context menu of a table object in the Database Structure View as shown in Figure 2-31.

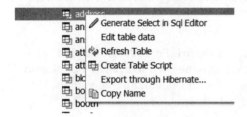

Figure 2-31. *Table operations in the Database Structure View*

The option Generate Select in SQL Editor opens a SQL editor with a SQL select statement for the selected table, which is useful as a template for your own select statements. The "Edit table data" feature enables you to edit the table data directly in a grid. The data set to be edited could be constrained by entering a "where" clause of a SQL statement as shown in Figure 2-32.

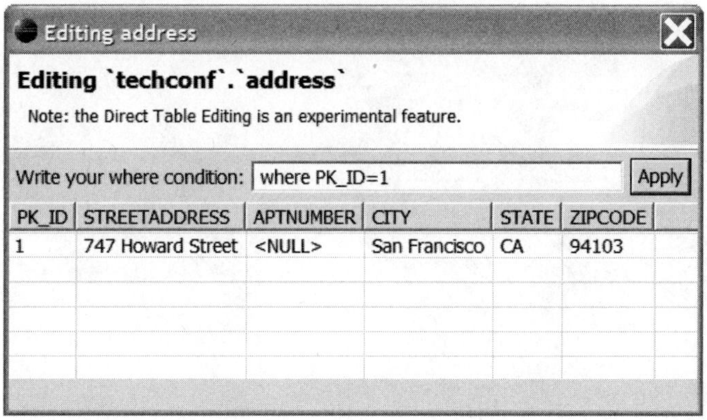

Figure 2-32. *"Edit table data" feature*

Another powerful database plug-in for Eclipse is the QuantumDB plug-in, which offers features similar to that of SQLExplorer. QuantumDB is also hosted at SourceForge and can be downloaded from `http://quantum.sourceforge.net`.

Web Development Plug-ins

There are many plug-ins, both commercial and open source, to accelerate and ease the development of J2EE Web applications. The Eclipse project has three subprojects dedicated to the creation of tools for the J2EE environment. Table 2-1 shows the Eclipse subprojects for J2EE and Web development.

Table 2-1. *Eclipse Tool Subprojects*

Project	Description	URL
Eclipse WST	Web standard tools	`http://eclipse.org/webtools/wst/main.html`
Eclipse JST	J2EE standard tools	`http://eclipse.org/webtools/jst/main.html`
Eclipse JSF	JavaServer Faces (JSF) tools	`http://eclipse.org/webtools/jsf/index.html`

For good coverage of the JST tools, an excellent reference is *Pro Eclipse JST* by Judd and Shittu (Apress, 2005). Another plug-in worth mentioning is the open source Lomboz plug-in, which supports the creation of EJB, servlets, Web services and other J2EE components. The Lomboz plug-in can be found at `http://lomboz.objectweb.org`.

Summary

In this chapter you learned the basics of using the Eclipse IDE to develop Java applications with ease. With the ever-growing ecosystem of Eclipse plug-ins, it is easy to turn Eclipse into your own personalized IDE. Eclipse has become in a relatively short time the number-one platform for the development of Java applications, and with the right combination of open source plug-ins, you can improve and streamline the development of J2EE Web applications.

CHAPTER 3

■ ■ ■

Building with Ant

The traditional definition of a build process entails converting source code into an executable deliverable. In the world of enterprise Java development this definition falls short. In this chapter you'll learn how to use the popular build tool Ant to set the stage for the build system used in the TechConf application. A production J2EE application build system will typically need to do much more than simply compiling and packaging your code. Some sample tasks that can be performed by a build include the following:

- **Version control:** Obtaining the latest version of a project's source code from a version control repository

- **Build plan:** Determining what to build

- **Generate:** Generating any source code from several sources such as annotated code, database tables, and Unified Modeling Language (UML) diagrams

- **Formatting:** Correcting syntax and style

- **Checking:** Validating syntax and style

- **Compiling:** Generating .class files from .java files

- **Testing:** Running automated tests

- **Validating:** Verifying components' validity

- **Javadoc:** Generating API documentation

- **Metrics:** Generating code metrics reports

- **Packaging:** Generating JAR, web archive (WAR), and enterprise archive (EAR) files

- **Deploying:** Deploying applications to servers

- **Distributing:** Distributing packaged applications

- **Notifying:** Notifying developers and managers of important build-related events

This relatively short list of activities should give you an idea of how involved the build process can become. How many times have you heard the dreaded, "But it was working just fine on my machine!" A reproducible build is of paramount importance for keeping your code base healthy and your project in a known state at all times. Having a reproducible and stable build process takes more than just having a dedicated team of developers. Without automation, even a small project with few developers can rapidly get out of hand.

By using an automated build tool, developers can define the steps in the process of building their software and execute those steps reliably under different environments and circumstances. Typically such tools will account for individual configuration differences between developers' environments and production systems. Most build tools have some sort of configuration or script that describes the build process in discrete, atomic steps.

A typical build process also covers aspects of both the production and the development stages of an application. For example, in a database-driven application, individual developers might need to initialize a database with sample data needed for testing, while in a production environment such a step would not be required.

Although integrated development environments (IDEs) have always provided a level of support for the building process, this support usually falls short of developers' needs and expectations. Most of these build solutions aren't portable across environments; it's hard enough to get one developer's IDE project file to work on any environment except for its creator's. Not only are these facilities IDE-independent, but they're also very different from the work that an application assembler or deployer has to do for a production application. Common sense should tell you that the closer your development environment is to the production environment, the fewer problems you'll have going into production. By having a build process that is consistent across development and production environments (and any other environments in between), you can eradicate many development maladies that come from using multiple IDEs, operating systems, and Java versions.

As the build process is automated and becomes transparent to programmers, other issues such as testing and documentation generation find their way into the build process. Most developers find that they begin with a build system that evolves to accomplish more than simply "building." From testing to document generation, a finely crafted build process eventually becomes a reflection of a team's development process.

In J2EE, a consistent build system brings together the roles of the application developer, assembler, and deployer. As part of the J2EE specification, Sun defined several roles in its definition of the J2EE platform. Newcomers to J2EE might quickly put themselves in one of these categories and disregard the details of the other roles. But the reality is that unless you have an understanding of every role's responsibility, your understanding of the J2EE platform will not be complete. In particular, the roles of the application assembler and the application deployer are reflected in the build process, and unless your developers can duplicate what happens in production you're likely to experience a painful transition from development into production.

Introduction to Ant

A project with a few files and very few dependencies makes the process of building almost not a process at all. By simply using the Java compiler and maybe the JAR command-line utility, you can build simple Java applications.

Before Ant, developers typically started with a set of simple batch files or shell scripts as an initial step towards automation. But as the number of files, components, target platforms, and virtual machine (VM) versions increases so does the build time, the complexity of the build, and the likelihood that human errors will contribute to irreproducible and inconsistent builds. After a while, you end up realizing that maintaining a non-portable, platform-dependent homemade solution is cumbersome and error-prone.

For the few teams in which developers actually agree on the choice of an IDE, the first choice is usually the build functionality provided by the IDE. Most IDEs provide wizards that build simple applications. These wizards cover only part of the equation, and they tie your team to the particular IDE.

Besides the aforementioned problems, both approaches treat development and production environments as being conceptually separate. What's needed is a low-level tool that can unify the build process across multiple IDEs, stages of development, platforms, and so on.

For many years, UNIX programmers have had a way to build their applications via the make utility and all of its variants (GNU Make, nmake, and so on). Like make, Ant is at its core a build tool, but as the Ant website states, Ant "is kind of like Make, but without Make's wrinkles" (http://ant.apache.org/).

Ant's simplicity has contributed to its rapid adoption and made it the de facto standard for building applications in the Java world. Ant, together with the Concurrent Versions System (CVS), has played an important role in fostering open source by providing a universal way for individuals to obtain, build, and contribute to the open source community. Ant has also become an indispensable tool for most Java developers, especially those developing J2EE applications.

Ant has made life easier for Java developers worldwide. Although far from perfect, it has demonstrated that it can cover what a Java developer needs, from gaining control over the build process to cutting the umbilical cord from proprietary build systems.

The most relevant reasons to choose Ant are as follows:

- **Platform independence:** A typical corporate Java environment includes development teams that work on Wintel machines and deploy to UNIX machines for production. Ant, being a pure Java tool, makes it possible to have a consistent build process regardless of the platform, thereby making the development, staging, integration, and production environments closer to each other. Ant also has built-in capabilities that handle platform differences. Your Java code is portable; your build should be too!!

- **Adoption:** Ant is everywhere! Yes, by itself this is a poor reason to favor a technology, but the strengths that ubiquity brings to the table are many, including hiring, training, and marketability of skills. Ant also has been integrated into many of the leading IDEs, thereby making it the one consistent factor between developers. This is partly due to the choice, for good and bad reasons, of XML as its language.

- **Functionality and flexibility:** For the majority of Java projects, Ant is extensible and highly configurable; it provides the required functionality right out of the box. For Java developers, any class can easily become an Ant task, although in our experience we seldom have to write our own tasks (because someone in the open source community always seems to beat you to the punch). If desired, you can plug scripting engines and run platform-specific commands.

- **Syntax:** Like it or not, XML has become a globally recognized data format. Most Java developers have worked with XML, and J2EE developers deal with XML on a daily basis. XML makes Ant buzzword-compliant. But XML also has some advantages. XML is ideal for representing structured data because of its hierarchical nature. The abundance of commercial and open source parsers, and the ability to easily check an XML file for being well-formed and valid has made the use of XML pervasive in the industry.

Ant's architecture is similar to the make utility in that it's based on the concept of a target. In Ant a target is a modular unit of execution that uses tasks to accomplish its work. An Ant target has dependencies and can be conditionally executed. A build is usually composed of some main targets that will accomplish some coarse-grained process related to an application's build, such as compiling the code or packaging a component. These main targets might make use of other subtargets (usually via dependencies) to accomplish their job.

Underneath the covers, tasks are plain Java classes that extend the org.apache.tools. ant.Task class, although any class that exposes a method with the signature void execute() can become an Ant task. One of Ant's great advantages is its extensibility. Ant tasks are pluggable plain Java classes. To write a task all you need to do is extend the Task class and add some code to the execute method. Ant comes loaded with myriad tasks to accomplish many of the things needed during a typical build. These tasks are referred to as the core tasks and the optional tasks. There are also a countless number of third-party tasks, whether they're commercial, freeware, or open source.

The scope of Ant's contribution to Java development isn't obvious at first, especially on small projects. But once complexity begins to creep in and you have multiple developers, you'll find that Ant becomes the glue that can help your team work in synchronization. It can basically remove the need for a full-time build "engineer." This is largely the case with most open source Java projects, and their success should be a testament to the effectiveness of the integration power of using Ant.

Ant isn't without its critics, however. Many have failed to understand that Ant was never meant to be a full-fledged scripting language but a Java-friendly way to automate the build process in a simple declarative, goal-oriented fashion. Since its inception, many scriptinglike features have been added to Ant in the form of custom tasks, and the arguments between camps that want a full scripting language and ones that want a simple, dependency-driven build system continue to this day. In my opinion there is no right answer; scripting is programming, and you know the issues that arise with that. On the other hand, Ant's simple declarative ways make it hard to do write-once and reuse builds across different projects. Ant's reusability is at the task level. In his essay "Ant in Anger" (http://ant.apache.org/ant_in_anger.html), Steve Loughran recommends that to achieve the level of complexity that most developers turn to scripting to achieve, Ant builds can be dynamically generated on a per-project basis using something like eXtensible Stylesheet Language Transformations (XSLT).

Fortunately, Ant version 1.6 provides new features that make Ant build reuse a reality. We will cover some of the relevant features that enable reuse later in this chapter.

Obtaining and Installing Ant

Ant can be obtained from http://ant.apache.org in binary and source distributions, or you can obtain the source code through CVS. Ant is a pure Java application. Therefore, the only requirement to run it is that you have a compliant JDK installed and a parser compliant with Java API for XML Processing (JAXP). Ant ships with the latest Apache Xerces2 parser. Ant is distributed as a compressed archive (.zip, tar.gz, and tar.bz2). Once the archive has been uncompressed to a directory (this directory is referred to as ANT_HOME), it's recommended that you add the environment variable ANT_HOME to your system and the bin directory under the ANT_HOME directory to your system's executable path. The bin directory contains scripts in many different formats for the most popular platforms. These scripts facilitate the execution of Ant and include DOS batch, UNIX shell, and Perl and Python scripts. Ant also relies on the JAVA_HOME environment variable to determine the JDK to be used.

■**Caution** If you have only the JRE installed (a rare case for most Java developers) many of Ant's tasks will not work properly.

To verify that Ant is installed correctly, at the command prompt type:

```
ant -version
```

If the installation was successful you should see a message showing the version of Ant and the compilation date:

```
Apache Ant version 1.6.5 compiled on June 2 2005
```

Ant's Command-Line Options

Ant is typically used from the command line by running one of the scripts in the bin directory. Ant's command line can take a set of options (prefixed with a dash) and any number of targets to be executed, as follows:

```
ant [options] [target target2 ... targetN]
```

Table 3-1 shows the options available from the command line. You can access them by typing ant -help. By default, Ant will search for a file named build.xml unless a different file is specified via the buildfile option.

Table 3-1. *Ant Command-Line Options*

Option	Purpose
help | h	Prints the help message showing all available options
projecthelp | p	Displays all targets for which the description attribute has been set
version	Prints the version of Ant
diagnostics	Prints a diagnostics report that shows information like file sizes and compilation dates; useful for reporting bugs

Table 3-1. *Ant Command-Line Options*

Option	Purpose
quiet | q	Minimizes the amount of console output produced by Ant
verbose | v	Maximizes the amount of console output produced by Ant
debug | d	Prints debugging information to the console
emacs | e	Removes all indentation and decorations from the console output
lib <path>	Configures a file system path to search for JARs and Java classes
logfile | l <file>	Redirects all console output to the specified log file
logger <classname>	Uses the specified class for logging (it must implement org.apache. tools.ant.BuildLogger)
listener <classname>	Adds an instance of a class that can receive logging events from the build (it must implement org.apache.tools.ant. BuildListener)
noinput	Prevents interactive input from blocking the build process
buildfile | file | f <file>	Specifies the buildfile to be processed
D <property>=<value>	Passes a property to the build
keep-going | k	Tells Ant to execute all targets whose dependencies succeed
propertyfile <filename>	Loads all properties in a properties file; properties passed with the D option take precedence.
inputhandler <class>	Specifies a class to handle input request; by default input requests are handled via the standard in (stdin)
find | s <file>	Tells Ant to search for the given filename by traversing upwards from the current directory until it finds the file
nice (1..10)	Specifies a niceness value for the main thread; 1 (lowest) to 10 (highest); 5 is the default
nouserlib	Tells Ant not to load any JAR files in the user's ${user.home}/.ant/lib directory
noclasspath	Tells Ant to run without using the System's CLASSPATH

A Simple Ant Example

Figure 3-1 shows a simplified view of what a simple Ant build entails. The root of an Ant build is the project element, which contains one or more targets and at least one default target. In this case the simple build contains three targets named Target A, Target B, and Target C, with Target C being the default target. As shown in the zoomed view of Target B, a target can contain zero or more tasks.

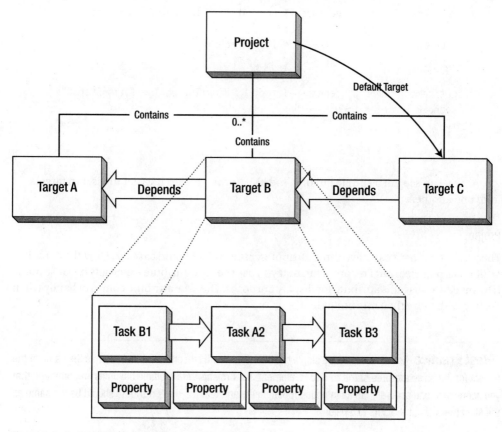

Figure 3-1. *A simplified view of an Ant build*

Ant controls the build process with a description file. In Ant the description file is typically referred to as a buildfile or build script. The Ant buildfile is an XML file whose root is the project element that contains child nodes that represent the targets. An Ant buildfile representing a build similar to the one depicted in Figure 3-1 would look like Listing 3-1.

Listing 3-1. *Simple Ant Buildfile*

```
<?xml version="1.0" encoding="UTF-8"?>
<project basedir="." default="Target C" name="MyProject">

    <target name="Target A" description="Performs Step A">
        <echo>Performing Step A</echo>
    </target>
```

```
        <target name="Target B" depends="Target A" description="Performs Step B">
            <echo>Performing Step B</echo>
            <echo>Echo is one of many Core Tasks</echo>
        </target>

        <target name="Target C" depends="Target B" description="Performs Step C">
            <echo>Performing Step C</echo>
        </target>

</project>
```

As you can see, for a simple buildfile the XML format makes it easier to discern targets from one another.

Project

The project element can have three attributes: name, default, and basedir. Only the default attribute is required, but I recommend that you use the name attribute especially because many IDE Ant editors use this attribute for display purposes. The name attribute comes in handy when dealing with more than one buildfile.

■**Best Practice**   For a project with a single buildfile (build.xml) I recommend that you use the name of the project for the name attribute of the project element. For projects with multiple buildfiles I recommend that you name each one according to its intended functionality and that the name attribute should be the same as the filename without the .xml extension.

The default attribute determines the default target to be executed for the buildfile. Finally, the basedir attribute determines the base directory for all file-related operations during the course of a build. In the previous example it's simply the current directory where the buildfile resides, and since this is the default value, the attribute could have been omitted. This setting is important especially if you're using multiple buildfiles in different subdirectories of an application directory structure and you want a uniform way to refer to paths across all buildfiles.

■**Best Practice**   Make the basedir directory the root directory of your project. This is a common convention, and it will make your buildfiles easy to understand.

The Build Stages

An Ant build has two stages: the parsing stage and the running stage. During the parsing stage the XML buildfile is parsed and an object model is constructed. This object model reflects the structure of the XML file in that it contains one project object at the root with several target objects, which themselves contain other objects representing the contents of a target such as tasks, datatypes, and properties.

■**Note** Ant scripts can contain top-level items other than targets. These can include certain tasks and datatypes. These elements are grouped in order of appearance into an implicit target that gets executed right after the parsing process ends and before any other targets are executed.

During the runtime phase Ant determines the build sequence of targets to be executed. This sequence is determined by resolving the target's dependencies. By default, unless a different target is specified, Ant will use the default target attribute as the entry point so it can determine the build sequence.

Let's execute the sample buildfile for the sample build shown in Figure 3-1 in order to get acquainted with Ant and some of the command-line options shown in Table 3-1. First type the contents shown in the listing to a text file and save it as build.xml. To run it, simply change to the directory where the buildfile is located and type the following:

```
ant
```

The output should look like this:

```
Buildfile: build.xml

Target A:
    [echo] Performing Step A

Target B:
    [echo] Performing Step B
    [echo] Echo is one of many Core Tasks

Target C:
    [echo] Performing Step C

BUILD SUCCESSFUL
Total time: 1 second
```

The output shows that Ant executed the buildfile successfully and that it took one second to execute (execution times will vary from system to system). From the output, you can see that the targets were executed in the following sequence: Target A, Target B, and Target C. To see a bit more detail you can run Ant again using the -v command-line option, which will show you some extra information:

```
Apache Ant version 1.6.5 compiled on June 2 2005
Buildfile: build.xml
...
Build sequence for target 'Target C' is [Target A, Target B, Target C]
Complete build sequence is [Target A, Target B, Target C]
...
BUILD SUCCESSFUL
Total time: 1 second
```

First, notice that the output shows that the intended target is Target C, which was defined as the build's default target. Ant resolved the default target dependencies to arrive at the build sequence [Target A, Target B, Target C] as shown at the top of the console output.

The text enclosed in the echo elements in each of the targets is shown on the console as each target is executed. The echo task is one of many built-in tasks provided by Ant. For example, a quick browse of the online documentation shows that the echo task sends the text enclosed to an Ant logger. By default Ant uses the DefaultLogger, which is a class that "listens" to the build and outputs to the standard out. Specific loggers can be selected on the command line by using the -logger option. Further examination shows that the echo task is well integrated with the logging system and that it can be provided with a level attribute to control the level at which the message is reported.

Note I decided against regurgitating the contents of the online documentation; therefore I'll explain some of Ant's tasks in context as you set out to build the tiers of the TechConf system. The best place to learn about all the available Ant tasks is from the online manual located at http://ant.apache.org/manual/index.html.

The previous run of the sample script assumed that you wanted to run the default target. To run a specific target you can indicate the target in the command line as follows:

```
ant "Target A"
```

Notice that target names are case sensitive and that double quotes are required for any target names that contain spaces. The resulting output should look like this:

```
Buildfile: build.xml

Target A:
    [echo] Performing Step A

BUILD SUCCESSFUL
Total time: 1 second
```

More on Targets

Targets are meant to represent a discrete step in the build process. Targets use tasks, datatypes, and property declarations to accomplish their work. Targets are required to have a name attribute and an optional comma-separated list of dependent targets.

■**Best Practice** Use simple action verbs to name your targets, such as "build," "test," or "deploy."

A typical buildfile is composed of several main targets: those that are meant to be called directly by the user and subtargets, which are targets that provide functionality to a main target.

■**Best Practice** Add a description attribute to a build's main targets. Targets containing a description are shown in the automatic project help, which is displayed when Ant is invoked with the -p or -projecthelp command-line options. For subtargets, prefix the name with a hyphen to make it easy to differentiate them from main targets.

Targets can be conditionally executed, and for this purpose Ant supports the if and unless attributes. Targets using either or both of these are said to be conditional targets. Both if and unless take the name of a property as a value, which is a test for existence. You can see an example of this if you modify Target A from the sample buildfile and add an if attribute with a value of do_a as shown in Listing 3-2.

Listing 3-2. *Conditional Ant Target*

```
<target name="Target A" description="Performs Step A" if="do_a">
    <echo>Performing Step A</echo>
</target>
```

The target should be executed only if the Ant property by the name do_a exists in the context of the build. Executing the buildfile produces the following result:

```
Buildfile: build.xml

Target A:

Target B:
    [echo] Performing Step B
    [echo] Echo is one of many Core Tasks

Target C:
    [echo] Performing Step C

BUILD SUCCESSFUL
Total time: 1 second
```

Notice that the output shows the banner for Target A but that the echo tasks contained within were never executed. You can run the buildfile again using the -D option to pass the property do_a to the build as shown:

```
ant -D "do_a="
```

The output now shows that Target A is being executed. You add the double quotes around the name-value pairs for the command-line argument parser so you can recognize the end of the argument. Any value could have been passed and the results would have been the same. Remember with if and unless, the value of the property is irrelevant; what matters is whether or not the property has been defined.

Target Dependencies

From the simple buildfile shown previously you can see that targets can depend on other targets. This example shows a very simple and linear dependency chain in which Target C depends on Target B, which in turn depends on Target A.

Ant will resolve any circular dependencies and will consequently fail the build. For example, you can modify the sample script to add Target C as a dependency of Target A as shown in Listing 3-3.

Listing 3-3. *Ant Target Dependencies*

```
<target name="Target A" depends="Target C" description="Performs Step A">
    <echo>Performing Step A</echo>
</target>
```

The resulting execution of the script will produce output similar to the following:

```
Buildfile: build.xml

BUILD FAILED
Circular dependency: Target C <- Target A <- Target B <- Target C

Total time: 1 second
```

Dependencies are resolved recursively using a topological sorting algorithm. The resulting build sequence ensures that a target in the dependency chain will only get executed once. You can see a great example of this in the Ant online manual, which shows a build with dependencies as shown in Figure 3-2.

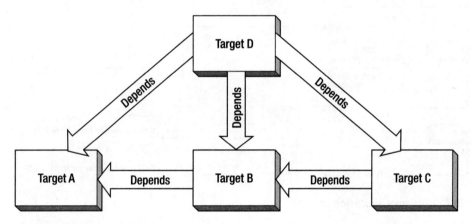

Figure 3-2. *Script dependencies*

A buildfile for the build in Figure 3-2 would look like Listing 3-4.

Listing 3-4. *Simple Ant Buildfile Showing Dependencies*

```xml
<?xml version="1.0" encoding="UTF-8"?>
<project basedir="." default="D" name="dependencies">
    <target name="A"/>
    <target name="B" depends="A"/>
    <target name="C" depends="B,A"/>
    <target name="D" depends="C,B,A"/>
</project>
```

Understanding how dependencies work is very important as your build process grows in complexity. Figure 3-3 shows a depiction of the dependency resolution process.

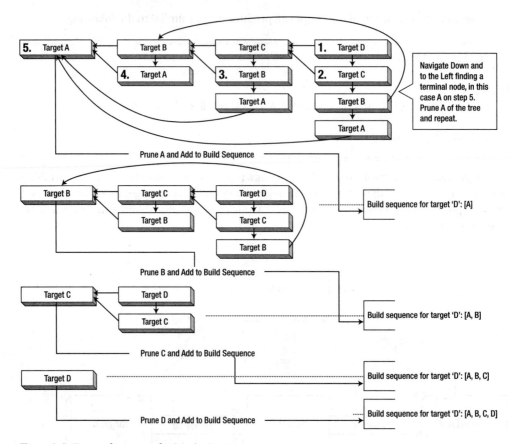

Figure 3-3. *Dependency resolution in Ant*

To test the dependencies example, save the buildfile as dependencies.xml and run it using Ant's -f parameter in order to indicate the buildfile as follows:

```
ant -f dependencies.xml -v
```

The output should look like this:

```
...
Buildfile: dependencies.xml
...
Build sequence for target 'D' is [A, B, C, D]
Complete build sequence is [A, B, C, D]

A:

B:

C:

D:
```

```
BUILD SUCCESSFUL
Total time: 1 second
```

■**Best Practice** Keep a build's dependencies as simple and linear as possible.

Tasks

Tasks are used within a target to achieve certain functionality. Think of a task element as a way to invoke a Java class's functionality. Ant provides a plethora of tasks that are divided in the following two categories:

- **Core:** Core tasks include basic foundational facilities needed in the build process like file manipulation, file dependencies, directory operations, source-code compilation, API document generation, archiving and packaging, XML file manipulation, SQL execution, and others.

- **Optional:** This includes tasks for some commercial products (like EJB/J2EE servers and third-party Version Control Systems) as well as nonbuild-specific tasks like unit testing, XML validation, and others.

Properties

Ant provides the ability for a project to have a set of properties. Properties are simple strings that you can access using the ${propertyName} notation. Whether you need to specify the location of a needed library many times or the name of a CVS repository, properties give you the flexibility to defer until runtime a set of values to be used in the build.

There are several ways to set a property. You can set it individually to the Ant buildfile via the D command-line option (see Table 3-1), or in bulk, from standard Java properties files by using the propertyfile option.

There are also several tasks that deal with properties. The property task enables the setting of a property by name. All property tasks are idempotent, which means that once a property's value has been set it will remain unchanged for the remainder of the build. The immutability of properties in Ant is often a source of confusion, because as developers you're often used to thinking with the use of variables.

■**Note** The <ant> and <antcall> tasks both span a new build by calling another buildfile. The <ant> task calls an external buildfile, and the <antcall> tasks calls a target on the current buildfile. Since version 1.6, Ant provides the <macro-def>, <import>, and <subant> tasks, which eliminate the need for using <ant> in most cases.

The simplest way to set a property's value is to use the property task. For example, to set a property named src, which could be later accessed using ${src}, you would use the property task as follows:

```
<property name="src" location="src" />
```

The src property would be an absolute path that refers to the location of the src directory relative to the basedir directory.

■**Best Practice**   Properties should be used with care. The two main uses of properties are for items whose value might change from build to build or for items whose value is calculated and used more than once during the build.

Many Ant properties are also available implicitly and are composed from the system properties, such as ${java.version}.

For any but the simplest project you can load a property file using the file attribute of the property task, thereby taking into account differences in user configurations, as follows:

```
<property file="build.properties"/>
```

Other tasks that deal directly with properties include the following:

- **LoadProperties:** Loads the contents of a file as properties (equivalent to using the file attribute for the property task).

- **LoadFile:** Load a text file into a single property.

- **XMLProperty:** Loads properties from an XML file. See the Ant documentation for the specific format of the XML file.

- **EchoProperties:** Displays all available properties in the project.

Many other tasks use properties as a way to take parameters in or out. For example, a common practice is for a task to have an attribute that takes the name of an inexistent property to be set in case of a specific event such as the possibility of the task failing.

■**Best Practice**   I recommend using a properties file named build.properties to store any overridden default values. This property file shouldn't be kept in the source-code repository but instead should add a sample properties file named build.properties.sample along with instructions on how to configure an individual build.properties file.

Datatypes

Ant's datatypes are primitive constructs that provide frequently required information in the processing of a buildfile. Their purpose is to simplify a task by encapsulating some information required and providing a simple way to manipulate it.

Several of Ant's built-in datatypes provide a structure that encapsulates information about a set of related resources such as files, environment variables, or even complex mappings between input and output files. Knowing how to properly use the Ant's datatypes will help you keep your buildfiles simple and efficient.

Datatypes and Properties in Action: A Simple Example

Many of Ant's tasks need to manipulate a file or groups of files. A typical need in a build is to specify a set of JAR files to be included in the classpath for certain tasks. Imagine that you're building a simple application with a directory structure, as shown in Figure 3-4.

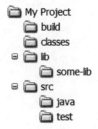

Figure 3-4. *Sample directory structure for datatypes and properties*

The sample buildfile in Listing 3-5 shows a build for which two path structures (datatypes) are defined, one with an id of class.path and the other with and id of all.source.path. These two datatypes are then used in the target named "compile", which uses the javac task to compile the classes referenced by the path reference by the id all.source.path.

Listing 3-5. *Simple Ant Buildfile Showing Datatypes*

```
<?xml version="1.0"?>
<project name="My Project" default="all" basedir=".">
...
    <property name="lib" location="lib"/>
    <property name="src" location="src"/>
    <property name="classes" location="classes"/>
    <property name="build" location="build"/>

    <property name="src-java" location="${src}/java"/>
    <property name="src-test" location="${src}/test"/>
    <property name="some-lib" location="${lib}/some-lib"/>
...
    <path id="class.path">
        <fileset dir="${lib}">
            <include name="*.jar"/>
```

```
        </fileset>
        <fileset dir="${some-lib}">
            <include name="*.jar"/>
        </fileset>
    </path>

    <path id="all.source.path">
        <pathelement path="${src-java}"/>
        <pathelement path="${src-test}"/>
    </path>
...
    <target name="compile" description="Compiles all sources.">
...
        <javac
            destdir="${classes}"
            classpathref="class.path"
            debug="on"
            deprecation="on"
            optimize="off">
            <src>
                <path refid="all.source.path"/>
            </src>
        </javac>
    </target>
```

The class.path path structure uses two instances of the fileset datatype to group under a common classpath all the JAR files included in the directories referenced by the lib and struts-lib properties. The pathelement is an example of an indispensable datatype that enables you to reuse path information in your builds. The fileset datatype is a typical example of Ant's pathlike structures. It encapsulates a group of files defined via nested patternset structures. For example, to create a fileset that includes all JAR files under the ${lib} directory, you can use the following fileset definition:

```
<fileset dir="${lib}">
    <patternset>
        <include name="*.jar"/>
    </patternset>
</fileset>
```

The fileset datatype contains an implicit patternset structure, which means that you can use shorthand to rewrite the fileset definition as follows:

```
<fileset dir="${lib}">
    <include name="*.jar"/>
</fileset>
```

We can further compact the fileset definition by using the include as a property rather than as a nested element:

```
<fileset dir="${lib}" include="*.jar" />
```

The path datatype can also make use of nested pathelements, as shown in the definition of the `all.source.path` path structure. It uses the pathelement datatype to reference the locations defined by `src-java` and `src-generated` properties.

Path is a typical Ant pathlike structure. When dealing with paths or classpaths, Ant's task makes use of pathlike structures to perform its function. In the previous example, you can see that the two pathelements defined at the top of the buildfile are then used by reference in the context of the javac task. The `class.path` path is passed to the `classpathref` attribute of javac to determine the classpath for compilation and the `all.source.path` is used by creating a new pathelement, which is nested inside the src nested element of the javac task.

As a build's complexity increases so do the patterns for selecting files. Pathlike structures enable the reuse of path information and help keep the growth of buildfiles under control.

■**Note** One of the criteria used in choosing many of the tools in this chapter was whether the tool provided an Ant task.

Case Study: Building TechConf with Ant

To set the stage for the development throughout the rest of the book, you need to first create a suitable directory structure (see Figure 3-5) as well as an initial Ant buildfile for the TechConf system.

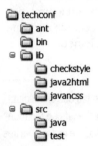

Figure 3-5. *Sample directory structure for the TechConf project*

The project's root directory is TechConf. Under this directory you'll place the project's main buildfile, named build.xml. The subdirectories under TechConf are organized as follows:

- **lib:** Contains any libraries required at runtime by the application(s)

- **ant:** Contains Ant macrodef in a single file, macros.xml

- **src:** The root directory for all non-generated sources

- **src/java:** The root directory for all non-J2EE Java sources

- **src/test:** The root directory for all test classes

- **src/j2ee:** The root directory for all J2EE source files

Now that you have a suitable directory structure, your next step should be to start putting together the TechConf buildfile. The `project` element contains the name of your project and a nested `description` element.

■**Best Practice** Use the `description` element, which allows you to enter a detailed description of the project. This description is shown on the console when invoking Ant with the `-projecthelp` or `-p` command-line option.

The default target will be the all target, which you'll develop later in the chapter. The basedir is set to be the directory where the buildfile resides, which in this case is the TechConf directory.

```
<?xml version="1.0"?>
<project name="TechConf" default="all" basedir=".">

    <description>
    This build script was developed to be a generic enterprise development
    build script using ANT 1.6.5 (ant.apache.org). To customize it or use it for
    other projects modify the build.properties file.
    </description>
...
```

Next, properties are defined for the created directories. Notice that you can define properties using other properties as with the `lib-dev` property. Properties that represent a directory are defined using the `location` attribute instead of the `value` attribute. The `location` attribute gets resolved to the full path relative to the basedir specified in the `project` element.

■**Best Practice** Making all paths relative to the project's basedir directory and avoiding the use of absolute paths guarantees that your buildfile will work anywhere. If your build depends on a resource whose location might change from environment to environment, you should place the location of said resource in a properties file or use environment variables such as ${os.name}.

The build directory is the root directory for all products of the build process, such as the classes directory, where the results of compiling the classes under src/java will be placed.

```
<!-- ================================================================ -->
<!-- Initialization                                                   -->
<!-- ================================================================ -->
<property file="build.properties"/>

<!-- =========== -->
<!-- Directories -->
```

```
<!-- =========== -->
<property name="build" location="build" />
<property name="lib" location="lib" />

<!-- Source -->
<property name="src" location="src" />
<property name="src-java" location="${src}/java" />
<property name="src-test" location="${src}/test" />
<property name="src-j2ee" location="${src}/j2ee" />

<property name="docs" location="docs" />
<property name="docs-api" location="${docs}/api" />
<property name="docs-html-source" location="${docs}/source" />
<property name="docs-test" location="${docs}/tests" />
<property name="src-web" location="web" />
```

Paths representing all the JAR files under the lib directory (class.path) and all class files under the classes directory are created.

Best Practice A common practice in Ant buildfiles is to have an init task that all other tasks depend on. I advocate not using the init task for setting up properties, loading properties files, paths, patternsets, or taskdefs. Instead, just place them before the first target, and they will be added to the implicit target. As mentioned earlier, the contents of the implicit target always get called and you don't have to remember making all other targets dependent on an init target.

A patternset is also used to filter a directory for non-source files. In the case where resources are part of the source directory such as property files or images, a patternset can be used to copy them to the location of the compiled classes which will require said resources.

```
<!-- Paths -->
<path id="class.path">
    <fileset dir="${lib}">
        <include name="*.jar"/>
    </fileset>
</path>

<path id="app.class.path">
    <pathelement location="${classes}"/>
    <path refid="class.path"/>
</path>

<!-- Patternsets -->
<patternset id="non.source.set">
    <exclude name="**/*.java"/>
    ...
```

```
    <exclude name="**/read-me.txt"/>
    <exclude name="**/package.html"/>
</patternset>
```

Compiling

Now it's time to add the first target to the buildfile, the compile target. This target will make use of the javac task, which is a wrapper to the javac command. In Listing 3-6, notice that before the javac task is invoked, all files under the ${src-java} directory that match the patternset non.source.set are copied to the ${classes} directory. This is done so that any resources such as Java properties files, images, and others are available to the compiled code under the classes directory. This is a common practice for many IDEs.

Listing 3-6. *Compile Target*

```
<!-- ================================================================ -->
<!-- Target: compile                                                  -->
<!-- Compiles all classes                                             -->
<!-- MUST use JDK 1.5 compiler                                        -->
<!-- ================================================================ -->

<target
    name="compile"
    depends="compile-init"
    description="Compiles all classes (JDK1.5)">
    <javac
        destdir="${classes}"
        classpathref="class.path"
        debug="on"
        deprecation="on"
        optimize="off"
        >
        <src>
            <path refid="all.source.path" />
        </src>
    </javac>
</target>

<target name="compile-init">
    <target-banner target="compile"/>
    <mkdir dir="${classes}"/>
    <copy todir="${classes}">
        <fileset dir="${src-java}">
            <patternset refid="non.source.set" />
        </fileset>
```

```
            <fileset dir="dd">
                <include name="*.properties"/>
            </fileset>
        </copy>
    </target>

    <target name="compile-clean">
        <delete includeemptydirs="true">
            <fileset dir="${classes}" includes="**/*"/>
        </delete>
    </target>
```

Notice that we've added two more targets other than compile. These are compile-init and compile-clean. The compile-init target simply creates the classes directory by making use of the mkdir task. The compile-clean target uses the delete task to remove the directory and all of its contents.

■**Best Practice** For each main target in the buildfile, add a target-init and a target-clean, where target is the name of the main target. This makes it fairly straightforward to determine the resources needed and created by a target and also makes it easier to maintain large buildfiles. For simple buildfiles a single clean target will usually suffice.

Buildfile Reuse with Macros

If you paid close attention to the compile-init target shown previously, you've notice that the first line is:

```
<target-banner target="compile"/>
```

The element target-banner is not a standard Ant task or a third-party task; it is a macro definition contained in a separate XML named macros.xml. Macro definitions, a feature introduced in Ant 1.6, help you avoid the tedious copy-paster reuse and enable you to modularize your builds. Macros can be invoked anywhere in the buildfile, and the macro definitions can be parameterized. In order to enable our build to use the macros, we use the import task as shown next:

```
<!-- ===================================================================== -->
<!-- Imports                                                               -->
<!-- ===================================================================== -->
<import file="ant/macros.xml"/>
```

Let's take a look at the file macros.xml, which is located in the ant directory at the root of the TechConf project and shown in Listing 3-7.

Listing 3-7. *Ant Macros File*

```
<?xml version="1.0"?>
<project name="techconf-ant-macros" default="test-macros" basedir="..">

    <!-- ================================================================ -->
    <!-- Prints a banner for the target being executed                    -->
    <!-- ================================================================ -->
    <macrodef name="target-banner">
        <attribute name="target"/>
        <attribute name="message" default="" />
        <sequential>
            <echo>==========================================================</echo>
            <echo>Executing Target @{target}</echo>
            <echo>@{message}</echo>
            <echo>==========================================================</echo>
        </sequential>
    </macrodef>

    <!-- ================================================================ -->
    <!-- Test the macros                                                  -->
    <!-- ================================================================ -->
    <target name="test-macros">
        <target-banner target="Compile"/>
        <target-banner target="Testing" message="This is a sample message"/>
    </target>
...
</project>
```

In macros.xml we define the target-banner macrodef. Ant macrodefs can take attributes; in this case there are two attributes, target and message. As you can guess from the snippet shown, the target-banner macrodef uses the echo task to print a banner to the console that informs the user of the current target being executed and also prints an optional message. The attributes are defined using the attribute element. The target attribute is required, but the message attribute is optional since it has a default value. Macro attributes are mutable and are expanded via @{attrname}.

■**Note** Macro attributes @{attr} are expanded before Ant properties ${property}. This is important if you are using properties in your macros.

On its own, the macros.xml file behaves just like any other Ant buildfile. If we execute the macros.xml file using Ant as follows:

```
ant -f macros.xml
```

The default target test-macros will execute, producing the following output:

```
Buildfile: macros.xml

test-macros:
    [echo] =====================================================================
    [echo] Executing Target Compile
    [echo] =====================================================================

    [echo] =====================================================================
    [echo] Executing Target Testing
    [echo] This is a sample message
    [echo] =====================================================================

BUILD SUCCESSFUL
Total time: 1 second
```

As you can see, macrodef in combination with the import task can help you create reusable, modularized Ant functionality that will help you keep your buildfiles simple. For the TechConf project we will use the macros.xml file to house most of the tasks peripheral to the build process. In the remainder of this chapter we will continue to enhance both the build.xml file and the macros.xml file to create a J2EE build system that's modular and reusable.

Javadoc Generation

For proper team communication and for enabling code reuse you must have a consistent, up-to-date set of API documentation. The Javadoc tool has existed for as long as Java has been around, and all developers are well acquainted with it. The problem has been that developers feel that they can run Javadoc only after they are finished with the code (which might be never). Running Javadoc at the end of a project provides very little help to others in the team and moves documentation to the end of process, when it isn't as helpful (waterfall).

With Ant you can ensure that Javadoc is generated as part of the daily build and that you don't hide the documentation process until the "end" of the development phase. The Ant Javadoc task provides a convenient way to generate Javadoc from within Ant.

To incorporate Javadoc generation into the TechConf build we will enhance the macros.xml file with a generic macrodef that defaults most of the common settings used with the Javadoc task. There are four required attributes—source.path, class.path, dest, year—and the optional company attribute, as shown in Listing 3-8.

Listing 3-8. *Javadoc Macrodef*

```
<!-- ===================================================================== -->
<!-- JavaDocs                                                              -->
<!-- ===================================================================== -->

<macrodef name="generate-javadoc" description="Generate JavaDocs.">
    <attribute name="company" default="Integrallis Software, LLC."/>
    <attribute name="source.path"/>
    <attribute name="class.path"/>
    <attribute name="year"/>
    <attribute name="dest"/>
    <sequential>
        <javadoc
            destdir="@{dest}"
            author="true"
            version="true"
            use="true"
            windowtitle="${ant.project.name}"
            sourcepathref="@{source.path}"
            classpathref="@{class.path}"
            packagenames="*.*"
            Verbose="false">
            <doctitle><![CDATA[<h1>${ant.project.name}</h1>]]></doctitle>
            <bottom>
        <![CDATA[<i>Copyright &#169; @{year} @{company} All Rights Reserved.</i>]]>
            </bottom>
            <tag name="todo" scope="all" description="To do:" />
        </javadoc>
    </sequential>
</macrodef>
```

Notice that the doctitle and the bottom nested elements make use of the XML character data (CDATA) section in order to be able to use HTML markup and not have it interfere with the markup of the buildfile.

To use the generate-javadoc macrodef in the TechConf buildfile we can create a target in our build.xml as shown in Listing 3-9.

Listing 3-9. *Generate-docs Target*

```
<!-- ===================================================================== -->
<!-- Target: docs                                                          -->
<!-- Generates documentation artifacts                                     -->
<!-- ===================================================================== -->
```

```
<target name="generate-docs" description="Generates all documentation">
    <target-banner target="generate-docs"/>
    <generate-javadoc
        class.path="class.path"
        dest="${docs-api}"
        source.path="all.source.path"
        year="2005"
    />
</target>

<target name="generate-docs-clean">
    <delete dir="${docs}" />
</target>
```

It is easy to see how much cleaner your main buildfile can become by using macrodefs effectively. For the rest of the chapter we will use the same technique to continue enhancing the build with other functionality.

Checking Code Conventions with Checkstyle

Even if you're using a formatting tool either at build time or with your favorite IDE, there are still style checks beyond the realm of formatting. Checkstyle is a tool that enables code to be checked against a convention. Checkstyle supports the Sun convention by default, although it can check for more than just simple formatting. For example, it can check for illegal regular expressions in the code, inline conditionals, double-checked locking, and other idioms or patterns that might be considered unsafe or problematic.

You can download Checkstyle from http://checkstyle.sourceforge.net. At the root of the Checkstyle distribution you'll find the checkstyle-all-4.0.jar file. Place this file in a directory named checkstyle under the lib directory of the TechConf project directory. The file containing the XML configuration representing the Sun convention is named sun_checks.xml, and it's located under the docs directory of the distribution directory. Copy this file to the lib/checkstyle directory also.

Checkstyle writes its output to the standard out by default or to a file in plain text or XML format. The Checkstyle distribution also provides several Extensible Stylesheet Language (XSL) stylesheets that can be used to convert the XML reports to HTML format for easier viewing. You can find these stylesheets in the Checkstyle distribution under the contrib directory. Copy the checkstyle-noframes-sorted.xsl file to the lib/checkstyle directory.

To use Checkstyle from within Ant, you first need to load the checkstyle task. As with the Javadoc task we will incorporate the checkstyle task in a macrodef contained in the macros.xml file. First we need to make the checkstyle task available to the macros.xml file by defining a taskdef for it:

```
<path id="checkstyle.class.path">
    <fileset dir="lib/checkstyle">
        <include name="*.jar"/>
    </fileset>
</path>
```

```
<taskdef
    resource="checkstyletask.properties"
    classpathref="checkstyle.class.path"
/>
```

The macrodef generate-checkstyle takes two required attributes: src to determine the directory containing the source files to check and checkstyle-reports for the location to place the generated reports. The rest of the attributes—checkstyle-checks-file, checkstyle-xml-report-file, checkstyle-html-report-file and checkstyle-stylesheet— are all optional. Notice that some of the default values for the optional attributes are generated from the values of the required attributes.

The checkstyle macrodef uses the checkstyle task to check the code under the @{src} directory against the conventions specified by the file @{checkstyle-checks-file} and uses a formatter of type XML to generate the report referred to in @{checkstyle-xml-report-file}. The failureProperty attribute is the property that's set if there are any errors encountered during the checking process. You can use this value to determine if any action is to be taken in the case of an error, such as emailing the report. The second part of the target uses the style task to transform the generated XML into an HTML report. The generate-checkstyle macrodef is shown in Listing 3-10.

Listing 3-10. *Generate-checkstyle Macrodef*

```
<!-- =================================================================== -->
<!-- CheckStyle                                                          -->
<!-- =================================================================== -->
<macrodef name="generate-checkstyle"
          description="Generates Code Convention Violations Report.">
    <attribute name="src" />
    <attribute name="checkstyle-reports" />
    <attribute name="checkstyle-checks-file"
               default="lib/checkstyle/sun_checks.xml"/>
    <attribute name="checkstyle-xml-report-file"
               default="@{checkstyle-reports}/checkstyle-report.xml"/>
    <attribute name="checkstyle-html-report-file"
               default="@{checkstyle-reports}/checkstyle-report.html"/>
    <attribute name="checkstyle-stylesheet"
               default="lib/checkstyle/checkstyle-noframes-sorted.xsl"/>
    <sequential>
        <mkdir dir="@{checkstyle-reports}" />
        <checkstyle
            config="@{checkstyle-checks-file}"
            failureProperty="checkstyle.failure"
            failOnViolation="false"
            >
            <formatter type="xml" tofile="@{checkstyle-xml-report-file}"/>
            <fileset dir="@{src}" includes="**/*.java"/>
        </checkstyle>
```

```
        <style
            in="@{checkstyle-xml-report-file}"
            out="@{checkstyle-html-report-file}"
            style="@{checkstyle-stylesheet}"
        />
    </sequential>
</macrodef>
```

A sample Checkstyle report is shown in Figure 3-6.

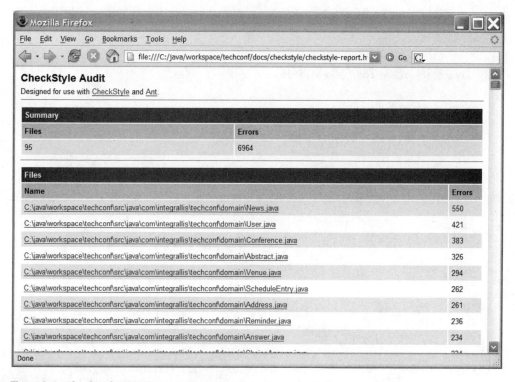

Figure 3-6. *Checkstyle HTML report*

Generating Source-Code Metrics

Although I don't advocate counting code lines, classes, or methods as a measure of a project's success, static code analysis can help you pinpoint some areas of unnecessary complexity that can lead to the discovery of potential bugs or high-maintenance code.

JavaNCSS is a simple source-measurement tool for Java that provides that following basic types of analysis:

- **NCSS:** Noncommenting source statements provide counts of many features of the code such as lines of code, declarations, methods, statements, constructors, and so on.

- **CCN:** Cyclomatic complexity number (McCabe metric). McCabe's cyclomatic complexity metric looks at a program's control flow graph as a measure of its complexity.

You can download JavaNCSS from www.kclee.de/clemens/java/javancss/ as a simple ZIP file that includes an Ant task. Place all JAR files located under the distribution's lib directory in a directory named javancss under the lib directory of the TechConf project. Next, create a directory named xslt under the lib/javancss and copy the contents of the xslt directory under the JavaNCSS distribution directory.

To make the JavaNCSS Ant task available in the macros.xml file we add the following path and taskdef definitions:

```
<path id="javancss.class.path">
    <fileset dir="lib/javancss">
        <include name="*.jar"/>
    </fileset>
</path>

<!-- Javancss - kclee.com/clemens/java/javancss -->
<taskdef
    name="javancss"
    classname="javancss.JavancssAntTask"
    classpathref="javancss.class.path"
/>
```

The Ant task can generate a report in plain text of the XML format. Similar to the checkstyle macrodef, you'll use the style task to transform the reports to HTML, as shown in Listing 3-11.

Listing 3-11. *Generate-metrics Macrodef*

```
<!-- ==================================================================== -->
<!-- Metrics                                                          -->
<!-- ==================================================================== -->
<macrodef name="generate-metrics">
    <attribute name="src" />
    <attribute name="report-name" />
    <attribute name="report-dir" default="." />
    <attribute name="xml-report" default="@{report-dir}/@{report-name}.xml" />
    <attribute name="html-report" default="@{report-dir}/@{report-name}.html" />
    <attribute name="stylesheet" default="lib/javancss/xslt/javancss2html.xsl" />
    <sequential>
        <mkdir dir="@{report-dir}" />
        <javancss
            srcdir="@{src}"
            includes="**/*.java"
            generateReport="true"
            outputfile="@{xml-report}"
            format="xml"
            functionMetrics="false"
        />
```

```
        <style
            in="@{xml-report}"
            out="@{html-report}"
            style="@{stylesheet}"
        />
    </sequential>
</macrodef>
```

The generated HTML reports look like the one shown in Figure 3-7.

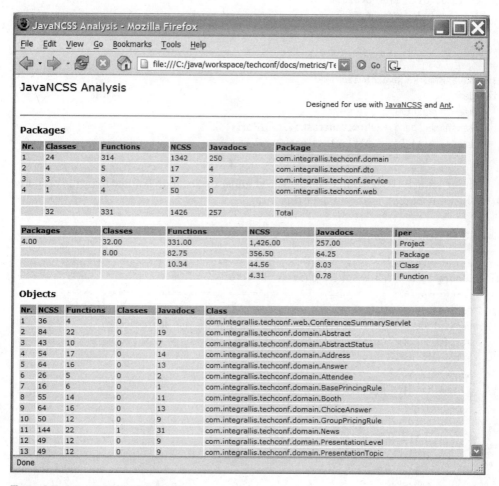

Figure 3-7. *A JavaNCSS HTML report*

Generating Browsable Source Code

One useful feature for sharing knowledge about a project is the ability to generate a browsable
version of the code for viewing online. Many open source projects use this as a way to allow
others to view the source to a particular class without having to download a source distribution

or having to use CVS. Java2Html is a tool that enables you to take a Java class or a snippet of Java code and generate a syntax-highlighted HTML version of the code.

The Java2Html tool can be obtained from www.java2html.de as a single ZIP file that contains one JAR file (java2html.jar). As with the other third-party Ant tasks, place the JAR file in a directory named java2html under the TechConf lib directory.

As mentioned previously, you should load the task using the taskdef task. First we add the path and taskdef to the macros.xml file as shown here:

```
<path id="java2html.class.path">
    <fileset dir="lib/java2html">
        <include name="*.jar"/>
    </fileset>
</path>

<!-- Java2Html - java2html.de -->
<taskdef
    name="java2html"
    classname="de.java2html.anttasks.Java2HtmlTask"
    classpathref="java2html.class.path"
/>
```

The generated HTML source will be placed under the location pointed to by the property ${browseable-source}, as shown in Listing 3-12.

Listing 3-12. *Generate-html Macrodef*

```
<!-- ================================================================ -->
<!-- Generates browsable source code in HTML format                 -->
<!-- ================================================================ -->
<macrodef name="generate-html"
    description="Generates browsable HTML version of the source code." >
    <attribute name="src"/>
    <attribute name="dest"/>
    <sequential>
        <mkdir dir="@{dest}" />
        <java2html
            srcdir="@{src}"
            destdir="@{dest}"
            includes="**/*.java"
            outputFormat="html"
            tabs="4"
            style="eclipse"
            showLineNumbers="true"
            showFileName="true"
            showTableBorder="true"
```

```
                includeDocumentHeader="true"
                includeDocumentFooter="true"
                addLineAnchors="true"
                lineAnchorPrefix="fff"
        />
    </sequential>
</macrodef>
```

Figure 3-8 shows an example of an HTML page generated by Java2Html.

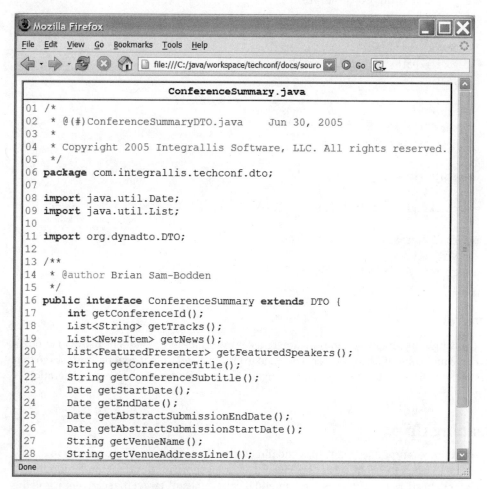

Figure 3-8. *An HTML page generated by Java2Html*

Document Generation

Finally we can group all of the document-generation tasks under one single target in the build.xml file as shown in Listing 3-13.

Listing 3-13. *Generate-docs Target*

```
<!-- ==================================================================== -->
<!-- Target: docs                                                         -->
<!-- Generates documentation artifacts: Javadoc, Browsable HTML, etc.   -->
<!-- ==================================================================== -->

<target name="generate-docs"
    description="Generates all documentation">
    <target-banner target="generate-docs"/>
    <generate-javadoc
        class.path="class.path"
        dest="${docs-api}"
        source.path="all.source.path"
        year="2005"
    />
    <generate-html
        src="${src}"
        dest="${docs-html-source}"
    />
    <generate-checkstyle
        src="${src}"
        checkstyle-reports="${checkstyle-reports}"
    />
    <generate-metrics
        src="${src}"
        report-dir="${metrics-reports}"
        report-name="${ant.project.name}"
    />
</target>
```

This single document-generation target makes the buildfile simpler. The use of macrodefs makes the main buildfile less verbose. I decided to group all document generation-tasks so that users of the build have to deal with only a single, simple target for all document-generation tasks.

Cleaning Up

The build process produces many files and directories. Getting the project directory to the same state as when the source was checked out of a repository is important for determining what has changed. Many Ant users recommend having a "clean" target that can remove all the products of the build process.

The problem with this approach is that for large builds it's easy to accidentally delete files that are needed, and it's also easy to miss files or directories that need to be deleted. For this reason you should include a clean sub target for each main target in the buildfile. By doing this you'll easily be able to determine what needs to be clean at the target level. Then for the global clean target you can simply invoke all individual clean sub targets by invoking them using the antcall task (or by listing them as dependencies), as shown in Listing 3-14.

Listing 3-14. *Clean-all Target*

```
<!-- ================================================================ -->
<!-- Target: clean-all                                               -->
<!-- Removes all build artifacts                                     -->
<!-- ================================================================ -->
<target name="clean-all" description="Removes all build artifacts">
    <antcall target="compile-clean" />
    <antcall target="generate-docs-clean" />
    <antcall target="test-clean" />
    ...
</target>
```

The All Target

Finally, it's a common practice to make the buildfile default target a target named "all", which has in its dependencies a list of the targets that represented a full build of the system. If your build process has any non-critical targets that take a fair amount of time to generate, you can create new targets that will do whatever the all target does in addition to any extra work. For example a target that does "all" and also generates documentation can be called "all-with-docs". The point is that you want to minimize the amount of time that it takes to build the application so that developers don't have noticeable interruptions in the flow of their work. A typical all target looks like that shown in Listing 3-15.

Listing 3-15. *The All Target*

```
<!-- ================================================================ -->
<!-- Does it all                                                     -->
<!-- ================================================================ -->

<target
    name="all"
    depends="compile,..."
    description="Generates, compiles, packages and deploys."
/>
```

Eclipse Integration

In Chapter 2 we learned how to get the Eclipse IDE installed and configured. Now that we have an Ant buildfile it will be ideal if we can achieve harmony between the command line and the IDE. Luckily for us, Eclipse ships with powerful Ant integration. Eclipse provides a great Ant XML editor with syntax highlighting, code completion, flyover evaluation of Ant elements, as well as immediate visual feedback about the validity of your buildfile.

For the TechConf application to work seamlessly, you can create an Ant Builder, which is a facility provided by Eclipse's external tools framework for Ant integration. An Ant Builder can be configured to run at specific times. For example, in my environment I configured the Ant build to run when a manual build is invoked or when the project "Clean" option is selected.

To create an Ant builder, select Project ➤ Properties from the Eclipse menu (alternatively you can right-click and select Properties or press Alt+Enter on the project's top node in the Navigator or Package Explorer). Next, select the Builders node as shown in Figure 3-9.

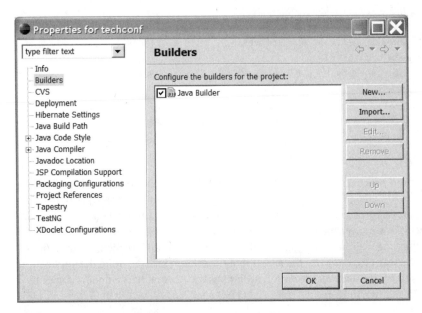

Figure 3-9. *TechConf Eclipse project properties dialog*

To create a new builder, click New in the Builders property dialog. Another dialog will appear asking to select the type of builder to create, as shown in Figure 3-10.

Select the Ant Build option and click OK. You should now be presented with the Ant builder property dialog as shown in Figure 3-11. Enter a suitable name for the builder in the Name field such as "TechConf Ant Builder". The dialog consists of several tabs of options. In the Main tab you can select the Ant buildfile to be used by the builder. Under the Buildfile field click Browse Workspace and find the build.xml file at the root of the techconf project.

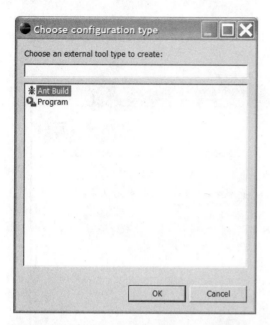

Figure 3-10. *External tool builder type selection*

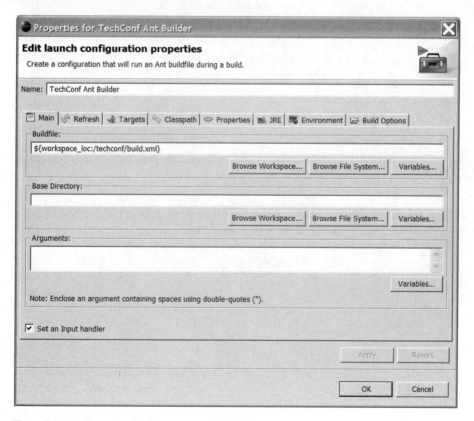

Figure 3-11. *Eclipse Ant builder properties dialog*

Under the Refresh tab, check the "Refresh resources upon completion" box, choose the radio button labeled "The project containing the selected resource", and check "Recursively include sub-folders" as shown in Figure 3-12.

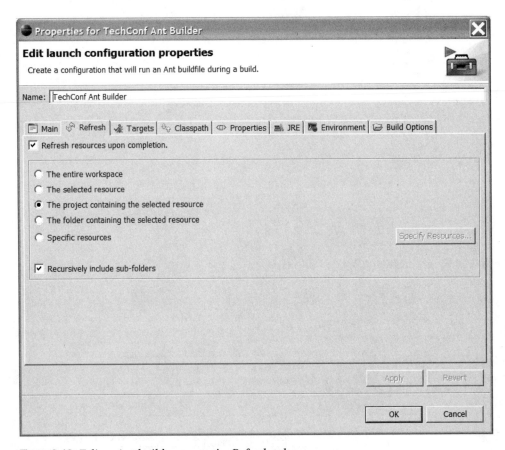

Figure 3-12. *Eclipse Ant builder properties Refresh tab*

Finally, under the Targets tab, you want the default target of the Ant build to be executed after a "Clean" and during a "Manual Build" as shown in Figure 3-13.

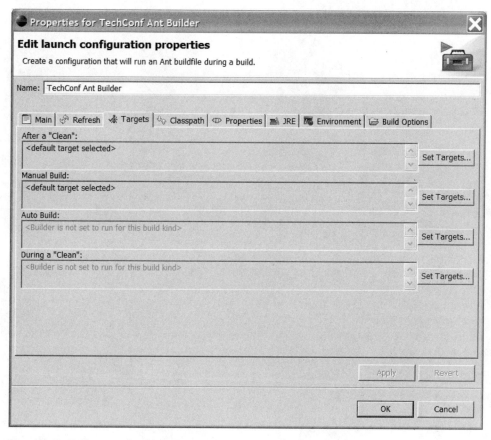

Figure 3-13. *Eclipse Ant builder properties Targets tab*

Summary

In this chapter you have learned the importance of having a solid build system in place and the basics of the Ant build tool. We crafted a reusable Ant build to automate the building process of the TechConf system by using several open source Ant tasks. The resulting base build reflects my experience building many Java and J2EE applications. You can apply most of the ideas used in this system to your existing and future projects. In the rest of the book we will continue to enhance the build to create the J2EE components and artifacts that compose the sample application.

The power of a well-crafted build will become even more apparent when we combine the building blocks learned in this chapter with the power of unit testing (Chapter 8) and continuous integration (Chapter 9).

CHAPTER 4

■ ■ ■

Object Relational Mapping with Hibernate

As a Java developer it's very likely that you'll find yourself retrieving data from a relational database and that you'll want to look at ways to move that data to and from your objects and components. The question is how to approach the problem of storing your objects' state in an RDBMS.

Like most software developers using a relational database to store objects, I find that this process is one that seems to consume a lot of my time. Some things are now clear to me about this process, and with each new project I find that how we go about hooking up a database to our object-oriented applications depends on several factors, including the following:

- How closely related the database schema is to the object model

- Whether the schema predates the application

- Whether the schema is a legacy schema with natural keys and compound primary keys

- What the degree of normalization is in the schema

- How much influence the schema had on the design of the object model and the user interface (and vice versa)

Object-oriented design and development is all about the trade-offs. An object-oriented purist view of the world might argue that the design of a domain model should not be influenced by an "implementation" detail such as where the state of the objects in that model will be stored when they are not in memory. On the other side of the spectrum, a relational data modeler might argue that the data will very likely outlive the application and that the design of the database schema should concentrate only on efficiently storing and accessing of the data. My view (and that of most of my colleagues) is that such broad statements are one-sided and only lead to problems down the line.

In a real-world application, with the sort of timelines we work against nowadays, agility is of the essence. In most enterprise environments you will have control of the object model and at best have influence on the design of the database schema. I find that the process of mapping your objects to databases is easier in places where there is the most cooperation between object modelers and data modelers. Designing the object model and the data model with the involvement of both parties will bring in compromises that will produce applications that reflect well the problem domain while ensuring the integrity, reusability, and efficient use of the data.

All of my previous remarks are based on the notion of having a domain model that represents the problem domain that your application is targeting. But domain modeling is just one approach to solving a problem. A lot of the typical Internet applications we use on a daily basis have a more data-driven, relational/procedural flavor to them and are better suited to be constructed in a way that exploits those characteristics, that is using a language that can take advantage of the relational model. Yes, you guessed it right, SQL. For very simple applications with very simple CRUD (create, read, update, and delete) interactions with the database and where performance is the number-one priority, raw SQL might still be the right choice.

That being said, it is important to foresee the evolution of an application to determine whether you should start with an object-relational mapping (ORM) tool from the onset, plain SQL or whether you will intermix both approaches in a single application.

OBJECT-RELATIONAL MAPPING

Object-relational mapping (ORM) is the name given to the technologies, tools, and techniques used to bridge the divide between objects and relational databases. ORM tools allow you to declaratively map data objects to data and relations in a relational database, allowing programmers to work with information from a relational database in the form of Java objects. This breed of tools generates all of the SQL code needed to interact with the database. Developers work at the object level, and the concept of queries and transactions are applied to the objects rather than database objects. Although they're under the same umbrella, the tools can vary greatly in the way they work, from the level of "transparency" to whether they work by generating code, modifying bytecode, or using runtime inspection.

The concept of transparency as applied to ORM tools is still very vague in the industry. Persistence transparency or orthogonality implies that objects are treated without any implicit notion of persistence. Most of the existing tools aren't truly transparent, yet they provide a good separation of concerns by isolating the persistence of objects behind very simple object-oriented constructs. In Hibernate for example, transparency means that the Plain Old Java Objects (POJOs) being mapped have no notion that they are persistent objects.

Also worthy of consideration is how to fit the way a certain tool works with the rest of your development process. With some tools, you start with an object model and derive a relational persistence model; with others, you start with a relational model and derive an object model. Most of the time you'll find that you have both an existing object model and a relational model, in which case most tools fall short of expectations and most of the mapping work is manual. Sometimes it is impossible to avoid the situation when trade-offs need to be made between your object model and the database schema. It's important that both models are developed in cooperation. An ORM tool can help this collaborative work, but it's the human factor that plays the larger role.

Object persistence is, like most hard problems, all about the trade-offs. The theme with Java persistence is about choices, as with many things in Java. No tool is perfect for every persistence scenario. Some tools trade transparency for performance or simplicity for capabilities. Some of the questions that arise during the selection (or creation) of an object-relational tool include the following:

- How to convert column values to Java objects and primitives. For example, a Java Date object can be mapped to many database types.

- How to model object relationships (such as inheritance, aggregation, and composition) on a database schema or how to model relations between tables in an object or group of objects.

- How to deal with database keys and object identity, which might not exist in the object model.

- How to optimize the resulting SQL calls.

- How to take advantage of proprietary database features such as updatable views and stored procedures.

- How to guarantee referential integrity without limiting the behavioral expressiveness of the object model.

- How to deal with transactions when the database is accessed concurrently from multiple sources. From a relational point of view, an object is nothing but an in-memory cache of the database data that must be invalidated and refreshed when appropriate.

- How to deal with expensive operations like loading many child objects in a one-to-many relationship (lazy loading, proxy objects, or caching).

Obviously, as the object graphs get more complex, the tools have to be more "intelligent." I've seen countless companies that start with a very simple system for which they write their own persistence layer from the ground up. We equate this to writing your own application server. Sooner or later you'll run into some of technical questions pondered previously by others and discover that you're spending most of your time "fine-tuning" your persistence framework. ORM tools take away the complexity of mapping classes in memory to databases. They provide interfaces that automatically select, insert, update, and delete tables in the database in order to reflect changes made to an object model.

Therefore my recommendation is that you choose a mapping tool earlier rather than later, before any "temporary" persistence logic in your application starts to look like a homemade framework. Using an ORM layer has proven to increase productivity by moving developer focus away from figuring out how to store objects (a nonfunctional concern) to solving the real business problems. Another positive side effect of using an ORM tool is that, like JDBC, it provides an isolating layer between the database and the application by providing an objectified view of the database. In a better case, it completely makes persistence "transparent," without the complexity of writing and maintaining straight JDBC code.

ORM tools also have drawbacks, including performance, portability (does the tool implement any of the known standards?), and the initial learning curve. If performance is of paramount importance in your application, isolate the key components of your application and test them against a significant amount of data.

Introduction to Hibernate

So you have a working object model! Your application has finally reached the state when a database is necessary. JUnit and mock unit tests have given you the confidence to declare your object model ready to be synchronized with some sort of data storage.

Depending on the complexity of your object model, this is when most of the headaches of developing an object-oriented application begin, the moment when you decide to hook it up to a relational database.

With relatively simple object models and simple querying requirements, a Java application that uses straight SQL can be easily ported, especially if you have externalized your queries. But the reality is that most applications will have either complex object-to-table mapping requirements, querying requirements, or in the worst case both. Also, with straight SQL we sometimes end up using a database vendor-specific feature, which can pretty much tie you up to that particular vendor.

Fortunately for us, the open source community has once again given us a choice. Hibernate is an ORM tool billed as a relational persistence service for idiomatic Java, which can be translated as a way of saying "object-oriented transparent persistence mechanism for Java." The transparency part here means that the objects being persisted don't have any code in them that exposes their ability to be persisted, as opposed to say, something like Entity EJBs, where the persistence capabilities are explicitly marked in the structure and relationships of the component in its environment, the EJB container.

Hibernate provides both persistence and object-querying capabilities that allow you to work in a fine-grained fashion with rich object models. It provides an object-oriented declarative programming model that doesn't depend on code generation or build-time bytecode modification, although it uses reflection and runtime code enhancement via Code Generation Library (cglib). Hibernate does not force you to implement any special interfaces or extend any particular class; you can work with clean and simple POJOs.

In Hibernate, the mappings between object and tables can be defined in XML documents, programmatically in Java code or via JSR-220 persistence annotations. Also, projects like XDoclet enable you to annotate pre-Java Standard Edition 1.5 applications with Javadoc comments which are used to generate the XML mappings. Hibernate works equally well in stand-alone applications or in managed environments such as a J2EE server.

The Hibernate project got started by Gavin King in late 2001 as the result of his experiences working with the earlier versions of CMP EJBs. Hibernate's easy-to-use SQL-like query language makes it easier for developers who are accustomed to writing SQL to make the transition from either Container-Managed Persistence (CMP) EJBs or straight JDBC. This project has become a successful example of an open source project, because it provides a large, clean amount of documentation and has very responsive community support. In late 2003, Hibernate became part of the JBoss project and is currently being used as the foundation for JBoss' CMP EJB3 engine and a great source of influence on the EJB3 specification. Hibernate provides a single, simple API that strives for familiarity (to SQL) rather than standards compliance. Figure 4-1 shows a simplified view of Hibernate's architecture.

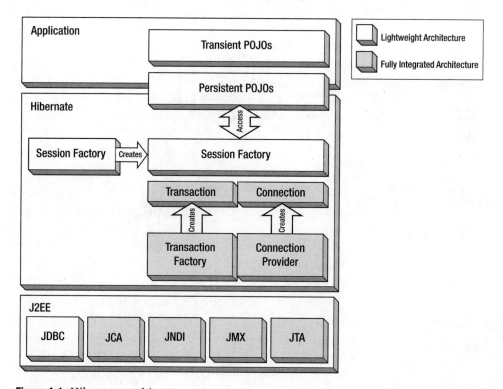

Figure 4-1. *Hibernate architecture*

As you can see from Figure 4-1, how much of Hibernate you use depends on your needs. At its simplest level Hibernate provides a lightweight architecture that deals only with ORM. Full-blown usage of Hibernate fully abstracts most aspects of persistence, such as transaction, entity/query caching, and connection pooling. To learn more about Hibernate's architecture go to www.hibernate.org/hib_docs/v3/reference/en/html/architecture.html.

How Hibernate Works

Hibernate's success lies in the simplicity of its core concepts. At the heart of every interaction between your code and the database lies the Hibernate Session. Figure 4-2 provides an overview of how Hibernate works.

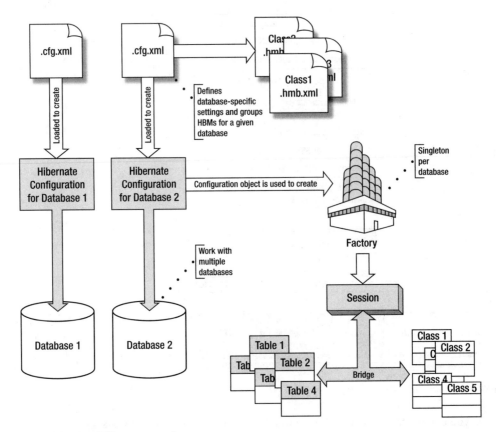

Figure 4-2. *How Hibernate works*

The Hibernate Session

The Hibernate Session embodies the concept of a persistence service (or persistence manager) that can be used to query and perform insert, update, and delete operations on instances of a class mapped by Hibernate. In an ORM tool you perform all of these interactions using object-oriented semantics; that is, you no longer are referring to tables and columns, but you use Java classes and object properties. As its name implies, the Session is a short-lived, lightweight object used as a bridge during a conversation between the application and the database. The Session wraps the underlying JDBC connection or J2EE data source, and it serves as a first-level cache for persistent objects bound to it.

The Session Factory

Hibernate requires that you provide it with the information required to connect to each database being used by an application as well as which classes are mapped to a given database. Each one of these database-specific configuration files, along with the associated class mappings, are compiled and cached by the SessionFactory, which is used to retrieve Hibernate Sessions. The SessionFactory is a heavyweight object that should ideally be created only once (since it is an expensive and slow operation) and made available to the application code that needs to perform persistence operations.

Each `SessionFactory` is configured to work with a certain database platform by using one of the provided Hibernate dialects. If you are prototyping an application you'll likely start with a database system you can easily install and run on your own machine. In my case this is usually MySQL, PostgreSQL or one of the flavors of pure embedded open source Java databases like HSQLDB. Most of us eventually have to migrate our schemas to an "enterprise" RDBMS such as Oracle, Sybase, or DB2. With its pluggable database architecture, Hibernate can make porting your application from database to database as simple as changing a few parameters in an XML file. The choice of Hibernate dialect is important when it comes to using database-specific features like native primary key generation schemes or `Session` locking. At the time of this writing Hibernate (version 3.1) supports 22 database dialects. Each of the dialect implementations are in the package `org.hibernate.dialect`. Figure 4-3 shows the available dialects.

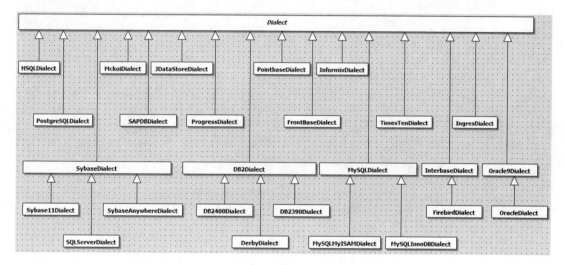

Figure 4-3. *Hibernate dialects*

The Hibernate Object Mappings

Hibernate specifies how each object state is retrieved and stored in the database via an XML configuration file. Hibernate mappings are loaded at startup and are cached in the `SessionFactory`. Each mapping specifies a variety of parameters related to the persistence lifecycle of instances of the mapped class such as:

- Primary key mapping and generation scheme

- Object-field-to-table-column mappings

- Associations/Collections

- Caching settings

- Custom SQL, store procedure calls, filters, parameterized queries, and more

Persistence Lifecycle

The last piece of information that I wish I had obtained earlier in my work with Hibernate is an understanding of the Lifecycle of an object as it pertains to Hibernate. There are three possible states for a Hibernate mapped object. Understanding these states and the actions that cause state transitions will become very important when dealing with the more complex Hibernate problems. Figure 4-4 shows how different methods provided by the Hibernate Session transition a mapped object from state to state.

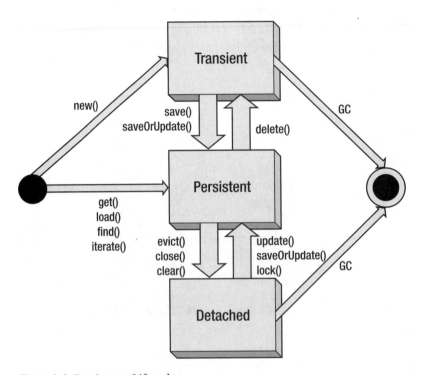

Figure 4-4. *Persistence Lifecycle*

In the transient state, the object is not associated with a database table. That is, its state has not been saved to a table, and the object has no associated database identity (no primary key has been assigned). Objects in the transient state are non-transactional, meaning that they do not participate in the scope of any transaction bound to a Hibernate Session. After a successful invocation of the save or saveOrUpdate methods an object ceases to be transient and becomes persistent. The Session delete method (or a delete query) produces the inverse effect making a persistent object transient.

Persistent objects are objects with database identity. (If they have been assigned a primary key but have not yet been saved to the database, they are referred to as being in the "new" state). Persistent objects are transactional, which means that they participate in transactions associated with the Session (at the end of the transaction the object state will be synchronized with the database).

A persistent object that is no longer in the Session cache (associated with the Session) becomes a detached object. This happens after a transaction completes, when the Session is closed, cleared, or if the object is explicitly evicted from the Session cache. Given Hibernate transparency when it comes to providing persistent services to an object, objects in the detached state can effectively become intertier transfer objects and in certain application architectures can replace the need to have DTOs (Data Transfer Objects). For a complete discussion of this pattern refer to Chapter 5.

The Process

So, how do you get started with Hibernate? Besides the obvious need to obtain and configure Hibernate to work with your environment, you need to create the mappings for each one of the classes that will be stored in the database. Aside from manually creating the POJOs, database schema, and HBM (HiBernate Mapping) files, there are three approaches to creating a complete ORM domain model.

POJO-Driven Approach

In the POJO-driven approach you start with an object/domain model, and using JSR-220 annotation or Javadoc metadata comments, you define how each field in a class maps to a database column. At runtime, Hibernate uses the annotations to dynamically create the mappings. Then using Hibernate's hbm2dll automatic feature, you can generate the database schema at runtime. In the case of pre-JSE1.5 applications you will use a code/metadata generator such as XDoclet to generate the HBM files and subsequently feed the HBM files to a tool such as Hibernate's own hbm2ddl and generate a schema for the relational database of your liking. This approach works very well for new applications for which a data model has not yet been designed or created. Figure 4-5 illustrates the POJO-driven approach.

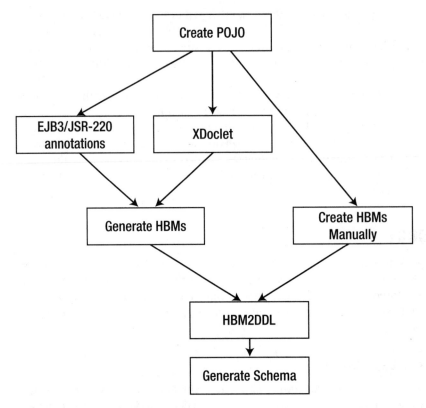

Figure 4-5. *POJO-driven approach*

Data Model–Driven Approach

In the model-driven approach you start with a database schema for the chosen database system, and using a tool like Middlegen or Hibernate Synchronizer, you generate mappings and POJOs for each table being mapped. This approach provides a fast start-up time for development but can potentially leave you with what Martin Fowler refers to as an anemic domain model with very little of the rich semantic that you would expect to find in a domain model.

   In such cases I sometimes like to think of the resulting model as more of a data-access model which will in turn be used by a richer domain model. Of course the issues of where the persistence interaction lies in your code become a hotly debated topic. Do you have your real domain objects peppered with persistence code in order to manipulate the data-driven table wrappers generated? Or do you take the more behavior/data separation model that most J2EE applications follow, where use cases are mapped to say a stateless session bean method which in terms manipulates the data mapper objects generated? Figure 4-6 illustrates the data model–driven approach.

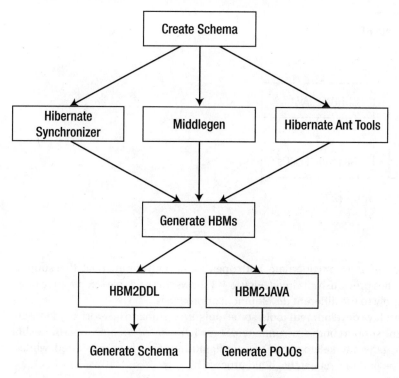

Figure 4-6. *Data model–driven approach*

HBM-Driven Approach

The two previous approaches, taking either a domain-model or data-model approach, typically result in HBM mappings that are not quite complete. Every time I use either of the approaches above in a moderately complex application, I find myself fine-tuning the HBM files to either get more accurate POJOs (in the data-driven approach) or more efficient, manageable database schema (in the POJO-driven approach). The third approach suggested here takes the stand that object-relational mapping is an inescapable, necessary evil that should be taken into consideration early and in a head-first fashion in the development of your application. By creating detailed, accurate HBM files you will end up with both a domain model and a database schema that meets your application needs and ensures the longevity of the data. This is by far the most tedious approach to map your domain model to a database, basically because it is a mostly manual process. Of course, based on the complexity of your object model and schema, you might be able to combine the different approaches outlined to maximize your productivity, therefore using one of the two automated approaches for most of your domain object mappings and resorting to manually created mappings for a few exceptional cases. Figure 4-7 illustrates the HBM-driven approach.

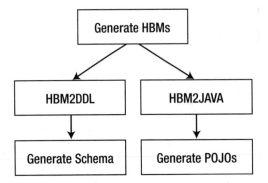

Figure 4-7. *HBM-driven approach*

The Tools

There is a great variety of tools for Hibernate, both open source and commercial, that support the different approaches previously outlined. Figure 4-8 shows the available open source offerings and how they apply to the different development approaches.

Also, as with most Java development tools, some tools are command line–driven, some are IDE-specific and some support both environments. Some IDE-centric tools are one-time-shot type of tools that will generate skeleton code and configurations for you to get started, while others are meant to be part of a repeatable build process.

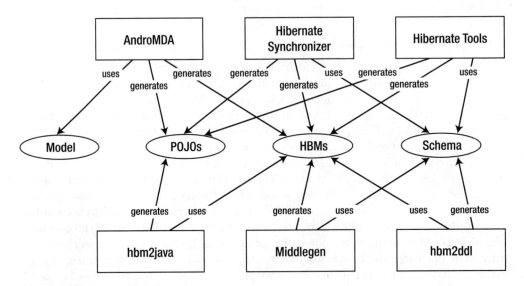

Figure 4-8. *Map of Hibernate-related tools*

Road Map

For the persistence needs of the TechConf application, we will use the HBM-driven method and work on developing a detailed set of HBM files, a domain model, and a database schema.

After configuring Hibernate to work with the local TechConf instance of MySQL, we will work on implementing some of the use cases of the TechConf system which will show the steps in creating Hibernate mappings and in generating POJO classes and a database schema as shown in Figure 4-9.

The order in which the use cases are implemented is based on the level of difficulty involved in creating the mappings and the different ORM concepts covered.

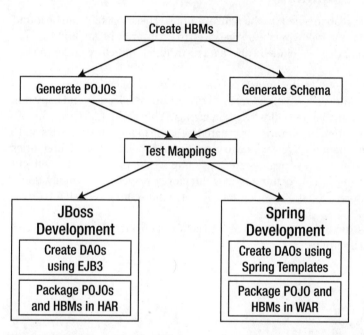

Figure 4-9. *Road map for the Hibernate-related development of the TechConf application*

Hibernate in J2SE

One of the advantages of a POJO-centric ORM tool like Hibernate is that it really helps you separate concerns, when it comes to development, by enabling you to work in the world of POJOs without worrying too much about the complexities introduced by the future needs of your application (such as distribution, clustering, and tier partitioning). As you will soon see with Hibernate, we can concentrate on developing a solid POJO domain model and design and test the persistence needs of the model before we plunge into the details of making a J2EE application.

Obtaining Hibernate

You can download Hibernate (version 3.X) from www.hibernate.org in both binary and source distributions. For the examples, you'll need the distribution file hibernate-3.X.zip, which you can unzip and save to any location, for example c:\java\hibernate. The Hibernate distribution contains the Hibernate JAR (hibernate3.jar) along with all third-party dependencies, full source code including tests, and reference and API documentation. In the rest of the chapter we will continue enhancing the directory structure developed in Chapter 3 to begin building the ORM layer of the TechConf application.

Setup for POJO Development

Table 4-1 lists the JAR files that are needed for the J2SE examples. These JAR files can be found in the Hibernate distribution, and following the advice given in Chapter 3 (the Ant build system chapter) we will place them under a versioned Hibernate distribution directory under the application's lib directory.

We will add the Hibernate JARs to the libraries of the TechConf application. To do this, create a hibernate directory under the lib directory of the TechConf application and copy the JAR files (hibernate3.jar, dom4j-1.6.1.jar, cglib-2.1.1.jar, asm.jar, ehcache-1.1.jar) listed in Table 4-1. Since the Jakarta Commons libraries are shared by some of the other libraries and tools we will be using in later chapters, I've decided to place them in their own set of directories as shown in Figure 4-10. The commons-logging-1.0.4 and commons-lang-2.0.jar files will end up in the lib/commons-logging and lib/commons-lang directories respectively. Finally, you'll need the file mysql-connector-java-3.0.14-production-bin.jar, which contains the JDBC driver for the MySQL instance.

Figure 4-10 shows the structure and contents of the TechConf lib directory after the necessary changes to work with Hibernate.

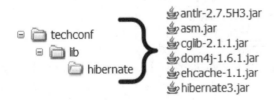

Figure 4-10. *Hibernate libraries in the TechConf directory structure*

Table 4-1. *Hibernate J2SE Application Dependencies*

File Name	Description
hibernate3.jar	The main hibernate classes
dom4j-1.6.1.jar	Dom4J XML library (used to load all XML definitions such as .cfg.xml and .hbm.xml files)
cglib-2.1.1.jar	Runtime code-generation library
asm.jar	Java Bytecode Manipulation Framework
ehcache-1.1.jar	Simple, non-distributed caching implementation

Table 4-1. *Hibernate J2SE Application Dependencies*

File Name	Description
commons-logging-1.0.4.jar	Jakarta commons used as a thin logging wrapper
commons-lang-2.0.jar	Used to simplify the POJO's implementation
mysql-connector-java-3.0.14-production-bin.jar	The JDBC driver used with MySQL

* Jar names and versions will vary from distribution to distribution.

Eclipse Setup

If you are using Eclipse and you've followed the steps in Chapter 2, in order for the examples in this chapter to work you'll have to add the Hibernate JARs to the TechConf project build path. To do so, go to the Project Properties page by selecting the project node in the Eclipse Package Explorer or Navigator, select Properties (by right-clicking on the node or via the main menu under Project ➤ Properties) and select Java Build Path. Click the Add Jars button to navigate to the lib directory and select the JARs shown in Figure 4-11.

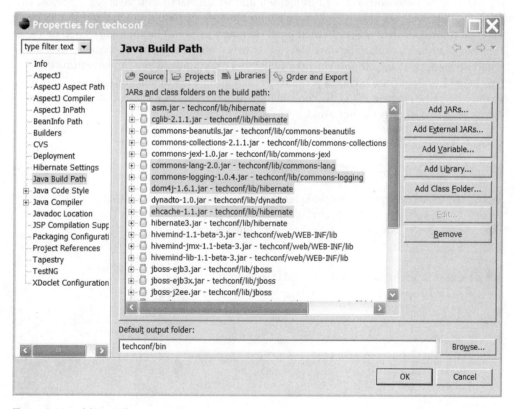

Figure 4-11. *Adding Hibernate JARs to the Eclipse project*

Database Setup

For the simple examples in this chapter you'll need to set up a MySQL instance. I used version 4.1.7-nt on a Windows XP machine. There are several tutorials online and plenty of books that can help you setup MySQL, including *The Definitive Guide to MySQL 5* by Michael Kofler (Apress, 2005) and *Pro MySQL* by Michael Kruckenberg and Jay Pipes (Apress, 2005). For JDBC connectivity I used the MySQL Connector/J 3.X JDBC Driver that is available from the MySQL website at `http://dev.mysql.com`.

Quick Start

We will create our first POJO, Hibernate mapping, and database table completely by hand so that you get an idea of what it takes to map an object to a table. In subsequent examples you might be able to use tools suited for your development style to streamline the process.

POJO Sample Code

The simple Address POJO follows the basic well-known JavaBean conventions, private fields exposed via getters and setters. That's the easy part; of paramount importance to how Hibernate manipulates persistent objects is the implementation of the equals and hashCode methods. The implementation of these methods is not a Hibernate-specific requirement, but it should be part of any Java business object. In their book *Hibernate in Action* (Manning, 2005), Bauer and King go the distance explaining the difference between object equality, object identity, and database identity. They promote the use of business key equality when implementing the equals method by using a business property or set of properties that are unique to a table row. In the case of the Address POJO the combination of StreetAddress, State, ZipCode, City and AptNumber fields identify a unique address as shown in Listing 4-1.

Listing 4-1. *Address POJO*

```
package com.integrallis.TechConf.domain;
...
import org.apache.commons.lang.builder.EqualsBuilder;
import org.apache.commons.lang.builder.HashCodeBuilder;
import org.apache.commons.lang.builder.ToStringBuilder;
...

public class Address implements Serializable {
    // primary key
    private Integer id;

    // fields
    private String streetAddress;
    private String state;
    private String zipCode;
    private String city;
    private String aptNumber;

    // constructors
    public Address () {}
```

```java
    // ...getters and setters

    /* Implementation of equals using Business Key Equality
     *
     * (non-Javadoc)
     * @see java.lang.Object#equals(java.lang.Object)
     */
    public boolean equals (Object object) {
        // short circuits
        if (object == null) return false;
        if (this == object) return true;
        if (!(object instanceof Address)) return false;

        final Address address = (Address) object;
        //NOTE always use getters on the passed object since it
        //       might be a Hibernate Proxy
        return new EqualsBuilder().
            append(streetAddress, address.getStreetAddress()).
            append(aptNumber, address.getAptNumber()).
            append(city, address.getCity()).
            append(state, address.getState()).
            append(zipCode, address.getZipCode()).
            isEquals();
    }

    public int hashCode () {
        // pick a hard-coded, randomly chosen, non-zero, odd number
        // ideally different for each class
        return new HashCodeBuilder(17, 37).
            append(streetAddress).
            append(aptNumber).
            append(city).
            append(state).
            append(zipCode).
            toHashCode();
    }

    public String toString () {
        return new ToStringBuilder(this).
            append("streetAddress", streetAddress).
            append("aptNumber", aptNumber).
            append("city", city).
            append("state", state).
            append("zipCode", zipCode).
            toString();
    }
}
```

Tip I use the Jakarta Commons Lang utility to implement the equals, hashCode and toString methods. Besides making a lot of the mundane coding simpler, they provide a clean and (most of the time) efficient way to deal with these three important methods of the Object class. The builders are EqualsBuilder, HashCodeBuilder and ToStringBuilder respectively, and they are located in the org.apache.commons. lang.builder package. The Jakarta Commons libraries can be found at http://jakarta.apache.org/ commons/. For a complete coverage of the available libraries I recommend Harshad Oak's *Pro Jakarta Commons* (Apress, 2004).

Technically you need to implement only equals and hashCode for your POJOs if they are going to be used as part of a composite primary key class or if an instance of that class loaded in a different session needs to be compared (either directly or by being in an ordered collection).

Mapping (HBM) File

For our first mapping I've selected the Address entity domain since it will be a straightforward object-to-table mapping with no associations. Listing 4-2 shows an HBM file that maps the class com.integrallis.TechConf.domain.Address.

Listing 4-2. *HBM File for Address Entity (Address.hbm.xml)*

```
<hibernate-mapping
    package="com.integrallis.TechConf.domain">
    <class name="Address">
        <id name="Id" column="PK_ID" type="integer">
            <generator class="identity" />
        </id>
        <property name="StreetAddress" />
        <property name="State" />
        <property name="ZipCode" />
        <property name="City" />
        <property name="AptNumber" />
    </class>
</hibernate-mapping>
```

Let's examine the address HBM file in detail. Hibernate mappings are XML documents whose root is the hibernate-mapping element. They are typically named after the class that it is mapped, followed by the .hbm and .xml extensions. In the case of the Address class the name would be Address.hbm.xml.

Note You can have multiple class mappings in a single HBM file, but I would recommend that you keep one HBM file per class. This practice will ease maintenance and will enable multiple developers to work on different mappings without stepping over each others' work.

The package attribute specifies where to look for the address POJO in the classpath at runtime. The class element denotes a class mapping. In this case we are mapping the Address class as the name attribute denotes. Hibernate will assume that the table we are mapping the class Address to is also named Address, since we did not include a table attribute.

The id element denotes the mapping of the database identity property to the primary key column in the target table. In this case we are mapping the Integer field Id to the database column PK_ID, and we are telling Hibernate to use the "identity" strategy to generate a new value for the PK every time a new row gets inserted in the database.

Note Hibernate uses smart defaults to minimize the amount of information needed in a mapping. This makes Hibernate mappings much less verbose than the equivalent EJB CMP 2.X deployment descriptors or many of the other existing ORM tools available.

The property elements map the POJO properties StreetAddress, State, ZipCode, City and AptNumber each to a column of the same name. Hibernate will guess that the properties are of type String in the POJO and the columns are of type VARCHAR in the database. You can be more exact in the mapping and provide the specific lengths and data types for a particular class.

Creating the Table

Now that we have a simple Address POJO class and the corresponding mapping, we just need to create a new ADDRESS table in the database. Listing 4-3 shows the SQL statement to create the ADDRESS table.

Listing 4-3. *SQL Create Statement for Table ADDRESS*

```
CREATE TABLE ADDRESS (
  PK_ID INTEGER NOT NULL PRIMARY KEY AUTO_INCREMENT,
  STREETADDRESS VARCHAR(64),
  APTNUMBER VARCHAR(32),
  CITY VARCHAR(32),
  STATE CHAR(2),
  ZIPCODE VARCHAR(10)
);
```

Figure 4-12 shows the MySQL Command Line Client displaying the list of commands needed to create the TechConf database instance and the Address table. Note that we could have chosen to let Hibernate create the table at application start-up time by configuring the hbm2ddl tool via the Hibernate configuration. The hbm2ddl tool generates a schema based on the loaded HBM files which Hibernate will use to create or update the database if necessary.

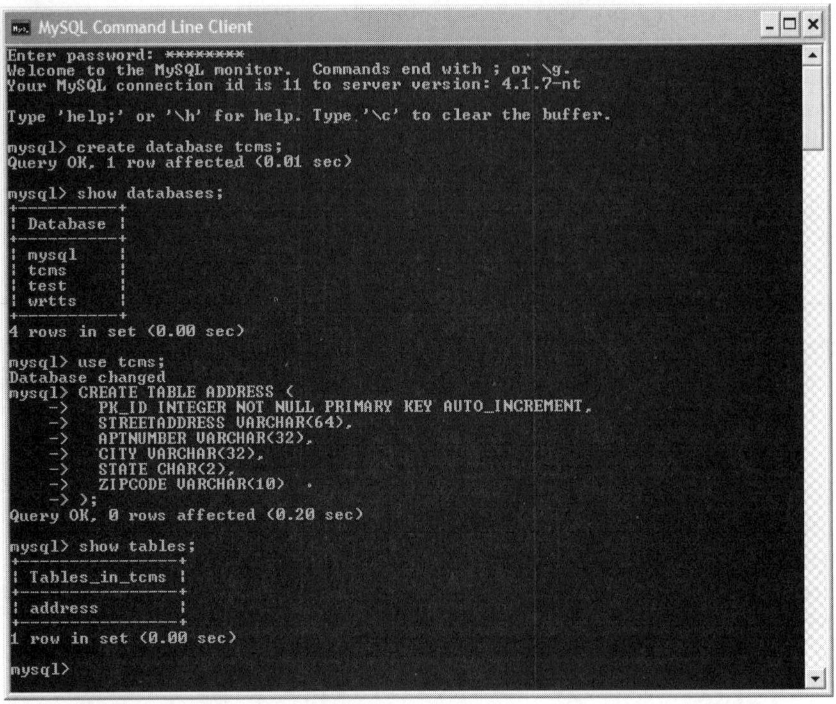

Figure 4-12. *MySQL command line client*

Primary Key Generation

Notice that we have selected the primary key field to be a MySQL AUTO_INCREMENT field. This is one case of a mapping in which the object property is optional but the table column is not. Remember, Hibernate mappings are class-centric. But in the case of the database identifier you can choose not to have the database identity reflected in your POJO classes. Although having a database ID field might seem like a leakage of concerns, it is highly recommended that you have one, since many of Hibernate's advanced features, such as the ability to use "detached" objects and the useful saveOrUpdate and merge methods of the Session object, depend on having the database identity reflected in your POJOs. You can minimize the impact of your POJO design by intelligently using the appropriate Java class member visibility when declaring your identity fields.

In an ORM tool it is important to know the persistent state of an object. Having a nullable, non-primitive primary key makes the job of knowing whether an object needs to be saved or updated much easier. Therefore in all examples we will typically use a surrogate integer primary key, and whenever possible we will rely on the database to generate new values for new objects.

■**Best Practice** When choosing a primary key for a new table, especially if you know that the table will be used in an object-oriented system by an ORM tool, use surrogate primary keys whenever possible. Surrogate primary keys are small, simple keys that have no business meaning and are normally not updated or even seen by end users. They provide an audit trail, result in small indexes, make joins easier to write and faster to execute, are more resilient to business changes (because they have no business meaning), and make referential integrity easier to maintain. An example of dangerous business-key usage as a primary key would be using telephone numbers as account identifiers. Because telephone numbers can and do change, maintenance or some sort of mapping would be required when a customer's telephone number changes, even worst in my opinion is the use of composite business/natural primary keys in which many such fields are used in combination as a primary key. The problem is that those fields are normally non-nullable, so there is no easy way (without doing a SELECT to check the row's existence) to determine if the object is already in the database.

Table 4-2 shows a quick summary of the generator strategies provided by Hibernate.

Table 4-2. *Hibernate's Identifier Generation Strategies*

Strategy	Description
increment	Generates integer-type identifiers (long, short, and int) using an in-memory scheme. Not recommended for clustered environments.
identity	Uses database identity columns for those databases that support it. Use it with an integer-type object property.
sequence	Uses a database sequence or internal database generator for those databases that support these features.
hilo	Uses an algorithm to determine the next value based on a column in a given table. Used when native database sequences are not supported and only in non-JTA environments or with user-supplied connections.
seqhilo	Uses a named database sequence and the hilo algorithm.
uuid	Uses an algorithm that generates a string representation of a 128-bit UUID (Universally Unique Identifier). The returned string is hex-encoded.
guid	Takes advantage of the capability of certain databases (Microsoft SQL Server and MySQL) to generate Globally Unique Identifiers (GUIDs)
foreign	Uses the identifier of an associated object.
native	Intelligently chooses the appropriate strategy. It's the recommended strategy for maximum portability.
select	Uses a database trigger or by issuing a SELECT against a unique key tables.
assigned	Used for applications that use provided business unique keys.

Choosing the right identity-generation strategy depends on many factors, including performance and portability. Native database strategies are usually more robust and perform better than the equivalent Java-based approach. In most cases I prefer to use simple integers for my primary keys in conjunction with the native database integer key generator.

Saving an Object

Now we need to tell Hibernate how to connect to the database and load the Address.hbm.xml class mapping in the SessionFactory. For this simple example we will do this directly in the Java code. Subsequent examples will use the preferred XML configuration file.

Listing 4-4 shows how to create a Hibernate configuration object in code, add a Hibernate mapped class, and retrieve an instance of the SessionFactory from the configuration. When you invoke the addClass method of the Configuration class, passing the class object for the Address class (Address.class), Hibernate will look for a HBM file named "Address.hbm.xml" in the class path. So the simplest way to ensure that Hibernate will find your mappings is to place them in the same location as the class they map. Once you have a SessionFactory, working with your persistent objects is as simple as obtaining a Session and invoking methods on it. Replace the user name and password with that required for your database.

Listing 4-4. *Configuring Hibernate in Code*

```
Configuration config = new Configuration().
    setProperty("hibernate.dialect", "org.hibernate.dialect.MySQLDialect").
    setProperty("hibernate.connection.driver_class", "com.mysql.jdbc.Driver").
    setProperty("hibernate.connection.url", "jdbc:mysql://localhost/techconf").
    setProperty("hibernate.connection.username", "mydbuser").
    setProperty("hibernate.connection.password", "mydbpassword").
    setProperty("hibernate.show_sql", "true");

config.addClass(Address.class);

SessionFactory factory = config.buildSessionFactory();
```

For example to create an Address object and save it to the database we take the following steps, reflected in Listing 4-5:

1. POJO is created and values are set.

2. SessionFactory is used to create a **Session**.

3. A Hibernate Transaction bound to the Session is started.

4. The object is saved using the Session persist method.

5. The Transaction is committed.

6. The Session is closed.

Listing 4-5. *Saving an Address*

```
Address address = new Address();
...
Session session = null;
Transaction tx = null;
try {
    session = factory.openSession();
    tx = session.beginTransaction();
    session.persist(address);
    tx.commit();
} catch (Exception e) {
    if (tx != null) tx.rollback();
} finally {
    session.close();
}
```

The code in Listing 4-5 follows the pattern you'll use when interacting with Hibernate mapped objects in a simple J2SE application. Behind the scenes the Hibernate Session just opened is given a JDBC connection for the database set in the SessionFactory configuration (this connection might be a new connection or might come from a pool of existing connections available to Hibernate). Once the Session is opened it acts as cache for mapped object entities, that is, any object you retrieve or save via the opened Session will now be in the Session cache. So, if you were to load the same object twice, in the first call Hibernate will issue a SQL statement to load the state of the object, but in any subsequent calls using the same Session, the object would be retrieved from the Session's internal cache and no database access would occur.

If the code in Listing 4-5 executes successfully, the Address instance that was passed to the persist method will now have its Id field populated with the identifier generated by the database and there will be a new row in the ADDRESS table. Hibernate's Session object provides several methods that persist the state of an object to the database, including persist, save, update, and saveOrUpdate. If an object's primary key attribute isn't set, Hibernate will detect this and automatically generate a primary key for the object based on the strategy selected on the id element. This will make the underlying operation a SQL INSERT.

■**Note** Hibernate detects that an object hasn't been saved by checking the primary key value for null, which is the default of the unsaved-value attribute. If your class required a value other than null, set this value in the unsaved-value attribute.

In the case of the saveOrUpdate method, if the primary key is set then the operation becomes a SQL UPDATE if the object exists and a SQL INSERT doesn't, while in the case of the persist, save and update methods, the semantics are clearly defined; a call to persist or save will always result in a SQL INSERT while a call to update will result in a SQL UPDATE.

Another important piece of information about Hibernate's functioning is that Hibernate interacts with the database in a transparent write-behind fashion. That means that you might not see SQL statements being executed against the database the moment the persist method is executed but possibly sometime after. This is a common technique employed by ORM tools to allow for runtime optimizations in the interaction with the database. For example, the actions in your code might result in several back-to-back identical SQL UPDATE statements which the ORM tool might combine into a single SQL UPDATE. In Hibernate, the moment when the Session is synchronized with the database is referred to as flushing. The Hibernate Session class also provides an explicit flush method which you can invoke. Typically you don't need to manually flush the Session, but in complex scenarios it might be useful for debugging purposes.

Finally, notice that in Listing 4-5 we wrapped the block of code saving the Address object in a try-catch-finally. In the finally clause we ensure that we invoke the close method of the Session. This ensures that any resources (like database connections) are released.

In the catch clause the Hibernate transaction is rolled back in the case of an exception to ensure the integrity of the operation. Note that the usage of the Hibernate transaction is not required, but it is recommended that you always use it since it insulates you from having to deal with the underlying JDBC connection (you could call the commit method of the JDBC connection associated with the Session).

The Hibernate transaction API is a very simple wrapper to whatever the underlying transaction mechanism might be for the environment your code is operating under. In the simple example above, the Transaction object represents the underlying JDBC transaction, while the same code running on a JTA-enabled environment would use the container JTA user transaction available in the context of the method. The end result is that you have consistent code that works in all environments, allowing you to test your POJOs outside of a container.

Listing 4-6 shows the complete listing for the example.

Listing 4-6. *Simple Hibernate Test for Saving an Address*

```
public static void main(String[] args) {
    Configuration config = new Configuration().
        setProperty("hibernate.dialect", "org.hibernate.dialect.MySQLDialect").
        setProperty("hibernate.connection.driver_class", "com.mysql.jdbc.Driver").
        setProperty("hibernate.connection.url", "jdbc:mysql://localhost/test").
        setProperty("hibernate.connection.username", "root").
        setProperty("hibernate.connection.password", "valencia").
        setProperty("hibernate.show_sql", "true");

    config.addClass(Address.class);

    SessionFactory factory = config.buildSessionFactory();

    Address address = new Address();
    address.setStreetAddress("1835 73rd Ave NE");
    address.setCity("Medina");
    address.setState("WA");
    address.setZipCode("98039");
```

```
        Session session = null;
        Transaction tx = null;
        try {
            session = factory.openSession();
            tx = session.beginTransaction();
            session.persist(address);
            tx.commit();
        } catch (Exception e) {
            if (tx != null) tx.rollback();
        } finally {
            session.close();
        }
    }
}
```

Running the example should produce output similar to that shown in the sample output. The relevant output messages have been highlighted. First, notice that Hibernate locates the mapping for the Address class in the Address.hbm.xml file, sets up the connection to the MySQL database using the MySQL Hibernate Dialect, sets up JDBC transactions to be the underlying transaction mechanism for the Hibernate transactions, and finally issues a SQL INSERT statement (the direct consequence of the call to the persist method).

```
Sep 21, 2005 1:42:22 PM org.hibernate.cfg.Environment <clinit>
INFO: Hibernate 3.1alpha1
...
Sep 21, 2005 1:42:23 PM org.hibernate.cfg.Configuration addClass
INFO: Reading mappings from resource:
com/integrallis/techconf/domain/Address.hbm.xml
...
INFO: Mapping class: com.integrallis.techconf.domain.Address -> Address
...
INFO: using driver: com.mysql.jdbc.Driver at URL: jdbc:mysql://localhost/test
Sep 21, 2005 1:42:24 PM org.hibernate.connection.DriverManagerConnectionProvider
configure
INFO: connection properties: {user=root, password=****}
Sep 21, 2005 1:42:24 PM org.hibernate.cfg.SettingsFactory buildSettings
INFO: RDBMS: MySQL, version: 4.1.7-nt
Sep 21, 2005 1:42:24 PM org.hibernate.cfg.SettingsFactory buildSettings
INFO: JDBC driver: MySQL-AB JDBC Driver, version: mysql-connector-java-3.0.14-pro-
duction ( $Date: 2004/04/24 15:49:43 $, $Revision: 1.27.2.39 $ )
Sep 21, 2005 1:42:24 PM org.hibernate.dialect.Dialect <init>
INFO: Using dialect: org.hibernate.dialect.MySQLDialect
Sep 21, 2005 1:42:24 PM org.hibernate.transaction.TransactionFactoryFactory
buildTransactionFactory
INFO: Using default transaction strategy (direct JDBC transactions)
...
```

```
Sep 21, 2005 1:42:25 PM org.hibernate.impl.SessionFactoryImpl <init>
INFO: building session factory
...
Sep 21, 2005 1:42:25 PM org.hibernate.impl.SessionFactoryObjectFactory addInstance
INFO: Not binding factory to JNDI, no JNDI name configured
Sep 21, 2005 1:42:25 PM org.hibernate.impl.SessionFactoryImpl checkNamedQueries
INFO: Checking 0 named queries
Hibernate: insert into Address (StreetAddress, State, ZipCode, City, AptNumber)
values (?, ?, ?, ?, ?)
```

If you use the SQL command-line tool to check the contents of the Address table, you should now see the newly inserted record as shown next:

```
mysql> select * from address;
```

```
+-------+------------------+-----------+--------+-------+---------+
| PK_ID | STREETADDRESS    | APTNUMBER | CITY   | STATE | ZIPCODE |
+-------+------------------+-----------+--------+-------+---------+
|     1 | 1835 73rd Ave NE | NULL      | Medina | WA    | 98039   |
+-------+------------------+-----------+--------+-------+---------+
1 row in set (0.00 sec)
```

Retrieving a Single Object

The Hibernate Session provides several convenient methods to retrieve an object via its primary key. No longer do you have to issue a full SQL statement to retrieve an object's data from the database. The Hibernate Session provides the load and get methods to retrieve an object by id. The main difference between these two methods is that load assumes that the object you are looking for exists while get can be equated with a find since you can check its result for null to test if a row exists in the database. The load method can throw an org.hibernate.ObjectNotFoundException if the entity does not exist in the database (this might not happen at all since load will attempt to return a proxy whenever possible). Both methods will check first in the Session cache to see if the entity has already been loaded, therefore preventing unnecessary database hits.

I prefer to use the get method and do a check for null in my code since this feels more in line with common Java semantics. Since load assumes existence of the entity, the thrown exception is assumed to be an unrecoverable exception, like most data access exceptions.

■**Note** In previous versions of Hibernate the root exception in Hibernate (org.hibernate. HibernateException) was a checked exception. Starting with version 3.0 it is now a runtime exception, which is more in line with the fact that most data-access exceptions are unrecoverable exceptions. This has been a welcome change in Hibernate, since it really simplifies the code by removing unnecessary exception wrapping code.

The code in Listing 4-7 shows the typical operation used to retrieve an object from the database using both the load and get methods. Assuming that you haven't deleted the Address object previously persisted and that the assigned primary key was 1, the code shown should showcase the interaction between the Hibernate Session and the database.

Listing 4-7. *Simple Hibernate Test for Retrieving an Address Object*

```
...
session = factory.openSession();

//
// first load - object is loaded from the database
//
System.out.println("[load] first Load - should hit the db");
Address addressUsingLoad = (Address) session.load(Address.class, 1);

//
// second load - object is retrieved from the session cache
//
System.out.println("[load] second Load - should not hit the db");
Address addressUsingLoad2 = (Address) session.load(Address.class, 1);

//
// compare the loaded objects - should be that same instance
//
System.out.println("[compare ==] comparing loaded objects using =="
    + (addressUsingLoad == addressUsingLoad2));
System.out.println("[compare equals()] comparing loaded objects using equals()"
    + (addressUsingLoad.equals(addressUsingLoad2)));

//
// now use get
//
System.out.println("[get] first get - should not hit the db");
Address addressUsingGet = (Address) session.get(Address.class, 1);

//
// compare to the objects retrieve using load
//
System.out.println("[compare load/get using ==] comparing load/get objects using =="
    + (addressUsingLoad == addressUsingGet));
System.out.println("[compare load/get using equals()]"
                + compare load/get objects using equals()"
                + (addressUsingLoad.equals(addressUsingGet)));
...
```

It is equally simple to update an existing object with the update method and to remove an object from the database by using the delete method. For more information on the capabilities of the Session in Hibernate consult the Javadoc for Hibernate (http://hibernate.org/hib_docs/ v3/api/), which shows all of the different methods exposed by the Session. The complexity when dealing with Hibernate is similar to that of regular SQL-based applications, which lies in the art of efficiently querying the database. As you'll see in the next few sections, Hibernate provides very advanced querying facilities.

Retrieving a Collection of Objects

Retrieving a single object is fairly easy, and you'll find yourself doing that frequently in a common Web application. Yet, in most cases you'll be getting a list of objects before you decide to retrieve the particular details of a single entity (since most likely you won't have previous knowledge of the database identifiers).

Hibernate provides a myriad of ways to retrieve a collection of persistent objects from the database. This flexibility can be a source of confusion for new users of Hibernate. In this section I will attempt to give you an overview of the available APIs in Hibernate used for querying your application persistent object space.

Finding Objects Using HQL

Hibernate provides an object query language known as HQL (Hibernate Query Language), which is a powerful query language similar in syntax to SQL but with classes and object properties at its heart rather than tables and columns. The similarity to SQL makes for a smoother transition from straight-JDBC applications to a Hibernate application. Hibernate also allows you to issue native SQL queries if necessary, but I recommend that you stick with HQL queries whenever possible. In my experience there are very few situations that might force you to use a native SQL query, and if one of those situations presents itself, you can also avoid such queries in your applications by using a custom query in your HBM mappings. For more information on using custom SQL queries in your HBMs, consult the Hibernate online reference documentation.

Listing 4-8 shows a simple HQL query to load all instances of the Address class from the database.

Listing 4-8. *Simple HQL Query to Retrieve All Instances of the Address Class*

```
List<Address> addresses = session.createQuery("from Address").list();
for (Iterator<Address> i = addresses.iterator(); i.hasNext();) {
    Address address = (Address) i.next();
    System.out.println(address);
}
```

As you can see, this query is completely expressed in the object terms, and the Hibernate team was kind enough to gives us a shorthand notation by allowing us to drop the "select" keyword. Notice that there is no intrusive result set class as an intermediary. The result is provided in a java.util.List, enabling us to do HQL work with familiar Java collections API.

In an HQL query you can have a FROM clause to narrow down the returned entity list, just like with SQL. The snippet in Listing 4-9 shows how you can select an Address object matching certain information.

Listing 4-9. *HQL Query to Retrieve All Address Instances for the State of Ohio*

```
List<Address> addresses = null;

// long version
Query query = session.createQuery("from Address as a where a.State = 'OH'");
addresses = query.list();

// short version
addresses = session
    .createQuery("from Address as a where a.State = 'OH'")
    .list();
```

Of course, in a real application you will most likely want to pass the parameter values dynamically to the query. HQL enables parameters to be passed positionally or by name as shown in Listing 4-10. I recommend that you use named parameters, which make the code more legible and will make any later modifications much simpler.

Listing 4-10. *HQL Query with Parameters*

```
List<Address> addresses = null;

// positional parameters
addresses = session
    .createQuery("from Address as a where a.State = ?")
    .setString("OH")
    .list();

// named parameters
addresses = session
    .createQuery("from Address as a where a.State = :mystate")
    .setString("mystate", "OH")
    .list();
```

HQL also provides you with other clauses typically found in SQL, like "order by", "join", "in", and a vast array of logical and arithmetic operators. Listing 4-11 shows a more complex example showcasing other HQL features.

Listing 4-11. *A More Elaborate HQL Query*

```
List<Address> addresses = null;

// parameter list
List states = new ArrayList();
states.add("OH");
states.add("KY");
```

```
// query string
String query = "from Address as a where a.State in (:listOfStates) " +
               "order by a.City desc";

// named parameters
addresses = session
    .createQuery(query)
    .setFirstResult(0)
    .setMaxResults(25)
    .setParameterList("listOfStates", states)
    .list();
```

The previous query selects the first 25 addresses for the states of Ohio and Kentucky, and it will order the resulting list by city in reverse alphabetical order.

Finding Objects by Example

Hibernate also provides a Query by Example (QBE) feature. Query by Example is part of the Hibernate criteria API. QBE provides a convenient way to find persistent entities by using a partially populated POJO as an example as shown in Listing 4-12.

Listing 4-12. *Query by Example*

```
// example pojo
Address exampleAddress = new Address();
exampleAddress.setCity("Columbus");
exampleAddress.setStreetAddress("main");

// create and configure the example object
Example example = Example.create(exampleAddress)
    .excludeZeroes()
    .ignoreCase()
    .enableLike();

List<Address> addresses = session
    .createCriteria(Address.class)
    .add(example)
    .list();
```

The query in Listing 4-12 will result is a SQL query similar to:

```
select * from Address a
    where (lower(a.StreetAddress) like ? and lower(a.City) like ?)
```

which would find all addresses where the street address contains the word "main" and the city contains the word "Columbus" regardless of case. The excludeZeroes method excludes any zeroed (null or zero) properties from appearing in the query.

Finding Objects by Criteria

The final query API we will discuss is the criteria API, which provides a very sophisticated and object-oriented way to construct queries. HQL is a great step forward from SQL since it lets us talk to a relational database as if it were an object database, but it is still a query language that is not Java. Therefore the same issues that we faced as Java developers when doing direct JDBC using straight SQL apply. Simply not all of us are experts when it comes to SQL. Furthermore, when it comes to multiple database platforms, SQL can vary widely, especially when you get to the boundaries of the specifications and into the world of vendor-specific extensions.

The Hibernate criteria API provides a way to create queries by chaining simple methods and simple objects that act as filters for a result set without using a specific query language.

Listing 4-13 shows some examples of criteria queries.

Listing 4-13. *Query by Criteria*

```
// retrieve all addresses
List<Address> allAddresses = session.createCriteria(Address.class).list();

// retrieve all addresses for the state of ohio
List<Address> addressesInOH = session
    .createCriteria(Address.class)
    .add(Expression.eq("State", "OH"))
    .list();

// retrieve the first 23 addresses where the city is like
// 'Columbus' and the street address is like 'main' and
// order them by state
List<Address> addresses = session
    .createCriteria(Address.class)
    .add(Expression.like("StreetAddress", "main"))
    .add(Expression.like("City", "Columbus"))
    .addOrder(Order.asc("State"))
    .setFirstResult(0)
    .setMaxResults(25)
    .list();
```

As you can see, the QBC and QBE facilities in Hibernate can make your code much less cryptic and much more maintainable by eliminating convoluted non-Java SQL and SQL-like code in your application. When we implement the DAO pattern in the middle/integration tier of the TechConf application, we will make extensive use of the Hibernate criteria API.

■**Note** If you use HQL extensively in your applications, it is recommended that you externalize your queries by placing them in the HBM files. Hibernate can locate named queries at runtime, which will make your code cleaner and less complex, avoids copy and paste reuse, and provides centralized control for your queries.

Case Study: Mapping the TechConf Domain Model

Now that you have seen how simple it is to map a simple POJO to a database table and interact with your data in an object-oriented fashion, it is time to move on to the development of the sample application. In a real application there will be not only a lot of simple mappings but also a lot of more complex situations involving more advanced ORM concepts. In this section we will tackle the development of the methods used by the TechConf application to retrieve and store data. As we flesh out each method, we will take a look at the POJOs involved, the HBM mappings, and the associated tables and its columns.

Most of the persistence code that we will develop in this section will eventually be used in the DAO layer of the TechConf application. We will cover in great detail this important pattern when we build the business tier of the TechConf application.

Conferences Home Page

The entry point into the TechConf system will be a page where the public can see the list of available conferences. A class diagram showing the Conference class and its relevant associations is shown in Figure 4-13.

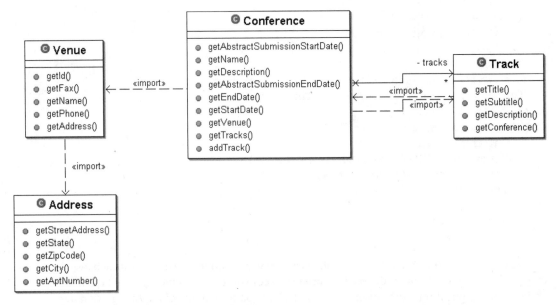

Figure 4-13. *Conference class and its associations*

As you can see from Figure 4-13, a conference can have one or more tracks (for example, a Java conference could have a JSE, JEE, and JME tracks) and a venue. Listing 4-14 shows the SQL statements needed to create the CONFERENCE, VENUE, and TRACK.

Listing 4-14. *SQL Create Statements for Tables ADDRESS, VENUE, CONFERENCE, and TRACK*

```
CREATE TABLE ADDRESS (
  PK_ID INTEGER NOT NULL PRIMARY KEY AUTO_INCREMENT,
  STREETADDRESS VARCHAR(64),
  APTNUMBER VARCHAR(32),
  CITY VARCHAR(32),
  STATE CHAR(2),
  ZIPCODE VARCHAR(10)
);

CREATE TABLE VENUE (
  PK_ID INTEGER NOT NULL PRIMARY KEY AUTO_INCREMENT,
  NAME VARCHAR(32),
  PHONE VARCHAR(12),
  FAX VARCHAR(12),
  FK_ADDRESS_ID INTEGER NOT NULL,
  CONSTRAINT VENUE_ADDRESS_FK FOREIGN KEY(FK_ADDRESS_ID) REFERENCES ADDRESS(PK_ID),
  CONSTRAINT UNIQUE_VENUE_NAME UNIQUE(NAME)
);

CREATE TABLE CONFERENCE (
  PK_ID INTEGER NOT NULL PRIMARY KEY AUTO_INCREMENT,
  NAME VARCHAR(64) NOT NULL,
  DESCRIPTION LONGTEXT NOT NULL,
  STARTDATE DATETIME NOT NULL,
  ENDDATE DATETIME NOT NULL,
  ABSTRACTSUBMISSIONSTARTDATE DATETIME NOT NULL,
  ABSTRACTSUBMISSIONENDDATE DATETIME NOT NULL,
  FK_VENUE_ID INTEGER,
  CONSTRAINT CONFERENCE_VENUE_FK FOREIGN KEY(FK_VENUE_ID) REFERENCES VENUE(PK_ID),
  CONSTRAINT UNIQUE_CONFERENCE_NAME UNIQUE(NAME)
);

CREATE TABLE TRACK (
  PK_ID INTEGER NOT NULL PRIMARY KEY AUTO_INCREMENT,
  TITLE VARCHAR(32) NOT NULL,
  SUBTITLE VARCHAR(32),
  DESCRIPTION LONGTEXT,
  FK_CONFERENCE_ID INTEGER NOT NULL,
  CONSTRAINT TRACK_CONFERENCE_FK FOREIGN KEY(FK_CONFERENCE_ID)
    REFERENCES CONFERENCE(PK_ID),
  CONSTRAINT UNIQUE_TRACK_TITLE UNIQUE(TITLE)
);
```

Let's start by creating the Conference POJO as shown in Listing 4-15. As you can see the Conference class has a typed `java.util.Set` of `Track` and a field for a `Venue` along with a collection of simple fields representing the name, description, and several dates of relevance to the running of a conference.

Listing 4-15. *Conference Class POJO*

```
package com.integrallis.techconf.domain;
...
import org.apache.commons.lang.builder.ToStringBuilder;

public class Conference implements Serializable {
    ...

    // primary key
    private Integer id;

    // fields
    private Date abstractSubmissionStartDate;
    private String name;
    private String description;
    private Date abstractSubmissionEndDate;
    private Date endDate;
    private Date startDate;

    // many to one
    private Venue venue;

    // collections
    private Set<Track> tracks;

    // constructors
    public Conference () {
    }

    ... getters and setters

    public Venue getVenue () {
        return venue;
    }

    public void setVenue (Venue venue) {
        this.venue = venue;
    }

    public Set getTracks () {
        return tracks;
    }
```

```
public void setTracks (Set<Track> tracks) {
    this.tracks = tracks;
}

public void addTrack(Track track) {
    if (null == this.tracks) this.tracks = new HashSet<Track>();
    track.setConference(this);
    tracks.add(track);
}
...
}
```

One-to-Many Mapping Using a Set

First we will map the one-to-many relationship between the Conference and Track POJOs.
Let's start with a basic Conference HBM file with the simple field-to-column property mappings
as shown in Listing 4-16.

Listing 4-16. *HBM Skeleton for the Conference Class*

```xml
<?xml version="1.0"?>
<!DOCTYPE hibernate-mapping PUBLIC
    "-//Hibernate/Hibernate Mapping DTD 3.0//EN"
    "http://hibernate.sourceforge.net/hibernate-mapping-3.0.dtd">

<hibernate-mapping package="com.integrallis.techconf.domain">
    <class name="Conference" table="conference">
        <id
            column="PK_ID"
            name="Id"
            type="integer"
        >
            <generator class="identity" />
        </id>
        <property
            name="AbstractSubmissionStartDate"
            length="19"
            not-null="true"
            type="timestamp"
        />
        <property
            name="Name"
            length="64"
            not-null="true"
            type="string"
        />
```

```
            <property
                name="Description"
                not-null="true"
                type="string"
             />
            <property
                name="AbstractSubmissionEndDate"
                length="19"
                not-null="true"
                type="timestamp"
             />
            <property
                name="EndDate"
                length="19"
                not-null="true"
                type="timestamp"
             />
            <property
                name="StartDate"
                length="19"
                not-null="true"
                type="timestamp"
             />
             ...
        </class>
    </hibernate-mapping>
```

To map the one-to-many relationship between the Conference and Track objects, we'll use a set element, as shown in Listing 4-17.

Listing 4-17. *Set Element Mapping Tracks in a Conference*

```
<set inverse="true" name="Tracks" cascade="all" lazy="false">
    <key column="FK_CONFERENCE_ID" />
    <one-to-many class="Track" />
</set>
```

The set element maps to the java.util.Set in the POJO, which enables you to work with a simple Java collection using typical Java semantics without worrying about whether the class is a persistent class or not.

The Tracks property is mapped to the class Track (in the same package) which is mapped to the TRACK table. The column attribute of the key element tells Hibernate that there is a foreign key constraint in the TRACK table to the CONFERENCE table via the FK_CONFERENCE_ID column:

```
CONSTRAINT TRACK_CONFERENCE_FK FOREIGN KEY(FK_CONFERENCE_ID) REFERENCES
```

We want to make the one-to-many relationship between Conference and Track bi-directional. In the POJOs this is represented by the java.util.Set "tracks" on the "one" side of the relationship and by a single Conference property on the "many" side. This type of bidirectional association can be very convenient, and it will permit us, given a track, to determine what conference it belongs to by accessing a Conference object via its getConference getter. The inverse attribute shown in the set element tells Hibernate that this is an inverse or bidirectional relationship.

Notice that in the implementation of the Conference class I have included a convenience method, the addTrack method, to add tracks to a given conference as shown in Listing 4-15. Notice that the addTrack method maintains both ends of the relationship by adding the passed Track object to the set of Tracks in the Conference object and also by setting the conference property in the Track being added. Encapsulating the maintenance of the relationship in a simple method will make the usage of both classes simpler.

The "lazy" attribute in the mapping is telling Hibernate to load the associated Track objects at the same time it loads the data for the Conference object. In the case of the Track association I've chosen to set the lazy attribute to false since our domain objects will be used from the middle tier to populate data transfer objects (DTOs) to be served to the Web tier. The decision on when to use lazy loading is an important one. In the previous case the factors influencing the decision were the architecture of the application (using DTOs versus using domain objects directly in the Web tier) and the number and size of the Track objects (which are few and fairly small).

■**Note** In Hibernate 3.X the default is for all associations to be lazy. If you are migrating an application from Hibernate 2.X to Hibernate 3.X, this can result in many Lazy Instantiation Exceptions, especially if you are using the Data Transfer Object pattern.

In the Conference class we created an association to the Track class in the form of a Set. To complete the other side of the association between conferences and tracks, we need to add an association to the Track class that will allow us to retrieve the associated conference object. The associated conference object's identity should match the value of the column FK_CONFERENCE_ID. We can use the many-to-one element to provide such a link as shown in Listing 4-18.

Listing 4-18. *Many-to-One Element Mapping Conference to a Track*

```
<many-to-one
    class="Conference"
    name="Conference"
    not-null="true"
    >
    <column name="FK_CONFERENCE_ID" />
</many-to-one>
```

Listing 4-19 shows the Track class, which has a property of type Conference as well as getters and setters.

Listing 4-19. *Track POJO*

```
package com.integrallis.techconf.domain;
...
public class Track implements Serializable {
    ...
    // primary key
    private Integer id;

    // fields
    private String title;
    private String subtitle;
    private String description;

    // tracks belong to a conference
    private Conference conference;

    // constructors
    public Track() {
    }

    // getters and setters
    ...

    public Conference getConference() {
        return conference;
    }

    public void setConference(Conference conference) {
        this.conference = conference;
    }
    ...
}
```

Testing Conference and Tracks

Before we delve into testing the mappings we just created, let's take a look at a Hibernate configuration file tailored to test the mappings for the classes shown in Figure 4-13. Listing 4-20 shows a Hibernate XML configuration file that does the equivalent of what we have done until now in Java code. This Hibernate configuration file is showing all of the mappings for the TechConf application. Most Hibernate applications use the XML format for their configurations, and it is the recommended way to configure Hibernate in your application. For a single database application, this file is usually named hibernate.cfg.xml.

Listing 4-20. *Hibernate XML Configuration File*

```xml
<?xml version="1.0" encoding="utf-8"?>
<!DOCTYPE hibernate-configuration
  PUBLIC "-//Hibernate/Hibernate Configuration DTD 3.0//EN"
  "http://hibernate.sourceforge.net/hibernate-configuration-3.0.dtd">

<hibernate-configuration>
  <!-- ==================================================================== -->
  <!-- SessionFactory used for Testing                                   -->
  <!-- ==================================================================== -->
  <session-factory>
    <property name="hibernate.connection.url">
      jdbc:mysql://localhost/test</property>
    <property name="hibernate.connection.driver_class">
      com.mysql.jdbc.Driver
    </property>
    <property name="hibernate.connection.username">yourUserName</property>
    <property name="hibernate.connection.password">yourPassword</property>
    <property name="dialect">org.hibernate.dialect.MySQLDialect</property>
    <property name="hibernate.show_sql">true</property>

    <!-- ==================================================================== -->
    <!-- Mappings                                                          -->
    <!-- ==================================================================== -->
    <mapping resource="com/integrallis/techconf/domain/Abstract.hbm.xml" />
    <mapping resource="com/integrallis/techconf/domain/AbstractStatus.hbm.xml" />
    <mapping resource="com/integrallis/techconf/domain/Address.hbm.xml" />
    <mapping resource="com/integrallis/techconf/domain/Answer.hbm.xml" />
    <mapping resource="com/integrallis/techconf/domain/AttendeeGroup.hbm.xml" />
    <mapping resource="com/integrallis/techconf/domain/BlogLink.hbm.xml" />
    <mapping resource="com/integrallis/techconf/domain/Booth.hbm.xml" />
    <mapping resource="com/integrallis/techconf/domain/ChoiceAnswer.hbm.xml" />
    <mapping resource="com/integrallis/techconf/domain/Conference.hbm.xml" />
    <mapping resource="com/integrallis/techconf/domain/News.hbm.xml" />
    <mapping resource="com/integrallis/techconf/domain/Presentation.hbm.xml" />
    <mapping resource="com/integrallis/techconf/domain/PresentationLevel.hbm.xml" />
    <mapping resource="com/integrallis/techconf/domain/PresentationTopic.hbm.xml" />
    <mapping resource="com/integrallis/techconf/domain/PresentationType.hbm.xml" />
    <mapping resource="com/integrallis/techconf/domain/PricingRule.hbm.xml" />
    <mapping resource="com/integrallis/techconf/domain/Question.hbm.xml" />
    <mapping resource="com/integrallis/techconf/domain/QuestionChoice.hbm.xml" />
    <mapping resource="com/integrallis/techconf/domain/Questionnaire.hbm.xml" />
```

```
        <mapping resource="com/integrallis/techconf/domain/QuestionType.hbm.xml" />
        <mapping resource="com/integrallis/techconf/domain/Reminder.hbm.xml" />
        <mapping resource="com/integrallis/techconf/domain/Role.hbm.xml" />
        <mapping resource="com/integrallis/techconf/domain/Room.hbm.xml" />
        <mapping resource="com/integrallis/techconf/domain/ScheduleEntry.hbm.xml" />
        <mapping resource="com/integrallis/techconf/domain/Session.hbm.xml" />
        <mapping resource="com/integrallis/techconf/domain/Track.hbm.xml" />
        <mapping resource="com/integrallis/techconf/domain/User.hbm.xml" />
        <mapping resource="com/integrallis/techconf/domain/UserRole.hbm.xml" />
        <mapping resource="com/integrallis/techconf/domain/Venue.hbm.xml" />
    </session-factory>
</hibernate-configuration>
```

Note The Hibernate configuration file shown in Listing 4-20 references all of the mappings in the TechConf application. If you are coding along for the example at hand, you can comment out the mappings that have not been created yet to have a working Hibernate XML configuration.

To load the XML configuration you'll need code similar to that shown in Listing 4-21.

Listing 4-21. *Java Code to Load a Hibernate XML Configuration File*

```
File configFile = new File("hibernate.cfg.xml");
Configuration configuration = new Configuration().configure(configFile);
SessionFactory factory = configuration.buildSessionFactory();
```

The code in Listing 4-22 creates a Conference object with its associated Tracks and then persist the Conference to the database.

Listing 4-22. *Testing the One-To-Many Set Mapping*

```
public static void main(String[] args) {
    File configFile = new File("hibernate.cfg.xml");
    Configuration configuration = new Configuration().configure(configFile);
    SessionFactory factory = configuration.buildSessionFactory();

    Session session = null;
    Transaction tx = null;
    try {
        // create a conference
        Conference conference = new Conference();
```

```java
        conference.setAbstractSubmissionEndDate(new Date());
        conference.setAbstractSubmissionStartDate(new Date());
        conference.setDescription("A Test Conference");
        conference.setEndDate(new Date());
        conference.setName("TestConf 2005");
        conference.setStartDate(new Date());

        // create some tracks
        Track jseTrack = new Track();
        jseTrack.setDescription(
            "Learn how to build powerful Java desktop applications");
        jseTrack.setSubtitle("Java Standard Edition");
        jseTrack.setTitle("JSE");

        Track jeeTrack = new Track();
        jeeTrack.setDescription(
            "Learn how to build powerful Enterprise applications");
        jeeTrack.setSubtitle("Java Enterprise Edition");
        jeeTrack.setTitle("JEE");

        Track jmeTrack = new Track();
        jmeTrack.setTitle("JME");
        jmeTrack.setDescription(
            "Learn how to bring cellphone and PDAs alive with Java");
        jmeTrack.setSubtitle("Java Micro Edition");

        // add the tracks to the conference
        conference.addTrack(jseTrack);
        conference.addTrack(jeeTrack);
        conference.addTrack(jmeTrack);

        // persist the conference
        session = factory.openSession();
        tx = session.beginTransaction();
        session.persist(conference);
        tx.commit();
    } catch (Exception e) {
        if (tx != null) {
            tx.rollback();
        }
    } finally {
        session.close();
    }
}
```

The code in Listing 4-22 will produce output similar to that shown here:

```
Hibernate: insert into conference (AbstractSubmissionStartDate, Name, Description,
AbstractSubmissionEndDate, EndDate, StartDate, FK_VENUE_ID) values (?, ?, ?, ?, ?,
?, ?)
Hibernate: insert into track (TITLE, SUBTITLE, DESCRIPTION, FK_CONFERENCE_ID)
values (?, ?, ?, ?)
Hibernate: insert into track (TITLE, SUBTITLE, DESCRIPTION, FK_CONFERENCE_ID)
values (?, ?, ?, ?)
Hibernate: insert into track (TITLE, SUBTITLE, DESCRIPTION, FK_CONFERENCE_ID)
values (?, ?, ?, ?)
```

As you can see from the sample output, Hibernate produced four SQL INSERTS, one for the Conference object and three for the Track objects. If you take a look back at the mapping shown in Listing 4-17 you'll notice that there is an attribute named "cascade" with a value of "all". In Hibernate every association can have a cascading style. The cascading style tells Hibernate how to treat associated objects in the scope of persistence operations. For example, if you set the cascading style to "save-update" in a one-to-many association, Hibernate will determine if any of the associated objects are "dirty" and generate SQL UPDATES for those objects, and similarly it will generate SQL INSERTS for new objects. The values for the cascade attribute are "none", "persist", "merge", "delete", "save-update", "evict", "replicate", "lock", "refresh", "delete-orphan", and "all". These values can be combined in a comma-separated list and correspond closely to the operations available on the Session class. Consult the Hibernate online reference for an in-depth coverage of cascading behavior and transitive persistence.

If you inspect the CONFERENCE and TRACK tables you should output results similar to that shown next.

```
mysql> select PK_ID, NAME from CONFERENCE;
```

```
+-------+---------------+
| PK_ID | NAME          |
+-------+---------------+
|     1 | TestConf 2005 |
+-------+---------------+
```

```
1 row in set (0.00 sec)mysql> select PK_ID, TITLE, SUBTITLE from TRACK;
```

```
+-------+-------+------------------------+
| PK_ID | TITLE | SUBTITLE               |
+-------+-------+------------------------+
|     1 | JSE   | Java Standard Edition  |
|     2 | JEE   | Java Enterprise Edition|
|     3 | JME   | Java Micro Edition      |
+-------+-------+------------------------+
3 rows in set (0.00 sec)
```

Many-to-One: Conferences and Venues

In the previous example we had a relationship where one or more tracks belonged to a conference, which is an owner parent-child relationship since we don't want the tracks to exist without an owning conference. In the case of a conference and a venue, we have an association where a venue can exist in the database without an associated conference and the same applies to a conference (since a site admin might create all the conference content in advance before choosing a suitable venue), and obviously many conferences can share the same venue (most likely not at the same time).

To satisfy this relationship we can use a many-to-one mapping in conference.hbm.xml as shown in Listing 4-23.

Listing 4-23. *Many-to-One Mapping Between Conference and Venue*

```
<many-to-one
    class="Venue"
    name="Venue"
    not-null="true"
    cascade="persist,save-update"
>
    <column name="FK_VENUE_ID" />
</many-to-one>
```

Since we don't want venues to be deleted when a conference is deleted, but we do want the venue information to be updated or inserted in the database when we update or create a conference, we set the cascade attribute to "persist,save-update". Therefore on any calls to persist, save or update against a Conference object, Hibernate will determine whether the associated Venue object needs to be saved or updated.

Inheritance

Of all of the differences between a database schema and an object graph, inheritance brings the most interesting challenges. The problem boils down to mapping "is a" relationships while retaining the power of the object-oriented language (polymorphism) and having the data stored in an efficient way that can be used not only by your object-oriented application but also by other (possibly procedural) applications (such as reports or ad-hoc queries). Hibernate supports three different approaches to mapping an inheritance hierarchy, which are outlined next.

Table-Per-Concrete-Class

In the Table-Per-Concrete-Class strategy you have a table per each class in the system. In this strategy, each class is mapped to a table that includes both the attributes of the implemented class as well as the attributes inherited from the parent class. This strategy basically discards polymorphism (polymorphic queries require you to query over all child classes), but it is very efficient in terms of storage space and record insertion (one SQL statement).

Table-Per-Class-Hierarchy

In the Table-Per-Class-Hierarchy strategy a single table is used to store all of the objects belonging to the class hierarchy. It uses a "type discriminator" column that specifies which specific subclass a row maps to. This strategy makes regular and polymorphic queries very simple and performant. The few drawbacks include maintenance, since each class you add to the inheritance hierarchy requires modifications to the table, and the requirement that all subclass columns be declared as nullable in the schema.

Table-Per-Subclass

In the Table-Per-Subclass strategy each subclass, interface, and abstract class have their own table containing only the properties for that particular class. In the tables, all associations are represented as foreign key constraints. To enable polymorphic queries, Hibernate uses the same primary key for all constituent parts of an object instance. From the standpoint of data storage, this strategy provides a completely normalized schema, and adding an object does not imply modification to existing tables but simply the addition of a new table. Major drawbacks are that it requires multiple SQL queries for saving and updating, and SQL join queries for data retrieval.

Choosing an Inheritance Mapping Strategy

Choosing one of the strategies previously outlined depends on the complexity of the inheritance graph you want to persist, the complexity of each class, how the classes will be used in your application, and whether the data is going to be used from outside of the application.

If you don't need polymorphic queries, the simplest route is to go with the Table-Per-Concrete-Class. If you need polymorphic queries and your subclasses differ mainly in behavior and not in data, use the Table-Per-Class-Hierarchy. On the other hand, if your classes differ mainly in the data, then the Table-Per-Subclass strategy might be a viable option.

In most cases I use the Table-Per-Class-Hierarchy strategy since it provides the best compromise between complexity and performance. Of course these choices all imply that you have control over the schema and that you are working in a top-down fashion.

Inheritance: Table-Per-Class Hierarchy

Now it's time to put some of the concepts about mapping inheritance into practice. In the first example from the TechConf system, we will map the User, Attendee, and Presenter class hierarchy. As you can deduce from Figure 4-14, an Attendee and a Presenter are types of User.

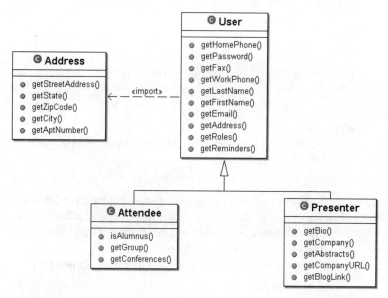

Figure 4-14. *User, Attendee, and Presenter class hierarchy*

Using the Table-Per-Class-Hierarchy strategy, we will use a single table named USER to hold the data for Users, Attendees, and Presenters. The SQL required to create this table is shown in Listing 4-24.

Listing 4-24. *SQL to Create the USER Table*

```
CREATE TABLE USER (
  PK_ID INTEGER NOT NULL PRIMARY KEY AUTO_INCREMENT,
  -- DISCRIMINATOR COLUMN
  USERTYPE VARCHAR(3) NOT NULL,
  PASSWORD VARCHAR(16) NOT NULL,
  FIRSTNAME VARCHAR(32) NOT NULL,
  LASTNAME VARCHAR(32) NOT NULL,
  EMAIL VARCHAR(64) NOT NULL,
  HOMEPHONE VARCHAR(12),
  WORKPHONE VARCHAR(12),
  FAX VARCHAR(12),
  FK_ADDRESS_ID INTEGER NOT NULL,
```

```
-- ATTENDEE
FK_ATTENDEEGROUP_ID INTEGER,
ALUMNUS BOOLEAN,
-- PRESENTER
BIO VARCHAR(255),
COMPANY VARCHAR(64),
COMPANYURL VARCHAR(64),
FK_BLOGLINK_ID VARCHAR(64),
CONSTRAINT USER_ADDRESS_FK FOREIGN KEY(FK_ADDRESS_ID) REFERENCES ADDRESS(PK_ID),
CONSTRAINT UNIQUE_USER_EMAIL UNIQUE(EMAIL)
);
```

Notice that the table has all of the fields required to store every element of the User-Attendee-Presenter class hierarchy. Also notice that all of the fields for the subclasses are nullable. The column USERTYPE—a VARCHAR(3)—will serve as the discriminator column that Hibernate will use to determine the type of object that's stored in a given row.

Now let's take a look at the HBM mapping file for the user class hierarchy shown in Listing 4-25.

Listing 4-25. *Table-Per-Class Hierarchy Mapping for User-Attendee-Presenter*

```xml
<?xml version="1.0"?>
<!DOCTYPE hibernate-mapping PUBLIC
    "-//Hibernate/Hibernate Mapping DTD 3.0//EN"
    "http://hibernate.sourceforge.net/hibernate-mapping-3.0.dtd">

<hibernate-mapping package="com.integrallis.techconf.domain">
    <class name="User" table="user" discriminator-value="USR">
        <id name="Id" column="PK_ID" type="integer">
            <generator class="identity" />
        </id>

        <discriminator column="USERTYPE" length="3"/>

        <!-- User fields -->
        <property name="HomePhone" not-null="false" />
        ...
        <many-to-one
            class="Address" name="Address"
            not-null="true" cascade="all" lazy="false"
        >
            <column name="FK_ADDRESS_ID" />
        </many-to-one>
        ...
        <!-- Attendee Subclass -->
        <subclass name="Attendee" discriminator-value="ATD">
            <property name="Alumnus" type="boolean" />
            <many-to-one name="Group" class="AttendeeGroup">
```

```
                <column name="FK_ATTENDEEGROUP_ID" />
            </many-to-one>
            ...
        </subclass>

        <!-- Presenter Subclass -->
        <subclass name="Presenter" discriminator-value="PST">
            <property name="Bio" />
            <property name="Company" />
            <property name="CompanyURL" />
            ...
        </subclass>
    </class>
</hibernate-mapping>
```

As you can see, the subclass element is used to map the subclasses Attendee and Presenter. For User objects the discriminator column value is "USR", for Attendee objects it is "ATD", and for Presenter objects it is "PST". Also, from this mapping we can see that Users can have an Address. I have omitted some sections of the mapping for clarity's sake.

Now we can write a simple test to create some User, Attendee, and Presenter objects and persist them to the database. Listing 4-26 shows some example code to create the objects. Notice that I am creating the required Address objects for each of the User, Attendee, and Presenter objects.

Listing 4-26. *Creating and Persisting Some User, Attendee, and Presenter Objects*

```
File configFile = new File("hibernate.cfg.xml");
Configuration configuration = new Configuration().configure(configFile);
SessionFactory factory = configuration.buildSessionFactory();

// create some addresses
Address address1 = new Address("123 Main Street", "N/A", "Columbus", "OH", "43081");
Address address2 =
    new Address("456 Vine Street", "N/A", "Cincinnati", "OH", "45202");
Address address3 = new Address("1 Easy Street", "N/A", "Columbus", "GA", "31901");

// create a user
User user = new User("Jim", "Smith", "jim@smith.com", "jimspassword");
user.setAddress(address1);

// create an attendee
Attendee attendee =
    new Attendee("Bob", "Smithers", "bsmithers@acme.com", "bobspassword");
attendee.setAlumnus(true);
attendee.setAddress(address2);
```

```
// create a presenter
Presenter presenter =
    new Presenter("Jackie", "Roberts", "jroberts@acme.com", "jackiespassword");
presenter.setBio("Jackie loves Java");
presenter.setCompany("Acme Java Corporation");
presenter.setCompanyURL("www.acme.com");
presenter.setAddress(address3);

Session session = null;
Transaction tx = null;
try {
    session = factory.openSession();
    tx = session.beginTransaction();
    // persist the objects
    session.persist(user);
    session.persist(attendee);
    session.persist(presenter);
    tx.commit();
} catch (Exception e) {
    if (tx != null) {
        tx.rollback();
    }
} finally {
    session.close();
}
```

Running the example shown in Listing 4-26 would produce the following SQL statements:

```
Hibernate: insert into Address (StreetAddress, State, ZipCode, City, AptNumber)
values (?, ?, ?, ?, ?)
Hibernate: insert into user (HOMEPHONE, PASSWORD, FAX, WORKPHONE, LASTNAME,
FIRSTNAME, EMAIL, FK_ADDRESS_ID, USERTYPE) values (?, ?, ?, ?, ?, ?, ?, ?, 'USR')
Hibernate: insert into Address (StreetAddress, State, ZipCode, City, AptNumber)
values (?, ?, ?, ?, ?)
Hibernate: insert into user (HOMEPHONE, PASSWORD, FAX, WORKPHONE, LASTNAME,
FIRSTNAME, EMAIL, FK_ADDRESS_ID, ALUMNUS, FK_ATTENDEEGROUP_ID, USERTYPE) values
(?, ?, ?, ?, ?, ?, ?, ?, ?, ?, 'ATD')
Hibernate: insert into Address (StreetAddress, State, ZipCode, City, AptNumber)
values (?, ?, ?, ?, ?)
Hibernate: insert into user (HOMEPHONE, PASSWORD, FAX, WORKPHONE, LASTNAME,
FIRSTNAME, EMAIL, FK_ADDRESS_ID, BIO, COMPANY, COMPANYURL, FK_BLOGLINK_ID,
USERTYPE) values (?, ?, ?, ?, ?, ?, ?, ?, ?, ?, ?, ?, 'PST')
```

As you can see, there are three SQL INSERT statements for the ADDRESS table and three for the USER table. Notice the values of the USERTYPE column in the different SQL INSERTS. If we inspect the USER table you should see the three records with their foreign key constraints to the three records in the ADDRESS table as shown next:

```
mysql> select PK_ID, FIRSTNAME, LASTNAME, EMAIL, USERTYPE, FK_ADDRESS_ID from USER;
```

PK_ID	FIRSTNAME	LASTNAME	EMAIL	USERTYPE	FK_ADDRESS_ID
1	Jim	Smith	jim@smith.com	USR	1
2	Bob	Smithers	bsmithers@acme.com	ATD	2
3	Jackie	Roberts	jroberts@acme.com	PST	3

3 rows in set (0.00 sec)

```
mysql> select * from ADDRESS;
```

PK_ID	STREETADDRESS	APTNUMBER	CITY	STATE	ZIPCODE
1	123 Main Street	N/A	Columbus	OH	43081
2	456 Vine Street	N/A	Cincinnati	OH	45202
3	1 Easy Street	N/A	Columbus	GA	31901

3 rows in set (0.02 sec)

The power of Hibernate's handling of inheritance lies in the ability to issue polymorphic queries. Before we jump into some examples, I will introduce you to the use of a tool that has saved me countless hours of coding and debugging when working with complex Hibernate queries. That tool is the Hibernate Console, which is a part of the collection of Eclipse plug-ins that encompasses the Hibernate Tools Project.

The Hibernate Console is an Eclipse perspective that gives several views to work with your mapped objects. The Hibernate Tools plug-ins can be obtained as part of the JBoss Eclipse IDE set of plug-ins or in a stand-alone distribution. For detailed information on how to obtain and install the Hibernate Tools, see the Hibernate Tools website at www.hibernate.org/255.html.

Once you have successfully installed the Hibernate Tools plug-ins, you are ready to work with your persistence objects without having to write a single line of Java code. Using any existing Eclipse project containing Hibernate mapped POJOs, you can select the Hibernate Console perspective for the Perspective toolbar. The Console is shown in Figure 4-15.

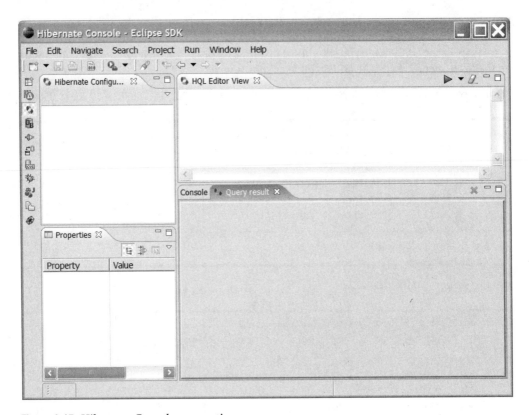

Figure 4-15. *Hibernate Console perspective*

The Console provides a tree view of Console configurations (a Console configuration is associated with a Hibernate configuration), an HQL editor view, and a Query results view. First we need a Hibernate configuration file to be used by our Console configuration, as opposed to the previous example shown in Listing 4-20. The file hibernate-no-mappings.cfg.xml we will be using has no mappings declared, as shown in Listing 4-27.

Listing 4-27. *Hibernate XML Configuration File with No Mappings*

```
<?xml version="1.0" encoding="utf-8"?>
<!DOCTYPE hibernate-configuration
    PUBLIC "-//Hibernate/Hibernate Configuration DTD 3.0//EN"
    "http://hibernate.sourceforge.net/hibernate-configuration-3.0.dtd">

<hibernate-configuration>
    <!-- ================================================================= -->
    <!-- Session Factory used for Testing                                 -->
    <!-- ================================================================= -->
    <session-factory>
        <property name="hibernate.connection.url">
            jdbc:mysql://localhost/test
```

```
        </property>
        <property name="hibernate.connection.driver_class">
            com.mysql.jdbc.Driver
        </property>
        <property name="hibernate.connection.username">yourUserName</property>
        <property name="hibernate.connection.password">yourPassword</property>
        <property name="dialect">org.hibernate.dialect.MySQLDialect</property>
        <property name="hibernate.show_sql">true</property>
    </session-factory>
</hibernate-configuration>
```

Now that we have a Hibernate configuration file ready, we can create a Console configuration by right-clicking on the Hibernate Configurations view and selecting Add Configuration from the popup menu, which will bring up a dialog as shown in Figure 4-16.

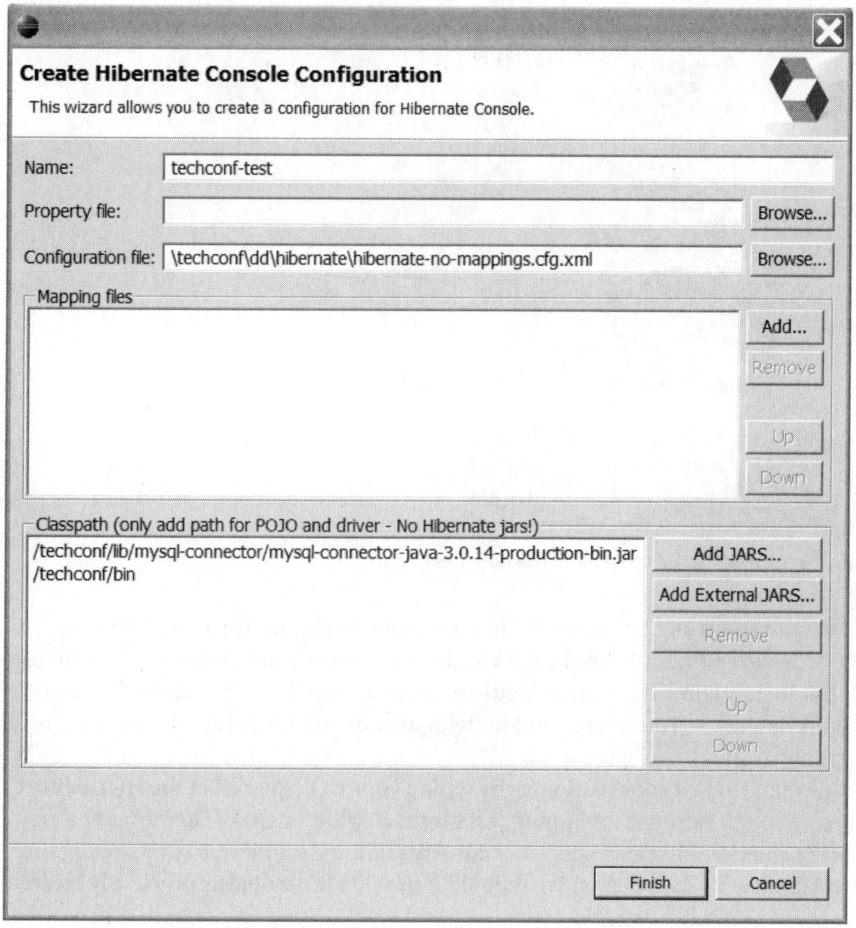

Figure 4-16. *Adding a Console configuration*

The Create Hibernate Console Configuration wizard asks you to specify the Hibernate configuration via a properties file in the "Property file" field or using an XML configuration in the "Configuration file" field. Click the Browse button next to the "Configuration file" field and select the file hibernate-no-mappings.cfg.xml previously created. Next, in the Classpath section add the JAR file containing the database driver as well as the path (directory) of your compiled POJO classes (you can simply add the bin directory of your Eclipse project).

Finally, we need to tell the Console which mappings to load by clicking Add next to the "Mapping files" field and selecting the HBM files as shown in Figure 4-17 and clicking OK.

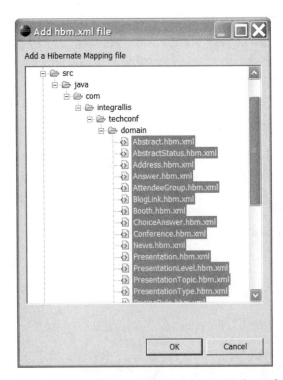

Figure 4-17. *Adding mapping files to a Console configuration*

Click Finish, and you should now see the new Console configuration in the tree view. To work with this Console configuration right-click and select Create SessionFactory. The node in the tree view should now show the mapped entities as under the "Mapped entities" node of Console configuration node. You can expand individual entity nodes to reveal the details of a particular mapping as shown in Figure 4-18.

You are now ready to test your mappings by typing your HQL queries in the HQL editor view. Going back to our inheritance mapping test for the Table-Per-Class-Hierarchy strategy, let's try some HQL queries. First let's check the contents of the User hierarchy by issuing the query shown in Figure 4-19. As expected, this should return the three objects previously created.

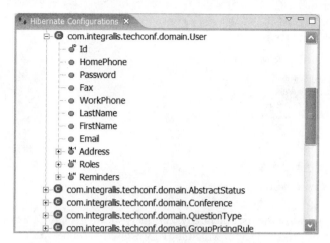

Figure 4-18. *A hierarchical view of a Hibernate mapping*

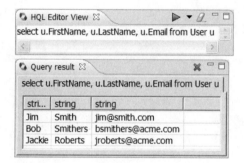

Figure 4-19. *Polymorphic query to retrieve all User objects*

We can also issue queries against the subclasses of User as shown in Figure 4-20 for the class, Attendee.

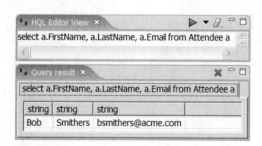

Figure 4-20. *Query to retrieve all Attendee objects*

Similarly, we can check the contents of the Address class by issuing the query shown in Figure 4-21.

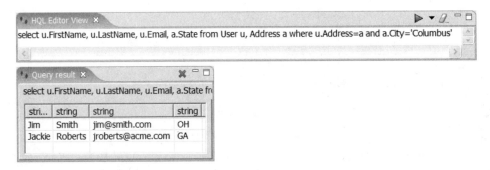

Figure 4-21. *Query to retrieve all Address objects*

Let's try a more interesting query against the User hierarchy. The query shown in Figure 4-22 finds all User objects containing an Address object for which the City property is equal to "Columbus".

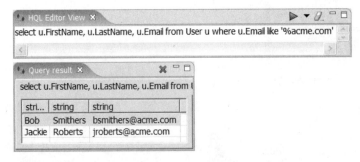

Figure 4-22. *A more complex polymorphic query*

As seen previously, you can also use some of the familiar SQL syntax in HQL queries as shown in Figure 4-23, a query to find all Users with an email address ending in "acme.com".

HQL Editor View ✕
select u.FirstName, u.LastName, u.Email from User u where u.Email like '%acme.com'

Query result ✕
select u.FirstName, u.LastName, u.Email from U

stri...	string	string
Bob	Smithers	bsmithers@acme.com
Jackie	Roberts	jroberts@acme.com

Figure 4-23. *HQL query using the "like" and "%" operators*

Inheritance: Table Per Subclass

In this example, the PricingRule hierarchy is mapped using the Table-Per-Subclass strategy. Pricing rules are applied at registration time when a conference attendee pays to attend the conference. The PricingRule hierarchy is composed of the interface PricingRule and the classes GroupPricingRule and RegistrationDatePricingRule, which implement the PricingRule interface. The PricingRule hierarchy is shown in Figure 4-24.

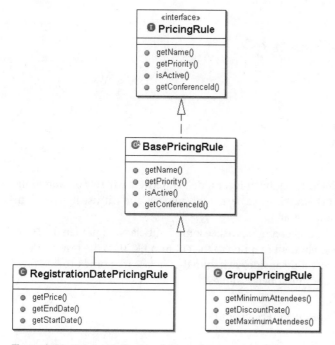

Figure 4-24. *PricingRule class hierarchy*

The three corresponding tables are shown in Listing 4-28. Notice that tables holding the subclasses data, GROUPPRICINGRULE and REGISTRATIONDATEPRICINGRULE, both have foreign key constraints referencing the PRICINGRULE table (the root of the class hierarchy).

Listing 4-28. *Pricing Rules Tables*

```
CREATE TABLE PRICINGRULE (
  PK_ID INTEGER NOT NULL PRIMARY KEY AUTO_INCREMENT,
  NAME VARCHAR(16) NOT NULL,
  PRIORITY INTEGER,
  ACTIVE BOOLEAN,
  FK_CONFERENCE_ID INTEGER NOT NULL,
  CONSTRAINT PRICINGRULE_CONFERENCE_FK FOREIGN KEY(FK_CONFERENCE_ID)
    REFERENCES CONFERENCE(PK_ID),
  CONSTRAINT UNIQUE_PRICINGRULE_NAME UNIQUE(NAME)
);
```

```
CREATE TABLE GROUPPRICINGRULE (
  PK_ID INTEGER NOT NULL PRIMARY KEY,
  MINIMUMATTENDEES INTEGER,
  MAXIMUMATTENDEES INTEGER,
  DISCOUNTRATE DOUBLE,
  CONSTRAINT GROUPPRICINGRULE_PRICINGRULE_FK
    FOREIGN KEY(PK_ID) REFERENCES PRICINGRULE(PK_ID)
);

CREATE TABLE REGISTRATIONDATEPRICINGRULE (
  PK_ID INTEGER NOT NULL PRIMARY KEY,
  STARTDATE DATETIME NOT NULL,
  ENDDATE DATETIME NOT NULL,
  PRICE DOUBLE NOT NULL,
  CONSTRAINT REGISTRATIONDATEPRICINGRULE_PRICINGRULE_FK
    FOREIGN KEY(PK_ID) REFERENCES PRICINGRULE(PK_ID)
);
```

In this strategy the data model mirrors the object model. Hibernate will rely on matching the primary keys to find all the data belonging to a particular subclass and will use it to perform joins when querying the PricingRule hierarchy.

To map these three tables to the object model, we use joined-subclass element in the HBM file as shown in Listing 4-29. The id element mapped to the column PK_ID is the primary key of the parent table, while the key elements inside each joined-subclass mapping provide the linkage between the parent table and the subclass tables.

Listing 4-29. *Table-Per-Subclass Mapping for Pricing Rules Hierarchy*

```xml
<?xml version="1.0"?>
<!DOCTYPE hibernate-mapping PUBLIC
    "-//Hibernate/Hibernate Mapping DTD 3.0//EN"
    "http://hibernate.sourceforge.net/hibernate-mapping-3.0.dtd">

<hibernate-mapping package="com.integrallis.techconf.domain">
    <class name="PricingRule" table="pricingrule">
        <id
            column="PK_ID"
            name="Id"
            type="integer"
        >
            <generator class="identity" />
        </id>
        <property name="Name" not-null="true" />
        ...
```

```
    <property
        column="FK_CONFERENCE_ID"
        name="ConferenceId"
        not-null="true"
        type="integer"
    />
    <!-- GroupPricingRule Subclass -->
    <joined-subclass name="GroupPricingRule" table="grouppricingrule">
        <key column="PK_ID"/>
        <property name="MinimumAttendees" type="integer" />
        <property name="DiscountRate" type="java.lang.Double" />
        <property name="MaximumAttendees" type="integer" />
    </joined-subclass>

    <!-- RegistrationDatePricingRule Subclass -->
    <joined-subclass name="RegistrationDatePricingRule"
                     table="registrationdatepricingrule">
        <key column="PK_ID"/>
        <property name="StartDate" not-null="true" type="timestamp" />
        <property name="EndDate" not-null="true" type="timestamp" />
        <property name="Price" not-null="true" type="java.lang.Double" />
    </joined-subclass>
  </class>
</hibernate-mapping>
```

Testing the Table-Per-Subclass mapping is similar to the testing previously performed for the Table-Per-Class-Hierarchy strategy, and it is left as an exercise for you.

Summary

In this chapter you have learned the foundations of object-relational mapping using Hibernate, the prevalent and by far richest mapping service available. Now that you know how to map simple classes and collections and how to deal with inheritance, you'll be ready to tackle the development of the TechConf application Data Access Objects (DAO) in subsequent chapters.

We will continue to learn about Hibernate features, including more advanced features such as caching and other facilities that will come into play when we transition into the world of J2EE by having our Hibernate-mapped POJOs working inside an EJB container. Also, in the Testing chapter, you'll learn how to apply some of the techniques of unit and integration testing to the testing of Hibernate-mapped POJOs and Hibernate-powered DAOs.

CHAPTER 5

■ ■ ■

Business Services with JBoss

For most of the last decade Java has reigned supreme in the server side of enterprise computing. In contemporary enterprise development the J2EE application server is positioned at the heart of it all and has come to replace the operating system as the new layer of abstraction upon which enterprise applications and services are created. The J2EE architecture represents the state of the art in middleware technology, drawing on the lessons learned from the fields of transaction processing monitors (TP monitors), object request brokers (ORBs), component technologies, distributed computing and relational and object databases. Java's foray into the enterprise started slowly with the introduction of the servlet API, followed by JavaServer Pages, the early EJB component models and a flurry of Model-View-Controller implementations. These helped Java compete in the Web applications arena, but what really brought the enterprise customers on board was the larger vision of the Java EE (formerly J2EE) specification. Java EE brought to the table a uniform way to deal with the big-picture issues faced by enterprises like directory services, distributed transactions, messaging, scalability, and integration. As a specification for an enterprise computing technology stack, Java EE provides an extensive and impressive list of technologies loosely coupled yet tightly integrated.

Like any technology that is mass-adopted, the shortcomings of the specification became apparent to those building database-driven web applications (which became the *raison d'etre* for the platform). These shortcomings were especially apparent in the areas of productivity and testability. J2EE was supposed to be about making simple things simple and the hard things possible, but it took some time for the specification to reach a level of maturity to realize that dream. Java EE was and still is a by-committee specification, and like any such entity, it moves at a snail's pace. One of the problems with a rich platform like Java EE is that it offers too many tools and possibilities. Architects and developers alike started building simple applications using the then heavyweight EJB technology. In the early version of the Java EE, there were a few well-defined reasons to use EJB, such as distributed transactions and the need for remoteness. If you were using EJBs and your application didn't meet those requirements, you were putting yourself and your team through a lot of unnecessary pain. Also, the component model proposed by EJB was too simplistic to create truly rich, object-oriented applications. While curtailing object-oriented expressiveness, previous incarnations of the Enterprise JavaBeans specification were too difficult and cumbersome to work. Besides the creation of the numerous deployment descriptors, they required the creation of many other "glue" files. The creation, maintenance, and synchronization of these files required a significant amount of overhead. Some applications servers even required platform-specific pre-compiling and packaging steps. All these factors added to a very steep learning curve for developers accustomed to working with rich, POJO-based Java SE applications or the simple HTTP wrappers provided by the servlet API or JavaServer Pages.

Fortunately, the Java community voiced its opinion about the state of development created by the early J2EE specification. Developers started to notice that they could not express a rich business object model with EJBs, and they grew frustrated by the amount of steps required to deploy a simple service component or to make a domain entity persistent. Frameworks and techniques started to appear to deal with the cumbersomeness of the API. Most of the agile, lightweight Java frameworks revolved around the notion of working with POJOs, Plain Old Java Interfaces (POJIs), minimizing the amount of configuration, inversion of control (IoC; also known as dependency injection or DI), and dynamic rather than static provision of container services.

Tools like XDoclet became a must-have for any development team looking to become productive with the API. These tools were crutches to deal with what was an apparent set of flaws in the specification. Frameworks like Spring showed what was possible by going back to basics, and rather than forcing your code to live by the rules of the environment (the J2EE container), you could have your code working unencumbered by the many services provided by the platform but with the ability to use them at will in a transparent way. Luckily for us, the complaints eventually made it into the specification via the Java Community Process (JCP) in the form of many JSRs influenced by what was wrong and what was missing in the world of Java EE.

The main message is that writing Java EE applications had to be easier. The JSR 220: Enterprise JavaBeans 3.0 sets out to "improve the EJB architecture by reducing its complexity from the developer's point of view." In this chapter we will explore the new world of development using the bleeding-edge technologies in the Java EE 1.4 stack, specifically the EJB3 specification as provided by the JBoss Application Server, a truly revolutionary vision of what the Java EE server of the future will be like.

In this chapter we will focus on extracting the essential services and processes from the design of the TechConf system and translating them into a system of components and pattern implementations that provide business services to the user-facing areas of the system while allowing us to maintain a rich domain model that can evolve to meet future needs.

JBoss

The JBoss Application Server started life as the EJBoss project back in March of 1999. Spear-headed by Marc Fleury, a former Sun Microsystems engineer, and an enthusiastic group of programmers ready to embrace the then-new EJB specification, it has grown to be the most popular open source application server in the market and a worthy contender to the likes of BEA WebLogic and IBM WebSphere (the two commercial leaders in the market).

Distributed under the GNU Lesser General Public License (LGPL), JBoss is a 100-percent compliant clean-room implementation that provides the full gamut of Java EE services. It is built on a pluggable architecture that leverages the JMX specification (Java Management Extensions) and advances in software engineering such as aspect-oriented programming (AOP) and (DI)/IoC techniques. JBoss was also one of the first application servers tailored to developers, with dynamic features like hot deployment and on-the-fly flexibility, for example, the ability to load and unload libraries at runtime and dynamic generation of container stubs and skeletons. Many of these features are still not found in some commercial offerings.

JBoss JEMS

JBoss is more than an application server, it is a full-featured platform for enterprise development providing the full Java EE stack of services under the umbrella of the JBoss Enterprise Middleware System (JEMS) brand. Positioned as a professionally supported choice for enterprises looking to implement a truly "service-oriented architecture" (SOA) built upon a foundation of reliable, battle-tested middleware components.

The JEMS products comprise an impressive list of offerings, including the following:

- **JBoss AS:** JBoss Application Server

- **Apache Tomcat:** Apache Tomcat Web container

- **Hibernate:** Object-relational persistence and query service

- **JBoss Portal:** Portal platform providing content aggregation and personalization based on the Porlet Specification (JSR-168). It evolved from the JBoss Nukes project

- **JBoss jBPM:** A powerful workflow and business process management engine

- **JBoss Rules:** Business rules engine based on the Drools Rule Engine

- **JBoss Cache:** Clustered, distributed object cache

- **JBoss Eclipse IDE:** A set of Eclipse plug-ins to develop JBoss Java EE 1.4 applications

JBoss AS Architecture

JBoss AS is built on a foundation that uses the JMX API to deliver a lightweight microkernel layer that provides an MBean-based component model that enables the lifecycle management of MBean-based services and provides an advanced and flexible class loading scheme.

The JMX specification allows the control and configuration of managed beans, or MBeans. MBeans are components that wrap the network entities such as other components, applications, and hardware devices. MBeans, just like EJBs, live in a container that abides by the JMX server standard, the MBean server. The MBean server is a lightweight process, similar to a Common Object Request Broker Architecture (CORBA) ORB, which serves as a repository or registry for MBeans. The JMX server in JBoss is the spinal cord of the system where MBeans plug in and interact with other MBeans. JMX was designed as a bridge and a consolidation point for other network management systems, just like Java Message Service (JMS) and JDBC are for the areas of enterprise messaging and database connectivity.

MBeans are designed for management, and they provide clients with the ability to receive notifications of relevant management events by registering with the MBean. JBoss' JMX-based flexible architecture allows you to select which components (or services) you want in a running server. JBoss enables developers to mix and match different implementations of specific J2EE services as long as there is a compliant JMX MBean. MBeans are registered and instantiated using MLets. MLets are management applets; the MBeans server provides a MLet service that loads a text file which specifies the information on the MBeans to be loaded. JBoss can be extended and customized by creating MBean services.

Out of the box, JBoss has a service layer that provides a set of services that implements the Java EE 1.4 stack. Later in this chapter you'll see how to use and manage the available JBoss services and how to add third-party services to fulfill the needs of your applications. The set of services that compose the Java EE 1.4 technology stack are provided by the following pre-packaged services available in the JBoss AS:

- **JBossServer:** An advanced EJB container and JMX "bus"

- **JBossMQ:** A JMS provider (to be replaced by JBoss Messaging)

- **JBossTX:** For JTA/JTS transactions

- **JBossCMP:** Container-Managed Persistence Engine

- **JBossSX:** For JAAS-based security

- **JBossCX:** For Java Connector Architecture (JCA) connectivity

- **JBossMail:** Java mail provider

- **JBossWeb:** An integrated Apache Tomcat container

Overseeing the deployment and inter-service messages is an aspect layer composed of pipelines of interceptors that decorate certain aspects of the functionality of a service and its interaction with other services. For example, in the JBoss EJB container is a pipeline of interceptors providing a myriad of services such as persistence and security, among others.

At the top of the hierarchy lies the application layer where your applications live. JBoss applications have the flexibility to use the services provided by the container either programmatically, via the use of deployment descriptors, or via Java SE version 1.5 metadata (JSR-175).

The Java metadata facility was introduced with Java SE version 1.5 in the form of annotations which are built in language constructs that can be applied at the class, property, or method level to provide meta information directly in a Java class. Annotations are preceded by the @ sign and can optionally take parameters. In Java EE they help to eliminate many glue classes, container contract classes, and many redundant XML deployment descriptors. Whenever possible and if adequate I will use annotations in code rather than external configuration files.

Figure 5-1 shows an architectural diagram of the JBoss AS.

Readers interested in finding out more on the inner workings of JBoss AS should start by exploring the JMX API, Java's Dynamic Proxy API, and Rickard Oeberg's "Interceptor Stack," the pattern at the heart of the JBoss containers. To learn more about the JBoss server architecture, see the JBoss Application Server Guide located at `http://docs.jboss.org/jbossas/jboss4guide/r4/html`.

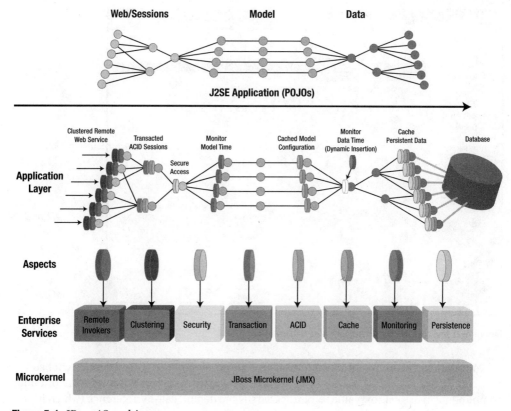

Figure 5-1. *JBoss AS architecture*

Installing and Configuring JBoss

JBoss AS is distributed as a single zip/tar file or as a convenient visual installer (also available via Java Web Start) and is hosted on www.sourceforge.net. Go to www.jboss.com/products/jbossas/downloads and follow the instructions to obtain a distribution.

I recommend that you use the visual installer since it simplifies the installation greatly. The version of JBoss used in this book is JBoss AS 4.0.3. If you're using the graphical installer, select the full product installation containing the EJB3 functionality.

The visual installer is distributed as an executable JAR file; for version 4.0.3 this file is jboss-4.0.3-installer.jar. To start the installation double-click the JAR file (in Windows XP) or on a command shell type:

```
java -jar jboss-4.0.3-installer.jar
```

The installation will present a step-by-step wizard that will allow you to select an installation directory, the language of the installation, and the type of installation. Figure 5-2 shows the installation type selection screen. As previously mentioned, for the examples in this book you'll need to select the "all" installation.

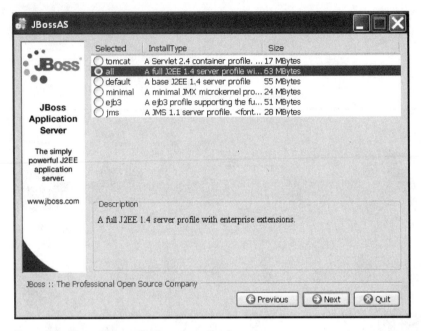

Figure 5-2. *JBoss AS installation type selection*

Another installation option of importance is shown in Figure 5-3. You need to choose between the available class loading schemes and whether to restrict calls between in-container components to use call-by-value semantics versus the default call-by-reference (which is much more efficient).

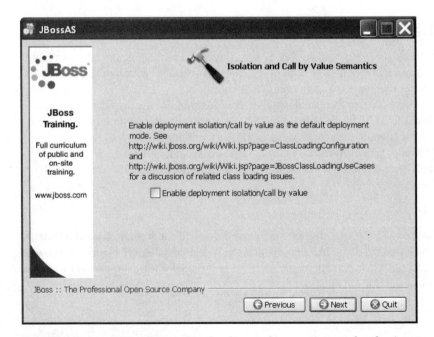

Figure 5-3. *JBoss AS installation class loading and invocation mode selection*

The final installation step of importance, as shown in Figure 5-4, allows for the JMX administrative interfaces to the application server to be secured. This is important if you are setting up a production environment; for a development installation you can choose to bypass this step.

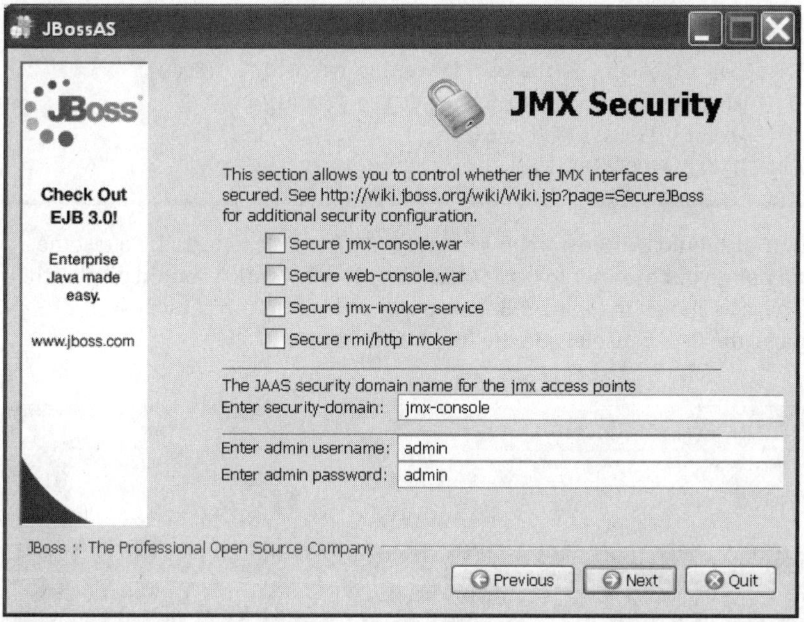

Figure 5-4. *JBoss AS installation JMX security settings*

Once the installation process has completed you can start the application server by changing directories to the bin directory under the JBoss AS installation directory and running the run.bat Windows batch file or the UNIX shell script run.sh. The console output should resemble the following:

```
===============================================================================
.
 JBoss Bootstrap Environment
.
 JBOSS_HOME: C:\java\jboss-4.0.3RC1\bin\\..
.
 JAVA: C:\jdk1.5.0_04\bin\java
.
 JAVA_OPTS:  -Dprogram.name=run.bat -Xms128m -Xmx512m
.
 CLASSPATH: C:\jdk1.5.0_04\lib\tools.jar;C:\java\jboss-4.0.3RC1\bin\\run.jar
.
===============================================================================
.
```

```
23:24:43,375 INFO  [Server] Starting JBoss (MX MicroKernel)...
23:24:43,375 INFO  [Server] Release ID: JBoss [Zion] 4.0.3RC1 (build:
CVSTag=JBoss_4_0_3_RC1 date=200506260220)
23:24:43,375 INFO  [Server] Home Dir: C:\java\jboss-4.0.3RC1
23:24:43,375 INFO  [Server] Home URL: file:/C:/java/jboss-4.0.3RC1/
...
23:25:33,375 INFO  [Http11Protocol] Starting Coyote HTTP/1.1 on http-0.0.0.0-8080
23:25:33,593 INFO  [ChannelSocket] JK: ajp13 listening on /0.0.0.0:8009
23:25:33,609 INFO  [JkMain] Jk running ID=0 time=0/109  config=null
23:25:33,625 INFO  [Server] JBoss (MX MicroKernel) [4.0.3RC1 (build:
CVSTag=JBoss_4_0_3_RC1 date=200506260220)] Started in 50s:235ms
```

The console output should be free from any exceptions after a clean install. To test the installation you can point your browser to http://localhost:8080/ which should display the JBoss AS welcome page as shown in Figure 5-5. This page has links to the Tomcat Web Container status page, the JMX console, and the JBoss Web Console.

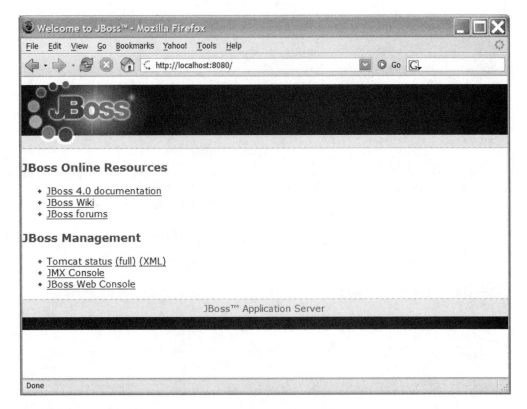

Figure 5-5. *JBoss AS welcome page*

The JMX console and the JBoss Web Console will come in handy when testing deployments and examining the application server Java Naming and Directory Interface (JNDI) tree contents.

The runtime management of the JBoss server is currently performed via the JBoss JMX Management Console shown in Figure 5-6.

Figure 5-6. *JBoss JMX Management Console*

The JBoss services are exposed as MBeans, which you can inspect with the console. The console provides a listing of all JBoss services (JMX agent view). From this list of services you can drill down to an individual view of the service to the MBean view in order to perform an operation on a particular MBean.

For example, to view the contents of the JNDI tree, select the `service=JNDIView` hyperlink under the "jboss" heading, which will take you to the MBean view for the JNDIView service. MBean operations are exposed in the raw in the JBoss console as method signatures that you can click to execute. On this page you'll see a list of MBean operations; select the list() operation. The list() operation will give you a listing of the items in the JNDI tree. Notice that you're able to select the value of the Boolean parameter. If you wonder about the meaning of the parameter, check the Javadoc documentation for the `org.jboss.naming.JNDIView` class and you'll find that the parameter is a verbose flag.

```
public java.lang.String list(boolean verbose)
```

The Javadoc also reveals the purpose of the method: "List deployed application java:comp namespaces, the java:namespace as well as the global InitialContext JNDI namespace."

Tip It comes in handy to bookmark the JBoss Javadoc API because the JMX console doesn't provide MBeans method details.

Service Objects

The last few years have seen the emergence of lightweight containers in combination with agile techniques as the new standard to strive for in Java enterprise development. But what does it mean to be doing "lightweight" Java? I see lightweight Java as the marriage of simplified programming models based on rich object-oriented models using POJOs and POJIs with responsive, intrusive, yet robust and full-featured component containers.

The accepted notion of a lightweight container such as those provided by the Spring framework, PicoContainer and NanoContainer, is for them to have a small memory footprint, fast start-up times, and the ability to hot-deploy components and applications without having to restart the server. Do you have to have a traditional lightweight container to be doing lightweight Java? In my opinion, lightweight Java is more about the programming model and the ability to shorten the code-compile-deploy-test cycle than the memory footprint or start-up times of a server as long as they are within reasonable boundaries. In that case, the main feature of lightweight Java contributing to increased developer productivity is a programming model that doesn't force your business and domain objects to conform to any specific component model, that allows you to use long-accepted best practices like that of programming to interfaces, and that has the ability to provide container services in a transparent way to the components living in the container without crippling their usability or testability outside of the container.

The EJB3 specification is an amalgamation of the lessons learned by the movement to make Java more lightweight and agile by reducing the unnecessary complexities introduced in previous specifications. In combination with the JSR-175 metadata facility and the use of techniques like IoC/DI and AOP, it makes JBoss AS a platform for lightweight and agile development.

In EJB3 development, components are POJOs, and POJOs are components. By using metadata in the form of annotations, any POJO can enjoy the benefits that a traditional managed service object has such as loose coupling, network independence, and the ability to have resource pooling transparently available.

Stateless Session Beans

For most Java EE applications, stateless session beans (SLSBs) have become the standard way to expose services provided by the middle tier. In combination with the Session Façade, Data Transfer Object (DTO), Command Pattern, and Data Access Object (DAO) design/implementation, patterns are one of the ways to define the functionality that our applications provide.

In previous incarnations of the EJB specification we had so many moving parts that getting started with our projects became an exercise in drudgery. Luckily for us, in EJB 3.0 the path of least resistance has been chosen, and all we have to do to create an SLSB is to have a POJO that implements (at least one) POJI describing the services being provided.

You could simply have a business interface `Business.java` and a bean implementation `BusinessBean.java`.

■Note The bean class may or may not implement a business interface although I recommend that you use interfaces to define the contracts between your application tiers and components. If you choose to not implement any business interfaces, a business interface will be dynamically generated using all the public methods. If only certain methods should be exposed in the business interface, all of those methods can be marked with the `@BusinessMethod` annotation.

Once we have this contract in place, all we need to do is annotate the POJO class with the EJB3 annotation `@Stateless`. This will flag this class as an SLSB so that at deployment time the JBoss EJB3 container can provide our simple class with all the enterprise services. But in order to keep our interfaces free from any EJB-specific annotations, we can subclass the business interface in order to provide specific interfaces to serve as remote and local interfaces. To do this we can create two interfaces, named `BusinessRemote.java` and `BusinessLocal.java`, and annotate them with `@javax.ejb.Remote` and `@javax.ejb.Local` respectively.

Following the trend of "convention over configuration," JBoss will by default bind the bean to JNDI by using the fully qualified name of the interfaces as the JNDI name, which makes the code more robust and simple by allowing JNDI lookups to simply use the getName() method of the Class object for a given interface, for example, `BusinessRemote.class.getName();`.

In order for our session bean to be properly handled, it must be first deployed. In JBoss 4, EJB3 non-persistent components are packaged in a familiar JAR archive with the extension .ejb3. There are no precompiling steps at build time; all enhancements are handled at deployment time by the JBoss EJB3 Deployer. Figure 5-7 shows a high-level view of the structure and features of the EJB3 specification.

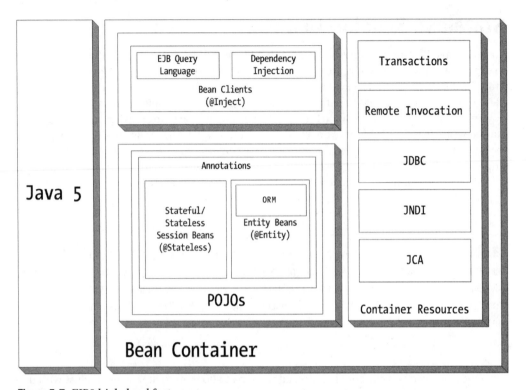

Figure 5-7. *EJB3 high-level features*

You might be wondering where all the different methods that were needed in the implementation of a version 2.X EJB have gone in version 3. Methods such as the callbacks provided for bean life cycle management. In EJB3 most of these methods are replaced with annotations applied to any method in the bean class in order to treat it as a life cycle callback method. In EJB3 the container automatically calls the annotated methods. The available annotations in EJB3 are described in Table 5-1.

Table 5-1. *EJB3 Lifecycle Callback Annotations*

Annotation	Description	Applicable Bean Type
@PostConstruct	Called right after instantiation	Stateful/Stateless Session Beans
@PreDestroy	Called before removal from the bean pool	Stateful/Stateless Session Beans
@PrePassivate	Called before passivation	Stateful/Stateless Session Beans
@PostActivate	Called right after activation when the instance is ready	Stateful Session Beans
@Init	Called right after instantiation but before PostConstruct	Stateful Session Beans
@Remove	Used on a particular method to indicate that the method should be invoked before the bean instance is removed	Stateful Session Beans

A good practice is to separate your life cycle methods in a separate class. To do this you'll need to annotate the bean class with the @CallbackListener tag that specifies the class to be used as a listener to the life cycle calls.

Roads to Persistence

There are several ways to fulfill the persistence needs of a Java EE application, but the two obvious choices when using JBoss are using Hibernate, as shown in Chapter 4, or using EJB3 persistence service. Under the covers, JBoss uses Hibernate to power the EJB3 persistence engine. Hibernate implements the EJB 3.0/JSR-220 persistence via its annotations and EntityManager implementations. Moving from Hibernate to EJB3 is a relatively simple process (if you need your application to use EJB3 persistence). In this chapter we will make use of the persistence-mapped POJOs developed in Chapter 4 since Hibernate, based on its popularity and pervasiveness in the industry, can also be considered a standard. Not to mention that JBoss AS offers the best integration with Hibernate of any application server.

Hibernate in JBoss

The JBoss AS provides for strong Hibernate integration via its HAR Deployer and Hibernate Service. Via the Hibernate Service you can have a Hibernate SessionFactory object bound to JNDI. The HAR Deployer is a specialized JBoss deployer that will scan the contents of a JAR archive with the extension .har and create a SessionFactory with any Hibernate mappings found (.hbm.xml files). HAR stands for Hibernate Archive, and it represents a custom deployment available in JBoss AS.

The HAR should contain the Hibernate mappings, the class files being mapped, and a JBoss service descriptor. Figure 5-8 shows the structure and contents of the HAR.

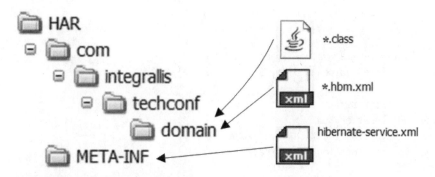

Figure 5-8. *Structure of a JBoss HAR*

Listing 5-1 shows a minimalist hibernate-service.xml file for the TechConf application. As you can ascertain from its contents, the hibernate-xml file allows for parameters almost identical to those in the previously used in hibernate.cfg.xml files except that it is not necessary to list the individual mappings.

Listing 5-1. *HAR Deployment Configuration via Hibernate-service.xml*

```
<mbean code="org.jboss.hibernate.jmx.Hibernate" name="jboss.har:service=Hibernate">
    <attribute name="DatasourceName">java:/jdbc/techconf</attribute>
    <attribute name="SessionFactoryName">java:/hibernate/SessionFactory</attribute>
    <attribute name="Dialect">org.hibernate.dialect.MySQLDialect</attribute>
    <attribute name="CacheProviderClass">
        org.hibernate.cache.HashtableCacheProvider
    </attribute>
    <attribute name="ShowSqlEnabled">true</attribute>
</mbean>
```

In the hibernate-service.xml file you'll need to specify the J2EE data source previously created which is bound to the JNDI name java:/jdbc/techconf and provide the name that will be used to bind the Hibernate SessionFactory object in JNDI.

For the purposes of the TechConf application, create a skeleton directory for the HAR under the directory dd/har at the root of the project directory. This directory will be used to create the HAR with the Ant target shown in Listing 5-2, which expands on the TechConf build-file started in Chapter 3. The property ${app.name} should be set to the value "techconf" via the properties file build.properties.

Listing 5-2. *Ant Buildfile Targets to Package HAR*

```
<!-- ===================================================================== -->
<!-- Initialization                                                        -->
<!-- ===================================================================== -->

<property file="build.properties"/>

<!-- ===== -->
<!-- Files -->
<!-- ===== -->
<property name="har-filename" value="${app.name}.har" />
<property name="har-file" value="${dist}/${har-filename}" />

<!-- Deployment Descriptors -->
<property name="dd" location="dd" />
<property name="dd-dynadto" location="${dd}/dynadto" />
<property name="dd-har" location="${dd}/har" />


<!-- ===================================================================== -->
<!-- Target: package-har                                                   -->
<!-- Package the JBoss Hibernate Archive (HAR)                             -->
<!-- ===================================================================== -->
```

```
<target name="package-har" depends="compile"
        description="Package the JBoss Hibernate Archive (HAR)">
    <target-banner target="package-har"/>
    <jar jarfile="${har-file}">
        <fileset dir="${classes}">
            <include name="**/domain/*.hbm.xml"/>
            <include name="**/domain/*.class"/>
        </fileset>
        <fileset dir="${dd-har}">
            <include name="**/*.xml"/>
        </fileset>
    </jar>
</target>

<target name="package-har-clean">
    <delete file="${har-file}"/>
</target>
```

With the Ant buildfile modified you can now execute the package-har to get the deployable archive techconf.har. The HAR can be deployed stand-alone or as part of a EAR deployment as shown later in the chapter.

During deployment you will see messages similar to the ones shown next. You should see all the mappings being processed.

```
22:35:50,234 INFO  [Environment] Hibernate 3.1alpha1
...
22:35:50,437 INFO  [Configuration] Searching for mapping documents in jar:
techconf.har
22:35:50,437 INFO  [Configuration] Found mapping document in jar: com/integrallis/
techconf/domain/Abstract.hbm.xml
22:35:50,609 INFO  [HbmBinder] Mapping class: com.integrallis.techconf.domain.
Abstract -> abstract
22:35:50,828 INFO  [Configuration] Found mapping document in jar: com/integrallis/
techconf/domain/AbstractStatus.hbm.xml
22:35:50,843 INFO  [HbmBinder] Mapping class: com.integrallis.techconf.domain.
AbstractStatus -> abstractstatus
22:35:50,859 INFO  [Configuration] Found mapping document in jar: com/integrallis/
techconf/domain/Address.hbm.xml
22:35:50,875 INFO  [HbmBinder] Mapping class: com.integrallis.techconf.domain.
Address -> address
22:35:50,906 INFO  [Configuration] Found mapping document in jar: com/integrallis/
techconf/domain/Answer.hbm.xml
22:35:50,921 INFO  [HbmBinder] Mapping class: com.integrallis.techconf.domain.
Answer -> answer
...
```

```
22:35:51,250 INFO   [Configuration] processing association property references
22:35:51,250 INFO   [Configuration] processing foreign key constraints
...
22:35:52,187 INFO   [DatasourceConnectionProvider] Using datasource: java:/jdbc/
techconf
22:35:52,390 INFO   [SettingsFactory] RDBMS: MySQL, version: 4.1.7-nt
..
22:35:52,437 INFO   [Dialect] Using dialect: org.hibernate.dialect.MySQLDialect
22:35:52,453 INFO   [TransactionFactoryFactory] Transaction strategy:
org.hibernate.transaction.JTATransactionFactory
...
22:35:53,750 INFO   [Hibernate] SessionFactory successfully built and bound into JN-
DI [java:/hibernate/SessionFactory]
```

To access the SessionFactory from within your SLSB code, you no longer have multiple lines of cumbersome JNDI lookup code since EJB3 supports an annotation-based dependency-injection facility. EJB3 dependency-injection annotations work with EJB components (POJOs annotated as EJBs). EJB3 dependency injection can inject EJBs into other EJBs with the @EJB annotation or any JNDI-bound resource using the @Resource annotation. For example, to inject the Hibernate SessionFactory object bound to java:/hibernate/SessionFactory, we could use code like that shown in Listing 5-3 from within an EJB3 SLSB.

Listing 5-3. *EJB3 Dependency Injection of a JNDI-bound Hibernate SessionFactory*

```java
package com.integrallis.techconf.ejb;

import javax.annotation.Resource;
import javax.ejb.Stateless;

import org.hibernate.SessionFactory;

@Stateless
public class ConferenceServiceBean implements
    ConferenceServiceLocal, ConferenceServiceRemote {

    // hibernate session factory (when not using DAOs)
    @Resource(name = "java:/hibernate/SessionFactory")
    protected SessionFactory sessionFactory;

...
```

By simply declaring a property of type SessionFactory and annotating it with the `@Resource` annotation, which takes as a parameter the JNDI name of the resource being looked up, you can now use the `SessionFactory` instance to construct Session objects in your code.

Implementing the DAO Pattern with Hibernate

Enterprise Java developers have been using the DAO pattern for quite some time now in order to abstract and encapsulate all access to one or more sources of data for an application. In an application dealing with multiple sources of data, the DAO pattern can make all the different sources seem the same to the application code by providing a unified and consistent interface for all data-related operations. A well-designed DAO layer should hide all of the technology-specific details of the underlying data-access mechanism whether it is a full-fledged ORM tool like Hibernate, simple JDBC, or something more esoteric like an object database or a prevalence system like Prevayler (`www.prevayler.org`).

The simple EJB3-based DAO implementation for the TechConf application is based on a very few simple principles:

- **Code to Interfaces:** DAOs are defined as interfaces. This provides the flexibility to plug in different implementations at runtime and simplifies testing by allowing the use of mock testing objects in the absence of a database.

- **EJB3 Component Model:** In EJB3, annotated components are POJOs, and being a component in an EJB3 environment enables your POJO to use the available container services. In particular, the ability to wire the application declaratively via annotations will come in handy when implementing the EJB3 TechConf DAOs.

- **Small Runtime Exception Hierarchy:** Most data-access exceptions are unrecoverable, and most data-access tools throw too many exceptions. Since we are striving for simplicity on the design of the DAO layer, a simple and meaningful exception hierarchy, rooted at `RuntimeException`, will be used.

- **Small Number of DAOs:** Having a single DAO per persistent entity can produce a parallel hierarchy that can quickly get out of control. I prefer to have a more cohesive DAO that covers a particular area of functionality for a related set of persistent entities.

- **Strongly Typed Methods:** I believe that (especially in large teams) using strongly typed methods in your DAOs can make the code more readable and minimize early usage errors.

Figure 5-9 shows the different DAO interfaces used in the TechConf application. As you can see, the TechConf application requires a small number of DAOs as compared to the number of persistent entities.

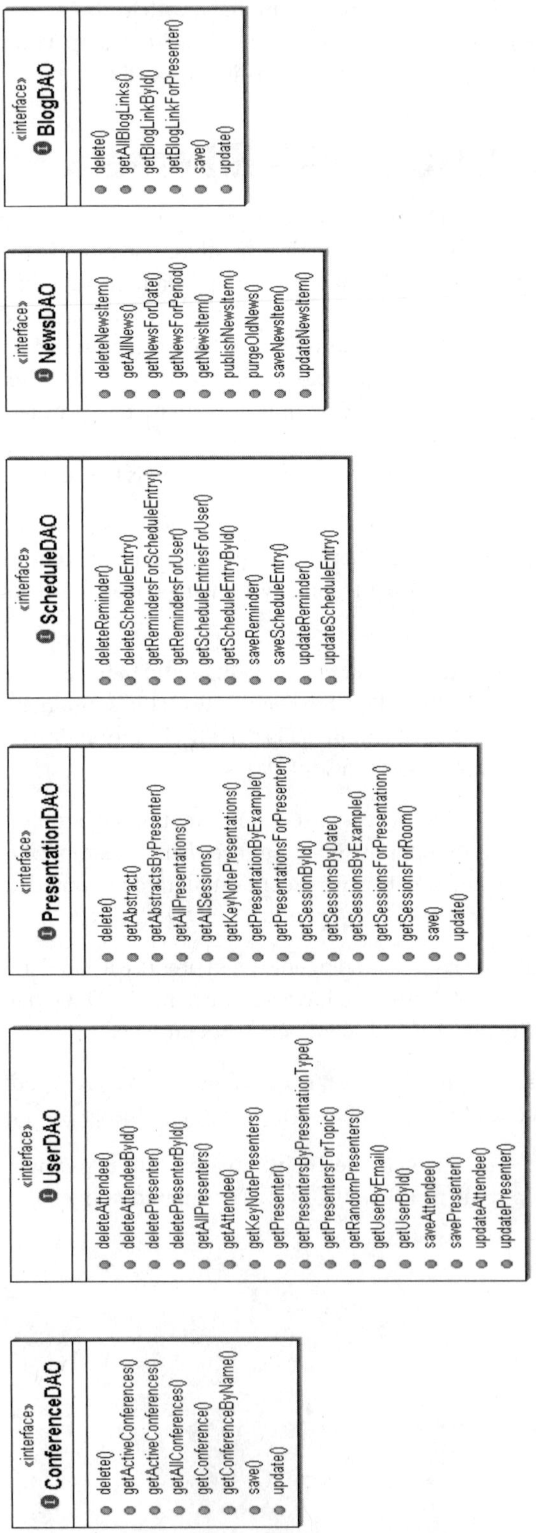

«interface»
ConferenceDAO
- delete()
- getActiveConferences()
- getActiveConferences()
- getAllConferences()
- getConference()
- getConferenceByName()
- save()
- update()

«interface»
UserDAO
- deleteAttendee()
- deleteAttendeeById()
- deletePresenter()
- deletePresenterById()
- getAllPresenters()
- getAttendee()
- getKeyNotePresenters()
- getPresenter()
- getPresentersByPresentationType()
- getPresentersForTopic()
- getRandomPresenters()
- getUserByEmail()
- getUserById()
- saveAttendee()
- savePresenter()
- updateAttendee()
- updatePresenter()

«interface»
PresentationDAO
- delete()
- getAbstract()
- getAbstractsByPresenter()
- getAllPresentations()
- getAllSessions()
- getKeyNotePresentations()
- getPresentationByExample()
- getPresentationsForPresenter()
- getSessionById()
- getSessionsByDate()
- getSessionsByExample()
- getSessionsForPresentation()
- getSessionsForRoom()
- save()
- update()

«interface»
ScheduleDAO
- deleteReminder()
- deleteScheduleEntry()
- getRemindersForScheduleEntry()
- getRemindersForUser()
- getScheduleEntriesForUser()
- getScheduleEntryById()
- saveReminder()
- saveScheduleEntry()
- updateReminder()
- updateScheduleEntry()

«interface»
NewsDAO
- deleteNewsItem()
- getAllNews()
- getNewsForDate()
- getNewsForPeriod()
- getNewsItem()
- publishNewsItem()
- purgeOldNews()
- saveNewsItem()
- updateNewsItem()

«interface»
BlogDAO
- delete()
- getAllBlogLinks()
- getBlogLinkById()
- getBlogLinkForPresenter()
- save()
- update()

Figure 5-9. *DAO interfaces for the TechConf application*

Let's start by looking at the ConferenceDAO interfaces for the TechConf application. As you can see in Listing 5-4, the interface provides some CRUD methods as well as some specific finder methods for Conference and Room objects.

Listing 5-4. *ConferenceDAO Interface*

```
package com.integrallis.techconf.dao;

import java.util.Date;
import java.util.List;

import com.integrallis.techconf.domain.Conference;
import com.integrallis.techconf.domain.Room;

public interface ConferenceDAO {
    Conference getConference(int conferenceId);
    Conference getConferenceByName(String name);
    List<Conference> getActiveConferences(Date beginDate, Date endDate);
    List<Conference> getActiveConferences(Date date);
    List<Conference> getAllConferences();
    List<Room> getRooms(int venueId);

    void save(Conference conference);
    void update(Conference conference);
    void delete(Conference conference);
    void delete(int conferenceId);
}
```

Listing 5-5 shows the BaseAbstractDAO class, which will serve as the base class for all of the Hibernate-specific DAO SLSBs. This class provides simplified methods against the Hibernate Session object and hides certain details of more complex Hibernate APIs like the Criteria API. Since the Hibernate DAOs depend on a Hibernate SessionFactory, we inject the Hibernate SessionFactory object via the @Resource annotation (javax.annotation.Resource). It also provides the ability to retrieve the Session object via the getCurrentSession() when working in a JTA-enabled environment like the JBoss AS or via the openSession() method when working in a non-JTA environment.

Methods wrapping the usage of the Criteria API are provided to findAll(), findFiltered(), findUnique(), and findUniqueFiltered(). These methods enable developers less experienced with Hibernate to quickly create DAO implementations. Since the TechConf application is using a very stateless architecture, the DAO layer doesn't have to deal with lazy transaction issues or detached domain objects, which would make the implementation slightly more complex.

Also notice that we use the getCurrentSession() method, which should avoid using a new Hibernate Session per operation. That can lead to poor performance. The SESSION_RETRIEVAL_STRATEGY_CREATE_NEW strategy is used mostly in the application's unit tests.

Listing 5-5. *BaseAbstractDAO, a Hibernate-specific Base DAO Implementation*

```
package com.integrallis.techconf.ejb.dao.hibernate;

import java.io.Serializable;
import java.util.List;
import javax.annotation.Resource;
import org.hibernate.Criteria;
import org.hibernate.Query;
import org.hibernate.Session;
import org.hibernate.SessionFactory;
import org.hibernate.criterion.Expression;
import org.hibernate.criterion.Order;

/**
 * Wraps some basic Hibernate methods to simplify the concrete
 * DAO implementations
 */
public abstract class BaseAbstractDAO {
    public static final int SESSION_RETRIEVAL_STRATEGY_USE_CURRENT = 0;
    public static final int SESSION_RETRIEVAL_STRATEGY_CREATE_NEW = 1;

    @Resource(name = "java:/hibernate/SessionFactory")
    protected SessionFactory sessionFactory;

    public BaseAbstractDAO() {}

    public BaseAbstractDAO(int sessionRetrievalStrategy) {
        this.sessionRetrievalStrategy = sessionRetrievalStrategy;
    }

    public void setSessionRetrievalStrategy(int sessionRetrievalStrategy) {
        this.sessionRetrievalStrategy = sessionRetrievalStrategy;
    }

    protected void setSessionFactory(SessionFactory sessionFactory) {
        this.sessionFactory = sessionFactory;
    }

    protected Session getSession() {
        return sessionFactory.getCurrentSession();
    }

    protected Criteria createCriteria(Class clazz) {
        return getSession().createCriteria(clazz);
    }
```

```
protected Query createQuery(String query) {
    return getSession().createQuery(query);
}

protected Object getEntityById(Class clazz, Serializable id) {
    return getSession().get(clazz, id);
}

protected void saveEntity(Object entity) {
    getSession().persist(entity);
}

protected void saveOrUpdateEntity(Object entity) {
    getSession().saveOrUpdate(entity);
}

protected void updateEntity(Object entity) {
    getSession().update(entity);
}

protected void deleteEntity(Object entity) {
    getSession().delete(entity);
}

protected void deleteEntityById(Class clazz, Serializable id) {
    Object entity = getEntityById(clazz, id);
    if (entity != null) {
        deleteEntity(entity);
    }
}

protected List findAll(Class clazz) {
    return getSession.createCriteria(clazz).list();
}

protected List findAll(Class clazz, String orderBy) {
    return getSession()
        .createCriteria(clazz)
        .addOrder(Order.asc(orderBy))
        .list();
}
```

```
    protected List findFiltered(Class clazz, String property, Object filter) {
        return getSession()
            .createCriteria(clazz)
            .add(Expression.eq(property, filter))
            .list();
    }

    protected List findFiltered(Class clazz, String property,
                                Object filter, String orderBy) {
        return getSession()
            .createCriteria(clazz)
            .add(Expression.eq(property, filter))
            .addOrder(Order.asc(orderBy))
            .list();
    }

    protected Object findUniqueFiltered(Class clazz, String property,
                                        Object filter) {
        return getSession()
            .createCriteria(clazz)
            .add(Expression.eq(property, filter))
            .uniqueResult();
    }

    protected Object findUniqueFiltered(Class clazz, String property,
                                        Object filter, String orderBy) {
        return getSession()
            .createCriteria(clazz)
            .add(Expression.eq(property, filter))
            .addOrder(Order.asc(orderBy))
            .uniqueResult();
    }
}
```

Listing 5-6 shows the class ConferenceDAOImpl, which is a Hibernate-specific EJB3 SLSB implementation of the ConferenceDAO interface. By making the DAO implementation SLSBs, we gain the ability to inject the SessionFactory into the DAO implementations using annotations (as well as the ability to inject the DAO implementations into the service implementations), and also we get pooling, which in most application servers can be controlled declaratively in a per-deployment fashion to (most likely) match the pooling characteristics of the SLSBs that will be using the DAO beans.

Listing 5-6. *ConferenceDAOImpl, a Hibernate-specific Concrete DAO Implementation*

```java
package com.integrallis.techconf.dao.hibernate;

import java.util.Date;
import java.util.List;

import javax.ejb.Stateless;

import org.hibernate.Criteria;
import org.hibernate.criterion.Restrictions;

import com.integrallis.techconf.dao.ConferenceDAO;
import com.integrallis.techconf.domain.Conference;
import com.integrallis.techconf.domain.Room;

@Stateless
public class ConferenceDAOImpl extends BaseAbstractDAO implements ConferenceDAO {

    public ConferenceDAOImpl(SessionFactory sessionFactory) {
        super(sessionFactory);
    }

    public Conference getConference(int conferenceId) {
        return (Conference) getEntityById(Conference.class, conferenceId);
    }

    public Conference getConferenceByName(String name) {
        return (Conference) findUniqueFiltered(Conference.class,
                                        Conference.PROP_NAME, name);
    }

    @SuppressWarnings("unchecked")
    public List<Conference> getActiveConferences(Date beginDate, Date endDate) {
        Criteria criteria = createCriteria(Conference.class)
            .add( Restrictions.between(Conference.PROP_START_DATE,
                                    beginDate, endDate))
            .add( Restrictions.between(Conference.PROP_END_DATE,
                                    beginDate, endDate));
        return criteria.list();
    }
```

```
@SuppressWarnings("unchecked")
public List<Conference> getActiveConferences(Date date) {
    Criteria criteria = createCriteria(Conference.class)
        .add( Restrictions.le(Conference.PROP_START_DATE, date))
        .add( Restrictions.ge(Conference.PROP_END_DATE, date));
    return criteria.list();
}

public void save(Conference conference) {
    saveEntity(conference);
}

public void update(Conference conference) {
    updateEntity(conference);
}

public void delete(Conference conference) {
    deleteEntity(conference);
}

public void delete(int conferenceId) {
    deleteEntityById(Conference.class, conferenceId);
}

@SuppressWarnings("unchecked")
public List<Conference> getAllConferences() {
    return findAll(Conference.class);
}

@SuppressWarnings("unchecked")
public List<Room> getRooms(int venueId) {
    return findFiltered(Room.class, "Venue.Id", venueId);
}
}
```

Notice that we are not wrapping the DAO methods to catch any of the Hibernate-specific runtime exceptions (rooted at org.hibernate.HibernateException). In the advanced topics chapter, you'll learn how to use aspect-oriented techniques to cleanly transform from the highly detailed Hibernate exception hierarchy to the TechConf data-access exception hierarchy. Figure 5-10 shows the simple exception hierarchy for the TechConf application.

Inspired by the Spring framework, I'm using unchecked exceptions since most data-access exceptions are unrecoverable and with a clean exception hierarchy is necessary only to catch the specific exception of interest while disregarding the base exception class (which you cannot do with a checked exception hierarchy). An unchecked exception hierarchy also prevents the dreaded anti-pattern of catching-logging-rethrowing or the even worse pattern of caching-swallowing exceptions.

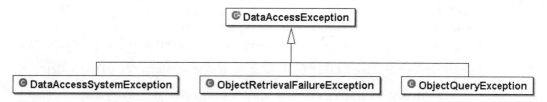

Figure 5-10. *TechConf DAO exception hierarchy*

Implementing DTO Pattern with DynaDTO

Another pattern that we typically find in an enterprise Java application is the Data Transfer Object pattern (DTO), which is also known as the value object pattern. DTOs are used when clients of the middle tier need to exchange data (traditionally with an EJB-based service layer).

Background

DTOs are typically lightweight objects that are used for intertier communications. Generally, in object-oriented, distributed, and middleware-driven Web applications there are three well-known tiers connected by what I define as two transformation layers. The three tiers are usually known as the *integration* tier (and/or the data tier), the *business* tier (where the business/domain objects reside) and the *presentation* tier (for a Web application this is the Web tier). Between these three tiers we typically encounter two transformation layers:

- **O/R Transformation Layer:** Between a relational database and the middleware-hosted domain objects (collectively referred to as the domain model)

- **DTO Transformation Layer:** Between the domain model and the user model. We define the user model as the collection of objects that the Web tier manipulates to interact with the middle tier.

The need for the DTO pattern became apparent to architects and developers based on the problems that arise for the multitier, distributed characteristics of many enterprise Java applications, including the following:

- **Coarse-Grained Entities:** Coarse-grained technologies like Entity EJBs are not meant to be manipulated directly by the Web tier, since every access can potentially become a remote call. Depending on temporal topology of an application (like collocation or vendor-specific optimizations), it can lead to portability problems and a brittle architecture.

- **Fine-Grained Entities:** A well-designed domain model reflects more about the problem domain than is normally exposed to a client. A domain model should represent a subset of the knowledge about the problem/solution domain. Martin Fowler coined the term Anemic Domain Model to refer to the anti-pattern where a domain model lacks behavior. We see a lot "tainted" domain models, tainted either by the data tier or by the presentation tier. Separation of concerns is usually disregarded in order to accelerate development. In other words, the user interface should deal with objects that are designed for the user interface to handle. You should not compromise the integrity of a domain model to satisfy the needs of the user interface.

- **Bulk-transfers:** Distribution brings a plethora of problems, including the need to minimize network traffic by using bulk transfers of data. Other typical issues affected by the granularity of the data exchanged between tiers include pagination schemes and caching.

These problems lead us to the forces behind the implementation of the DTO pattern:

- Potential remote calls when accessing a field of a remote object using coarse-grained technologies like entity EJBs.

- Web applications are typically read-mostly and save-update-occasionally.

- Viewing requirements per page are typically composed of multiple attributes from multiple domain objects. Transferring all domain objects needed to satisfy these requirements can result in a large object graph being serialized across tiers.

- Hand-coded DTO means that code needs to be developed to instantiate a DTO at runtime and populate its values from one or more sources.

Developers typically end up creating objects that are lightweight counterparts to the domain entities. They create transfer objects to encapsulate business data. For most use cases these translate to one DTO per use case that encapsulates the needs of the user interface. The traditional implementations of the DTO pattern still have some undesirable side effects, including:

- **Parallel-Object Hierarchy:** As pointed out by Gavin King of the Hibernate project, a parallel class hierarchy to maintain is "smelly." We see this as a sign that the domain has been flattened by the influence of either the Web tier requirements or the underlying data model. Although there will be obvious similarities between the domain objects and the DTOs, we believe that a well-designed domain model will be fairly dissimilar to the DTO model in both structure and content. Remember, the domain model should be reusable between different applications dealing with the same problem domain.

- **Code Maintenance:** We find that maintaining these transformation and transport objects can add quite a bit of overhead to a project. We find this problem similar to the problem of maintaining a custom object-relational mapping layer.

DynaDTO

For the implementation of the TechConf DTO layer I'm using DynaDTO (`https://dynadto.dev.java.net/`), which is a solution to the screen-domain mapping problem similar to what Hibernate is to the object-relational mapping problem. DynaDTO is a project that provides a library that enables you to dynamically generate DTOs that implement a given Java interface. Created to ease the burden of hand-coding DTOs, DynaDTO eases the enforcement of separation of concerns between your application domain model and the user interface, reduces the amount of code required to implement the pattern, and provides a consistent way to declaratively define simple and complex mappings between your domain model and your user interface model (your DTOs).

DynaDTO is configured via an XML file that configures the DTO builder factory for a given DTO. A DTO builder factory serves DTO builders which can construct a given type of DTO from one or more domain objects (any JavaBean or POJO). A DynaDTO configuration file uses simple property mappings (DTOs can also be configured inline using Java), nested properties, and expressions using Jakarta Commons Java Expression Language (JEXL) found at `http://jakarta.apache.org/commons/jexl/`.

To implement the TechConf application DTO layer, we define the DTOs using Java interfaces that represent the contract between the middle tier service layer and the Web tier. Let's work on a example using the Conference domain POJO as shown in Listing 5-7.

Listing 5-7. *Conference Domain POJO*

```java
package com.integrallis.techconf.domain;
...
import org.apache.commons.lang.builder.ToStringBuilder;

public class Conference implements Serializable {
    ...

    // primary key
    private Integer id;

    // fields
    private Date abstractSubmissionStartDate;
    private String name;
    private String description;
    private Date abstractSubmissionEndDate;
    private Date endDate;
    private Date startDate;

    // many to one
    private Venue venue;

    // collections
    private Set<Track> tracks;

    // constructors
    public Conference () {}

    ... getters and setters

    public Venue getVenue () {
        return venue;
    }

    public void setVenue (Venue venue) {
        this.venue = venue;
    }
```

```
    public Set getTracks () {
        return tracks;
    }

    public void setTracks (Set<Track> tracks) {
        this.tracks = tracks;
    }

    public void addTrack(Track track) {
        if (null == this.tracks) this.tracks = new HashSet<Track>();
        track.setConference(this);
        tracks.add(track);
    }
    ...
}
```

Listing 5-8 shows the DTO interface ConferenceSummary, which represents the information required by the user interface about a Conference domain object.

Listing 5-8. *ConferenceSummary DTO Interface*

```
package com.integrallis.techconf.dto;

import java.util.Date;
import java.util.List;
import org.dynadto.DTO;

public interface ConferenceSummary extends DTO {
    int getConferenceId();
    List<TrackSummary> getTracks();
    List<NewsItem> getNews();
    List<PresenterSummary> getFeaturedSpeakers();
    String getConferenceTitle();
    String getConferenceSubtitle();
    Date getStartDate();
    Date getEndDate();
    Date getAbstractSubmissionEndDate();
    Date getAbstractSubmissionStartDate();
    String getVenueName();
    String getVenueAddressLine1();
    String getVenueAddressLine2();
    String getVenuePhone();
}
```

As you can see, the ConferenceSummary DTO interface is a read-only interface providing only getters and no setters. In a typical Web application you'll find that most of your DTOs will follow this pattern with a few read-write DTOs typically associated with data submitted via HTTP POST forms.

Listing 5-9 shows the DynaDTO configuration file ConferenceSummary.dto.xml, which is needed to dynamically create an instance of an object implementing the ConferenceSummary interface given an instance of a Conference domain object.

Listing 5-9. *ConferenceSummary DTO Configuration File*

```xml
<?xml version="1.0" encoding="UTF-8"?>
<dtos>
    <!-- ********************************************************** -->
    <!-- ConferenceSummary                                         -->
    <!-- ********************************************************** -->
    <dto target="com.integrallis.techconf.dto.ConferenceSummary" useProxy="yes">
        <sources>
            <!-- ********************************************************** -->
            <!-- Conference                                                -->
            <!-- ********************************************************** -->
            <source type="com.integrallis.techconf.domain.Conference">
                <!-- aliases, used by the expressions -->
                <alias source="venue" name="venue" />
                <!-- mappings -->
                <mapping from="id" to="conferenceId" />
                <mapping from="name" to="conferenceTitle" />
                <mapping from="description" to="conferenceSubtitle" />
                <mapping property="startDate" />
                <mapping property="endDate" />
                <mapping property="abstractSubmissionStartDate" />
                <mapping property="abstractSubmissionEndDate" />
                <mapping from="venue.name" to="venueName" />
                <mapping from="venue.phone" to="venuePhone" />
                <mapping from="venue.address.streetAddress"
                        to="venueAddressLine1" />
                <mapping-collection
                    action="list"
                    collection-property="tracks"
                    target="tracks"
                    target-type="com.integrallis.techconf.dto.TrackSummary"
                />
            </source>
        </sources>
        <!-- ********************************************************** -->
        <!-- Expressions                                               -->
        <!-- ********************************************************** -->
        <expressions>
            <expression target="VenueAddressLine2"
                    value="venue.getAddress().getCity() + ',' +
                        util.space() + venue.getAddress().getState() +
                        util.space() + venue.getAddress().getZipCode()" />
```

```
            </expressions>
            <!-- ************************************************************ -->
            <!-- Comparator                                                 -->
            <!-- ************************************************************ -->
            <comparator useSuper="false" useReflection="false">
                <compare property="conferenceId" />
            </comparator>
        </dto>
</dtos>
```

Notice that the .dto.xml root element is <dtos>, which can contain one or more <dto>. The <dto> element defines the recipe of how one or more domain objects can be used to populate a POJO or a dynamic proxy instance of a POJI (as is the case with ConferenceSummary DTO). Although you can have more than one <dto> element, I recommend that, except for small applications with very few DTOs, you stick with one <dto> element per file and name your DTO configuration files after the interface or class that they map. The useProxy attribute denotes that DynaDTO should create a dynamic proxy instance of the DTO interface.

Let's explore some of the details of the mapping. The <mapping> element provides several ways to take information from one object to another. First notice that when mapping two properties with an identical name, you can simply use the property attribute as shown in the mapping of the startDate property (<mapping property="startDate" />). For different named properties you can use the from and to attributes as shown in the mapping from Conference. name to ConferenceSummary.conferenceTitle (<mapping from="name" to="conferenceTitle" />). For nested objects you can use dot notation to access a property value as shown in the mapping of the venueAddressLine1 (<mapping from="venue.address.streetAddress" to="venueAddressLine1" />). For more complex mappings, DynaDTO provides the ability to use expressions using JEXL. Expressions are declared inside of the <expressions> element of the <dto> element. The <expressions> element can contain one or more <expression> elements, which take a target and value attributes. For example, in the mapping of the venueAddressLine2 property, the target is VenueAddressLine2, and the values is venue.getAddress().getCity() + ',' + util.space() + venue.getAddress().getState() + util.space() + venue.getAddress(). getZipCode(). DynaDTO provides an object named util, which is available inside of your expressions, to do simple things like adding spaces via util.space(int), where the integer parameter denotes the number of spaces. DynaDTO has other utilities. There is also an object named self, which provides you with access to the DTO being built. DynaDTO will handle nested DTOs by attempting to find a configuration for the nested DTO that matches the source object.

The last feature worth mentioning is DynaDTO's ability to manipulate collections via the <mapping-collection> element. For example, in the ConferenceSummary mapping there is a collection mapping that reads the property tracks of the Conference instance and for each element in it creates a DTO of type TrackSummary. The resulting TrackSummary collection is stored in the tracks property of the TrackSummary instance as shown in Listing 5-10.

Listing 5-10. *Mapping a Collection of Objects in DynaDTO*

```
<mapping-collection
    action="list"
    collection-property="tracks"
    target="tracks"
    target-type="com.integrallis.techconf.dto.TrackSummary"
/>
```

The TrackSummary.dto.xml mapping for the nested TrackSummary objects is shown in Listing 5-11.

Listing 5-11. *TrackSummary DTO Configuration File*

```
<?xml version="1.0" encoding="ISO-8859-1" ?>
<dtos>
    <!-- ********************************************************** -->
    <!-- TrackSummary                                             -->
    <!-- ********************************************************** -->
    <dto target="com.integrallis.techconf.dto.TrackSummary" useProxy="yes">
        <sources>
            <!-- ********************************************************** -->
            <!-- Track                                                   -->
            <!-- ********************************************************** -->
            <source type="com.integrallis.techconf.domain.Track">
                <mapping property="id" />
                <mapping property="title" />
                <mapping property="subtitle" />
                <mapping property="description" />
            </source>
        </sources>
        <!-- ********************************************************** -->
        <!-- Comparator                                              -->
        <!-- ********************************************************** -->
        <comparator useSuper="false" useReflection="false">
            <compare property="id" />
        </comparator>
    </dto>
</dtos>
```

For cases when the source and target objects are identical, DynaDTO provides the automap attribute of the <dto> element. This will tell DynaDTO that the source and the target objects have identical structure, and it should attempt to copy each property in the source object to an equally named property in the target object. Listing 5-12 shows the simplest DynaDTO configuration file (for the AddressInfo DTO).

Listing 5-12. *The Simplest DTO Configuration File*

```
<?xml version="1.0" encoding="ISO-8859-1" ?>
<dtos>
    <!-- ******************************************************** -->
    <!-- AddressInfo                                             -->
    <!-- ******************************************************** -->
    <dto target="com.integrallis.techconf.dto.AddressInfo" useProxy="yes">
        <sources>
            <!-- ********************************************************* -->
            <!-- Address                                                  -->
            <!-- ********************************************************* -->
            <source type="com.integrallis.techconf.domain.Address" automap="true" />
        </sources>
        <!-- ********************************************************* -->
        <!-- Comparator                                               -->
        <!-- ********************************************************* -->
        <comparator useSuper="false" useReflection="false">
            <compare property="id" />
        </comparator>
    </dto>
</dtos>
```

DynaDTO also provides other facilities to the dynamically generated DTOs, like built-in implementations of `toString()`, a facility to check which properties have changed since the DTO was created, as well as a facility to create a comparator as shown in the previous configurations.

DynaDTO in a JSE Environment

Once you have the DTO interfaces and the DynaDTO configurations in place, all you need to do to use them in a JSE environment is to use the DynaDTO ConfigurationLoader to load the required mappings. When working in a JSE environment, DynaDTO caches the DTO mappings statically and then makes DTO builders available via the `BuilderFactory` class. Using a particular builder returned from the factory, you can simply invoke the build method passing an instance of the domain object in order to get a fully populated DTO as shown in Listing 5-13.

Listing 5-13. *Using DynaDTO in a JSE Environment*

```
ConfigurationLoader.loadMapping(new File("ConferenceSummary.dto.xml"));
ConfigurationLoader.loadMapping(new File("TrackSummary.dto.xml"));

Conference conference = new Conference();
// ... set object values
Builder builder = BuilderFactory.getInstance().getBuilder(ConferenceSummary.class);
ConferenceSummary conferenceSummary =
    (ConferenceSummary) builder.build(conference);
```

DynaDTO in JBoss

The DynaDTO project provides for JBoss integration via its DDTO deployer and DynaDTO Service. Via the DynaDTO Service you can have a DynaDTO BuilderFactory object bound to JNDI. The DDTO deployer is a specialized JBoss deployer that will scan a JAR archive with the extension .ddto and create a BuilderFactory with any DynaDTO mappings found (.dto.xml files).

The HAR should contain the Hibernate mappings, the class files being mapped, and a JBoss service descriptor. Figure 5-11 shows the structure and contents of the DDTO archive.

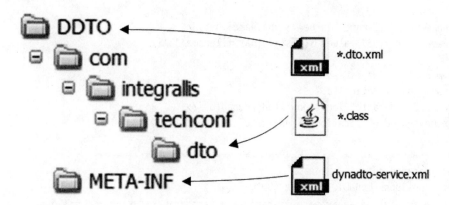

Figure 5-11. *Structure of a JBoss DynaDTO DDTO archive*

Listing 5-14 shows a typical dynadto-service.xml file for the TechConf application.

Listing 5-14. *DDTO Deployment Configuration via Dynadto-service.xml*

```
<mbean code="org.dynadto.jboss.deployment.DynaDTOService"
      name="org.dynadto:service=DynaDTOService">
   <attribute name="BuilderFactoryName">java:dynadto/BuilderFactory</attribute>
   <attribute name="TestMappings">false</attribute>
</mbean>
```

In dynadto-service.xml, you'll need to specify the JNDI name used to bind the DynaDTO BuilderFactory object. For the purposes of the TechConf application I created a skeleton directory for the DDTO under the directory dd/ddto at the root of the project directory. This directory will be used to create the DDTO archive with the Ant target shown in Listing 5-15, which expands on the TechConf buildfile started in Chapter 3.

Listing 5-15. *Ant Buildfile Targets to Package DDTO Archive*

```
<!-- ================================================================= -->
<!-- Initialization                                                    -->
<!-- ================================================================= -->

<property file="build.properties"/>


<!-- ===== -->
<!-- Files -->
<!-- ===== -->
<property name="har-filename" value="${app.name}.har" />
<property name="har-file" value="${dist}/${har-filename}" />

<!-- Deployment Descriptors -->
<property name="dd" location="dd" />
<property name="dd-dynadto" location="${dd}/dynadto" />
<property name="dd-ddto" location="${dd}/ddto" />


<!-- ================================================================= -->
<!-- Target: package-ddtp                                              -->
<!-- Package the JBoss DynaDTO Archive (DDTO)                          -->
<!-- ================================================================= -->

<target name="package-ddto" depends="compile"
        description="Package the JBoss DynaDTO Archive (DDTO)">
    <target-banner target="package-ddto"/>
    <jar jarfile="${ddto-file}">
        <fileset dir="${classes}">
            <include name="**/dto/*.class"/>
        </fileset>
        <fileset dir="${dd-ddto}">
            <include name="**/*.xml"/>
        </fileset>
        <!-- add the mappings -->
        <fileset dir="${dd-dynadto}">
            <include name="**/*.dto.xml"/>
        </fileset>
    </jar>
</target>

<target name="package-ddto-clean">
    <delete file="${ddto-file}"/>
</target>
```

With the Ant buildfile modified, you can now execute the package-ddto to get the deployable archive techconf.ddto. The DDTO archive can be deployed stand-alone or as part of an EAR deployment. During deployment you will see messages similar to the ones shown next. You should see all the mappings being processed.

```
00:23:12,859 INFO  [DynaDTOService] Creating DynaDTO Service
00:23:12,859 INFO  [DynaDTODeployer] Deploying .ddto; create; org.jboss.
deployment.DeploymentInfo@8ff608c3 { url=file:/C:/java/jboss-4.0.3RC1/server/
default/tmp/deploy/tmp33273techconf.ear-contents/techconf.ddto }
00:23:18,671 INFO [DynaDTOService] Starting DynaDTO Service org.dynadto.jboss.
deployment.DynaDTOService@1376afa
00:23:18,671 INFO [DynaDTOService] Building BuilderFactory;
org.dynadto.jboss.deployment.DynaDTOService@1376afa
00:23:18,687 INFO [Configuration] Searching for mapping documents in jar:
techconf.ddto
00:23:18,687 INFO [Configuration] Found mapping documents in jar:
AddressInfo.dto.xml
00:23:18,812 INFO [Configuration] Found mapping documents in jar: AnswerInfo.dto.xml
00:23:18,828 INFO [Configuration] Found mapping documents in jar:
AttendeeInfo.dto.xml
00:23:18,828 INFO [Configuration] Found mapping documents in jar: BlogEntry.dto.xml
00:23:18,843 INFO [Configuration] Found mapping documents in jar:
ConferenceSummary.dto.xml
...
00:23:18,921 INFO  [Configuration] Found mapping documents in jar:
TrackSummary.dto.xml
00:23:18,921 INFO  [Configuration] Found mapping documents in jar:
UserSummary.dto.xml
00:23:18,921 INFO  [DynaDTOService] Bound Dynadto Builder Factory to java:dynadto/
BuilderFactory
00:23:18,921 INFO  [DynaDTOService] BuilderFactory successfully built and bound
into JNDI [java:dynadto/BuilderFactory]
```

To access the BuilderFactory you will again use the EJB3 annotation-based dependency injection facility via the @Resource annotation. For example, to inject the DynaDTO BuilderFactory object bound to java:/dynadto/BuilderFactory, we could use code like that shown in Listing 5-16 from within an EJB3 SLSB.

Listing 5-16. *EJB3 Dependency Injection of a JNDI-bound DynaDTO BuilderFactory*

```
package com.integrallis.techconf.ejb;

import javax.annotation.Resource;
import javax.ejb.Stateless;

import org.dynadto.BuilderFactory;

@Stateless
public class ConferenceServiceBean implements
    ConferenceServiceLocal, ConferenceServiceRemote {

    @Resource(name = "java:/dynadto/BuilderFactory")
    protected BuilderFactory builderFactory;
...
```

Implementing Service Layer for TechConf

In this section we will see how to put together TechConf service implementations using EJB3-based DAOs and using a JNDI-bound DynaDTO builder factory. Let's take the Schedule Service as an example. The Schedule Service provides methods to schedule/unschedule a conference session for a given user as well as create email remainders which will be sent at a specified time before a scheduled session start time. Listing 5-17 shows the ScheduleService Business Interface.

Listing 5-17. *Schedule Service Business Interface*

```
package com.integrallis.techconf.service;

import java.util.Date;
import java.util.List;

import com.integrallis.techconf.dto.ReminderInfo;
import com.integrallis.techconf.dto.ScheduleEntryInfo;

public interface ScheduleService {
    ScheduleEntryInfo scheduleSessionForUser(Integer userId, Integer sessionId);

    void unscheduleSessionForUser(Integer scheduleEntryID);

    List<ScheduleEntryInfo> getScheduleForUser(Integer userId);

    ReminderInfo createReminder(Integer scheduleEntry, Date dateTime,
                                String message);
}
```

Let's build the service implementation from the outside in, starting at one end with the DTO layer. The first thing to notice in Listing 5-17 is that all return values are DTO interfaces. We have two interfaces, the `ScheduleEntryInfo` and `ReminderInfo` DTOs.

Listing 5-18. *ScheduleEntryInfo DTO Interface*

```
public interface ScheduleEntryInfo extends DTO {
    Integer getId();
    String getName();
    void setName(String name);
    String getDescription();
    void setDescription(String description);
    Integer getUserId();
    void setUserId(Integer userId);
    Integer getSessionId();
    void setSessionId(Integer session);
}
```

Listing 5-18 shows the `ScheduleEntryInfo` DTO which provides a very simple view into the contents of a `ScheduleEntry` business object, which is shown in Listing 5-19.

Listing 5-19. *ScheduleEntry Persistent POJO*

```
public class ScheduleEntry implements Serializable {

    ...

    public static String PROP_SESSION = "Session";
    public static String PROP_DESCRIPTION = "Description";
    public static String PROP_USER = "User";
    public static String PROP_NAME = "Name";
    public static String PROP_ID = "Id";

    // primary key
    private Integer id;

    // fields
    private String name;
    private String description;

    // many to one
    private User user;
    private Session session;

    // collections
    private Set<Reminder> reminders;
```

```java
// constructors
public ScheduleEntry() {
}

// getters and setters
public Integer getId() {
    return id;
}

public void setId(Integer id) {
    this.id = id;
}

public String getName() {
    return name;
}

public void setName(String name) {
    this.name = name;
}

public String getDescription() {
    return description;
}

public void setDescription(String description) {
    this.description = description;
}

public User getUser() {
    return user;
}

public void setUser(User user) {
    this.user = user;
}

public Session getSession() {
    return session;
}

public void setSession (Session session) {
    this.session = session;
}
```

```
public Set getReminders () {
    return reminders;
}

public void setReminders(Set<Reminder> reminders) {
    this.reminders = reminders;
}

public void addToReminders(Reminder reminder) {
    if (null == this.reminders) this.reminders = new HashSet<Reminder>();
    this.reminders.add(reminder);
}

public boolean equals(Object object) {
    if (object == null) return false;
    if (this == object) return true;
    if (!(object instanceof ScheduleEntry)) return false;

    final ScheduleEntry scheduleEntry = (ScheduleEntry) object;
    return new EqualsBuilder().
        append(getDescription(), scheduleEntry.getDescription()).
        append(getName(), scheduleEntry.getName()).
        append(getSession().getId(), scheduleEntry.getSession().getId()).
        append(getUser().getId(), scheduleEntry.getUser().getId()).
        isEquals();
    }
}
```

To map the POJO to the DTO we need a DynaDTO mapping configuration as shown in the previous section. The configuration for the ScheduleEntry to ScheduleEntryInfo is shown in Listing 5-20.

Listing 5-20. *ScheduleEntryInfo DynaDTO Mapping Configuration*

```xml
<?xml version="1.0" ?>
<dtos>
    <!-- *********************************************************** -->
    <!-- ScheduleEntryInfo                                         -->
    <!-- *********************************************************** -->
    <dto target="com.integrallis.techconf.dto.ScheduleEntryInfo" useProxy="yes">
        <sources>
            <!-- *********************************************************** -->
            <!-- ScheduleEntry                                            -->
            <!-- *********************************************************** -->
```

```
            <source type="com.integrallis.techconf.domain.ScheduleEntry" >
                <mapping property="id" />
                <mapping property="name" />
                <mapping property="description" />
                <mapping from="user.id" to="userId" />
                <mapping from="session.id" to="sessionId" />
            </source>
        </sources>
        <!-- *********************************************************** -->
        <!-- Comparator                                                 -->
        <!-- *********************************************************** -->
        <comparator useSuper="false" useReflection="false">
            <compare property="id" />
        </comparator>
    </dto>
</dtos>
```

With the DTO mapped to the domain object we can now move to the other end of the spectrum and look at how the ScheduleEntry POJO is mapped to the database via a HBM file as shown in Listing 5-21.

Listing 5-21. *ScheduleEntry Hibernate Mapping*

```xml
<?xml version="1.0"?>
<!DOCTYPE hibernate-mapping PUBLIC
    "-//Hibernate/Hibernate Mapping DTD 3.0//EN"
    "http://hibernate.sourceforge.net/hibernate-mapping-3.0.dtd">

<hibernate-mapping package="com.integrallis.techconf.domain">
    <class name="ScheduleEntry" table="scheduleentry">
        <id
            column="PK_ID"
            name="Id"
            type="integer"
        >
            <generator class="identity" />
        </id>
        <property
            length="64"
            name="Name"
         />
        <property
            length="32"
            name="Description"
         />
```

```
        <many-to-one
            class="User"
            name="User"
        >
            <column name="FK_USER_ID" />
        </many-to-one>
        <many-to-one
            class="Session"
            name="Session"
        >
            <column name="FK_SESSION_ID" />
        </many-to-one>
        <set inverse="true" name="Reminders">
            <key column="FK_SCHEDULEENTRY_ID" />
            <one-to-many class="Reminder" />
        </set>
    </class>
</hibernate-mapping>
```

Now we can move to the implementation of the required DAOs. The Schedule Service needs three DAOs to accomplish its work; the ScheduleDAO, PresentationDAO, and UserDAO. The ScheduleDAO implementation is shown in Listing 5-22.

Listing 5-22. *ScheduleDAOBean: An EJB3-Hibernate DAO Implementation*

```
package com.integrallis.techconf.ejb.dao.hibernate;

import java.util.List;
import javax.ejb.Stateless;
import com.integrallis.techconf.dao.ScheduleDAO;
import com.integrallis.techconf.domain.Reminder;
import com.integrallis.techconf.domain.ScheduleEntry;
import com.integrallis.techconf.domain.User;

@Stateless
public class ScheduleDAOBean extends BaseAbstractDAO implements ScheduleDAO {

    public ScheduleDAOBean() {}

    public ScheduleEntry saveScheduleEntry(ScheduleEntry scheduleEntry) {
        saveEntity(scheduleEntry);
        return scheduleEntry;
    }

    public ScheduleEntry updateScheduleEntry(ScheduleEntry scheduleEntry) {
        updateEntity(scheduleEntry);
        return scheduleEntry;
    }
```

```java
    public void deleteScheduleEntry(ScheduleEntry scheduleEntry) {
        deleteEntity(scheduleEntry);
    }

    public void deleteScheduleEntry(int scheduleEntryId) {
        deleteEntityById(ScheduleEntry.class, scheduleEntryId);
    }

    @SuppressWarnings("unchecked")
    public List<ScheduleEntry> getScheduleEntriesForUser(int userId) {
        return findFiltered(ScheduleEntry.class, ScheduleEntry.PROP_USER,
                        new User(userId));
    }

    public ScheduleEntry getScheduleEntryById(int scheduleEntryId) {
        return (ScheduleEntry) getEntityById(ScheduleEntry.class, scheduleEntryId);
    }

    public Reminder saveReminder(Reminder reminder) {
        saveEntity(reminder);
        return reminder;
    }

    public Reminder updateReminder(Reminder reminder) {
        updateEntity(reminder);
        return reminder;
    }

    public void deleteReminder(Reminder reminder) {
        deleteEntity(reminder);
    }

    public void deleteReminder(int reminderId) {
        deleteEntityById(Reminder.class, reminderId);
    }

    @SuppressWarnings("unchecked")
    public List<Reminder> getRemindersForScheduleEntry(int scheduleEntryId) {
        return findFiltered(Reminder.class, Reminder.PROP_SCHEDULE_ENTRY,
                        new ScheduleEntry(scheduleEntryId));
    }

    @SuppressWarnings("unchecked")
    public List<Reminder> getRemindersForUser(int userId) {
        return findFiltered(Reminder.class, Reminder.PROP_USER, new User(userId));
    }
}
```

As you can see in Listing 5-22, the DAO implementation becomes fairly simple by using the utility methods provided in the abstract DAO base class. Notice that in the methods that take the name of any property of a POJO, I've added utility final static String fields to the POJOs in order to minimize the possibility of errors as shown in the getScheduledEntryForUser, getRemindersForScheduleEntry, and getRemindersForUser methods.

Now that we have all the constituents in place, we can assemble the ScheduleService implementation as shown in Listing 5-23. The DynaDTO builder factory is injected as shown before using the @Resource annotation, and the DAOs are injected using the @EJB annotation. The @EJB annotation is used to inject EJB stubs. It replaces the cumbersome lookup code previously needed with EJB 2.X. In the ScheduleServiceBean class I decided to use EJB stub injection using a class field, but like most dependency-injection facilities, it can also be applied to setter methods. For example, the field scheduleDAO is of type ScheduleDAO, which happens to be the local interface of the ScheduleDAOBean. At runtime the container will look up the stub for the ScheduleDAOBean and inject it into the ScheduleServiceBean.

Note In situations when there are multiple bean implementations of a service interface, the @EJB annotation can take attributes to specify how the EJB container locates the specific bean instance.

Listing 5-23. *ScheduleServiceBean: An EJB3 SLSB Service*

```java
package com.integrallis.techconf.ejb;

...

@Stateless
public class ScheduleServiceBean implements ScheduleService {

    @Resource(name = "java:/dynadto/BuilderFactory")
    protected BuilderFactory builderFactory;

    @PostConstruct
    public void initialization() {
        // constructs the DynaDTO builders
        scheduleEntryInfoBuilder = builderFactory
            .getBuilder(ScheduleEntryInfo.class);
        reminderInfoBuilder = builderFactory.getBuilder(ReminderInfo.class);
    }

    // DAOs
    @EJB protected ScheduleDAO scheduleDAO;
    @EJB protected PresentationDAO presentationDAO;
    @EJB protected UserDAO userDAO;
```

```java
// DynaDTO Builders
protected Builder scheduleEntryInfoBuilder;
protected Builder reminderInfoBuilder;

public ScheduleEntryInfo scheduleSessionForUser(Integer userId,
                                                Integer sessionId) {
    // look up the Session
    Session session = presentationDAO.getSessionById(sessionId);
    Presentation presentation = session.getPresentation();
    User user = userDAO.getUserById(userId);

    String name = presentation.getAbstract().getTitle();
    String description = "In room " + session.getRoom().getName()
                        + " starting at " + session.getDateTimeBegin();

    ScheduleEntry scheduleEntry = new ScheduleEntry();
    scheduleEntry.setName(name);
    scheduleEntry.setDescription(description);
    scheduleEntry.setSession(session);
    scheduleEntry.setUser(user);

    scheduleDAO.saveScheduleEntry(scheduleEntry);

    return (ScheduleEntryInfo) scheduleEntryInfoBuilder.build(scheduleEntry);
}

public void unscheduleSessionForUser(Integer scheduleEntryId) {
    scheduleDAO.deleteScheduleEntry(scheduleEntryId);
}

@SuppressWarnings("unchecked")
public List<ScheduleEntryInfo> getScheduleForUser(Integer userId) {
    List<ScheduleEntry> entities =
        scheduleDAO.getScheduleEntriesForUser(userId);
    return scheduleEntryInfoBuilder.buildList(entities);
}

public ReminderInfo createReminder(Integer scheduleEntryId, Date dateTime,
                                   String message) {
    ScheduleEntry scheduleEntry = new ScheduleEntry();
    scheduleEntry.setId(scheduleEntryId);

    Reminder reminder = new Reminder();
    reminder.setDateAndTime(dateTime);
    reminder.setMessage(message);
    reminder.setScheduleEntry(scheduleEntry);
```

```
        scheduleDAO.saveReminder(reminder);

        return (ReminderInfo) reminderInfoBuilder.build(reminder);
    }
}
```

The DynaDTO builders for the two DTO interfaces are constructed in the `initialization` method, which is marked with the annotation `@PostConstruct`, which is called right after instantiation.

The methods in the service implementation look up Hibernate-mapped domain objects using the DAOs, perform certain business logic, and finally return DTOs. As you can see, using the DAO and DTO patterns (with the help of DynaDTO) makes the service implementation deal mainly with business logic while minimizing the amount of plumbing code required.

Message-Driven POJOs

The vast majority of operations in a typical Web-based application will be synchronous, but there are cases in which there is a need to perform an operation in an asynchronous way, especially if that operation can take longer than what is considered acceptable for a typical Web user to wait (a few seconds at most).

A typical case of an asynchronous operation is sending email from a service method. This is needed for example to provide the typical "forgotten password page" in a Web application. In the TechConf application we provide this functionality via the `sendPassword` method of the User Service as shown here:

```
void sendPassword(String email) throws ServiceException;
```

Obviously we could implement the asynchronous functionality needed from the Mail Service by using Message Driven Beans (MDBs) or straight JMS. But this would require us to agree on a message format and a destination to use between the producer of the message and the consumer, which is the nature of working with a flexible, loosely coupled messaging system.

Luckily for us, the JBoss server provides a very powerful extension to do message-driven remote procedure calls (RPCs) by supporting "message-driven POJOs." A message-driven POJO works in similar fashion to an SLSB with the exception that all method calls are dispatched via a JMS message queue.

The first step for implementing a message-driven POJO is to annotate the business interface with the `@Producer` annotation as shown in Listing 5-24.

Note Methods annotated with the `@Producer` annotation must have a return type of void since the caller will not block to receive a response.

Listing 5-24. *MailService Business Interface Using the @Producer Annotation*

```
package com.integrallis.techconf.service;

import java.util.List;
import org.jboss.annotation.ejb.Producer;
import com.integrallis.techconf.service.exception.ServiceException;

@Producer
public interface MailService {
    void sendEmail(String to, String from,
                    String subject, String text) throws ServiceException;
    void sendEmail(List<String> recipients, String from,
                    String subject, String text) throws ServiceException;
}
```

Listing 5-25 shows the MailServiceBean, which is the message-driven POJO implementation of the MailService. The MailServiceBean implements the two sendEmail methods using JavaMail API (the JavaMail Session at java:/Mail is injected using the @Resource annotation). To fulfill the rest of the message-driven POJO contract, the implementation is annotated with the @Consumer annotation. The @Consumer annotation specifies the name of the message queue to be used, which if not defined will be automatically created at deployment time.

Listing 5-25. *MailServiceBean Message-driven POJO Implementation*

```
package com.integrallis.techconf.ejb;

import java.util.Iterator;
import java.util.List;

import javax.annotation.Resource;
import javax.ejb.ActivationConfigProperty;
import javax.mail.Message;
import javax.mail.MessagingException;
import javax.mail.Session;
import javax.mail.Transport;
import javax.mail.Message.RecipientType;
import javax.mail.internet.InternetAddress;
import javax.mail.internet.MimeMessage;

import org.jboss.annotation.ejb.Consumer;

import com.integrallis.techconf.service.MailService;
import com.integrallis.techconf.service.exception.ServiceException;
```

```java
@Consumer(activateConfig =
{
  @ActivationConfigProperty(propertyName="destinationType",
    propertyValue="javax.jms.Queue"),
  @ActivationConfigProperty(propertyName="destination",
    propertyValue="queue/techconfmailqueue")
})
public class MailServiceBean implements MailService {

    @Resource(name = "java:/Mail")
    protected Session session;

    public void sendEmail(String to, String from, String subject, String text) {
        try {
            if (session != null) {
                Message message = new MimeMessage(session);
                message.setContent(text, "text/plain");
                message.setFrom(new InternetAddress(from));
                message.setRecipients(RecipientType.TO,
                                    InternetAddress.parse(to, false));
                message.setSubject(subject);
                message.setText(text);
                Transport.send(message);
            }
        } catch (MessagingException me) {
            throw new ServiceException("could not send email to " + to, me);
        }


    }

    public void sendEmail(List<String> recipients, String from,
                        String subject, String text) throws ServiceException {
        try {
            if (session != null) {
                Message message = new MimeMessage(session);
                message.setContent(text, "text/plain");
                message.setFrom(new InternetAddress(from));

                InternetAddress[] recipientAddresses =
                    new InternetAddress[recipients.size()];
                for (int i = 0; i < recipients.size(); i++) {
                    recipientAddresses[i] = new InternetAddress(recipients.get(i));
                }
                message.setRecipients(RecipientType.TO, recipientAddresses);
                message.setSubject(subject);
                message.setText(text);
                Transport.send(message);
            }
```

```
        } catch (MessagingException me) {
            Iterator i = recipients.iterator();
            StringBuffer sb = new StringBuffer();
            while (i.hasNext()) {
                sb.append((String) i.next());
                if (i.hasNext()) {
                    sb.append(", ");
                }
            }
            throw new ServiceException("could not send email to "
                                + sb.toString(), me);
        }
    }
}
```

To use the message-driven POJO, you need a generic object of type `org.jboss.ejb3.`
`mdb.ProducerManager`, which is used to manage the underlying JMS connection used. The
ProducerManager is obtained calling the method getProducerManager on an instance of
ProducerObject. To obtain the `ProducerObject` instance you need to cast the stub object of the
@Producer interface which we injected into the field `mailService` using the @Resource annota-
tion as shown in Listing 5-26.

The implementation of the sendPassword method entails looking up the User domain
object using the UserDAO and then sending the password associated with the retrieved User
using the MailService. Listing 5-26 shows the implementation of the sendPassword method in
the UserServiceBean.

Listing 5-26. *UserServiceBean Using Message-driven POJO*

```
package com.integrallis.techconf.ejb;

import javax.annotation.EJB;
import javax.annotation.Resource;
import javax.ejb.PostConstruct;
import javax.ejb.Stateless;
import javax.jms.JMSException;


...
import org.jboss.ejb3.mdb.ProducerManager;
import org.jboss.ejb3.mdb.ProducerObject;

import com.integrallis.techconf.dao.UserDAO;
import com.integrallis.techconf.domain.User;
import com.integrallis.techconf.service.MailService;
import com.integrallis.techconf.service.UserService;
import com.integrallis.techconf.service.exception.NoSuchUserException;
```

```
@Stateless
public class UserServiceBean implements UserService {

    ...

    @Resource(name = "com.integrallis.techconf.service.MailService")
    protected MailService mailService;

    ProducerManager manager;

    @PostConstruct
    public void initialization() {
        ...

        // initialize the producer manager
        ProducerObject producerObject = (ProducerObject) mailService;
        manager = producerObject.getProducerManager();
    }

    // DAOs
    @EJB protected UserDAO userDAO;

    ...

    public void sendPassword(String email) {
        User user = userDAO.getUserByEmail(email);
        if (user != null) {
            try {
                manager.connect(); // internally create a JMS connection
                mailService.sendEmail(email,
                                "noreply@techconf.org",
                                "Your Techconf Password",
                                "Your Password is " + user.getPassword());
            } catch (JMSException jmse) {
                Throw new ServiceException("Error sending email", jmse);
            } finally {
                try {
                    // clean up the JMS connection
                    manager.close();
                } catch (JMSException e) {
                    // do nothing
                }
            }
        }
    }
```

```
        else {
            throw new NoSuchUserException("There is no user with email " + email);
        }
    }
}
```

Summary

In this chapter you've learned how to build a robust application using the JBoss application server as an agile development application platform. Using the power of the EJB3 specification in combination with Java annotations and JBoss extensions, you've learned that the power of Java EE platform is now easier to harness. Using an intelligent combination of open source tools, frameworks, and design patterns, you've learned how to create an end-to-end implementation of a service for a distributed Web application.

CHAPTER 6

■ ■ ■

The Spring Framework

The Spring Framework is an open source Dependency Injection (DI) and Aspect Oriented Programming (AOP) lightweight container and full-stack Java EE application framework leading the pack in the movement towards making enterprise Java development simpler, faster, less error-prone, and more enjoyable. Spring helps you assemble components declaratively into a working system.

Spring is based on the principle that good object-oriented design should come first and not be hindered by the choice of technology being used. Spring grew from the experiences of a seasoned and dedicated team of developers led by Rod Johnson dealing with real applications on a daily basis and looking for a way to address end-to-end application requirements in a consistent fashion across application tiers. The Spring Framework brings back some of the good object-oriented aspects that were missing from the previous versions of Java EE platform, such as the use of POJOs, programming by contract using interfaces, and clean, layered architecture. Spring eliminates the need to deal with most middle-tier glue as opposed to heavyweight component models like EJB 2.X, allowing you to build truly portable, object-oriented Java SE and Java EE applications. The Spring Framework is licensed under the terms of the Apache License, Version 2.0.

Coding to Interfaces

The first aspect of the Spring Framework that you'll notice is that it makes your Java code cleaner and easier to test by promoting the practice of coding to interfaces, a practice well-known in object-oriented programming. Exposing a public contract (the interface) and being able to provide a suitable implementation of that interface seems like a no-brainer to most Java programmers, but unfortunately, previous versions of the Java EE framework, particularly EJB, made this very difficult with its heavy and bloated container contracts.

The side effect of the pre-3.0 EJB APIs was that although they promoted a component-oriented development style, their particular implementation disregarded good object-oriented practices. Developers had to go through hoops implementing their own frameworks to test their components in isolation outside of the J2EE container. Most developers who came from building good object-oriented applications, when thrown under the wheels of the EJB bus, decided to take the path of *most* resistance, using EJB in an inverted fashion by first building robust, interface-driven "by contract", object-oriented applications and using EJB as a layer to leverage multithreading, object pooling, and other container services. After all, there is much more to J2EE than just EJB, but unfortunately, the previous ill-designed versions of the EJB specification took the limelight from the rest of the specification, especially from the real gems of the specification—in my humble opinion, JNDI and JMS. Those developers who took the path of least resistance ended up with so-called components that were not truly reusable, were hard to test, and contained more plumbing code that actual application code of value to the business.

Frameworks like Spring emerged from the philosophy of using the best parts of the specification, masking those parts that are cumbersome, and simplifying the APIs, all the while making good, object-oriented design priority number one. As you'll soon learn, Spring lets you approach the design of your application using interfaces in a loosely coupled way without compromising good, object-oriented principles.

Dependency Injection

Spring is primarily known as a Dependency Injection container. Dependency Injection is the more appropriate term coined by Martin Fowler, Rod Johnson, and the PicoContainer team in late 2003 for what was once known as "Inversion of Control." An alternative view is that DI is a strategy or flavor of IoC. Most explanations of DI also referred to it as the Hollywood Principle: "Don't call us, we'll call you."

Early in my forays into DI containers and the Spring Framework, I found some of the explanations of IoC/DI overly complex. The best explanation I can give for DI is that it is a technique by which you externalize the choice of which implementation of a given interface you'll use at runtime. In Spring, a system is designed using interfaces, and the Spring framework plugs or injects the right implementations at runtime. In Spring you typically inject specific implementations of an interface into other beans via an XML configuration file referred to as an application context.

Therefore in a Spring application your POJOs or beans do not have their dependencies explicitly constructed in the code. Instead, dependencies are "injected" by the container at runtime. For example, in a typical Spring Web application using the DAO pattern, you'll have interfaces defining the DAOs and interfaces defining the services. In the implementation of a service, a property for a DAO is defined (using the interface) along with a setter or a constructor that takes the DAO as a parameter. The Spring application context XML configuration contains a definition of the specific implementation of the DAO interface that will be injected into the service class (using the setter or the constructor provided). At runtime, the Spring container using the application context will correctly wire the beans and the collaborators needed to fulfill its functions. This is contrary to the lookup-based approached of EJB 2.X, in which the service locator pattern along with factories and straight object construction is used to wire all collaborators in a system. In a typical EJB 2.X system, a service locator is used as a way to pull the dependencies (typically from JNDI) into a component (all this is done programmatically from within the component itself). This doesn't mean that JNDI isn't a powerful abstraction for resource management, but the implementation in EJB 2.X forced this "pull" usage of JNDI and a dependence on the JNDI API (making it harder to test without having JNDI available and therefore in most cases a container) and requiring a lot of code to perform lookups. As we saw in Chapter 5, the EJB3 specification allows for JNDI-bound resources to be injected into a component in a loosely coupled fashion via Java annotations. Similarly, Spring allows for the injection of JNDI-bound resources. Figure 6-1 depicts the dependency injection pattern as supported by the Spring Framework.

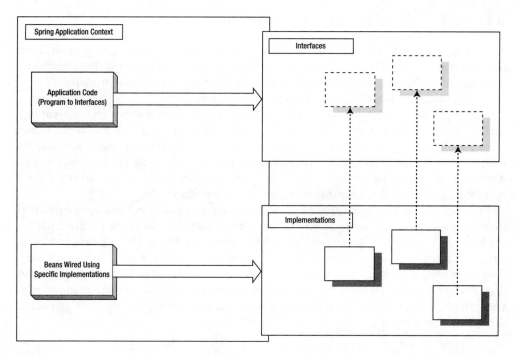

Figure 6-1. *Dependency Injection in Spring*

Dependency Injection moves the responsibility of configuring application objects and resource lookups to the container in a declarative fashion. The main advantages of DI are that it removes the requirement of business objects to implement any container-specific interfaces and eliminates redundant lookup code or the need for service locator implementations. By removing container-specific dependencies, objects can be tested without a container, and legacy code can also be easily adapted to work in new environments.

I mentioned before that the implementations to be injected with a resource need to provide either a setter or a constructor that is used by the container to inject the given resource. This brings us to the different types of dependency injection: constructor-based injection and setter-based injection. Both methods provide advantages and disadvantages. Renowned technologist Martin Fowler provides the explanation of IoC/DI in an online article at `www.martinfowler.com/articles/injection.html`.

In this book and in the Spring implementation of the TechConf application, I used setter-based DI, mostly because it makes it easier in the scenarios when multiple resources are being injected and prevents the proliferation of too many constructors, which I found is the result of trying to account for the possible combinations or required parameters. Of course, by providing constructors that take the required resources (and without a no-arguments constructor) you effectively guarantee that the object being constructed will be in a valid state upon creation.

In combination with the practice of coding to interfaces, DI provides for a very testable environment that makes it easier to take a test-first approach to development, providing reduced development effort and increasing test coverage and overall quality. Using a different application context during testing, one could, for example, inject mock implementations of certain collaborators to test a component in isolation.

Aspect Oriented Programming

Another facility provided by the Spring framework and one on which Spring itself builds a lot of its internal functionality upon its AOP stack. Although Spring's doesn't provide a complete language-level AOP implementation, it provides the necessary AOP features to deal with common problems encountered in enterprise applications.

As you'll learn in depth in Chapter 10, AOP provides the ability to deal with cross-cutting concerns of an application in a declarative fashion. Aspects are behaviors or functionality that are required by the application but that might not necessarily belong alongside business application code. By defining pointcuts (where to apply an aspect) AOP techniques provide a clean way to deal with common services such as logging, persistence, transactions, and any other non-functional aspect that will otherwise litter your application code.

Spring AOP was designed with usability in a Java EE environment in mind. Spring provides a coarse-grained dynamic proxy based AOP implementation that uses runtime-generated proxies to add concerns. Following the prevailing theme in Spring, any Spring bean can be advised in a declarative fashion. Spring itself uses several predefined aspects to handle transactions, security, tracing, logging, contention management, and integration with technologies like EJB and JMS. So if you are using Spring today, you are already (and perhaps unknowingly) using AOP. In Chapter 10 we will explore AOP techniques as they apply to the development of the TechConf application.

Full-featured Application Framework

The Spring framework is much more than just another IoC/AOP lightweight container. Spring is a very non-invasive framework that will let you use as much as you need but not more. By providing a comprehensive and consistent feature set built upon the best offerings available in the open source arena, it provides a complete, feature-rich application framework that focuses of solving common Java EE problems.

Spring provides abstractions to deal in a simple way with such concerns as transaction management, object-relational mapping, integration with MVC frameworks, and others. The abstraction of common services makes Spring applications completely portable across application servers or Web containers and provides a consistent way to deal with resource management and exception handling. Figure 6-2 depicts the extent of the Spring Framework and the myriad of tools and projects that it seamlessly integrates under a single roof.

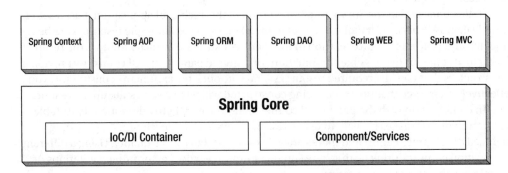

Figure 6-2. *Overview of the Spring Framework*

As seen in Figure 6-2, Spring consists of 12 modules in the main distribution and 5 subprojects. The main Spring modules are:

- **Spring Core:** Commons classes and interfaces not specific to any part of the framework, including exception handling and JDK and collections utilities

- **Spring Beans:** Utilities to manipulate Java beans and the core implementation of the Inversion of Control container

- **Spring AOP:** Spring AOP implementation (AOP alliance compliant); tightly integrated with Spring application context

- **Spring Context:** Provides utilities for consistent resource lookup and sharing (including JNDI bound resources, EJBs, email, internationalization, validation, and scheduling); also provides support for message sources, data binding, validation and the Observer design pattern

- **Spring Support:** Provides support for JMX, JCA, scheduling, mail, and caching

- **Spring Mock:** Provides mock testing classes for JNDI, servlet API, and general JUnit integration

- **Spring JDBC:** Provides an abstraction over JDBC by providing template and callback interfaces, thread-safe classes for JDBC operations, and other utilities such as large data-base object-handling classes

- **Spring ORM:** Provides support for various ORM technologies, including iBATIS SQL maps, Apache OJB, TopLink, and JDO

- **Spring DAO:** Provides a clean, unchecked exception hierarchy for DAO implementations independent of the underlying data access technology

- **Spring Hibernate:** Provides ORM support for Hibernate version 2.X and 3.X

- **Spring Web:** Provides integration with many popular Web technologies, including Struts, Velocity, and JSF; also provides a multipart file upload framework and other Web utilities

- **Spring MVC:** A full-featured MVC Web framework implementation that can be integrated with numerous view technologies including JSP, Velocity, Tiles, iText, and POI

The five current Spring subprojects are:

- **Spring Security:** Provides a comprehensive set of security services to the Spring frame-work, including support for single sign-on (SSO)

- **Spring Web Flow:** Spring Web Flow (SWF) provides facilities to define and orchestrate page flow in Web applications

- **Spring Rich Client:** Principles of the Spring Framework applied to the creation of professional Swing applications

- **Spring BeanDoc:** A tool for documenting in a graphical way the structure of a Spring Bean Factory

- **Spring IDE for Eclipse:** A collection of Eclipse plug-ins to work with Spring configuration files

Spring also integrates with most Web application frameworks including the Apache Struts project, JSF, Tapestry, and most recently Wicket.

Installing and Configuring Spring

The Spring Framework is distributed as a ZIP file containing source, prepackaged JAR files, and supporting files available at `www.springframework.org/download`. There are two available download types, one including all third-party (open source) dependencies and one without. I recommend that you download the one containing all dependencies. At the time of this writing the archive is spring-framework-1.2.5-with-dependencies.zip. Inside the archive you'll find eight folders:

- **dist:** Spring Framework distribution files

- **docs:** Reference and API documentation and a Spring MVC tutorial

- **lib:** All third-party dependencies, organized by project/product

- **mock:** Web and JNDI mock objects

- **samples:** Several sample applications

- **src:** The complete source code base for the Spring Framework

- **test:** Comprehensive set of JUnit tests

- **tiger:** JSE 5.0 specific features, including annotation support for certain features like transactions and Hibernate 3.0 annotations

The focus of this book is building Web applications; therefore you'll need a Web container such as Tomcat or Jetty supporting the servlet API. As before, we will be using JSE 5.0 for all examples.

Working with Spring Bean Factories

Spring Bean Factories are implementations of the factory design pattern that serve beans or objects of a specific type and configure them using metadata provided in the form of property files or XML documents. By far the most used part of Spring Bean Factory is the `XMLBeanFactory`, which can instantiate an implementation of an interface from an XML definition that describes which concrete class to use and how to configure it.

In Listing 6-1 we have a Java interface defining a simple service called `GreetingService`. The `GreetingService` interface provides two methods that return a greeting message. (Yes, you guessed it! It's a "hello world" example.)

Listing 6-1. *A Simple Service Interface*

```
package com.integrallis.spring.basic;

public interface GreetingService {
    String greet();
    String greet(String subject);
}
```

Listing 6-2 shows an implementation of the GreetingService interface. As you can see, we have provided a private property greeting that will hold the string representing the greeting used by the service. The greeting property can be set via a constructor or via the setGreeting setter method.

Listing 6-2. *A Simple Service Implementation*

```
package com.integrallis.spring.basic;

public class GreetingServiceImpl implements GreetingService {
    //
    // constructors
    //

    public GreetingServiceImpl() {}

    /**
     * Constructor used for Dependency Injection
     * @param greeting
     */
    public GreetingServiceImpl(String greeting) {
        this.greeting = greeting;
    }

    //
    // Service Business Methods
    //

    public String greet() {
        return greeting;
    }

    public String greet(String subject) {
        return greeting + " " + subject;
    }

    //
    // Setters for dependency injection
    //
```

```
    public void setGreeting(String greeting) {
        this.greeting = greeting;
    }

    private String greeting;
}
```

In a traditional tightly coupled Java application, one would probably declare a property of type GreetingService (or sometimes even disregard the interface and directly expose an instance of GreetingServiceImpl). You would then either use the constructor that takes the greeting property or the no-arguments constructor along with the setGreeting method to configure the instance before usage.

The problems with this type of tight coupling become painfully obvious when it comes to testing, and the specific implementation of a resource depends on external factors such as a database, a JNDI context, or a remote Web service. Of course after seeing this pattern repeat itself many times, you might choose to implement some of your own plumbing using property files or some other way of externalizing the system variant parameters.

At the lowest level this is the simplest function of the Spring Framework, except that the Spring Framework creators have gone through all the evolutionary steps that make a simple utility into an application framework. For example, in Listing 6-3 we have a simple Spring XML configuration file. At the root we have the beans element which contains one or more bean elements. The single bean element in this simple file defines a bean with an id of greetingService implemented by the class GreetingServiceImpl and sets the property greeting via the setter setGreeting with the value "Hello".

Listing 6-3. *Simple Spring Configuration*

```
<?xml version="1.0" encoding="UTF-8"?>
<!DOCTYPE beans PUBLIC "-//SPRING//DTD BEAN//EN"
 "http://www.springframework.org/dtd/spring-beans.dtd">
<!-- ===================================================================== -->
<!-- A Simple Spring Bean Configuration                                    -->
<!-- ===================================================================== -->
<beans>
    <!-- ================================================================= -->
    <!-- Greeting Service Bean Configuration                               -->
    <!-- ================================================================= -->
    <bean id="greetingService"
        class="com.integrallis.spring.basic.GreetingServiceImpl">
        <property name="greeting">
            <value>Hello</value>
        </property>
    </bean>
</beans>
```

Place the XML file in the same package (com.integrallis.spring.basic). To use the greetingService bean we initialize the Spring Bean Factory by reading the XML configuration file (using a `ClassPathResource`) and using the `getBean` method to retrieve an instance of the bean by its `id`, as shown in Listing 6-4.

Listing 6-4. *Simple Client for the Simple Service*

```
package com.integrallis.spring.basic;

import org.springframework.beans.factory.BeanFactory;
import org.springframework.beans.factory.xml.XmlBeanFactory;
import org.springframework.core.io.ClassPathResource;
import org.springframework.core.io.Resource;

public class GreetingServiceClient {

    public static void main(String[] args) {
        Resource configuration =
            new ClassPathResource("com/integrallis/spring/basic/beans.xml");
        BeanFactory factory = new XmlBeanFactory(configuration);
        GreetingService bean = (GreetingService)factory.getBean("greetingService");
        System.out.println(bean.greet(args[0]));
    }
}
```

To compile the simple example, you'll need spring.jar (found in the dist) and commons-logging.jar (found in lib/Jakarta-commons directory) in the classpath. If you compile and run the simple test class using as a parameter the string "World", you should see output similar to:

```
Nov 7, 2005 11:21:43 AM
org.springframework.beans.factory.xml.XmlBeanDefinitionReader loadBeanDefinitions
INFO: Loading XML bean definitions from class path resource
[com/integrallis/spring/basic/beans.xml]
Hello World
```

In the previous example, Setter Dependency Injection was used. Similarly, you could use Constructor Dependency Injection to accomplish the same effect as shown in Listing 6-5.

Listing 6-5. *Constructor Dependency Injection*

```
<bean id="greetingService"
    class="com.integrallis.spring.basic.GreetingServiceImpl">
    <constructor-arg>
        <value>Howdy</value>
    </constructor-arg>
</bean>
```

Another thing to notice about how Spring is managing your beans based on the simple XML file shown is that the greetingService bean is in fact a singleton. All bean definitions in a Spring XML file are singletons by default, which is typically the type of behavior you would need for stateless services. Therefore if we were to instantiate another instance of the greetingService bean, you'll find that all instances are indeed the same instance.

If we were to change the previous XML declarations as shown in Listing 6-6, you'll find out that now you would get a separate instance for each invocation of getBean method. This type of bean is referred to as a prototype bean.

Listing 6-6. *Making greetingService a Prototype Bean*

```
<bean id="greetingService"
    class="com.integrallis.spring.basic.GreetingServiceImpl"
    singleton="false">
```

A prototype bean is useful when you are instantiating an object that might be a collaborator to another object that will carry or hold state information for the collaborator or that is configured based on the state of the collaborator object. In Spring, beans are deployed as singletons by default. Prototype beans are completely non-managed since Spring simply instantiates the object and hands it over to the client.

A Simple Spring Web Application

In the previous section you've learned how to use the Spring Framework for its basic dependency injection features (available via a BeanFactory) to

- Decouple a simple service interface from its implementation

- Configure a service declaratively via an XML file

- Easily switch the service from being a singleton or getting a new instance each time

A BeanFactory is a very powerful construct that provides DI and basic service management, but for most applications (especially Web applications) you'll likely need to move up to using a Spring ApplicationContext. An ApplicationContext is a subinterface of BeanFactory and provides all the power of a BeanFactory along with many features typically needed by a full-featured application such as text message resolution, internationalization, resource loading, and more complete object life cycle management and notifications.

From this point on we'll use a Spring application context in a Web application environment.

Spring's Starter Web Application

Luckily for us, the Spring folks provide a starter Web application along with the Spring distribution. This application provides a skeleton for a Spring MVC Web application along with an Ant buildfile. We will modify this application slightly to create our version of a simple Spring Web application.

Let's begin by making a copy of the samples/webapp-minimal directory. This minimal Spring Web application has a directory structure like that shown in Figure 6-3. As explained in the readme.txt located at the root of the Web application, the directories have the following purpose:

- **src:** All Java source code that will be compiled into class files that will be available in the target WAR file WEB-INF/classes directory

- **war:** Contains the Web application documents (JSP and HTML pages) along with the Web deployment descriptors and Spring application context in the WEB-INF

- **lib:** Contains the JAR files to be included in the WAR archive WEB-INF/lib directory

- **dist:** Directory to be created by the build script which will contain the WAR deployment archive

Figure 6-3. *Minimal Spring Web application*

JAR Dependencies

Once again you'll need a few JARs required for our application. Copy the following JARs into the lib directory of the Web application:

- **spring.jar** (found in the dist directory)

- **commons-logging.jar** (found in lib/jakarta-commons directory)

- **servlet-api.jar** (found in lib/j2ee, only needed for compilation)

Java Code

Next let's copy the Java files created in our stand-alone greeter service example to the src directory of the Web application, maintaining the package structure.

Modify the file `ExampleController.java` in the example package to look like Listing 6-7.

Listing 6-7. *Simple Spring MVC Controller*

```
...
public ModelAndView handleRequest(
    HttpServletRequest request,
    HttpServletResponse response) throws ServletException, IOException {

    String greeting = greetingService.greet();

    return new ModelAndView("/test.jsp", "greeting", greeting);
}
```

```
private GreetingService greetingService;

// Used for dependency injection
public void setGreetingService(GreetingService greetingService) {
    this.greetingService = greetingService;
}
...
```

We would go into greater detail about the Spring MVC framework later in this chapter. For the time being the important facts about the ExampleController class is that it is the code that will be used to respond to an HTTP request for a simple application and that it is the bridge between the presentation tier (the Web tier) and our service tier (the Spring-managed greetingService singleton).

Listing 6-7 shows that the controller class provides the setter setGreetingService for the GreetingService property that we will use to wire the greetingService bean to the controller class.

Configuring the Spring Application Context

The Spring application context distributed with the starter Web application is named example-servlet.xml and is located in the war/WEB-INF directory. Modify the example-servlet.xml to look like Listing 6-8.

Listing 6-8. *Spring Application Context for Simple Web Application*

```
<?xml version="1.0" encoding="UTF-8"?>
<!DOCTYPE beans PUBLIC "-//SPRING//DTD BEAN//EN"
"http://www.springframework.org/dtd/spring-beans.dtd">
<!-- ================================================================ -->
<!-- A Simple Spring Web Application                                   -->
<!-- ================================================================ -->
<beans>
    <!-- ============================================================= -->
    <!-- Greeting Service Bean Configuration                          -->
    <!-- ============================================================= -->
    <bean id="greetingService"
        class="com.integrallis.spring.basic.GreetingServiceImpl">
        <property name="greeting">
            <value>Hello!</value>
        </property>
    </bean>
```

```
<!-- =================================================================== -->
<!-- Web MVC Controller mapped the URI /test                             -->
<!-- with GreetingService injected                                       -->
<!-- =================================================================== -->
<bean name="/test" class="example.ExampleController">
    <property name="greetingService"><ref bean="greetingService"/></property>
</bean>
</beans>
```

As you can see, the application context definition uses the same DTD as the configuration file used with the Bean Factory in the stand-alone example. The only difference here is the addition of the bean named "/test", which is mapped to the ExampleController class and injected with the greetingService bean. By naming the bean with a URL path, it simplifies the configuration file by implicitly creating a URL mapping. (We will explicitly create URL mappings when we wire up the TechConf application Spring edition).

JSP Test Page

With the model, implemented by the greetingService and the controller, implemented by the ExampleController class, the only missing element of our MVC implementation is the view, which we'll provide in the form of a JSP file as shown in Listing 6-9.

Listing 6-9. *Simple JSP View (test.jsp)*

```
<h1>Simple Spring Web Application</h1>
<h2>Spring says, ${greeting}!</h2>
```

The test.jsp displays the value (toString) of the object bound to the name greeting which, as you'll remember, is the name of the String object (model) passed to the view in the controller code new ModelAndView("/test.jsp", "greeting", greeting).

We'll also include a JSP page, index.jsp, to redirect to test.jsp, since the Servlet API doesn't allow for a redirect to use a virtual URL. The index.jsp is shown in Listing 6-10.

Listing 6-10. *Redirect JSP (index.jsp)*

```
<jsp:forward page="example/test" />
```

The index.jsp will be included in the welcome-file-list element of the web.xml deployment descriptor.

Deployment Descriptors and Build Configuration

The final configuration step required is to modify the included web.xml file (located in the WAR/web-inf directory) as shown in Listing 6-11.

Listing 6-11. *Web Deployment Descriptor (web.xml)*

```xml
<?xml version="1.0" encoding="ISO-8859-1"?>

<web-app xmlns="http://java.sun.com/xml/ns/j2ee"
    xmlns:xsi="http://www.w3.org/2001/XMLSchema-instance"
    xsi:schemaLocation="http://java.sun.com/xml/ns/j2ee web-app_2_4.xsd"
    version="2.4">

    <servlet>
        <servlet-name>example</servlet-name>
        <servlet-class>
        org.springframework.web.servlet.DispatcherServlet
        </servlet-class>
        <load-on-startup>1</load-on-startup>
    </servlet>

    <servlet-mapping>
        <servlet-name>example</servlet-name>
        <url-pattern>/example/*</url-pattern>
    </servlet-mapping>

    <welcome-file-list>
        <welcome-file>index.jsp</welcome-file>
    </welcome-file-list>

</web-app>
```

As you can see in the URL pattern, /example/* is mapped to the servlet named "example",
which in turn resolves to the Spring Framework DispatcherServlet. As mentioned previously,
the welcome-file index.jsp redirects all requests to the URL /example.

■Note The included web.xml in the starter Web application complies with the Servlet specification 2.3. The
web.xml shown in Listing 6-11 complies with the 2.4 specification and uses JavaServer Pages Standard Tag
Library 1.1 version.

The included build script uses a properties file named build.properties in which you can
change the directories being used for source, compiled classes, libraries, and the name of the
generated WAR (controlled by the name property).

Running the Ant script from the command line as follows:

```
ant warfile
```

should produce output similar to that shown next:

```
Buildfile: C:\java\workspace\webapp-minimal\build.xml
build:
    [javac] Compiling 4 source files to C:\java\workspace\webapp-minimal\.classes
warfile:
    [mkdir] Created dir: C:\java\workspace\webapp-minimal\dist
     [war] Building war: C:\java\workspace\webapp-minimal\dist\minimal.war
BUILD SUCCESSFUL
Total time: 6 seconds
```

Deploying to Tomcat

We are now to deploy the simple Spring Web application to a servlet container. In this chapter I will be deploying to an instance of Jakarta Tomcat version 5.5.12. To get started with Tomcat, visit http://tomcat.apache.org/tomcat-5.5-doc/introduction.html.

Once you have Tomcat installed and running, you can simply copy the WAR minimal.war from the dist directory to the Tomcat webapps directory. The output on the Tomcat console should look like:

```
Nov 7, 2005 9:29:54 PM org.apache.catalina.startup.HostConfig deployWAR
INFO: Deploying web application archive minimal.war
Nov 7, 2005 9:29:55 PM org.springframework.web.servlet.HttpServletBean init
INFO: Initializing servlet 'example'
Nov 7, 2005 9:29:55 PM org.springframework.web.servlet.FrameworkServlet
  initServletBean
INFO: FrameworkServlet 'example': initialization started
Nov 7, 2005 9:29:55 PM org.springframework.beans.factory.xml
  .XmlBeanDefinitionReader loadBeanDefinitions
INFO: Loading XML bean definitions from ServletContext resource [/WEB-INF/example
servlet.xml]
Nov 7, 2005 9:29:55 PM org.springframework.context.support.
AbstractRefreshableApplicationContext
refreshBeanFactory
INFO: Bean factory for application context [WebApplicationContext for namespace
'example-servlet']:
org.springframework.beans.factory.support.DefaultListableBeanFactory defining
beans [greetingService,/test]; root of BeanFactory hierarchy
Nov 7, 2005 9:29:55 PM
org.springframework.context.support.AbstractApplicationContext refresh
INFO: 2 beans defined in application context [WebApplicationContext for namespace
'example-servlet']
...
INFO: Pre-instantiating singletons in factory
[org.springframework.beans.factory.support.DefaultListableBeanFactory defining
beans [greetingService,/test]; root of BeanFactory hierarchy]
Nov 7, 2005 9:29:55 PM org.springframework.web.servlet.FrameworkServlet
```

```
initWebApplicationContext
INFO: Using context class
[org.springframework.web.context.support.XmlWebApplicationContext] for servlet
'example'
...
INFO: FrameworkServlet 'example': initialization completed in 500 ms
Nov 7, 2005 9:29:55 PM org.springframework.web.servlet.HttpServletBean init
INFO: Servlet 'example' configured successfully
```

You can now test the servlet by opening your browser and pointing it to the URL http://localhost:8080/minimal/example/test as shown in Figure 6-4.

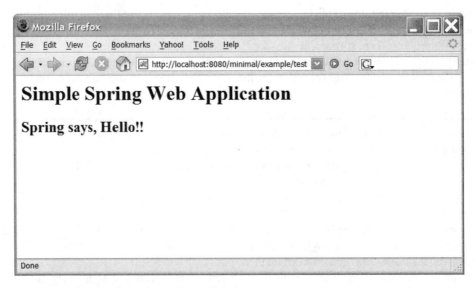

Figure 6-4. *The Simple Spring Web Application*

Business Services with Spring

Now that we know how to wire together the components in a Spring application, we can put this knowledge to use in the Spring implementation of the TechConf application.

The approach we will take is fairly similar to the implementation using EJB3 on JBoss covered in Chapter 5. We actually will reuse the same service, DAO, and DTO interfaces. (After all, that's the point of using interfaces; reusability and the ability to swap implementations.) We will start by developing a set of Spring-Hibernate DAOs and DynaDTO DTOs. These DAOs and DTOs will then be injected into the implementations of the service interfaces.

We will also showcase the power of the Spring Framework by dealing with other cross-cutting concerns of a typical enterprise Web application such as transactions, security, and email needs.

From Figure 6-5 you can see that we have decided to break up the application context into three different files. There is one XML file per application tier:

- **techconf-data:** Wires up basic JDBC connectivity, configures Hibernate and Spring's Hibernate integration beans, and declares DAO implementations

- **techconf-service:** Wires up all business services including DynaDTO builder factory and JavaMail mail sender, declares service implementations, and sets up transactional proxy wrappers for services

- **techconf-servlet:** Defines Spring MVC controllers, configures Tiles, and sets up view resolution and URL mappings

Separating the Spring application context across tiers makes your application more modular and pluggable, allowing you to replace the implementation of a whole tier easily and allowing different developers to work on different parts of the application without stepping over each others' work.

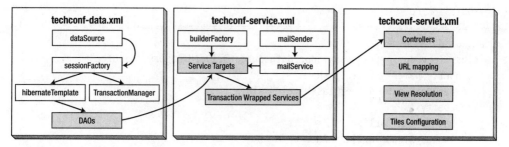

Figure 6-5. *Dependency Injection in the Spring version of the TechConf application*

Spring and Hibernate

In Chapter 4 you learned how to work with the powerful ORM framework Hibernate. Fortunately for us, the Spring Framework offers great integration with Hibernate. In Chapter 5, the EJB3 JBoss implementation of the TechConf application depended on a Hibernate `SessionFactory` instance stored in JNDI.

In the Spring implementation we could choose to use JNDI, but it is much more common for a Spring application to rely on the container to manage this singleton. In order to configure a bean of type `SessionFactory`, we first need a suitable JDBC data source.

Listing 6-12 shows the portion of the Spring application context file techconf-data.xml showing a JDBC data source configured from the values contained in a properties file named jdbc.properties, which is located in the WEB-INF directory of the WAR file containing the Spring Web application.

Listing 6-12. *Data Source Configuration Using a Spring Property Configurer*

```
<!-- ================================================================= -->
<!-- Resolve placeholder properties ${...} in beans from values in     -->
<!-- properties file                                                   -->
<!-- ================================================================= -->
<bean id="configurer"
    class="org.springframework.beans.factory.config.PropertyPlaceholderConfigurer">
    <property name="location">
        <value>/WEB-INF/jdbc.properties</value>
    </property>
</bean>


<!-- ================================================================= -->
<!-- Data Source                                                       -->
<!-- ================================================================= -->
<bean id="dataSource"
    class="org.springframework.jdbc.datasource.DriverManagerDataSource">
    <property name="driverClassName">
        <value>${jdbc.driverClassName}</value>
    </property>
    <property name="url">
        <value>${jdbc.url}</value>
    </property>
    <property name="username">
        <value>${jdbc.username}</value>
    </property>
    <property name="password">
        <value>${jdbc.password}</value>
    </property>
</bean>
```

With the data source in place, a Hibernate SessionFactory is configured as shown in Listing 6-13. I'm using the Hibernate 3 LocalSessionFactoryBean integration class which, when used as a bean reference, behaves just like a Hibernate SessionFactory. The use of this class is recommended for most Spring-Hibernate applications, from single database applications to those requiring distributed two-phase commit (2PC) transactions.

Notice that the data source previously declared is injected as we have seen before with other dependencies. To load the Hibernate HBM XML files, which are assumed to be located alongside the classes they map in the com.integrallis.techconf.domain package, we could list each individual HBM file in a property of type mappingResources, but instead I'm opting for a less verbose approach by telling the bean to scan the classpath at a certain location (given by the value classpath:/com/Integrallis/techconf/domain) for all HBM files.

Listing 6-13. *Hibernate SessionFactory Configuration*

```
<!-- ==================================================================== -->
<!-- Hibernate SessionFactory                                             -->
<!-- ==================================================================== -->
<bean id="sessionFactory"
    class="org.springframework.orm.hibernate3.LocalSessionFactoryBean">
    <property name="dataSource">
        <ref local="dataSource"/>
    </property>

    <property name="mappingDirectoryLocations">
        <list>
            <value>classpath:/com/integrallis/techconf/domain</value>
        </list>
    </property>

    <property name="hibernateProperties">
        <props>
            <prop key="hibernate.dialect">${hibernate.dialect}</prop>
            <prop key="hibernate.show_sql">${hibernate.show_sql}</prop>
            <prop key="hibernate.cglib.use_reflection_optimizer">true</prop>
        </props>
    </property>
</bean>
```

Finally, we configure other Hibernate properties via the hibernateProperties property, which allows us to pass arbitrary name-value pairs of properties to the underlying SessionFactory. In this case the properties hibernate.dialect and hibernate.show_sql are defined in the jdbc.properties file for convenience. We now have a Hibernate SessionFactory available to any bean in our Spring application.

Implementing the DAO Pattern with Spring

As we learned in Chapter 5, we could have easily created our DAO implementations by injecting the Hibernate SessionFactory into the DAOs and creating a session using the openSession method of the SessionFactory and reusing the session for the life of the DAO, thus avoiding the new-session-per-operation antipattern.

Spring provides the HibernateTemplate utility class to deal with the managing of Hibernate Session instances in the context of the current thread (similar to what SessionFactory method getCurrentSession does in a JTA environment) and handling conversion of the fairly fine-grained Hibernate exception hierarchy to the more manageable (from an application's point of view) Spring DAO exception hierarchy.

The HibernateTemplate implements the Hibernate Session interface wrapping the thread-bound Hibernate Session or creating one when necessary. Spring's HibernateTemplate is an application of IoC to simplify interaction with Hibernate. Using Spring template objects will reduce the amount of code required in your DAOs (especially if compared to the typical DAO implementation using Hibernate 2.X) since it removes the need to close the session and catch the (typically fatal) data access exceptions.

To configure a Hibernate Template bean we inject the previously configured `SessionFactory` as shown in Listing 6-14.

Listing 6-14. *Configuring the Spring `HibernateTemplate`*

```
<!-- ==================================================================== -->
<!-- Spring's HibernateTemplate                                           -->
<!-- ==================================================================== -->
<bean id="hibernateTemplate"
    class="org.springframework.orm.hibernate3.HibernateTemplate">
    <property name="sessionFactory"><ref bean="sessionFactory"/></property>
</bean>
```

The `HibernateTemplate` will be injected into the DAO implementations, which will extend the `HibernateDAOSupport` base class that provides convenience methods for Hibernate-based DAOs. As we did in Chapter 5, I'm using a base abstract DAO class to simplify the concrete implementations of the DAO interfaces. The TechConf Spring-Hibernate `BaseAbstractDAO` as shown in Listing 6-15 shows the usage of the `HibernateTemplate` available within the `HibernateDAOSupport` base class.

Listing 6-15. *Spring-Hibernate `BaseAbstractDAO`*

```
package com.integrallis.techconf.spring.dao;

import java.io.Serializable;
import java.util.List;

import org.hibernate.criterion.DetachedCriteria;
import org.hibernate.criterion.Expression;
import org.hibernate.criterion.Order;
import org.springframework.dao.support.DataAccessUtils;
import org.springframework.orm.hibernate3.support.HibernateDaoSupport;

public class BaseAbstractDAO extends HibernateDaoSupport {

    protected Object getEntityById(Class clazz, Serializable id) {
        return getHibernateTemplate().get(clazz, id);
    }

    protected void saveEntity(Object entity) {
        getHibernateTemplate().persist(entity);
    }

    protected void saveOrUpdateEntity(Object entity) {
        getHibernateTemplate().saveOrUpdate(entity);
    }
```

```
protected void updateEntity(Object entity) {
    getHibernateTemplate().update(entity);
}

protected void deleteEntity(Object entity) {
    getHibernateTemplate().delete(entity);
}

protected void deleteEntityById(Class clazz, Serializable id) {
    Object entity = getEntityById(clazz, id);
    if (entity != null) {
        deleteEntity(entity);
    }
}

protected List findAll(Class clazz) {
    return getHibernateTemplate().loadAll(clazz);
}

protected List findAll(Class clazz, String orderBy) {
    return getHibernateTemplate().findByCriteria(
            DetachedCriteria.forClass(clazz).addOrder(Order.asc(orderBy)));
}

protected List findFiltered(Class clazz, String property, Object filter) {
    return getHibernateTemplate().findByCriteria(
            DetachedCriteria.forClass(clazz).add(
                    Expression.eq(property, filter)));
}

protected List findFiltered(Class clazz, String property,
                            Object filter, String orderBy) {
    return getHibernateTemplate().findByCriteria(
            DetachedCriteria.forClass(clazz).add(
                    Expression.eq(property, filter)).addOrder(
                    Order.asc(orderBy)));
}

protected Object findUniqueFiltered(Class clazz, String property,
                                    Object filter) {
    return DataAccessUtils.requiredUniqueResult(getHibernateTemplate()
            .findByCriteria(
                    DetachedCriteria.forClass(clazz).add(
                            Expression.eq(property, filter))));
}

protected Object findUniqueFiltered(Class clazz, String property,
                                    Object filter, String orderBy) {
```

```
        return DataAccessUtils.requiredUniqueResult(getHibernateTemplate()
            .findByCriteria(
                    DetachedCriteria.forClass(clazz).add(
                            Expression.eq(property, filter)).addOrder(
                            Order.asc(orderBy))));
    }

}
```

Finally, implementing a concrete DAO becomes almost trivial. For example, in Listing 6-16 we have the DAO interface related to the Conference domain object.

Listing 6-16. *The ConferenceDAO Interface*

```
public interface ConferenceDAO {
    Conference getConference(int conferenceId);
    Conference getConferenceByName(String name);
    List<Conference> getActiveConferences(Date beginDate, Date endDate);
    List<Conference> getActiveConferences(Date date);
    List<Conference> getAllConferences();
    List<Room> getRooms(int venueId);

    void save(Conference conference);
    void update(Conference conference);
    void delete(Conference conference);
    void delete(int conferenceId);
}
```

Using the BaseAbstractDAO, our concrete DAO implementation becomes fairly simple to understand and maintain, as shown in Listing 6-17.

Listing 6-17. *The ConferenceDAO Spring-Hibernate Implementation*

```
package com.integrallis.techconf.spring.dao;

...

public class ConferenceDAOImpl extends BaseAbstractDAO implements ConferenceDAO {

    public ConferenceDAOImpl() {}

    public Conference getConference(int conferenceId) {
        return (Conference) getEntityById(Conference.class, conferenceId);
    }

    public Conference getConferenceByName(String name) {
        return (Conference) findUniqueFiltered(Conference.class,
                                        Conference.PROP_NAME, name);
    }
```

```java
@SuppressWarnings("unchecked")
public List<Conference> getActiveConferences(Date beginDate, Date endDate) {
    return getHibernateTemplate().findByCriteria(
            DetachedCriteria.forClass(Conference.class).add(
                    Restrictions.between(Conference.PROP_START_DATE,
                            beginDate, endDate)).add(
                    Restrictions.between(Conference.PROP_END_DATE,
                            beginDate, endDate)));
}

@SuppressWarnings("unchecked")
public List<Conference> getActiveConferences(Date date) {
    return getHibernateTemplate().findByCriteria(
            DetachedCriteria.forClass(Conference.class)
        .add( Restrictions.le(Conference.PROP_START_DATE, date))
        .add( Restrictions.ge(Conference.PROP_END_DATE, date)));
}

public void save(Conference conference) {
    saveEntity(conference);
}

public void update(Conference conference) {
    updateEntity(conference);
}

public void delete(Conference conference) {
    deleteEntity(conference);
}

public void delete(int conferenceId) {
    deleteEntityById(Conference.class, conferenceId);
}

@SuppressWarnings("unchecked")
public List<Conference> getAllConferences() {
    return findAll(Conference.class);
}

@SuppressWarnings("unchecked")
public List<Room> getRooms(int venueId) {
    return findFiltered(Room.class, "Venue.Id", venueId);
}
}
```

Finally, in the Spring application context we need to declare the DAO bean and inject the `hibernateTemplate` previously defined as shown in Listing 6-18.

Listing 6-18. *Wiring the conferenceDAO Bean*

```
<bean id="conferenceDAO"
      class="com.integrallis.techconf.spring.dao.ConferenceDAOImpl">
    <property name="hibernateTemplate">
        <ref bean="hibernateTemplate"/>
    </property>
</bean>
```

■**Tip** For those applications making use of Hibernate in the view of a Web application via Spring-Hibernate DAOs, Spring provides a solution to the possible problem of accessing a persistent object that has only been partially loaded—the dreaded lazy loading and closed session exceptions that can baffle developers new to Hibernate and Spring. This is not a concern for the TechConf application since we are using completely detached DTOs between the Web and service tiers. For those choosing to expose domain objects with lazy loading of associations in the view, Spring provides an implementation of the "Open Session In View" strategy proposed by the Hibernate Team which basically enables a session to be opened to retrieved associated objects lazily. This strategy is based on servlet filters and AOP interception. Spring provides a servlet filter in the class `OpenSessionInViewFilter`, which is of course configured in the Web deployment descriptor and the `OpenSessionInViewInterceptor`, which can be configured from within a Spring application context. Both serve the same function, as they open a Hibernate Session during the request, binding the Session to the current thread.

With the DAO layer completed, now we can move to wire the rest of the collaborators required by the TechConf services. Hibernate provides a powerful ORM framework, and Spring adds value by reducing and simplifying the amount of plumbing code required to use Hibernate.

Implementing DTO Pattern with DynaDTO

Implementing the DTO pattern using DynaDTO is fairly easy since DynaDTO provides a convenient class for Spring integration in the `LocalBuilderFactoryBean`. The `LocalBuilderFactoryBean` is configured in a similar fashion to the Hibernate `LocalSessionFactoryBean` class seen in the previous section.

Listing 6-19 shows the Spring configuration for DynaDTO assuming that the DTO mappings (.dto.xml files) are located in the WEB-INF/dynadto directory of the Web application WAR.

Listing 6-19. *Configuring DynaDTO in Spring*

```
<!-- ===================================================================== -->
<!-- DynaDTO BuilderFactory                                                 -->
<!-- ===================================================================== -->
<bean id="builderFactory" class="org.dynadto.spring.LocalBuilderFactoryBean">
    <property name="mappingDirectoryLocations">
        <list>
            <value>/WEB-INF/dynadto</value>
        </list>
    </property>
</bean>
```

To make use of the DynaDTO builder factory in your beans, simply create a field that will hold the builder factory and corresponding getter and setter as shown next:

```
// DynaDTO BuilderFactory
private BuilderFactory builderFactory;

public BuilderFactory getBuilderFactory() {
    return builderFactory;
}

public void setBuilderFactory(BuilderFactory builderFactory) {
    this.builderFactory = builderFactory;
}
```

Then, simply inject the builder factory into the bean at configuration time using the property element as shown next:

```
<property name="builderFactory"><ref bean="builderFactory"/></property>
```

Implementing Service Layer for TechConf

With the foundation now in place we can put together the service layer for the TechConf application using Spring. We will, of course, reuse the service interfaces already created for the EJB3 implementation in Chapter 5. Let's implement a few of the conference-related methods in the ConferenceService interface as shown in Listing 6-20.

Listing 6-20. *ConferenceService Interface*

```
List<ConferenceSummary> getActiveConferences();
List<ConferenceSummary> getAllConferences();
ConferenceSummary getConferenceSummary(int conferenceId);
List<RoomInfo> getRooms(int venueId);
```

First we'll start with simple POJO implementing the `ConferenceService` interface. This implementation will need a field to hold the required DAOs, DynaDTO factory, and builder objects. We initialize the DynaDTO builders in a method called `initialization` (you can use any name you prefer since this will be configured in the Spring application context). The typical implementation of our service read-only methods is fairly simple; first we retrieve that data required in the form of Hibernate-mapped POJOs and then use the DynaDTO builders to create the DTOs that are exposed to the service's clients as shown in Listing 6-21.

Listing 6-21. *ConferenceService Spring Implementation*

```
public class ConferenceServiceImpl implements ConferenceService {

    // DAOs
    protected ConferenceDAO conferenceDAO;
    ...

    // DynaDTO BuilderFactory
    private BuilderFactory builderFactory;

    // DynaDTO Builders
    protected Builder conferenceBuilder;
    protected Builder roomBuilder;
    ...

    public void initialization() {
        // constructs the DynaDTO builders
        conferenceBuilder = builderFactory.getBuilder(ConferenceSummary.class);
        roomBuilder = builderFactory.getBuilder(RoomInfo.class);
    }

    public ConferenceSummary getConferenceSummary(int conferenceId) {
        Conference conference = conferenceDAO.getConference(conferenceId);

        ConferenceSummary conferenceSummary = null;
        if (conference != null) {
            conferenceSummary =
                (ConferenceSummary) conferenceBuilder.build(conference);
        }
        return conferenceSummary;
    }
```

```
@SuppressWarnings("unchecked")
public List<ConferenceSummary> getActiveConferences() {
    List<Conference> entities = conferenceDAO.getActiveConferences(new Date());
    return conferenceBuilder.buildList(entities);
}

@SuppressWarnings("unchecked")
public List<ConferenceSummary> getAllConferences() {
    List<Conference> entities = conferenceDAO.getAllConferences();
    return conferenceBuilder.buildList(entities);
}

@SuppressWarnings("unchecked")
public List<RoomInfo> getRooms(int venueId) {
    List<Room> entities = conferenceDAO.getRooms(venueId);
    return roomBuilder.buildList(entities);
}
...
}
```

Finally, to glue everything together at runtime we need to tell the Spring IoC container how to wire the service bean. This can be accomplished with the bean configuration shown in Listing 6-22. We define the bean with an id of "conferenceServiceTarget" that will be backed by the concrete class ConferenceServiceImpl as a prototype bean and upon instantiation the method "initialization" will be invoked. In the body of the bean definition we inject the DAOs and the DynaDTO builder factory.

Listing 6-22. *Wiring the conferenceServiceTarget Bean with Spring*

```
<bean id="conferenceServiceTarget"
    class="com.integrallis.techconf.spring.service.ConferenceServiceImpl"
    singleton="false"
    init-method="initialization">
    <property name="conferenceDAO"><ref bean="conferenceDAO"/></property>
    ...
    <property name="builderFactory"><ref bean="builderFactory"/></property>
</bean>
```

Spring provides powerful transaction demarcation capabilities that can be transparently applied to any POJO without forgoing the power of any available transactional engine that might be available (such as a JTA transaction manager).

In Listing 6-22 you probably noticed that we named the bean "conferenceServiceTarget". This was done in order to have a bean named "conferenceService", which uses the Spring TransactionProxyFactoryBean to wrap the "conferenceServiceTarget" and provide transactional capabilities as shown in Listing 6-23.

Listing 6-23. *Wiring the conferenceService Bean with Spring*

```
<bean
    id="conferenceService"
    class="org.springframework.transaction.interceptor.TransactionProxyFactoryBean"
    >
    <property name="transactionManager"><ref bean="transactionManager"/></property>
    <property name="target"><ref bean="conferenceServiceTarget"/></property>
    <property name="transactionAttributes">
        <props>
            <prop key="get*">PROPAGATION_REQUIRED,readOnly</prop>
            <prop key="submit*">PROPAGATION_REQUIRED</prop>
        </props>
    </property>
</bean>
```

In Listing 6-23 the bean conferenceService is an example of how to apply transaction demarcation to your bean methods declaratively. Although Spring provides both programmatic and declarative transaction management capabilities, it is recommended that you use declarative transactions for maximum flexibility and simpler code. For the conferenceService bean we are saying that for all methods whose name start with "get", we will apply "readOnly" semantics, which provides a "hint" to the underlying transaction manager that can lead to runtime optimizations. We define the propagation behavior (whether to use, support/join, or create a new transaction) as PROPAGATION_REQUIRED, which means that the method will support the current transaction or create a new one if there is no transaction in context. PROPAGATION_REQUIRED is the most commonly used behavior and provides a pretty portable default choice for your transactions.

There are more advanced features that can be applied to your transactions, such as timeouts and whether to rollback a transaction based on a given exception. Those features are out of the scope of this chapter, but you should investigate, especially if your application has complex transactional requirements like multiple distributed data sources or requirements on sometimes faulty third-party network services.

The transactionManager property points to a bean of the same id. Spring offers several transaction managers to choose from, including a simple JDBC, JTA, and in the case of the TechConf application, the HibernateTransactionManager (for Hibernate version 3 as implied by the package name) shown in the bean configuration in Listing 6-24.

Listing 6-24. *Declaring the Transaction Manager*

```
<bean id="transactionManager"
      class="org.springframework.orm.hibernate3.HibernateTransactionManager">
    <property name="sessionFactory"><ref local="sessionFactory"/></property>
</bean>
```

The HibernateTransactionManager is an implementation of Spring's PlatformTransactionManager, which taps into Hibernate transaction API and works in conjunction with any Session retrieved using Hibernate's SessionFactory getCurrentSession method (as done in Chapter 5 DAO implementations) or by using the HibernateTemplate (as done in the Spring DAO implementations).

Sending Email

The Spring Framework provides a simple facility for sending email from a Java application. The MailSender interface provides a simple interface for sending an email message or a collection of email messages.

Listing 6-25 shows how simple it is to send an email message with Spring by using a MailSender implementation.

Listing 6-25. *Sending Email with Spring*

```
package com.integrallis.techconf.spring.service;

import java.util.List;

import org.springframework.mail.MailException;
import org.springframework.mail.MailSender;
import org.springframework.mail.SimpleMailMessage;

import com.integrallis.techconf.service.MailService;
import com.integrallis.techconf.service.exception.ServiceException;

public class MailServiceImpl implements MailService {

    private MailSender mailSender;

    public void sendEmail(String to, String from, String subject, String text)
            throws ServiceException {
        SimpleMailMessage message = new SimpleMailMessage();
        message.setTo(to);
        message.setFrom(from);
        message.setSubject(subject);
        message.setText(text);
        try{
            mailSender.send(message);
        }
        catch(MailException mex) {
            throw new ServiceException("Problem sending email", mex);
        }
    }
```

```java
    public void sendEmail(List<String> recipients, String from, String subject,
            String text) throws ServiceException {
        SimpleMailMessage message = new SimpleMailMessage();
        message.setTo(recipients.toArray(new String[0]));
        message.setFrom(from);
        message.setSubject(subject);
        message.setText(text);
        try{
            mailSender.send(message);
        }
        catch(MailException mex) {
            throw new ServiceException("Problem sending email", mex);
        }
    }

    public void setMailSender(MailSender mailSender) {
        this.mailSender = mailSender;
    }

}
```

To configure the MailSender instance we use the bean definition shown in Listing 6-26.

Listing 6-26. *Configuring Spring's MailSender*

```xml
<!-- ================================================================= -->
<!-- JavaMail Sender                                                   -->
<!-- ================================================================= -->

<bean id="mailSender"
    class="org.springframework.mail.javamail.JavaMailSenderImpl">
    <property name="username"><value>techconf@gmail.com</value></property>
    <property name="password"><value>PASSWORD</value></property>
    <property name="protocol"><value>smtp</value></property>
    <property name="host"><value>smtp.gmail.com</value></property>
    <property name="port"><value>465</value></property>
    <property name="javaMailProperties">
        <props>
            <prop key="mail.store.protocol">pop3</prop>
            <prop key="mail.transport.protocol">smtp</prop>
            <prop key="mail.user">techconf@gmail.com</prop>
            <prop key="mail.pop3.host">pop.gmail.com</prop>
            <prop key="mail.smtp.host">smtp.gmail.com</prop>
            <prop key="mail.smtp.port">465</prop>
            <prop key="mail.smtp.user">techconf@gmail.com</prop>
            <prop key="mail.smtp.password">PASSWORD</prop>
            <prop key="mail.smtp.auth">true</prop>
            <prop key="mail.smtp.starttls.enable">true</prop>
```

```
            <prop key="mail.from">noreply@techconf.org</prop>
            <prop key="mail.debug">true</prop>
            <prop
                key="mail.smtp.socketFactory.class">javax.net.ssl.SSLSocketFactory
            </prop>
            <prop key="mail.smtp.socketFactory.port">465</prop>
        </props>
    </property>
</bean>
```

The configuration shown in Listing 6-26 also shows how to pass more specific JavaMail properties. In the example, the extra properties are required to properly configure a Google Gmail account to be used for the application.

Spring MVC

The Spring Framework integrates well with many frameworks, including simple servlets and JSPs, Struts, JSF, WebWork, Tapestry, and its own MVC implementation Spring MVC. Spring MVC is a simpler implementation of MVC that provides a way to plug in several view technologies such as Struts, WebWork, Tapestry, or simple JSPs as shown in the simple example earlier in the chapter.

In the MVC implementation provided by Spring, the model is not abstracted away as in the case of Struts and its ActionForm, but it can be any simple POJO (a DTO or a domain object). All model objects are stored in a simple map structure. The controller prepares the model map for the view to pull data from and for forming backing objects to modify data in the model.

Creating an MVC Controller

Let's start by creating the entry page for the Techconf system, in which we will list the available conferences. First we start by implementing the controller class, ListConferenceController as shown in Listing 6-27.

Listing 6-27. *ListConferencesController Class*

```
package com.integrallis.techconf.spring.web;

import java.util.List;

import javax.servlet.http.HttpServletRequest;
import javax.servlet.http.HttpServletResponse;

import org.springframework.web.servlet.ModelAndView;
import org.springframework.web.servlet.mvc.AbstractController;

import com.integrallis.techconf.dto.ConferenceSummary;
import com.integrallis.techconf.service.ConferenceService;
```

```
public class ListConferencesController extends AbstractController {

    protected ModelAndView handleRequestInternal(HttpServletRequest request,
            HttpServletResponse response) throws Exception {

        List<ConferenceSummary> conferences = conferenceService
                .getAllConferences();

        return new ModelAndView("conferenceList", "conferences", conferences);
    }

    private ConferenceService conferenceService;

    public void setConferenceService(ConferenceService conferenceService) {
        this.conferenceService = conferenceService;
    }
}
```

This class extends Spring's AbstractController, which in turn implements the Controller interface. A controller implementation is responsible for handling, in a thread-safe manner, an HttpServletRequest and ultimately return a ModelAndView object. A ModelAndView object is a construct that groups the model and view together so that a controller can return them as a single return value. AbstractController provides caching, session synchronization, and method filters and is a convenient base class for your controller implementations. Spring provided other controller implementations such as the ParameterizedViewController, FileNameViewController and MultiActionController.

The bulk of the controller implementation lies in the development of the handleRequestInternal method, which follows servlet semantics by taking an HttpServletRequest and HttpServletResponse objects as parameters. The implementation of the ListConferencesController uses an instance of the ConferenceService to retrieve a list of ConferenceSummary DTOs using the method getAllConferences. The list of DTOs is passed to the constructor of the ModelAndView class under the identifier "conferences" as seen in the second and third parameters of the constructor call.

To be able to use ConferenceService we need to provide a field to hold an instance of the previously configured service and a setter that we will use to inject the service via the application context. Listing 6-28 shows the definition of listConferencesController that is implemented by class ListConferencesController shown in Listing 6-27 and for which we are injecting the previously created conferenceService bean.

Listing 6-28. *ListConferencesController Bean Definition*

```
<bean id="listConferencesController"
    class="com.integrallis.techconf.spring.web.ListConferencesController">
    <property name="conferenceService"><ref bean="conferenceService"/></property>
</bean>
```

Creating a JSP View

With the controller configured, we can turn our attention to the view. The first parameter on the constructor call for ModelAndView is the name of the view, which will be resolved by the framework's view resolver. Alternatively, the ModelAndView can also be constructed with a reference to a view object. The conferenceList view is represented by the conferenceList.jsp page shown in Listing 6-29. All JSP pages are stored in a directory named jsp under the WEB-INF Web application directory.

Listing 6-29. *JSP View conferenceList.jsp*

```
<%@ page contentType="text/html; charset=UTF-8" %>
<%@ taglib uri="http://java.sun.com/jsp/jstl/core" prefix="c" %>

<p>Currently Available Conferences</p>
<ul>
  <c:forEach var="conference" items="${conferences}">
    <li>
      <a href="displayConference.htm?id=${conference.conferenceId}">
      ${conference.conferenceTitle}
      </a>
    </li>
  </c:forEach>
</ul>
```

In the conferenceList.jsp page we use core JSTL forEach tag to iterate over the list of ConferenceSummary DTOs (accessed as ${conferences}). For each object we are creating a link that points to the displayConference.html page, displays the conferenceTitle, and passes the conferenceId field as the parameter id.

Using Tiles

For the TechConf application we will configure the view resolution using the Tiles framework. In a typical website you'll have common elements to every page such as the header, footer, and navigation menu. Tiles is a framework that enables the usage of template layouts and reusability of common elements for JSP-based Web applications. Spring MVC integrates with the Tiles seamlessly. In Listing 6-30 shows the configuration elements in the application context needed to configure and use Tiles.

Listing 6-30. *View Resolution Strategy Using Tiles*

```
<!-- ==================================================================== -->
<!-- View Resolution using Tiles                                          -->
<!-- ==================================================================== -->

<bean id="tilesConfigurer"
    class="org.springframework.web.servlet.view.tiles.TilesConfigurer">
    <property name="definitions">
        <list>
            <value>/WEB-INF/tiles-defs.xml</value>
        </list>
    </property>
</bean>

<bean id="viewResolver"
    class="org.springframework.web.servlet.view.InternalResourceViewResolver">
    <property name="viewClass">
        <value>org.springframework.web.servlet.view.tiles.TilesView</value>
    </property>
</bean>
```

The `tilesConfigurer` bean backed by an instance of `TilesConfigurer` is used to configure objects representing one or more Tiles views. In Listing 6-30 we load a tiles definition contained in the file tiles-defs.xml, which is located in the WEB-INF directory of the Web application. Before we take a look a the tiles configuration, let's create a simple template in the form of a JSP. The simple template, template.jsp, is shown in Listing 6-31.

Listing 6-31. *A Simple Tiles JSP Template*

```
<%@ taglib uri="/WEB-INF/struts-tiles.tld" prefix="tiles" %>
<html>
  <head>
    <title>TechConf - <tiles:getAsString name="pageTitle"/></title>
    <link rel="stylesheet" type="text/css" href="css/style.css"/>
  </head>
  <body>
    <h1><a href="index.html" style="color: #E9601A">TechConf</a></h1>
    <p id="titleblock" style="font-size: larger;">
        <tiles:getAsString name="pageTitle"/>
    </p>
    <tiles:insert attribute="body"/>
  </body>
</html>
```

As shown in Listing 6-31, a Tiles JSP uses Tiles tags to insert attributes into the template page. The tiles-defs.xml file shown in Listing 6-32 contains a single definition for the view conferenceList, which uses the template (template.jsp) as the frame for the page. Inside the definition element we define the value to be inserted for the property pageTitle and more importantly the value to be used for the body property defined in the template, which corresponds to the conferenceList.jsp page previously created.

Listing 6-32. *Tiles Definition File*

```
<!DOCTYPE tiles-definitions PUBLIC
    "-//Apache Software Foundation//DTD Tiles Configuration 1.1//EN"
    "http://jakarta.apache.org/struts/dtds/tiles-config_1_1.dtd">

<tiles-definitions>
  <definition name="conferenceList" page="/WEB-INF/jsp/template.jsp">
    <put name="pageTitle" value="Conferences" />
    <put name="body" value="/WEB-INF/jsp/conferenceList.jsp" />
  </definition>
  ...
</tiles-definitions>
```

The second bean shown in Listing 6-30 is the viewResolver bean, which tells Spring MVC to use a TilesView, which is a view implementation corresponding to a Tiles definition. This resolution strategy takes the URL as the name of the Tiles definition. The viewResolver bean depends implicitly on the Tiles DefinitionsFactory object which was also implicitly created via the tilesConfigurer bean.

Configuring the Web Deployment

Before we test the first page of the TechConf Spring application, we need to configure the Web deployment descriptor web.xml. This web.xml descriptor will be a little more involved than the previous one created for a simple introductory example. As mentioned previously and outlined in Figure 6-5, the Spring application context for the TechConf application has been modularized into three separate XML files, one per application tier. Listing 6-33 shows the Web deployment descriptor for the TechConf application. The "contextConfigLocation" property is the location of the Spring beans application context files. By default, Spring loads the application context "techconf-servlet.xml"; therefore we only need to load the two remaining application contexts for the data and service tiers.

Listing 6-33. *Web Deployment Descriptor for TechConf Spring Application*

```
<?xml version="1.0" encoding="ISO-8859-1"?>

<web-app xmlns="http://java.sun.com/xml/ns/j2ee"
    xmlns:xsi="http://www.w3.org/2001/XMLSchema-instance"
    xsi:schemaLocation="http://java.sun.com/xml/ns/j2ee web-app_2_4.xsd"
    version="2.4">
```

```xml
<!-- ================================================================ -->
<!-- Load Spring application context files                            -->
<!-- ================================================================ -->
<context-param>
  <param-name>contextConfigLocation</param-name>
  <param-value>
  /WEB-INF/techconf-service.xml,/WEB-INF/techconf-data.xml
  </param-value>
</context-param>


<!-- ================================================================ -->
<!-- Load Spring Log4J configuration                                 -->
<!-- ================================================================ -->
<context-param>
  <param-name>log4jConfigLocation</param-name>
  <param-value>/WEB-INF/log4j.properties</param-value>
</context-param>


<!-- ================================================================ -->
<!-- Listeners                                                       -->
<!-- ================================================================ -->
<listener>
  <listener-class>
  org.springframework.web.util.Log4jConfigListener
  </listener-class>
</listener>

<listener>
  <listener-class>
  org.springframework.web.context.ContextLoaderListener
  </listener-class>
</listener>


<!-- ================================================================ -->
<!-- Configure TechConf servlet as Spring's DispatcherServlet        -->
<!-- ================================================================ -->
<servlet>
  <servlet-name>techconf</servlet-name>
  <servlet-class>org.springframework.web.servlet.DispatcherServlet</servlet-class>
  <load-on-startup>1</load-on-startup>
</servlet>
```

```
<servlet-mapping>
  <servlet-name>techconf</servlet-name>
  <url-pattern>*.htm</url-pattern>
</servlet-mapping>
```

```
</web-app>
```

In the Web deployment descriptor we are also configuring Log4J. The "log4jConfigLocation" is one of the parameters used to configure the Log4jWebConfigurer, which is a utility class that enables Log4J initialization in a Web container, keeping log files within the Web application (for expanded WAR deployments) and the ability to check for live changes to the logging configuration. For the TechConf application the configuration file log4j.properties is located under the WEB-INF directory (to use Log4J you'll also need the Log4J JARs).

Mapping URLs to Controllers

Listing 6-34 shows the urlMapping bean in the Spring application context for the Web tier. To expose your application pages using a simple HTML extension, we map simple .htm files to our controllers.

Listing 6-34. *URL Mappings in Application Context for the Web Tier*

```
<!-- ===================================================================== -->
<!-- URL Mappings                                                          -->
<!-- ===================================================================== -->

<bean id="urlMapping"
    class="org.springframework.web.servlet.handler.SimpleUrlHandlerMapping">
    <property name="mappings">
        <props>
            <prop key="/displayConference.htm">
            displayConferenceController
            </prop>
            <prop key="/listConferences.htm">listConferencesController</prop>
            ...
        </props>
    </property>
    ...
</bean>
```

After building and deploying the application you can access the first page by using the URL http://localhost:8080/techconf-spring/listConferences.htm. The output should resemble that shown in Figure 6-6.

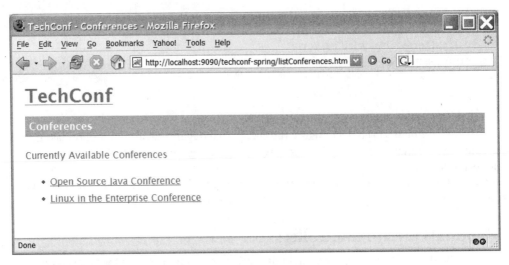

Figure 6-6. *The listConferences page of the Spring TechConf application*

The resulting HTML for the listConference page is shown in Listing 6-35.

Listing 6-35. *HTML Generated for the listConferences Page*

```html
<html>
  <head>
    <title>TechConf - Conferences</title>
    <link rel="stylesheet" type="text/css" href="css/style.css"/>
  </head>
  <body>
    <h1><a href="index.html" style="color: #E9601A">TechConf</a></h1>
    <p id="titleblock" style="font-size: larger;">Conferences</p>
    <p>Currently Available Conferences</p>
    <ul>
      <li><a href="displayConference.htm?id=1">Open Source Java Conference</a></li>
      <li>
        <a href="displayConference.htm?id=2">
        Linux in the Enterprise Conference
        </a>
      </li>
    </ul>
  </body>
</html>
```

Page Navigation and Parameter Passing

With the listConferences page in place, we can move to the development of the conferenceDetail page. In this page we will show a summary of the selected conference. For this example we work through setting the Tiles template for the rest of the application and show how to handle the transition from the listConference page to the detail view of a chosen conference.

For the rest of the pages in the application, a more elaborate template will be used. This template is conferenceTemplate.jsp as shown in Listing 6-36.

Listing 6-36. *JSP Template for All Conference Pages*

```
<%@ taglib uri="/WEB-INF/struts-tiles.tld" prefix="tiles" %>
<%@ taglib uri="http://java.sun.com/jsp/jstl/core" prefix="c" %>
<%@ taglib uri="http://java.sun.com/jsp/jstl/fmt" prefix="fmt" %>

<html>
  <head>
    <title>TechConf - <tiles:getAsString name="pageTitle"/></title>
    <link rel="stylesheet" type="text/css" href="css/style.css"/>
  </head>
  <body>
    <h1><a href="index.html" style="color: #E9601A">TechConf</a></h1>
    <p id="titleblock" style="font-size: larger;">
      <tiles:getAsString name="pageTitle"/>
    </p>
    <div id="header" class="borderedBlock">
     <table width="100%">
      <tr>
        <td>
          <h1>${conference.conferenceTitle}</h1>
        </td>
      </tr>
      <tr>
       <td>
         <!-- dates and locale -->
         <h5>
           <fmt:formatDate value="${conference.startDate}"
                           type="date"
                           dateStyle="full"/> -
           <fmt:formatDate value="${conference.endDate}"
                           type="date"
                           dateStyle="full"/> -
           <c:out value="${conference.venueAddressLine1}"/> ,
           <c:out value="${conference.venueAddressLine2}"/> -
           <c:out value="${conference.venuePhone}"/>
         </h5>
       </td>
      </tr>
     </table>
    </div>
```

```
    <table width="100%">
      <tbody>
        <tr>
          <th style="width: 20%; text-align: justify;"
              id="left" class="borderedBlock">
          <a href="index.html">Home</a><br>
          <a href="listKeynotes.htm?id=${conference.conferenceId}">Keynotes</a><br>
          <a href="listSpeakers.htm?id=${conference.conferenceId}">Speakers</a><br>
          <a href="listSessions.htm?id=${conference.conferenceId}">Sessions</a><br>
          <a href="listBlogs.htm?id=${conference.conferenceId}">Blogs</a><br>
          Schedule<br>
          </th>
          <td id="body" class="borderedBlock"><tiles:insert attribute="body"/></td>
        </tr>
      </tbody>
    </table>
    <div id="footer" class="borderedBlock">
     Copyright&copy; <a href="http://www.integrallis.com">
     Integrallis Software, LLC
     </a>.
    </div>
  </body>
</html>
```

This template handles the main navigation for the application and displays the date and location (venue) or the given conference. In the Tiles definition file we add the definition for the conferenceDetail page using the template conferenceTemplate.jsp as shown next:

```
<definition name="conferenceDetail" page="/WEB-INF/jsp/conferenceTemplate.jsp">
  <put name="pageTitle" value="Conference Detail" />
  <put name="body" value="/WEB-INF/jsp/conferenceDetail.jsp" />
</definition>
```

The controller implementation for the conferenceDetail page is shown in Listing 6-37. This controller implementation shows the retrieval of the "id" parameter that is passed from the listConferences pages. Just like with normal servlet development, the parameter is extracted from HttpServletRequest, converted to an integer, and used to retrieve a ConferenceSummary DTO from the conferenceService. The DTO is then passed to the view under the name "conference".

Listing 6-37. *DisplayConferenceController Class*

```
public class DisplayConferenceController extends AbstractController {

    public DisplayConferenceController() {
    }

    protected ModelAndView handleRequestInternal(HttpServletRequest request,
            HttpServletResponse response) throws Exception {
```

```
    int conferenceId = Integer.parseInt(request.getParameter("id"));

    ConferenceSummary conference = conferenceService
            .getConferenceSummary(conferenceId);

    return new ModelAndView("conferenceDetail", "conference", conference);
}


private ConferenceService conferenceService;

public void setConferenceService(ConferenceService conferenceService) {
    this.conferenceService = conferenceService;
}
}
```

Finally, the view conferenceDetail.jsp shows the dates for which the conference is accepting abstracts for presentation, as well as list of the tracks available for the conference. Again, as previously done, JSTL tags are used to format the dates and iterate over retrieved collections, as shown in Listing 6-38.

Listing 6-38. *JSP View for Conference Detail View (conferenceDetail.jsp)*

```
<%@ page contentType="text/html; charset=UTF-8" %>
<%@ taglib uri="http://java.sun.com/jsp/jstl/core" prefix="c" %>
<%@ taglib uri="http://java.sun.com/jsp/jstl/fmt" prefix="fmt" %>

<table width="100%">
  <tr>
    <td>
      <h4>Abstract Submissions</h4>
    </td>
  </tr>
  <tr>
    <td>
      Abstracts accepted from
      <fmt:formatDate
          value="${conference.abstractSubmissionStartDate}"
          type="date"
          dateStyle="full"
      />
      until
      <fmt:formatDate
          value="${conference.abstractSubmissionEndDate}"
          type="date"
          dateStyle="full"
      />
```

```
        </td>
      </tr>
      <tr>
        <td>
          <h4>Tracks</h4>
        </td>
      </tr>
      <tr>
        <td>
          <ul>
            <c:forEach var="track" items="${conference.tracks}">
              <li><a href="displayTrack.htm?id=${track.id}">${track.title}</a></li>
            </c:forEach>
          </ul>
        </td>
      </tr>
    </table>
```

Clicking on one of the conference links in the listConferences page navigates to the conferenceDetail page as shown in Figure 6-7.

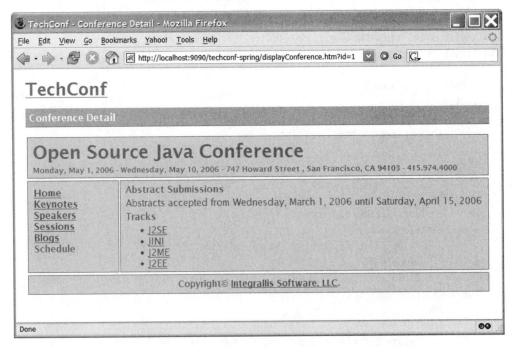

Figure 6-7. *The conferenceDetail Page of the Spring TechConf application*

Summary

In this chapter we have learned how to implement and wire together a fairly complex, database-driven Web application using the Spring Framework. Spring lets your code use POJOs and POJIs and allows you to declaratively mix and match beans to create complete applications. Using the simple yet powerful concept of Inversion of Control, the Spring Framework simplifies and reduces the amount of plumbing code required in an enterprise application.

We briefly looked at the Spring MVC framework, which should make for an easy transition from Struts (the most popular MVC framework to date). Like Struts, Spring MVC rides on top of the servlet API semantics. This chapter was intended as a light introduction to this new choice in Java Web development. To learn about Spring MVC's more advanced options, I recommend the wonderful *Pro Spring* by Rob Harrop and Jan Machacek (Apress, 2005).

Coupled with a great deal of functionality needed for most enterprise applications, Spring has become the leading application framework for Java that doesn't rely on specifications or committees but on the working experience of the Java community. If you are building Web applications, Spring can significantly improve the experience and the quality of your applications.

CHAPTER 7

■ ■ ■

Tapestry

In no other place is the diversity of the Java landscape more apparent than in the arena of Web development frameworks. The rise of the Internet as an application platform coupled with the stateless nature of the HTTP protocol gave rise to the servlet API as the workhorse API used to bring Java to the Web.

The servlet API helped formalize the usage of HTTP in Java and provide some simple constructs for dealing with the need to maintain state as required by dynamic applications. Servlets provided an initial avenue for Java on the Web. We built many pure servlet Web applications at it was soon apparent that for any application with more than a few pages and with medium to complex user interface requirements, servlets did not provide a high enough abstraction as separation of concerns between the business logic, presentation logic, and the actual view composed of HTML.

With servlet development, developers often received mocked-up HTML pages from Web designers. Form that point, developers had to extract the HTML and place it in the servlet code using `println` statements and escaping common HTML characters like double quotes. Development time was also painfully slow with servlets since code changes could not be quickly tested without complete recompilation and redeployment.

The shortcomings of the servlet API and inspiration from some of the early commercial and open source Web frameworks led to the creation of JavaServer Pages (JSP). This was a definitive improvement, especially in the area of productivity. JSPs changed the way Web applications were developed in Java. Instead of embedding HTML markup in Java, the metaphor flipped to embedding Java code in the HTML. Productivity increased because there was no longer a need to manually recompile and redeploy since JSPs are dynamically compiled into servlets on demand after a modification. Initially, JSPs seemed to solve a lot of the problems with servlet development, allowing Web designers to make ongoing changes to the HTML during the development process. Unfortunately, no good deed goes unpunished, and JSP-based applications, with their ability to embed Java code in the HTML via scriptlets, led to poor Web development practices such as placing heavy business logic in the presentation tier. In addition, JSPs didn't provide any good means of reusing the code placed in scriptlets which led to duplication of code and all of the headaches associated with copy-and-paste reuse. This is what most people refer to as JSP Model 1, in which JSP pages serve both as controllers or dispatchers and the model is accessed via beans used to communicate with back-end technologies such as EJBs. Model 1 coupled view and the dispatcher and effectively created many controllers. The problems with this approach became apparent in larger applications as the controller code grew out of proportion, rendering the almost-like-HTML JSPs to look more like pure Java code surrounded by HTML. This coupling becomes problematic for both Java developers and HTML designers.

Finally, developers realize that an old true-and-tried architectural pattern, the Model-View-Controller (MVC), was the solution to the problem of scaling and maintaining Web applications. The MVC pattern separates the data (model) from the presentation (view) and the work flow (controller). In Model 2 architectures, JSP and servlets were used in combination and taking advantage of their respective strengths. Servlets are used to dispatch the views and glue (and maybe transform) data coming from a back end such as a database or EJBs. This is the controller part of the MVC pattern providing application flow and service and resource discovery and allocation for the view generation technology, the JSP pages.

JSP/Servlet Model 2 represented a huge leap forward in terms of maintainability and development time. It allowed for separation of concerns between HTML designers and Java developers as well as between Java developers of varied skills; more-seasoned developers usually ended up writing most of the controlling code while more-junior developers deal with the JSPs. As more and more Model 2 applications were being built, many developers noticed the repetition of effort from application to application. The typical question became, how do we avoid recreating the wheel over and over again? And most developers' conclusion culminated with the creation of frameworks to provide uniform ways to deal with MVC applications and removing the need for the plumbing code.

Today we have many frameworks based on the MVC pattern, and they provided a great deal of functionality that you no longer have to create from scratch. They also standardized Web development in the Java world to an extent. The different frameworks all implement MVC in slightly different ways. Some have one chosen technology for view generation such as JSPs or some sort of template engine as Velocity, while others allow pluggable view implementations. One thing that most have in common is that although they are built on top of the servlet API, they still work under the same underlying principle of the request/response paradigm that makes your development and the resulting code very procedural. Many technologists' feelings were these frameworks help us deal with the Web as an application platform, but they have also flattened and taken away some of the power of object orientation provided by Java.

Meanwhile, a little-known framework was already providing a framework for Web development based on the MVC pattern but with components that embraced object-orientation at its core. That framework was NeXT WebObjects, which appeared in 1996 and later became Apple's WebObjects. WebObjects had a great deal of interest behind it and attracted a significant number of large players looking for a robust platform on which to build large-scale Web applications. WebObjects today remains a closed source proprietary system that until just recently had a price tag that placed it out of most developers' hands. WebObjects is a J2EE-compliant Web development framework providing more than just Web development—a suite of tools, advanced ORM, scalability, and performance features. For example, one of the largest applications running on WebObjects is Apple's iTunes Music Store.

Fortunately for most of us, an alternative as powerful and flexible as WebObjects is available from the open source community in the Jakarta Tapestry Web application framework. Tapestry began life as a SourceForge project in 2000 loosely based on the way WebObjects worked. It gained enough public acceptance to become an Apache Jakarta project in 2003.

What Is Tapestry?

Tapestry is an open source Java Web application framework created by Howard Lewis-Ship and a talented group of contributors. Tapestry is distributed under the Apache Software License version 2.0. In Tapestry, as opposed to other frameworks like Struts, you deal with components and pages (which are themselves components), and interactivity is provided via listeners which interpret the user's actions associated with a component.

A Tapestry application is made of pages. Each page consists of a template and a number of components. The templates are standard HTML pages decorated with span tags declaring the Tapestry components.

Tapestry is built on top of the servlet API, but unlike other frameworks, it completely abstracts the procedural request-response nature of the Web by allowing you to work with pages and components in a similar way that a Java Swing developer works with forms and components. As with many Web frameworks, Tapestry takes the drudgery out of common tasks and functionality like state management, input validation, localization and internationalization, and error reporting. But instead of dealing with URLs, HTTP requests, and responses, you work at a higher level of abstraction dealing with user interaction with the pages and components in an object-oriented way. As in a Swing application, components and pages know how to respond to events which are mapped from the HTML component view representation to the Java implementation.

One of the greatest strengths of Tapestry for a Web development team lies in its strong separation of concerns between Web designers and Java developers. It also brings true object-oriented development to Web applications. As a former Delphi and Swing developer, I was initially attracted to experiment with Tapestry by this factor. In Tapestry you create plain HTML pages, and using span tags or any other HTML tags, you embed Tapestry components. Tapestry allows you to use static markup in the location of the components to accurately represent the look and feel of the page at design time. These static placeholders (for example, a drop-down field) are replaced at runtime with a live Tapestry component. This allows HTML designers to work with the actual templates used by the application, guaranteeing that the responsibility for the application look stays with the designers and functionality stays with the application developers.

The components view in the HTML and any possible actions taken by a user on a component are glued together with small amounts of Java code and optionally with very simple XML configuration files. Tapestry uses the HiveMind IoC framework/microkernel under the covers to deal with resource and service configuration. We will learn more about HiveMind as we work to integrate a Tapestry Web application with an EJB3 back end. Tapestry also comes with a large collection of prepackaged components, provides good support for JavaScript (for client-side validation and interaction) and has several third-party libraries that provide AJAX-enabled components. Tapestry is a battle-tested Web framework that can be used to create scalable and robust Web applications.

Tapestry 4 Features

I ran into Tapestry late in its life. When I started using Tapestry, version 3.0 had just been released. At that point it was obvious to me that Tapestry was a robust, fully-featured Web framework.

Tapestry takes care of all the mundane and not-so-mundane tasks that Web developers face, such as URL construction, simplification and dispatching, client- and server-side state management, form input validation, localization, internationalization, and exception handling and reporting.

Version 4 of Tapestry brings even more features to an already feature-rich framework, including the following:

- **Friendly URLs:** URLs that depend more on path information and less on query parameters, which makes for cleaner-looking URLs and for easier configuration with path-based utilities like J2EE security

- **Listener Methods:** Easier configuration and syntax

- **Message Catalogs:** Component message catalogs and a global message catalog, which will be searched if a message is not found at the component level

- **Portlet Support:** Full, native support for developing JSR-168 portlets

- **Performance:** Less reliance on reflection and ONGL and more on conventions and smart configuration

- **Integration:** The ability to inject both HiveMind and Spring (see Chapter 6) service objects into Tapestry pages and components

- **Validation:** Complete overhaul of input validation, enabling complex validations using custom extensions, and providing many built-in validations

- **Annotations:** Support for Java 5.0 annotations for specifying in code certain configuration, customization, and operations that would otherwise be specified in the page or component specification

- **Error Reporting:** Line-precise error reporting that can display and highlight the exact contents of the files containing errors

- **Advanced Form Handling:** The ability to cancel forms, therefore bypassing client-side validation logic, and the ability to invoke an alternate "cancellation" listener on the server side

- **Server-side State:** In contrast to objects holding application state being limited to the old `Global` and `Visit` objects, a removal of the limit to the number of application state objects

Downloading and Configuring Tapestry

Tapestry is distributed as a ZIP file or a TAR file containing both the source and binaries from `http://jakarta.apache.org/tapestry/downloads.html`. Tapestry consists of four JAR files: tapestry-4.0.jar, tapestry-contrib-4.0.jar, tapestry-annotations-4.0.jar, and tapestry-portlet-4.0.jar.

Tapestry depends on several third-party libraries. The easiest way to obtain all the dependencies is to go to http://jakarta.apache.org/tapestry/dependencies.html and follow the links to download the required JARs from ibiblio.org. Table 7-1 shows the Tapestry 4 JARs as well as the dependencies. Alternatively, you can use the Tapestry Ant build script, which will automatically download the dependencies from ibiblio.org.

For those developers wanting to build Tapestry from scratch, instructions on how to build Tapestry can be found in the Tapestry Wiki located at http://wiki.apache.org/jakarta-tapestry/ BuildingTapestry (which requires HiveMind 1.1, Ant 1.6.2, and Java 1.5).

Your First Tapestry Application

Nothing helps when working with a new Web framework as actually building a functioning Web application. Like any other Java servlet or JSP-based framework, the deployable unit for a Tapestry application is a WAR file. Let's take a step-by-step approach at building our first Tapestry application. This application would start as a very simple single page application producing some content dynamically.

Dynamic content is what differentiates a Web application from a static website, and it means only that the information your website or application displays varies based on some conditions. Examples of dynamic content include news sites, product catalogs where entries change and users can accumulate a shopping cart of items, and online polls and statistics.

Before we get started, let's create a directory structure for the application. Figure 7-1 shows the directory structure for the tapestry-time application.

Figure 7-1. *Directory structure for simple Tapestry application*

Configuring Tapestry

To run Tapestry in a Web container you need to make the Tapestry classes and its dependencies available to the Tapestry applications. There are two ways to accomplish this. If you are running multiple Tapestry applications in the same Web container, you can place the JARs in a shared location that your Web container will make available to all deployed applications. In Tomcat 5.X, for example, this shared location is $TOMCAT_HOME/shared/lib.

The other option is to place the required JARs in the WEB-INF/lib directory, which guarantees that you can deploy the JAR to any compliant Web container without any special configuration. For this chapter we'll use the WEB-INF/lib location for the Tapestry dependencies. Table 7-1 shows the required JARs.

Table 7-1. *Tapestry JARs and Dependencies*

File	Description
tapestry-4.0.jar	Tapestry Core
tapestry-annotations-4.0.jar	Java 5 annotation support
tapestry-contrib-4.0.jar	Community contributed components
hivemind-1.1.jar	Services and configuration microkernel core
hivemind-lib-1.1.jar	Common HiveMind functionality
commons-codec-1.3.jar	Encoder implementations
commons-fileupload-1.0.jar	File uploading and multipart support
commons-logging-1.0.4.jar	Logging package
javassist-3.0.jar	Reflection and bytecode manipulation
ognl-2.6.7.jar	Object-Graph Navigation Language
oro-2.0.8.jar	Regular expression package

HTML Page

Let's start by creating a simple HTML page for our application. Tapestry page templates are regular HTML documents decorated with tags and attributes for Tapestry to replace dynamically at runtime.

The initial template for our simple application is shown in Listing 7-1.

Listing 7-1. *Tapestry Time HTML Template (Home.html)*

```
<html>
    <body>
    <h1>Tapestry Time</h1>
    The current time is <span jwcid="time">high noon</span>!
    </body>
</html>
```

Save this page template as Home.html in the context directory. Like any good framework, Tapestry follows the convention-over-configuration philosophy. At start-up time Tapestry will look for a page named "Home" and render it. (You can override this default behavior, but this is an easy convention to follow, and most Tapestry applications do so it is easy to find an application main page easily.)

The HTML document looks like any other HTML document. It is viable in any compliant Web browser and more importantly, editable in any WYSIWYG HTML editor such as HomeSite or Macromedia's Dreamweaver as shown in Figure 7-2.

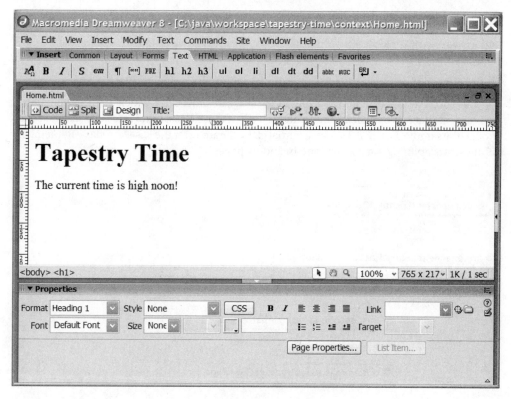

Figure 7-2. *Simple HTML page in a WYSIWYG editor*

In the Home.html template we use a span tag with an attribute jwcid attribute which stands for Java Web Component Id. There are two ways to declare Tapestry components in an HTML template: explicitly as shown in the example or implicitly by prefixing the component name with @. Implicit declarations are like anonymous inner classes in Java; you are declaring and using a component on the spot. Since we are using an explicit declaration, the meat and potatoes of the components must be defined somewhere else so that we can refer to it by name.

The Java Code

The code that will provide the backing for the component is contained in the file Home.java. The Home class provides one simple method called getTime, which returns a new java.util. Date object as shown in Listing 7-2.

Listing 7-2. *Java Class Extending BasePage, Which Implements IPage*

```
package com.integrallis.time;

import java.util.Date;

import org.apache.tapestry.html.BasePage;
```

```
public abstract class Home extends BasePage {
    public Date getTime() {
        return new Date();
    }
}
```

This abstract class extends the Tapestry BasePage abstract class, which in turn implements the IPage interface. We will learn more about both of these classes and interfaces as we work through the sample. Figure 7-3 shows a partial class hierarchy for the BasePage class. Remember, in Tapestry everything is a component, including pages.

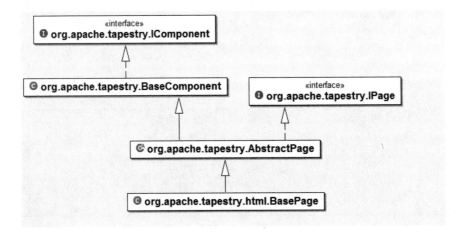

Figure 7-3. *BasePage class hierarchy*

Page XML Descriptor

The page specification file is an XML file with the extension "page". Remember, pages are a special type of Tapestry component, and this is the configuration file for the Home page component of our application. Pages can contain components, and in this case our page contains one component of type Insert. The Insert component is one of many built-in Tapestry components. Insert gives you the ability to insert text dynamically in the HTML response with the option of filtering special characters or formatting by using a java.text.Format instance. Listing 7-3 shows the contents of the Home.page file.

Listing 7-3. *The Page Specification XML File (Home.page)*

```xml
<?xml version="1.0"?>
<!DOCTYPE page-specification PUBLIC
  "-//Apache Software Foundation//Tapestry Specification 4.0//EN"
  "http://jakarta.apache.org/tapestry/dtd/Tapestry_4_0.dtd">
<page-specification class="com.integrallis.time.Home">
  <component id="time" type="Insert">
    <binding name="value" value="ognl:time"/>
  </component>
</page-specification>
```

The DTD located at `http://jakarta.apache.org/tapestry/dtd/Tapestry_4_0.dtd` gives us a clue as to what types of elements can be configured via XML in Tapestry. Figure 7-4 shows a graphical depiction of the `page-specification` element showing the detail of the `component` element.

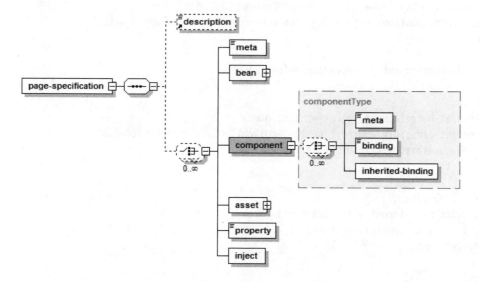

Figure 7-4. *DTD definition for the page-specification element*

The Home.page file specifies that:

- This is the page specification for a Home page as deduced by the name of the file Home.page, the associated Home.html template, and the class `com.integrallis.time.Home` as defined in the class attribute of the page-specification element.

- It defines one component with an id of "time" which is of type `Insert`.

- The component time binds the value of the expression `ognl:time` to the value of the component.

Web Deployment Descriptor

As with any Java Web application, you will need a Web deployment descriptor (web.xml) in the WEB-INF directory. As with most Web frameworks, the entry point into the framework is a servlet. In the case of Tapestry, it is `org.apache.tapestry.ApplicationServlet`. In a Tapestry application you'll name the `ApplicationServlet` after your application; in our case as shown in Listing 7-4, the `servlet-name` element values is "tapestry-time".

The first `servlet-mapping` maps to the URL pattern /app to Tapestry application servlet. The purpose of the rest of the mappings will become apparent as we work through the example. Finally, at the end of the descriptor we have the `welcome-file` element in which we are declaring the file Home.html as a welcome file. Notice that there is also a servlet mapping that maps *.html to the Tapestry application servlet.

Listing 7-4. *Web Deployment Descriptor*

```xml
<?xml version="1.0" encoding="ISO-8859-1"?>

<web-app xmlns="http://java.sun.com/xml/ns/j2ee"
    xmlns:xsi="http://www.w3.org/2001/XMLSchema-instance"
    xsi:schemaLocation="http://java.sun.com/xml/ns/j2ee web-app_2_4.xsd"
    version="2.4">

  <display-name>tapestry-time</display-name>

  <servlet>
    <servlet-name>tapestry-time</servlet-name>
    <servlet-class>org.apache.tapestry.ApplicationServlet</servlet-class>
    <load-on-startup>1</load-on-startup>
  </servlet>

  <servlet-mapping>
    <servlet-name>tapestry-time</servlet-name>
    <url-pattern>/app</url-pattern>
  </servlet-mapping>

  <servlet-mapping>
    <servlet-name>tapestry-time</servlet-name>
    <url-pattern>*.html</url-pattern>
  </servlet-mapping>

  <servlet-mapping>
    <servlet-name>tapestry-time</servlet-name>
    <url-pattern>*.external</url-pattern>
  </servlet-mapping>

  <servlet-mapping>
    <servlet-name>tapestry-time</servlet-name>
    <url-pattern>*.direct</url-pattern>
  </servlet-mapping>

  <servlet-mapping>
    <servlet-name>tapestry-time</servlet-name>
    <url-pattern>*.sdirect</url-pattern>
  </servlet-mapping>

  <servlet-mapping>
    <servlet-name>tapestry-time</servlet-name>
    <url-pattern>*.svc</url-pattern>
  </servlet-mapping>
```

```
<servlet-mapping>
  <servlet-name>tapestry-time</servlet-name>
  <url-pattern>/assets/*</url-pattern>
</servlet-mapping>

<welcome-file-list>
  <welcome-file>Home.html</welcome-file>
</welcome-file-list>

</web-app>
```

Building and Running the Example

To run the example we need to create a WAR file from the contents of the context directory. You could simply compile the code so that the class files end up in the context/WEB-INF/classes directory and then create a JAR file out of the contents of the context directory, or you could simply use the Ant buildfile in Listing 7-5.

Listing 7-5. *Ant Buildfile for the Tapestry Time Application*

```
<?xml version="1.0"?>
<project name="tapestry-time" default="package-web" basedir=".">

    <!-- =========== -->
    <!-- Directories -->
    <!-- =========== -->

    <!-- Source -->
    <property name="src" location="src" />

    <!-- Source Web Folders -->
    <property name="context" location="context" />
    <property name="web-inf" location="${context}/web-inf" />

    <!-- Build Artifact Destinations -->
    <property name="classes" location="${web-inf}/classes" />
    <property name="dist" location="dist" />

    <!-- Libraries in WEB-INF/lib -->
    <property name="lib" location="${web-inf}/lib" />

    <!-- ===== -->
    <!-- Files -->
    <!-- ===== -->

    <property name="war-filename" value="${ant.project.name}.war" />
    <property name="war-file" value="${dist}/${war-filename}" />
```

```xml
<!-- ===== -->
<!-- Paths -->
<!-- ===== -->

<path id="all.source.path">
    <pathelement path="${src}"/>
</path>

<!-- =========== -->
<!-- Class Paths -->
<!-- =========== -->

<path id="class.path">
    <fileset dir="${lib}">
        <include name="*.jar"/>
    </fileset>
</path>

<path id="app.class.path">
    <pathelement location="${classes}" />
    <path refid="class.path"/>
</path>

<!-- =============================================================== -->
<!-- Target: compile                                                 -->
<!-- Compiles all classes                                            -->
<!-- =============================================================== -->

<target name="compile" description="Compiles all classes (JDK1.5)">
    <javac
        destdir="${classes}"
        classpathref="class.path"
        debug="on"
        deprecation="on"
        optimize="off"
        >
        <src>
            <path refid="all.source.path" />
        </src>
    </javac>
</target>

<!-- =============================================================== -->
<!-- Target: package-web                                             -->
<!-- Package the web module                                          -->
<!-- =============================================================== -->
```

```
<target name="package-web" depends="compile"
    description="Package the web module" >
    <mkdir dir="dist" />
    <jar basedir="${context}" jarfile="${war-file}" />
</target>

</project>
```

Save the Ant buildfile to the root of the project directory and build the WAR file by running Ant. You should now have a WAR in the dist directory of your application ready to be deployed to your Web container. In the case of Tomcat, WARs are deployed to the webapps directory. Deploying the WAR should result in output similar to that shown here:

```
INFO: Deploying web application archive tapestry-time.war
Dec 14, 2005 9:51:15 AM org.apache.tapestry.ApplicationServlet init
INFO: Initialized application servlet 'tapestry-time': 1,234 millis to create
HiveMind Registry, 2,562 millis overall.
```

To see the application running, open a browser window and point it to the URL http://localhost:8080/tapestry-time as shown in Figure 7-5.

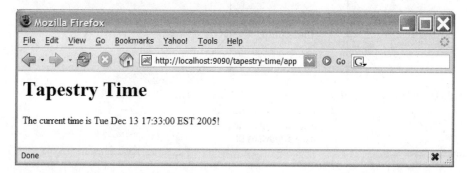

Figure 7-5. *A simple Tapestry application*

■**Tip** As you can see in Figure 7-5, the port used is 9090 rather than the default 8080. I changed the default Tomcat port in order to run other servers on port 8080. To do this, edit the file server.xml located in the TOMCAT_HOME/conf directory and modify the port attribute of the Connector element.

The Big Picture

In our simple application, Tapestry binds dynamically the value of a component to the result of a method call on a simple object. The Home.page file configures the component to be used in the HTML by defining the source of the value element for an instance of the Insert Tapestry component.

The expression `ognl:time` tells Tapestry to evaluate the contents after the semicolon as an OGNL expression. OGNL stands for Object-Graph Navigational Language, which is an expression language for getting and setting properties of Java objects. In the page file, we defined the class attribute as `com.integrallis.time.Home` under the `page-specification` element. This causes the evaluation of the expression to result in a call to the `getTime` method of the `com.integrallis.time.Home` to get the value to display. Before returning the Web page to the browser, Tapestry converts the component's HTML code shown in Listing 7-1 to markup similar to that shown in Listing 7-6.

Listing 7-6. *HTML Tapestry Sends to the Web Browser*

```
<html>
    <body>
    <h1>Tapestry Time</h1>
    The current time is Wed Dec 14 08:44:22 EST 2005!
    </body>
</html>
```

Figure 7-6 shows the interactions between the different components in Tapestry in the context of the simple example.

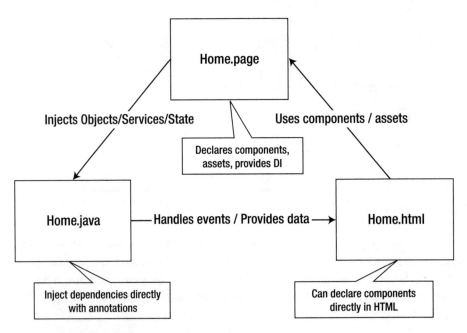

Figure 7-6. *The big picture*

The Power of Components

The great thing about having a solid component library is that most of the changes to the user interface and the user experience of the application require simple changes to the configuration of a component rather than hours of Java coding. That's the beauty of building with components. They are little black boxes of functionality that you wire together to create an application.

So far in our example, we have used one of the simplest Tapestry components, the Insert component. Tapestry provides an online component reference located at http://jakarta. apache.org/tapestry/tapestry/ComponentReference. If we look up the Insert component we find out that it provides more capabilities than simply outputting text.

Table 7-2 shows the parameters available in the Insert component.

Table 7-2. *Insert Component Parameters*

Name	Type	Direction	Requires	Default	Description
value	Object	in	no		Value to be inserted. Uses toString() on non-string objects.
format	Format	in	no		Format object (java.text.Format) use to format the value.
class	String	in	no		Wraps the output in a span tag using the passed CSS class.
raw	boolean	in	no	false	Ignores (doesn't attempt to fix) markup interfering text.

For example, to format the Date object used by the Insert component we can modify the page specification as shown next:

```
<component id="time" type="Insert">
  <binding name="value" value="ognl:time" />
  <binding name="format" value="ognl:timeFormat" />
</component>
```

Now we need to provide an object of type java.text.Format as shown in the additions to Home.java:

```
private Format timeFormat;

public Format getTimeFormat() {
    if (timeFormat == null) {
        timeFormat = new SimpleDateFormat("h:mm a");
    }

    return timeFormat;
}
```

The output should now reflect the name of the application and return a time string according to the format string as shown in Figure 7-7.

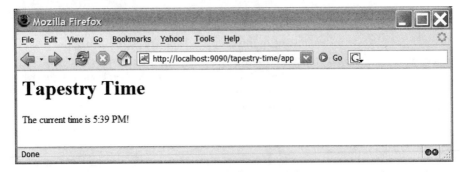

Figure 7-7. *Result of using the format parameter on the* Insert *component*

Simplifying the Simple Example

I mentioned previously that you can declare a Tapestry component implicitly in the HTML template by using the syntax "@Type", where type is the specific component type. The page file provides a level of indirection that gives you flexibility to keep changes to the HTML templates to a minimum. But if most of the bindings in your page files are as simple as the ones shown in the example, then you might get a proliferation of page files that can clutter your project.

Listing 7-7 shows a version of the HTML template for the Home.html page using implicit components.

Listing 7-7. *HTML Template Using Implicit Components*

```
<html>
    <body>
    <h1>Tapestry Time</h1>
    The current time is <span jwcid="@Insert" value="ognl:time" >high noon</span>!
    </body>
</html>
```

With these additions you could now remove the Home.page file. However, you'll need a way to tell the Tapestry template parser and consequently the OGNL expression evaluation where to find the getTime method. Tapestry uses a global configuration file for your application, which should be named with the same name as the servlet mapping name and end with the .application extension. In the case of the tapestry-time application, the configuration file is tapestry-time.application and should be located WEB-INF directory. The application XML file format is also defined in the Tapestry_4_0.dtd. This file is used to declare global locations for classes, components, and third-party component libraries. Listing 7-8 shows a minimal application XML file for the tapestry-time application with a meta element defining the package (com.integrallis.time) for the property org.apache.tapestry.page-class-packages, which tells Tapestry where to look for the Java code for a page component.

Listing 7-8. *Tapestry Application Configuration File*

```
<!DOCTYPE application PUBLIC
  "-//Apache Software Foundation//Tapestry Specification 4.0//EN"
  "http://jakarta.apache.org/tapestry/dtd/Tapestry_4_0.dtd">
<application name="Tapestry Demo">

    <!-- ================================================================ -->
    <!-- Global location for page Java implementations                    -->
    <!-- ================================================================ -->
    <meta
        key="org.apache.tapestry.page-class-packages"
        value="com.integrallis.time"
    />

</application>
```

Figure 7-8 shows a graphical depiction of the `application` element.

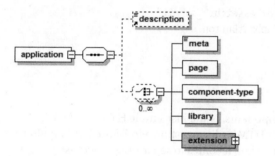

Figure 7-8. *DTD definition for the application element*

As we add more functionality to the application we will continue enhancing the tapestry-time.application file through the chapter.

User Input

A Web application is fairly useless if it can't take input from its users. Tapestry provides a large built-in collection of components to handle user input. First, we will enhance the application by allowing the users to select the formatting of the date on the page from a drop-down of choices.

First let's start by modifying the page template as shown in Listing 7-9.

Listing 7-9. *A More Elaborate Home.html*

```html
<html>
    <body>
    <h1>Tapestry Time</h1>
    <p>The current time is <span jwcid="time">high noon</span>!</p>
    <form jwcid="@Form" listener="listener:formSubmit">
        <h2>Select format:</h2>
        <p>
          <span jwcid="@PropertySelection"
                model="ognl:@com.integrallis.time.Home@FORMAT_MODEL"
                value="ognl:formatString">
          <select>
            <option value="0" selected="selected">h:mm a</option>
            <option value="1">EEE, MMM d, ''yy</option>
          </select>
          </span>
        </p>
        <p>
          <img jwcid="@ImageSubmit" image="asset:btn_submit"
               alt="Submit" src="images/submitButton.png" />
        </p>
    </form>
    </body>
</html>
```

This template, although it has more components, is still just simple HTML and it will render properly on any compliant browser or HTML editor as shown in Figure 7-9. Hopefully you are starting the see the power of Tapestry when it comes to separating concerns.

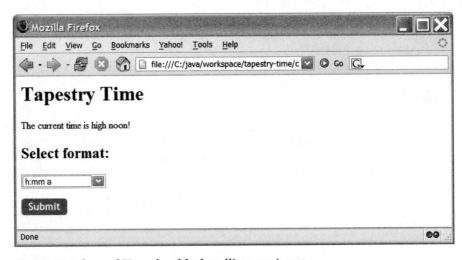

Figure 7-9. *Enhanced Home.html for handling user input*

Let's break down the different elements used in this example. Besides the previously used Insert component named "time", we now have a Form component defined as:

```
<form jwcid="@Form" listener="listener:formSubmit">
...
</form>
```

The Form component encapsulates and extends the functionality of an HTML form. Just like an HTML form, it encloses other components, and it handles the submission of the form, known as "rewinding" the form in Tapestry lingo. Unlike an HTML form, the Form component really makes dealing with form submissions simple by handling all the naming of the generated HTML forms and each enclosed component.

For the Home.html template, we define the Form component implicitly by using the @ sign in the jwcid attribute. To handle the form submission we need to declare a listener method. In this case it is the formSubmit method that we will add to the Home.java class.

Inside the form we have two components. The first component is a PropertySelection component, which provides a drop-down list:

```
<span jwcid="@PropertySelection"
      model="ognl:@com.integrallis.time.Home@FORMAT_MODEL"
      value="ognl:formatString">
  <select>
    <option value="0" selected="selected">h:mm a</option>
    <option value="1">EEE, MMM d, ''yy</option>
  </select>
</span>
```

Similar to a Swing component, the PropertySelection component has an associated selection model which is an implementation of the IPropertySelectionModel interface. The model provides the values for the drop-down to be populated and also serves to determine the value selected by the user.

Having models really changes the dynamics of Web development. They give you flexibility regarding how the data that populates a component is stored and retrieved. Models also provide a centralized data structure that can be shared between different entities, avoiding replication, and depending on their context, they can have multiple listeners to which changes in the model can be propagated. This is especially useful when dealing with Asynchronous JavaScript Technology and XML (AJAX) techniques.

The PropertySelection component is also defined implicitly. The model property tells the component where to get its data, which we define as the FORMAT_MODEL property in the Home class. The value attribute tells Tapestry where to place the user selection during the form submission, which we define as the formatString property, also in the Home page class.

The select element inside the body of the PropertySelection component is just plain HTML that gives us a preview of the drop-down at design time. If you explore the documentation for the component, you'll find out that it states that the contents of the body will be removed at rendering time (shown in the documentation as "Body: removed"). This is a very powerful construct that's at the core of Tapestry philosophy that HTML should be HTML.

Finally we need a way for the form to be submitted. Although we could have used a simple button for the form submission, we've chosen to use an image button to show how assets are handled in Tapestry. The ImageSubmit component is used to generate the image button to be used for a form submission. It extends the much simpler Submit component as shown:

```
<img jwcid="@ImageSubmit"
     image="asset:btn_submit"
     alt="Submit"
     src="images/submitButton.png" />
```

Another side effect of the rich object-oriented nature of the Tapestry component library is the amount of reuse; complex components can be created by extending or aggregating simpler components. In the ImageSubmit component we are declaring that the image will be provided by the Tapestry asset manager and that the name of the asset is btn_submit. Also, alternate text is provided in the case that the user browser has images disabled. Finally, to enable an accurate HTML static page, the actual image is presented using the src attribute. As you'll learn, assets eliminate the confusion of finding assets (resources such as images and other media) typically encountered in sites with multiple pages in multiple directories.

To create an asset for the submitButton.png image, add an asset element to the Home.page definition file as shown next (which assumes that the image is in the images directory under the context directory).

```
<asset name="btn_submit" path="images/submitButton.png" />
```

With the HTML template modifications in place, we need to update the Home class to satisfy the components in the template. Listing 7-10 shows the modified Home class.

Listing 7-10. *A More Elaborate Home.java*

```
public abstract class Home extends BasePage implements PageBeginRenderListener {
    private static String[] FORMAT_STRINGS =
        new String[] { "h:mm a",
                       "EEE, MMM d, ''yy",
                       "hh 'o''clock' a, zzzz",
                       "K:mm a, z"};

    public static final IPropertySelectionModel FORMAT_MODEL =
        new StringPropertySelectionModel(FORMAT_STRINGS);

    private Format timeFormat;

    public void pageBeginRender(PageEvent event) {
        if (getFormatString() == null) {
            setFormatString(FORMAT_STRINGS[0]);
        }
    }

    public Format getTimeFormat() {
        timeFormat = new SimpleDateFormat(getFormatString());
```

```
        return timeFormat;
    }

    public Date getTime() {
        return new Date();
    }

    public abstract String getFormatString();

    public abstract void setFormatString(String formatString);

    public void formSubmit(IRequestCycle cycle) {
        System.out.println("The form has been submitted!");
    }
}
```

Let's start with definition of the FORMAT_MODEL, for which we will use the simple StringPropertySelectionModel, which enables a string array to be used as the source of the labels in the drop-down and uses a simple integer index as the value. A String[] containing several format strings that can be used with a java.text.SimpleDateFormat instance is created and is then used in the constructor of the StringPropertySelectionModel.

The getFormatString method will return the value of the selected format string after a form submission. This value is used in the getTimeFormat method to return a Format object. The formSubmit method returns void and has an empty implementation. Returning void signifies that the page to be rendered after the submission is the current page and the method body is empty of any functionality since the value of the drop-down selection has already been assigned to the formatString property.

You might notice that the getFormatString and setFormatString are abstract methods. At runtime Tapestry will create a concrete implementation of the Home class and will provide implementations for all abstract getter and setter methods as well as a field to hold the value of the property. Developers new to Tapestry and who haven't encountered this clever usage of abstract classes might feel a bit apprehensive about coding to abstract classes. But this is one of the greatest strengths of Tapestry, and it shows the best possible way to intermix concrete user provided code while still exploiting the dynamic features of the environment.

Finally, we need to assign a value to the format string when the page is being rendered, not as the result of a form submission. To accomplish this we need to be aware of the Page life cycle. Tapestry pages produce several different events which can be listened to by implementing the right listener interface. In this case we implement the org.apache.tapestry.event.PageBeginRenderListener, which is used to determine when a page is about to be rendered. The implementation of the void pageBeginRender(PageEvent event) method checks if the formatString is null, and if so it assigns the first value in the array.

The running application is shown in Figure 7-10. Selecting a format string from the drop-down and clicking the Submit button should result in the displayed string changing to the selected format.

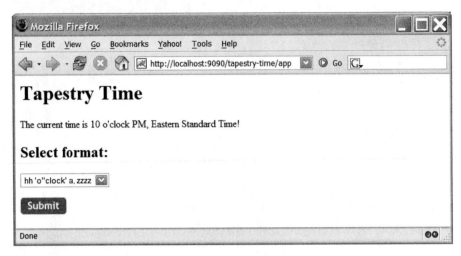

Figure 7-10. *Tapestry Time application handling user input*

To understand the amount of work that Tapestry is doing behind the scenes, one can simply inspect the generated HTML sent to the browser as shown in Listing 7-11.

Listing 7-11. *HTML Rendered by the Browser*

```html
<html>
    <body>
    <h1>Tapestry Time</h1>
    <p>The current time is 12:33 AM!</p>
    <form method="post" action="/tapestry-time/app" name="Form" id="Form">
    <div style="display:none;">
      <input type="hidden" name="formids" value="PropertySelection,ImageSubmit"/>
      <input type="hidden" name="component" value="$Form"/>
      <input type="hidden" name="page" value="Home"/>
      <input type="hidden" name="service" value="direct"/>
      <input type="hidden" name="submitmode" value=""/>
      <input type="hidden" name="submitname" value=""/>
    </div>
        <h2>Select format:</h2>
        <p>
          <select name="PropertySelection" id="PropertySelection">
            <option value="0" selected="selected">h:mm a</option>
            <option value="1">EEE, MMM d, ''yy</option>
            <option value="2">hh 'o''clock' a, zzzz</option>
            <option value="3">K:mm a, z</option>
          </select>
        </p>
```

```
    <p>
      <input type="image" name="ImageSubmit" border="0"
             src="/tapestry-time/images/submitButton.png"
             id="ImageSubmit" alt="Submit"/>
    </p>
  </form>
  </body>
</html>
```

Building the TechConf UI with Tapestry

The TechConf application user interface is a dynamic Web application. In Chapter 6 we built portions of the TechConf Web application using the Spring MVC Web framework with a middle tier consisting of Spring bean services. In this chapter we'll approach the same problem using a different technology stack. Instead of Spring MVC we'll use Tapestry, and instead of Spring bean services we'll use EJB3 stateless session bean services developed in Chapter 5, and we'll inject them into our Tapestry pages using HiveMind. In the Tapestry implementation we will also implement more of the TechConf Web tier than we did in Chapter 6. In order to better understand the TechConf user interface, Figure 7-11 shows a website map for the TechConf application. We won't develop every single page shown in Figure 7-11 but we will tackle a significant and representative set of functionality.

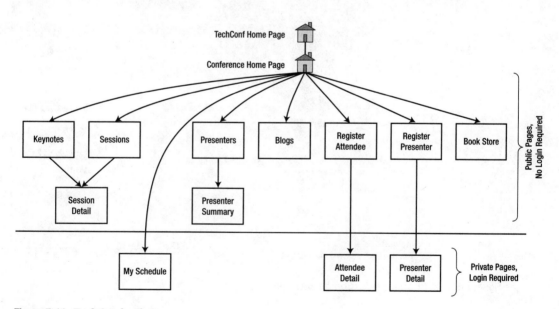

Figure 7-11. *TechConf website map*

Building the Home Page

Let's start by building the opening page of the TechConf application, which shows the list of available conferences. We'll work from the outside in, starting with the HTML template. In the HTML template for the application's home page we want to list the available conferences and create hyperlinks that will take the user to each individual conference page where detailed information about the particular conference is shown.

Figure 7-12 shows the template for the TechConf home page Home.html.

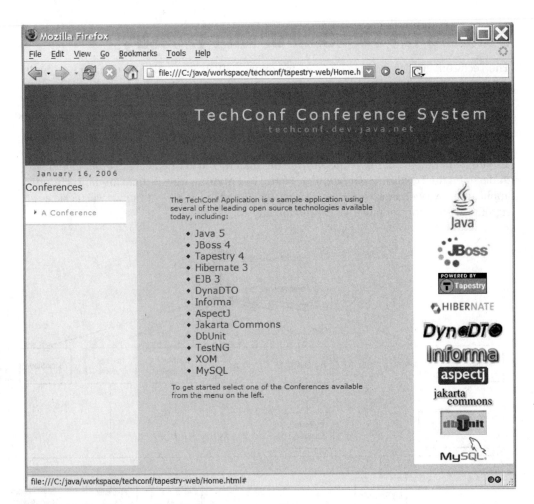

Figure 7-12. *TechConf application home page template*

In the HTML template, we will make use of the For component to loop over a collection of ConferenceSummary DTOs. The For component allows you to iterate over a collection of values. Listing 7-12 shows the snippet of HTML that makes up the navigation bar shown on the left of the template in Figure 7-12.

Listing 7-12. *Relevant Portions of the HTML Template Home.html*

```
<tr jwcid="@For" element="tr"
    source="ognl:conferences" value="ognl:conference">
  <td width="165">
  <span jwcid="@ExternalLink" page="conference/Summary"
        parameters="ognl:conference.conferenceId" class="navText">
    <span jwcid="@Insert" value="ognl:conference.conferenceTitle" />
  </span>
</tr>
<span jwcid="$remove$">
  <tr>
    <td width="165">
      <a href="#" class="navText">A Conference</a>
    </td>
  </tr>
</span>
```

In Listing 7-12 the For component is being used to loop over the collection provided by the OGNL expression "ognl:conferences" as declared in the source attribute. The value attribute indicates that we can access the current value that we're iterating over using the expression "ognl:conference". The value of the element attribute tells Tapestry to wrap the content with the specified HTML element. Informal parameters (those parameters not formally defined in the component specification) become attributes of the HTML element. Tapestry allows for this pass-through of informal parameters which allows you to still use common HTML syntax to configure resulting HTML markup.

Notice that right below the tr element, we have a tr element wrapped in a span tag with attribute jwcid="$remove$". The tr element is shown in the template as a preview of how an item on the navigation menu will appear. The "$remove$" value tells Tapestry to remove this span tag (and its contents) when rendering the page. This is another example of how Tapestry allows designers to work with pure HTML that can be easily maintained without the need of any Java knowledge.

To provide the values required by the HTML template, a Tapestry page specification file serves as a bridge or binding between the HTML template and any underlying Java code or HiveMind services.

Listing 7-13 shows the Home.page file showing how to inject a HiveMind service using the inject element. The property attribute is the name under which the property will be exposed, and the object attribute is the identifier used to locate the value. In the template we're also defining the property conference, which serves as the placeholder for the individual element of the collection being iterated over in Listing 7-12.

Listing 7-13. *Home Page Tapestry Page Specification*

```xml
<?xml version="1.0"?>
<!DOCTYPE page-specification PUBLIC
  "-//Apache Software Foundation//Tapestry Specification 4.0//EN"
  "http://jakarta.apache.org/tapestry/dtd/Tapestry_4_0.dtd">

<page-specification>

    <inject property="conferenceService"
            object="service:app.ConferenceService"/>

    <property name="conference"/>

    <!-- Assets -->
    <asset name="stylesheet" path="css/techconf.css"/>
    <asset name="spacer" path="images/spacer.gif" />
    <asset name="arrow"  path="images/arrow.gif" />

</page-specification>
```

The Java code for the Home page needs to provide the method to access the collection of conferences. To accomplish this it also needs an instance of ConferenceService (which is injected in the page specification shown in Listing 7-13). Listing 7-14 shows the code for the Home page.

Listing 7-14. *Home Page Page Class*

```java
package com.integrallis.techconf.web.tapestry.pages;

import java.util.List;

import org.apache.tapestry.event.PageBeginRenderListener;
import org.apache.tapestry.event.PageEvent;
import org.apache.tapestry.html.BasePage;

import com.integrallis.techconf.dto.ConferenceSummary;
import com.integrallis.techconf.service.ConferenceService;

public abstract class Home extends BasePage implements PageBeginRenderListener {

    public void pageBeginRender(PageEvent event) {
        setConferences(getConferenceService().getAllConferences());
    }
```

```
    public abstract ConferenceService getConferenceService();

    public abstract void setConferences(List<ConferenceSummary> s);
    public abstract List<ConferenceSummary> getConferences();
}
```

As with most Tapestry pages, the Home class extends Tapestry's BasePage and implements PageBeginRenderListener. In the pageBeginRender method, we retrieve the collection of conference from the conference service using the getAllConferences method, and we assign the returned collection to the List of conferences implicitly created by Tapestry to support the setConferences and getConferences method.

HiveMind Services

Tapestry uses HiveMind, which is a services and configuration microkernel. Similarly to Spring, HiveMind provides a framework for IoC which can be used to configure services and the collaborations among those services and components using simple XML configuration files. HiveMind services are defined in terms of interfaces or simple POJOs. As an IoC container, HiveMind instantiates and wires together services. As a configuration framework, HiveMind enables you to wire and manage highly complex systems composed of multiple services. HiveMind uses the concept of modules, which are a collection of services packaged as JARs, each with its own XML configuration. Tapestry itself uses HiveMind to configure a large number of modules that work in conjunction to provide Tapestry's runtime capabilities.

In Tapestry, services are added to the HiveMind registry by specifying them in the hive-module.xml configuration file (located in the WEB-INF directory for the TechConf application). In Tapestry you can have any number of objects whose state can be maintained. Those objects are also declared in the HiveMind configuration file. Tapestry bootstraps HiveMind on start-up and initializes the HiveMind registry.

To make the "conferences" object available to the page we need a way to wrap the EJB3 service implementing the ConferenceService interface as a HiveMind service which will be then injected into the page as using the inject property as shown in Listing 7-13.

HiveMind includes a service that creates proxy objects to work with EJB 2.X. The EJBProxyFactory service is used to create a proxy object to wrap an EJB stateless session bean. This wrapper takes care of doing JNDI lookup and invocation of the create method on the returned home interface to obtain an instance of the bean. Since we are using EJB 3.0, we have created a simple service to retrieve our EJB3 stateless session bean instances using JNDI. Listing 7-15 shows how simple it is to create a HiveMind service by implementing the ServiceImplementationFactory interface and returning the desired object in the createCoreServiceImplementation method.

Listing 7-15. *HiveMind EJB3Factory*

```
package com.integrallis.techconf.web.tapestry.hivemind;

import javax.naming.InitialContext;

import org.apache.commons.logging.Log;
import org.apache.commons.logging.LogFactory;
import org.apache.hivemind.ApplicationRuntimeException;
import org.apache.hivemind.ServiceImplementationFactory;
import org.apache.hivemind.ServiceImplementationFactoryParameters;
import org.apache.hivemind.internal.Module;

/**
 * An implementation of {@link org.apache.hivemind.ServiceImplementationFactory}
 * that retrieved a stateless session EJB via JNDI.
 */
public class EJB3Factory implements ServiceImplementationFactory {
    private static Log log = LogFactory.getLog(EJB3Factory.class);

    public Object createCoreServiceImplementation(
            ServiceImplementationFactoryParameters factoryParameters) {
        EJB3FactoryParameters proxyParameters =
            (EJB3FactoryParameters) factoryParameters.getParameters().get(0);
        String remoteInterfaceClass = proxyParameters.getRemoteInterface();

        Module module = factoryParameters.getInvokingModule();

        Class remoteInterface = module.resolveType(remoteInterfaceClass);

        Object result = null;
        try {
            InitialContext context = new InitialContext();
            result = context.lookup(remoteInterface.getName());
        } catch (Exception ex) {
            log.error("Could not retrieve service", ex);
            throw new ApplicationRuntimeException(ex);
        }
        return result;
    }
}
```

In the body of the createCoreServiceImplementation method we use the parameter
remoteInterface of type Class and use the full class name as the JNDI lookup string to
retrieve the stateless session bean. Notice that the method takes a parameter of type
ServiceImplementationFactoryParameters. Luckily you don't have to implement this
interface since HiveMind will take any simple POJO and create an instance of

`ServiceImplementationFactoryParameters` that includes the contents of the POJO. Listing 7-16 shows the simple POJO used to hold the configuration parameters for the `EJB3Factory`.

Listing 7-16. *EJB3FactoryParameters*

```
public class EJB3FactoryParameters {
    private String remoteInterface;

    public String getRemoteInterface() {
        return remoteInterface;
    }

    public void setRemoteInterface(String remoteInterface) {
        this.remoteInterface = remoteInterface;
    }
}
```

The next step is to make our service available by declaring it in the HiveMind configuration. The HiveMind configuration is a simple XML file akin to the Spring application context in which you can define services and wire collaborators. Listing 7-17 shows the service point definition for the `EJB3Factory` and the `ConferenceService` which uses the EJB3Factory.

Listing 7-17. *EJB3FactoryParameters in HiveMind Configuration (hivemodule.xml)*

```
<?xml version="1.0"?>
<module id="app" version="1.0.0" package="com.integrallis.techconf">
  ...

  <!-- ================================================================== -->
  <!-- Service Point for EJB3 Factory                                     -->
  <!-- ================================================================== -->
  <service-point id="EJB3Factory"
                 interface="org.apache.hivemind.ServiceImplementationFactory">
    <parameters-schema>
      <element name="construct">
        <attribute name="remote-interface" required="true" />
        <conversion
class="com.integrallis.techconf.web.tapestry.hivemind.EJB3FactoryParameters">
          <map attribute="remote-interface" property="remoteInterface"/>
        </conversion>
      </element>
    </parameters-schema>

    <invoke-factory model="singleton">
      <construct
        class="com.integrallis.techconf.web.tapestry.hivemind.EJB3Factory"
      />
    </invoke-factory>
```

```
    </service-point>

    <!-- ================================================================= -->
    <!-- TechConf EJB3 Services                                           -->
    <!-- ================================================================= -->

    <service-point id="ConferenceService" interface="service.ConferenceService">
      <invoke-factory service-id="app.EJB3Factory">
        <construct remote-interface="service.ConferenceService"/>
      </invoke-factory>
    </service-point>
    ...
</module>
```

At the highest level, the hivemodule.xml file defines a module which defines an id prefix for all services and a default package prefix. Factory services can be defined as singletons or as pooled instances.

HiveMind is a very powerful IoC framework that enables the creation of service-driven frameworks and applications by providing decentralized configuration. Looking deeper into HiveMind is outside of the scope of this chapter, but I highly recommend that you explore this powerful framework that is becoming one of the tools of choice of the toolmakers.

Testing the Home Page

The Tapestry WAR file for the TechConf application will be packaged as part of the EAR deployment created in Chapter 5. Figure 7-13 shows the location of the files that make up the home page in the tapestry-web directory under the TechConf project directory.

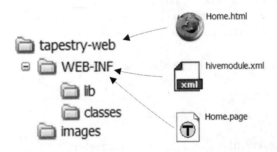

Figure 7-13. *Location of home page files under the TechConf project directory*

Figure 7-14 shows the TechConf application's home page at http://localhost:8080/ TechConf/ displaying the available conferences loaded in the database.

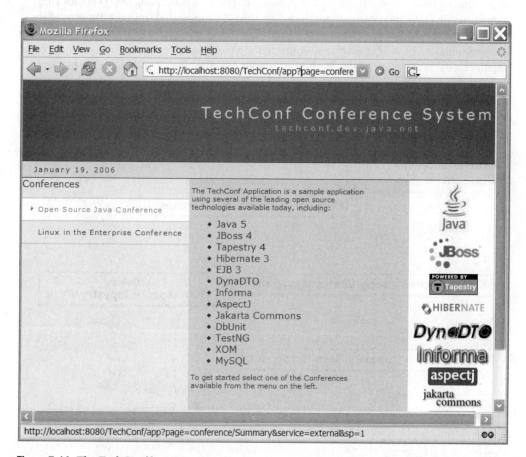

Figure 7-14. *The TechConf home page*

Creating a Border Component

The home page is a fairly simple page. For the rest of the application we have more complex requirements and a fair amount of common elements amongst the pages. Similarly to what you can do with Tiles (as seen in Chapter 6) we can create a custom Tapestry component to server as a border for the rest of the pages in the application. This custom component will also be responsible for handling user logins and logouts.

In Tapestry, creating your own components is very similar to creating pages. After all, pages are themselves Tapestry components. Components can be assembled in two different ways depending on how the resulting HTML is produced. If you are generating the HTML for your component in code, your component Java class should be inherited from the Tapestry class org.apache.tapestry.AbstractComponent. On the other hand, if you want to use an HTML template as the foundation of your component's output, then you'll need to inherit from the class org.apache.tapestry.BaseComponent. Figure 7-15 shows the component and page core hierarchy.

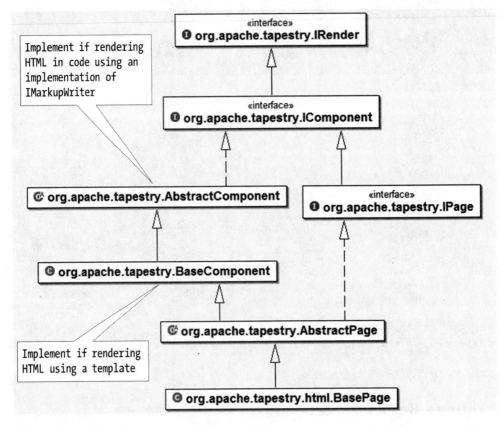

Figure 7-15. *Tapestry component and page hierarchy*

The Component HTML Template

To create the component that will serve as a frame for all the conference pages, we'll start with the HTML template. The template is shown in Figure 7-16.

The ConferenceBorder.html template is divided into four clearly demarcated areas as shown in Figure 7-17.

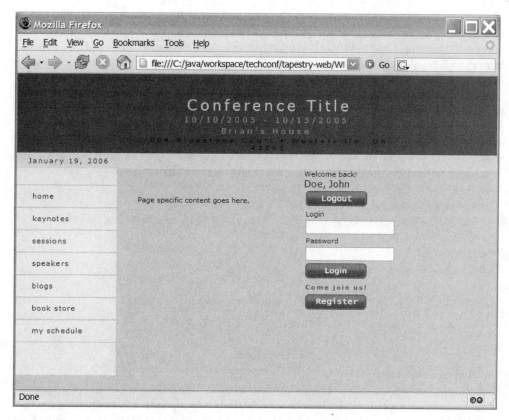

Figure 7-16. *Preview of the Conference border HTML template*

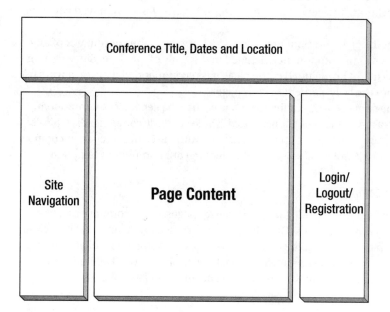

Figure 7-17. *Structure of the Conference border template*

At the top of the template we have an area that will display the conference title, date range, and location. On the left side we have a typical navigation menu that will take the user to the other available pages in the site. On the right-hand side there is a common login box, a logout button, a placeholder to display the name of the logged in user, and a button that will take the user to the conference registration page. Listing 7-18 shows the relevant HTML.

Listing 7-18. *ConferenceBorder.html Template*

```
<html jwcid="@Shell" title="ognl:title" stylesheet="asset:stylesheet">
<head>
  <meta http-equiv="Content-Type" content="text/html; charset=iso-8859-1" />
  ...
  <span jwcid="$remove$">
    <link rel="stylesheet" type="text/css" href="../css/techconf.css"/>
  </span>
</head>
<body jwcid="@Body">
  ...
  <span class="bodyText" jwcid="@RenderBody">Page specific content goes here.</span>
  ...
</body>
</html>
```

As you can see the template is a normal HTML page. In the html root element we add a Shell component which, as its name indicates, constructs the outer shell of an HTML page. In the html element we are also inserting the title of the page dynamically and setting the CSS style sheet for the page to the value of the asset with an id equal to stylesheet. Inside the head element we include a reference to the relative location of the CSS style sheet used by the page in order to provide an accurate preview of the page. This reference will be removed when the page is rendered.

In the body element the Body component is used which serves as the coordinator of any JavaScript contributions by any components included in the body of the page. Since we don't know what components might be included in the page, it is recommended that you always use the Body component with the body element of your pages.

Finally, to insert the content of the individual page we use the RenderBody component, which renders the body of any component or page used. The RenderBody component is typically used for the type of templating that we are looking to provide with the ConferenceBorder component. You should have exactly one RenderBody component in your component template.

The Component Specification

Similar to the page specification XML file (.page) used with pages, every component has a component specification XML file (.jwc). The component specification defines the Java class for the component, the parameter that the components takes, and any other collaborators used by the component such as other components, state holding objects, or HiveMind services.

Figure 7-18 shows the structure of the component specification XML file.

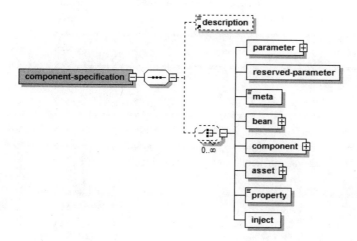

Figure 7-18. *DTD definition for the component-specification element*

Listing 7-19 shows the component specification for the `ConferenceBorder` component. In the component-specification element the component is linked to the Java code using the class attribute, which in this case points to the class `ConferenceBorder` in the package `com.integrallis.techconf.web.tapestry.pages`. The `allow-body` attribute tells Tapestry that this component will render the contents of its body. Many components in Tapestry replace the contents of the body at rendering time. That's why in some templates we can simply add sample content to the body of an element for previewing purposes, while in others we use `$remove$` directive to explicitly tell Tapestry to remove the sample content.

The `parameter` element is used to define parameters for your component. Similarly you can `prevent` users of your component from passing a specific informal parameter by using the `reserved-parameter` element.

Listing 7-19. *ConferenceBorder Component Specification (.jwc)*

```
<?xml version="1.0" encoding="UTF-8"?>
<!DOCTYPE component-specification
  PUBLIC "-//Apache Software Foundation//Tapestry Specification 4.0//EN"
  "http://jakarta.apache.org/tapestry/dtd/Tapestry_4_0.dtd">
<component-specification
  class="com.integrallis.techconf.web.tapestry.pages.ConferenceBorder"
  allow-body="yes"
  allow-informal-parameters="no"
  >


  <!-- ================================================================= -->
  <!-- Service and State objects Injection                         -->
  <!-- ================================================================= -->
  <inject property="webRequest" object="infrastructure:request"/>
  <inject property="userService"
          object="service:app.UserService"/>
```

```xml
<inject property="userInformation" type="state" object="logged-in-user-data"/>

<!-- =============================================================== -->
<!-- Pass-through Parameters                                         -->
<!-- =============================================================== -->
<parameter name="title" required="yes"/>

<!-- =============================================================== -->
<!-- Base URL property used to simplify the location of resources    -->
<!-- =============================================================== -->
<property name="baseURL" initial-value="webRequest.contextPath" />

<!-- =============================================================== -->
<!-- Date Formatters                                                 -->
<!-- =============================================================== -->
<property name="dateStartFormater"
          initial-value="new java.text.SimpleDateFormat('EEE, d MMM')"/>

<property name="dateEndFormater"
          initial-value="new java.text.SimpleDateFormat('EEE, d MMM yyyy')"/>

<component id="conferenceTitle" type="Insert">
  <binding name="value"
          value="ognl:userInformation.conferenceSummary.conferenceTitle"/>
</component>

<!-- =============================================================== -->
<!-- Conference Summary Fields                                       -->
<!-- =============================================================== -->
<component id="startDate" type="Insert">
  <binding name="value"
          value="ognl:userInformation.conferenceSummary.startDate"/>
  <binding name="format" value="ognl:dateStartFormater"/>
</component>

<component id="endDate" type="Insert">
  <binding name="value"
          value="ognl:userInformation.conferenceSummary.endDate"/>
  <binding name="format" value="ognl:dateEndFormater"/>
</component>

<component id="venueName" type="Insert">
  <binding name="value"
          value="ognl:userInformation.conferenceSummary.venueName"/>
</component>
```

```
<component id="venueAddressLine1" type="Insert">
  <binding name="value"
           value="ognl:userInformation.conferenceSummary.venueAddressLine1"/>
</component>

<component id="venueAddressLine2" type="Insert">
  <binding name="value"
           value="ognl:userInformation.conferenceSummary.venueAddressLine2"/>
</component>

...

</component-specification>
```

In the component specification file we also inject the EJB3 service UserService as we learned previously. The UserService will be used to handle the login, logout, and registration functions.

Formatting Output

In the component specification we bind and format a lot of the values contained in the DTO ConferenceSummary to Insert components. An example of Tapestry's formatting capabilities is the formatting of the conference start and end dates which will be displayed below the conference title. Listing 7-20 shows how a formatter object is defined as a property and then applied as a formatter to the contents of an Insert component.

Listing 7-20. *Formatting the Contents of an Insert Component*

```
<property name="dateEndFormater"
          initial-value="new java.text.SimpleDateFormat('EEE, d MMM yyyy')"/>

<component id="endDate" type="Insert">
  <binding name="value"
           value="ognl:userInformation.conferenceSummary.endDate"/>
  <binding name="format" value="ognl:dateEndFormater"/>
</component>
```

Aside from the component-specific features, the component specification file can handle assets, services, and object injection just as we learned earlier with the page specification.

Managing State

The ConferenceBorder is also responsible for login and logout functionality. To handle keeping the state of the logged in user we declare a state object contribution in the HiveMind configuration.

The state object is a simple POJO that can be reference by the id logged-in-user-data and is mapped to the Java class LoggedInUser located in the package com.integrallis.techconf. web.tapestry.domain. This object is scoped to the session, which is exactly what the lifetime of a user login should be. This contribution has a configuration-id of tapestry.state. ApplicationObjects. The term "contribution" here implies that HiveMind is making a contribution to the Tapestry-specific configuration, in this case the Tapestry application objects, as shown in Listing 7-21.

Listing 7-21. *Configuring an Application State Object Using HiveMind*

```xml
<?xml version="1.0"?>
<module id="app" version="1.0.0" package="com.integrallis.techconf">
  ...
  <!-- ==================================================================== -->
  <!-- Server-side State                                                    -->
  <!-- ==================================================================== -->
  <contribution configuration-id="tapestry.state.ApplicationObjects">
    <state-object name="logged-in-user-data" scope="session">
      <create-instance
        class="com.integrallis.techconf.web.tapestry.domain.LoggedInUser"
      />
    </state-object>
    ...
  </contribution>
  ...
</module>
```

Listing 7-22 shows the LoggedInUser POJO, which is a simple wrapper to hold both the UserSummary and the ConferenceSummary DTOs.

Listing 7-22. *Simple LoggedInUser Application State POJO*

```java
public class LoggedInUser implements Serializable {
    private UserSummary userSummary;
    private ConferenceSummary conferenceSummary;

    public ConferenceSummary getConferenceSummary() {
        return conferenceSummary;
    }

    public void setConferenceSummary(ConferenceSummary conferenceSummary) {
        this.conferenceSummary = conferenceSummary;
    }

    public UserSummary getUserSummary() {
        return userSummary;
    }

    public void setUserSummary(UserSummary userSummary) {
        this.userSummary = userSummary;
    }

}
```

For the login and logout functionality we need to handle two states with their corresponding changes to the user interface. When there is no user logged in, the form with the fields for the username and password need to be shown, as well as the Register button. Upon a successful login, the login form and Register button should be hidden, and instead a user greeting and the Logout button should be shown. To handle the conditional HTML sections, we define two components. The ifLoggedIn component is a Tapestry If component which will render the content of its body if the value of the condition attribute evaluates to true (for a non-boolean object value true equates to not null). The complement of the ifLoggedIn component is the elseNotLoggedIn component which is a Tapestry Else component. The Else component renders the contents of its body if the previous If component condition evaluates to false. Listing 7-23 shows the login and logout functionality.

Listing 7-23. *Login and Logout Functionality in Component Specification*

```
<component-specification
    class="com.integrallis.techconf.web.tapestry.pages.ConferenceBorder"
    allow-body="yes" allow-informal-parameters="no">

    ...

    <!-- ===================================================================== -->
    <!-- Login Handling                                                        -->
    <!-- ===================================================================== -->

    <property name="login"/>
    <property name="password"/>

    <component id="ifLoggedIn" type="If">
        <binding name="condition" value="ognl:userInformation.userSummary"/>
    </component>

    <component id="elseNotLoggedIn" type="Else"/>

    <component id="displayLoggedInLinks" type="If">
        <binding name="condition" value="ognl:userInformation.userSummary"/>
    </component>

    <component id="login" type="TextField">
        <binding name="value" value="ognl:login"/>
        <binding name="displayName" value="literal:Email Login"/>
    </component>

    <component id="loginLabel" type="FieldLabel">
        <binding name="field" value="component:login"/>
    </component>
```

```
    <component id="passwd" type="TextField">
        <binding name="value" value="ognl:password"/>
        <binding name="displayName" value="literal:Password"/>
      <binding name="hidden" value="true"/>
    </component>

    <component id="passwdLabel" type="FieldLabel">
        <binding name="field" value="component:passwd"/>
    </component>

    <component id="displayName" type="Insert">
        <binding name="value"
                value="ognl:userInformation.userSummary.displayName"/>
    </component>
    ...
</component-specification>
```

The rest of the components define the field and corresponding labels for the login form. Listing 7-24 shows the usage of the login and logout functionality components in the HTML template of the ConferenceBorder component.

Listing 7-24. *Login and Logout Markup in the HTML Template*

```
<!-- ================================================================== -->
<!-- User Logged In                                                     -->
<!-- ================================================================== -->
<span jwcid="ifLoggedIn">
  Welcome back!<br/>
  <!-- Show Greeting -->
  <span jwcid="displayName" class="mediumText">Doe, John</span>
  <!-- Logout Form -->
  <form jwcid="@Form" listener="ognl:listeners.logout">
    <table width="100%" border="0" summary="logout">
      <tr><td>
        <img jwcid="@ImageSubmit" image="asset:btn_logout" alt="Logout"
            src="../images/btn-logout.gif"/>
      </td></tr>
    </table>
  </form>
</span>
```

```
<!-- ================================================================ -->
<!-- User Not Logged In                                              -->
<!-- ================================================================ -->
<span jwcid="ElseNotLoggedIn">
  <!-- Login Form -->
  <form jwcid="@Form" listener="ognl:listeners.login">
    <table width="100%" border="0" summary="login">
      <tr><td><span jwcid="loginLabel">Login</span></td></tr>
      <tr><td><input type="text" jwcid="login"/></td></tr>
      <tr><td><span jwcid="passwdLabel">Password</span></td></tr>
      <tr><td><input type="text" jwcid="passwd"/></td></tr>
      <tr><td>
        <img jwcid="@ImageSubmit" image="asset:btn_login" alt="Login"
             src="../images/btn-login.gif"/>
      </td></tr>
    </table>
  </form>

  <!-- Register Message and Link -->
  <table width="100%" border="0" summary="register">
    <tr><td><span class="subHeader">Come join us!</span></td></tr>
    <tr><td>
      <a href="../attendee/Register.html"
         jwcid="@PageLink" page="attendee/Register">
        <img jwcid="@Image" image="asset:btn_register"
             border="0" alt="Register" src="../images/btn-register.gif"/>
      </a>
    </td></tr>
  </table>
</span>
```

The last section of the ConferenceBorder template is the site navigation menu on the left portion of the page. For each menu item, we need to create a link to a Tapestry page. The PageLink component creates a hyperlink to a Tapestry page in the current application. Listing 7-25 shows the portions of the HTML template that create the navigation menu using PageLink components.

Listing 7-25. *Navigation Menu Using* `PageLink` *Component*

```
<table border="0" cellspacing="0" cellpadding="0" width="165" id="navigation">
   ...
   <!-- ================================================================ -->
   <!-- Page Link to Conference Summary Page                          -->
   <!-- ================================================================ -->
   <tr><td width="165">
     <a href="#" jwcid="@PageLink"
        page="conference/Summary" class="navText">home</a>
   </td></tr>
   <!-- ================================================================ -->
   <!-- Page Link to Conference Keynote Page                          -->
   <!-- ================================================================ -->
   <tr><td width="165">
     <a href="#" jwcid="@PageLink" page="conference/Keynote"
        class="navText">keynotes</a>
   </td></tr>
   <!-- ================================================================ -->
   <!-- Page Link to Conference Sessions Page                         -->
   <!-- ================================================================ -->
   <tr><td width="165">
     <a href="#" jwcid="@PageLink" page="conference/Sessions"
        class="navText">sessions</a>
   </td></tr>
   <!-- ================================================================ -->
   <!-- Page Link to Conference Speakers Page                         -->
   <!-- ================================================================ -->
   <tr><td width="165">
     <a href="#" jwcid="@PageLink" page="conference/Speakers"
        class="navText">speakers</a>
   </td></tr>
   <!-- ================================================================ -->
   <!-- Page Link to Conference Speakers Blogs Page                   -->
   <!-- ================================================================ -->
   <tr><td width="165">
     <a href="#" jwcid="@PageLink" page="conference/Blogs"
        class="navText">blogs</a>
   </td></tr>
   <!-- ================================================================ -->
   <!-- Page Link to Conference Speakers Books Page                   -->
   <!-- ================================================================ -->
   <tr><td width="165">
     <a href="#" jwcid="@PageLink" page="conference/Books"
        class="navText">book store</a>
   </td></tr>
```

```
<!-- ======================================================================= -->
<!-- Page Link to Logged in User Schedule                                    -->
<!-- ======================================================================= -->
<span jwcid="displayLoggedInLinks">
  <tr><td width="165">
    <a href="#" jwcid="@ExternalLink" page="attendee/ConfSessions"
       class="navText">my schedule</a>
  </td></tr>
</span>
</table>
```

The final element of the ConferenceBorder component is the Java code that handles the login and logout logic. The ConferenceBorder class contains the login method, which uses the application state object LoggedInUser to store the UserSummary DTO returned by the injected EJB3 UserService if the username and password supplied to the UserService login method pass authentication. The logout method simply sets the user information to null in the LoggedInUser object. Listing 7-26 shows the implementation of ConferenceBorder.

Listing 7-26. *ConferenceBorder Java Implementation*

```java
package com.integrallis.techconf.web.tapestry.pages;

import org.apache.tapestry.BaseComponent;
import org.apache.tapestry.IRequestCycle;

import com.integrallis.techconf.dto.UserSummary;
import com.integrallis.techconf.service.UserService;
import com.integrallis.techconf.web.tapestry.domain.LoggedInUser;

public abstract class ConferenceBorder extends BaseComponent {
    /**
     * Handles the user login
     * @param cycle
     */
    public void login(IRequestCycle cycle) {
        LoggedInUser user = getUserInformation();

        // Attempt the log in, a null return signifies a failed login
        UserSummary userSummary = getUserService()
                                    .login(getLogin(), getPassword());

        user.setUserSummary(userSummary);
        setUserInformation(user);
    }
```

```
/**
 * Handles the user logout
 * @param cycle
 */
public void logout(IRequestCycle cycle) {
    LoggedInUser user = getUserInformation();
    user.setUserSummary(null);
    setUserInformation(user);
}

// Login objects
public abstract void setLogin(String s);
public abstract String getLogin();
public abstract void setPassword(String s);
public abstract String getPassword();

// get and store the user information
public abstract LoggedInUser getUserInformation();
public abstract void setUserInformation(LoggedInUser u);

// the page service
public abstract UserService getUserService();
}
```

Conference Summary Page

With the ConferenceBorder in place we can now begin fleshing out the pages of the TechConf application. The first page that is shown after the user selects a particular conference from the TechConf home page is the conference Summary page. The details page shows information such as:

- A description of the conference

- The dates the conference is accepting abstract submissions from potential speakers

- The conference tracks

- A list of featured speakers

- News headlines from the list of conference news items

- Blog headings from the speaker blogs

Figure 7-19 shows a preview of the HTML template for the Summary page.

To use the ConferenceBorder component as the template for the Summary page, we simply declare the component in the html element of the page template as shown next:

```
<html jwcid="@ConferenceBorder" title="Conference Summary">
...
</html>
```

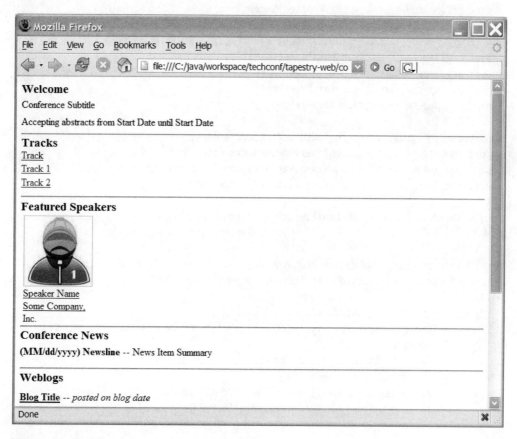

Figure 7-19. *Conference Summary page template*

The class `ActiveConferencePage` extends the Tapestry `BasePage`. The `ActiveConferencePage` will serve as the base class for all conference pages, and it handles redirection to the `Home` page if a `ConferenceSummary` is not found. This class also showcases the use of annotations to inject application state objects, Tapestry pages, and services using the `InjectState`, `InjectPage`, and `InjectObject` annotations respectively. Annotations provide an alternate way to the page and component specifications to inject dependencies into your pages and components.

Listing 7-27. *Base Page for All Conference-Specific Pages (ActiveConferencePage)*

```java
package com.integrallis.techconf.web.tapestry.pages.common;

import org.apache.tapestry.PageRedirectException;
import org.apache.tapestry.annotations.InjectObject;
import org.apache.tapestry.annotations.InjectPage;
import org.apache.tapestry.annotations.InjectState;
import org.apache.tapestry.event.PageBeginRenderListener;
import org.apache.tapestry.event.PageEvent;
import org.apache.tapestry.html.BasePage;

import com.integrallis.techconf.dto.ConferenceSummary;
import com.integrallis.techconf.service.ConferenceService;
import com.integrallis.techconf.web.tapestry.domain.LoggedInUser;
import com.integrallis.techconf.web.tapestry.pages.Home;

public abstract class ActiveConferencePage extends BasePage
                                        implements PageBeginRenderListener {
    /**
     * This checks to make sure that there is an active conference always loaded.
     * If not it redirects one to the home page of the site.
     */
    public void pageBeginRender(PageEvent event) {
        ConferenceSummary summary = getUserInformation().getConferenceSummary();
        if (summary == null) {
            // if it is null, no active conference is present
            // forward to the home page
            // the exception will force the page to the home page.
            throw new PageRedirectException(getHomePage());
        }
    }

    /**
     * Gets the conference id.
     * @return int the id of the current conference
     */
    protected int getConferenceId() {
        return getUserInformation().getConferenceSummary().getConferenceId();
    }
```

```
// get and store the user information
@InjectState("logged-in-user-data")
public abstract LoggedInUser getUserInformation();
public abstract void setUserInformation(LoggedInUser u);

@InjectPage("Home")
public abstract Home getHomePage();

// The conference service is needed across all conference pages
@InjectObject("service:app.ConferenceService")
public abstract ConferenceService getConferenceService();
}
```

The Summary page is the entry point page for any given conference. Therefore we wish to be able to access the page externally using a fixed URL that a user should be able to bookmark in their browser. This can also allow for the setting of subdomains on a Web server to provide each conference with a unique, easy-to-remember URL.

To create a Tapestry page that can be referenced externally, the page class must implement the IExternalPage interface. The IExternalPage interface contains only one method, activateExternalPage, which takes as parameters an Object array and the current request cycle.

Listing 7-28 shows the implementation of the Summary page, which extends the ActiveConferencePage base class and implements the IExternalPage interface. In the implementation of the activeExternalPage method, we retrieve the id of the conference being requested. The id is used to invoke the retrieveConferenceSummary method, which retrieves all the values needed to populate the Summary page. Those values are contained in the ConferenceSummary DTO returned by the getConferenceSummary method of the EJB3 ConferenceService.

To avoid retrieving the conference summary information for every page under a given conference, the retrieved ConferenceSummary object is also stored in the application state object LoggedInUser, which is the location where the ConferenceBorder component looks for the ConferenceSummary object.

Listing 7-28. *Summary Page Java Implementation*

```
package com.integrallis.techconf.web.tapestry.pages.conference;

import java.util.List;

import org.apache.tapestry.IExternalPage;
import org.apache.tapestry.IRequestCycle;
```

```java
import com.integrallis.techconf.dto.BlogEntry;
import com.integrallis.techconf.dto.ConferenceSummary;
import com.integrallis.techconf.dto.PresenterSummary;
import com.integrallis.techconf.web.tapestry.domain.LoggedInUser;
import com.integrallis.techconf.web.tapestry.pages.common.ActiveConferencePage;

public abstract class Summary extends ActiveConferencePage
                                implements IExternalPage {
    private static final int BLOG_ENTRIES = 2;
    private static final int FEATURED_PRESENTERS = 3;

    /**
     * This method is used when being activated from an external page.
     * This will load up the conference based on the conference id passed
     * setting it on the state object.
     */
    public void activateExternalPage(java.lang.Object[] parameters,
                                     IRequestCycle cycle) {
        // get the id of the requested conference
        Integer conferenceId = (Integer)parameters[0];

        // retrieve the conference Summary and stores it to the user information
        ConferenceSummary summary = retrieveConferenceSummary(conferenceId);

        // set the summary object on the user object
        LoggedInUser user = getUserInformation();
        user.setConferenceSummary(summary);
    }

    private ConferenceSummary retrieveConferenceSummary(Integer id) {
        // Get the summary for a particular conference
        ConferenceSummary summary = getConferenceService().getConferenceSummary(id);

        // Get the featured speakers
        summary.setFeaturedSpeakers(
            getConferenceService().
                getFeaturedPresenters(id, FEATURED_PRESENTERS)
        );

        // get the news
        summary.setNews(getConferenceService().getNews(id));
```

```
    // also retrieve the blogs
    try {
        List<BlogEntry> blogEntries = getConferenceService()
            .getBlogEntries(id, BLOG_ENTRIES);
        setBlogEntries(blogEntries);
    } catch(Exception e) {
        // do nothing, this allows for development in
        // a machine without internet access
    }

    return summary;
}


/**
 * Return the relative URL for the image for the speaker using the presenter id.
 * @return String a relative URL to the speaker image
 */
public String getSpeakerImage() {
    return "../speakerImages/" + getSpeaker()
        .getPresenterId().toString() + ".jpg";
}

public abstract PresenterSummary getSpeaker();
public abstract void setBlogEntries(List<BlogEntry> blogs);
}
```

The page definition file for the Summary page is responsible for declaring and formatting the components used in the HTML template. It uses For, Insert, and If components. It also uses the Any component. The Any component is a very versatile component that can emulate any HTML element. In the following example, the value of the OGNL expression speakerImage is bound to the attribute src of the surrounding tag.

```
<component id="speakerPicture" type="Any">
    <binding name="src" value="ognl:speakerImage"/>
</component>
```

The HTML snippet shown next uses an img tag with the speakerPicture component. At runtime, the src attribute will be replaced with the value of the speakerImage expression.

```
<img jwcid="speakerPicture" border="0" src="../speakerImages/1.jpg"/>
```

Figure 7-20 shows the Conference Summary page on the running application showing the conference with id equals to 1, which corresponds to the URL localhost:8080/TechConf/app?page=conference%2FSummary&service=external&sp=1.

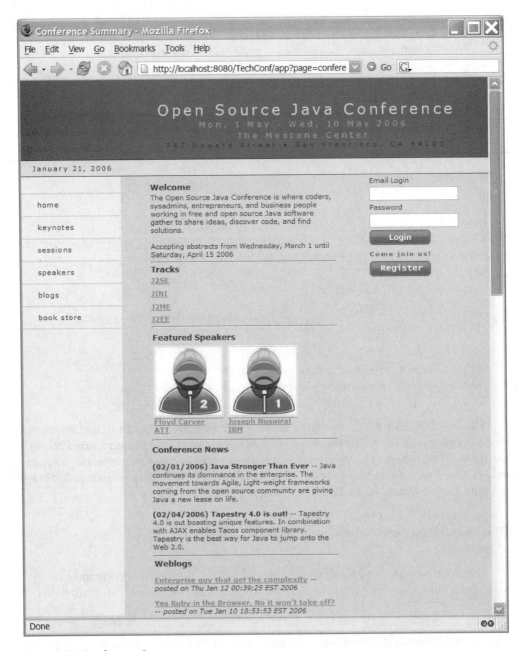

Figure 7-20. *Conference Summary page*

AJAX with Tacos

No, we are not talking about a potentially deadly new concoction at Taco Bell. The term AJAX is today's hot buzzword and stands for Asynchronous JavaScript and XML and was coined in early 2005 by Jesse James Garrett of Adaptive Path, a design and user experience consulting firm in San Francisco. AJAX encompasses a set of Web development techniques for creating rich, interactive Web applications. AJAX is being defined even as you read this text. The combination of these technologies has been referred to as DHTML and remote scripting in the past. Many claim that AJAX is a new name for old things that have been around for almost the last 10 years, while others point out that it is the evolution and the synergistic usage of these technologies that is new. The even newer term Web 2.0 is being used to refer to AJAX and other technologies that are taking the Web user experience and capabilities to a new level.

The impact of websites like Google Maps, Google Suggest, Gmail, Flickr, Amazon's A9, and the many spin-offs and clones that their success have created are being used as the foundation to define AJAX. In his original article Garrett defines AJAX as

- Standards-based presentation using XHTML and CSS

- Dynamic display and interaction using the Document Object Model (DOM)

- Data interchange and manipulation using XML and XSLT

- Asynchronous data retrieval using `XMLHttpRequest`

- JavaScript binding everything together

In the past we all have used websites where a page had certain dynamic elements that did not require a page reload such as a folding and expanding of information triggered by hovering over a particular image or text. The difference between those earlier JavaScript-enabled sites and an AJAX website is that in the former case the data was preloaded in its entirety and simply hidden from view. With AJAX the UI is dynamic, and the data behind the user interface is also dynamic. In a typical AJAX interaction a user action results in asynchronous HTTP requests to the server using the JavaScript `XMLHttpRequest` object that results in HTML, XML, plain text or even JavaScript returned from the server. The information returned from the server is used to modify the DOM tree of the current page dynamically without a page reload.

The gains are all in the user experience as it approaches the richness of standard desktop applications. With careful planning, users are no longer tied to the traditional request-response dance. The interaction with a website becomes a chain of dynamic, behind-the-scenes asynchronous requests, bound by few full round trips to the server. The typical side effects include the added complexity to development with a need for tighter integration between the client and the server and a slew of other technical hurdles including

- Browser incompatibilities

- Accessibility and internationalization concerns

- Testing and debugging complexity

- Asynchronous requests outside of the application domain (sandboxing)

- Security and the implication of mobile code

- Network throughput and traffic concerns

Some of these concerns are being addressed by encapsulating solutions and common patterns of usage in frameworks. The technology glue that has advanced AJAX from simple client-side scripting to the hot item of the day is the evolution of projects like Dojo (`www.dojotoolkit.org/`), script.aculo.us (`http://script.aculo.us/`), Prototype (`http://prototype.conio.net/`), Rico (`http://openrico.org/`), and DWR (`http://getahead.ltd.uk/dwr`).

Luckily for Tapestry users, AJAX-enabled components are available via the Tacos component library. Taco is a small but robust framework for building AJAX-enabled Tapestry components as well as a complete library of ready-to-use Ajaxian Tapestry components. Tacos was created by Viktor Szathmary and is actively maintained by Jesse Kuhnert. The Tacos project is hosted at SourceForge (`http://tacos.sourceforge.net/`) and distributed under the Apache open source license.

Tacos provides all the power of AJAX without the complications of dealing with constructs like `XMLHttpRequest` and complex JavaScript. Tacos takes advantages of the most mature JavaScript AJAX libraries available. It depends primarily on Dojo, but it also relies on Prototype and script.aculo.us for certain components.

As you will see in the TechConf Tacos example in this section, you rarely need to interact directly with JavaScript. Tacos also provides a built-in logging and debugging console that simplifies the development of rich Web applications.

Using Tacos in your Tapestry Application

Tacos is distributed in source and binary form. Documentation and samples are also distributed separately. Table 7-3 shows the Tacos distribution files.

Table 7-3. *Tacos Distribution Files*

File	Description
tacos-alpha-7-lib.zip	Includes the core JAR file (tacos-alpha-7-lib.jar) and JavaScript libraries
tacos-alpha-7-src.jar	Source distribution, including demos source code
tacos-alpha-7-docs.zip	Javadoc and User Guide documents (complete content of Tacos site)
tacos-alpha-7-demo.war	Deployable Web archive containing examples of every Tacos component

By far the easiest way to get started with Tacos is to use the demo WAR file as a skeleton for your WAR archive. Figure 7-21 shows the location of the different Tacos elements in the TechConf tapestry-web directory (the template directory for the WAR file). Figure 7-21 also shows the structure and location of the Tapestry page and component specification, as well as the HTML templates.

To get acquainted with Tacos, I recommend test-driving the Demo application. You can access the demo application online, or better yet, you can simply deploy the demo WAR file in Tomcat or JBoss. Figure 7-22 shows the Tacos demo application running under Tomcat.

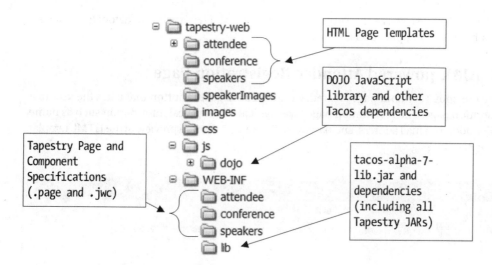

Figure 7-21. *Tacos in TechConf*

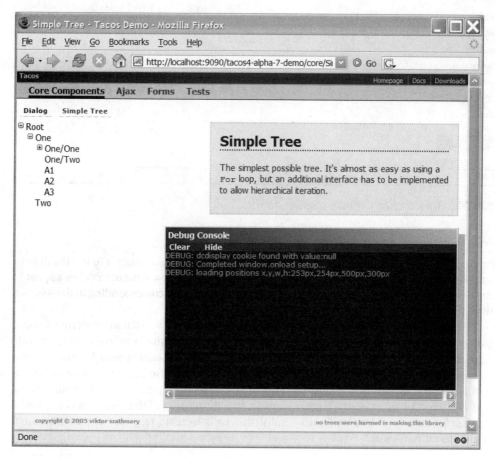

Figure 7-22. *Tacos demo application running under Tomcat*

Figure 7-22 also shows the Tacos Debug Console, which is a very useful tool for debugging Tacos-based AJAX applications.

The AJAX-powered Attendee Registration Page

In the previous TechConf page created, we added a "Register" button that takes the user to a registration page. The registration page takes typical biographical information such as name, mailing address, email address, and password. Figure 7-23 shows a preview of the HTML template for the Register page.

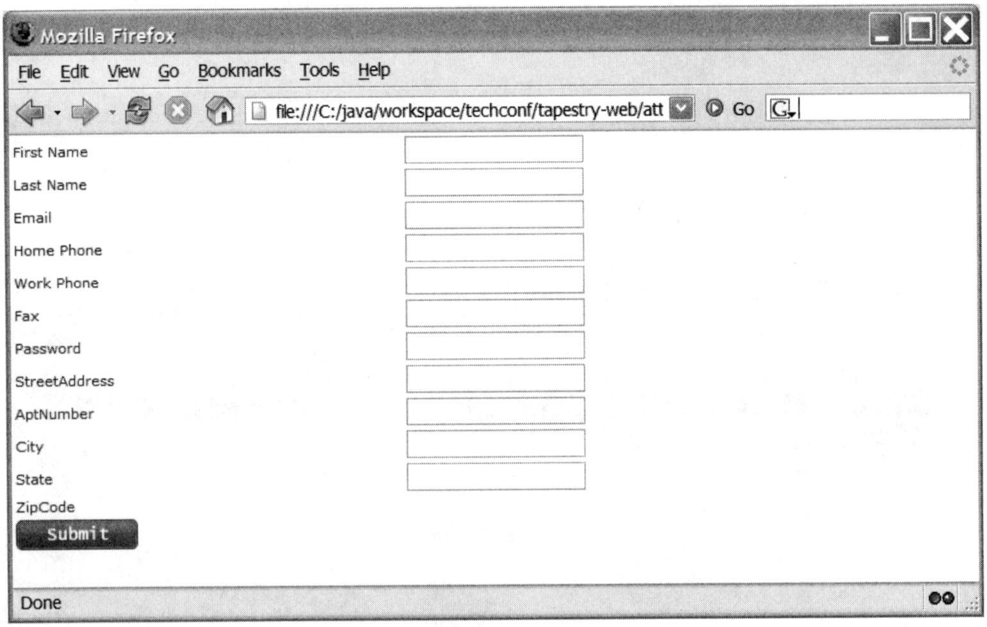

Figure 7-23. *Attendee Register page (register.html)*

AJAX Features

One of the AJAX features that we want to accomplish on the Register page is to use the auto-complete effect to allow users to partially enter a ZIP code and have a list of matches appear in a drop-down menu. Once they select a ZIP code, the city and state corresponding to the selected ZIP code should appear in their respective fields.

The other feature of the Register page is dynamic user input validation. In a typical non-AJAX application, the user will enter data in the form and submit the form to the server for validation. If errors exist, the new page rendered will contain error messages or some kind of indicator as to what fields are in error. The goal for the Register page is to use Tacos components to submit the form data asynchronously and update the display dynamically to show any errors.

To display the errors on the page, we need a specific portion of the page to serve as the container for the error messages. To accomplish this, we can create a simple custom component to render error messages.

The ErrorDisplay Component

The `ErrorDisplay` component will construct the output HTML in code; therefore it will inherit from the `org.apache.tapestry.AbstractComponent`. For this component we are making full use of Tapestry annotations to define the component. Instead of having a component specification file (.jwc), we use the `org.apache.tapestry.annotations.ComponentClass` and `org.apache. tapestry.annotations.Parameter` annotations to define the component and its parameters respectively.

The `renderComponent` method is responsible for rendering the component's body. To create the HTML, we use an instance of `IMarkupWriter`, which is passed as a parameter to the method. Listing 7-29 shows the implementation of the `ErrorDisplay` component.

Listing 7-29. *ErrorDisplay Custom Component*

```
package com.integrallis.techconf.web.tapestry.components;
...

@ComponentClass(allowBody = false, allowInformalParameters = false)
public abstract class ErrorDisplay extends AbstractComponent {

    @Parameter(required = true)
    public abstract IValidationDelegate getDelegate();

    @SuppressWarnings("unchecked")
    public void renderComponent(IMarkupWriter writer, IRequestCycle cycle) {
        if (cycle.isRewinding()) return;

        IValidationDelegate delegate = getDelegate();
        // check the validation delegate, if there are no errors just return
        if (delegate != null) {
            if (!delegate.getHasErrors()) return;

            writer.begin("table");
            writer.attribute("class", "red");
            writer.begin("tr");
            writer.attribute("valign", "top");
            writer.begin("td");
            writer.beginEmpty("img");
            writer.attribute("src", "../images/warning.png");
            writer.attribute("width", 42);
            writer.attribute("height", 42);
            writer.end();
            writer.begin("td");
            writer.attribute("class", "message");
```

```
        List<IRender> errorRenders = delegate.getErrorRenderers();
        writer.begin("ul");
        for (IRender render : errorRenders) {
            writer.begin("li");
            render.render(writer, cycle);
            writer.end();
        }
        writer.end();
        writer.end("table");
    }
}
}
```

HTML Template

The HTML template for the registration page is shown in Listing 7-30. Like other conference pages, it uses the ConferenceBorder component previously created. At the very top of the template we place an instance of the ErrorDisplay component created in the previous section.

Listing 7-30. *Register Page HTML Template*

```
<html jwcid="@ConferenceBorder" title="Register">
  <span jwcid="@ErrorDisplay" delegate="bean:delegate"/>
  <form jwcid="@tacos:AjaxForm"
        delegate="bean:delegate"
        listener="ognl:listeners.add">
        ...
  </form>
</html>
```

In previous examples submitting user information we used the Tapestry Form component. Tacos provides its own form component called AjaxForm, which provides a form that can handle AJAX and DHTML effects. AjaxForm descends from Tapestry's Form, therefore they are used in nearly identical ways. The delegate attribute refers to the object to which the validation of the form is delegated. The delegate is a class implementing the IValidationDelegate interface. A validation delegate keeps track of the user input, and it's responsible for decorating form fields and field labels. The listener attribute determines the listener method that will be invoked when the form is submitted.

Listing 7-31 shows a sample of the input fields and field labels in the form of the Register page.

Listing 7-31. *Register Page HTML Template*

```
<table width="100%" border="0" summary="register">
  <tr>
    <td><span jwcid="firstNameLabel"><label>First Name</label></span></td>
    <td><span jwcid="firstName"><input type="text" alt="First Name" /></span></td>
  </tr>
```

```
<tr>
  <td><span jwcid="lastNameLabel"><label>Last Name</label></span></td>
  <td><span jwcid="lastName"><input type="text" alt="Last Name" /></span></td>
</tr>
<tr>
  <td><span jwcid="emailLabel"><label>Email</label></span></td>
  <td><span jwcid="email"><input type="text" alt="Email" /></span></td>
</tr>
...
<tr>
  <td><span jwcid="cityLabel"><label>City</label></span></td>
  <td><span jwcid="city"><input type="text" alt="City" /></span></td>
</tr>
<tr>
  <td><span jwcid="stateLabel"><label>State</label></span></td>
  <td><span jwcid="state"><input type="text" alt="State" /></span></td>
</tr>
<tr>
  <td><span jwcid="zipCodeLabel"><label>ZipCode</label></span></td>
  <td><span class="auto_complete" jwcid="zipCode"/></td>
</tr>
<tr>
  <td><img jwcid="@ImageSubmit" image="asset:btn_submit"
          alt="Submit" src="../images/btn-submit.gif" /></td>
</tr>
</table>
```

Java Code

In the Java code, we need to handle the form submission and the creation of the objects used to hold the registration information. Since the EJB3 service methods that we will be interacting with take DTOs as parameters, we need an instance of the DynaDTO builder factory to create the necessary objects. Listing 7-32 shows the Java implementation of the Register page. In the pageBeginRender listener, we create and set the DTO objects that will carry the data from the form to the form listener all the way down to the EJB3 service.

Listing 7-32. *Register Page Implementation*

```
package com.integrallis.techconf.web.tapestry.pages.attendee;
...
public abstract class Register extends ActiveConferencePage {
    /** DynaDTO builders */
    private Builder attendeeBuilder = null;
    private Builder addressBuilder = null;
    ...
```

```
    public void pageBeginRender(PageEvent event) {
        super.pageBeginRender(event);
        if (getUser() == null) {
            // get the builders if necessary
            if (attendeeBuilder == null) {
                attendeeBuilder = getBuilderFactory()
                    .getBuilder(AttendeeInfo.class);
            }
            if (addressBuilder == null) {
                addressBuilder = getBuilderFactory().getBuilder(AddressInfo.class);
            }
            // set the user/address empty DTOs if one is not already set
            setUser((AttendeeInfo)attendeeBuilder.build());
            getUser().setAddress((AddressInfo) addressBuilder.build());
        }
    }

    public String add(IRequestCycle cycle) {
        IValidationDelegate delegate =
            (IValidationDelegate)getBeans().getBean("delegate");

        if (delegate.getHasErrors()) return null;

        // if it passes validation then register them
        setUser( getUserService().registerAttendee(getUser()));

        // back to the page
        return "attendee/Register";
    }

    public abstract void setUser(AttendeeInfo i);
    public abstract AttendeeInfo getUser();

    public abstract UserService getUserService();
    public abstract BuilderFactory getBuilderFactory();
}
```

The add method processes the form submission. It first checks the form for errors using the validation delegate, and if there are no errors, it uses the UserService to invoke the registerAttendee method passing the AttendeeInfo DTO populated with the form data.

Page Specification

The Register page will use the UserService EJB3 service to attempt to register a new user and the DynaDTO builder to create the instance of the AttendeeInfo DTO (and the enclosed AddressInfo DTO). Therefore we need to make the service available to the page by injecting it in the page specification as shown next:

```
<!-- User Service -->
<inject property="userService" object="service:app.UserService"/>
```

To inject the DynaDTO builder factory, we need to first define it in the hivemodule.xml file as follows:

```
<!-- ================================================================ -->
<!-- DynaDTO Builder Factory                                          -->
<!-- ================================================================ -->
<service-point id="DynaBuilderFactory" interface="org.dynadto.BuilderFactory">
  <invoke-factory service-id="app.JndiLookupFactory">
    <construct resource="java:/dynadto/BuilderFactory" />
  </invoke-factory>
</service-point>
```

The service point app.JndiLookupFactory is another custom HiveMind service created for the TechConf application that, similar to the EJB3Factory, does a simple JNDI lookup to return an object. Since the DynaDTO builder factory is available in the JNDI tree as shown in Chapter 5, we can use this HiveMind service to locate it. In the Register page definition we inject the builderFactory property as follows:

```
<inject property="builderFactory"
        object="service:app.DynaBuilderFactory"/>
```

In the page definition for the Register page, we define the components for the fields and labels used in the HTML template and any validation required. The simplest type of validator is the required validation which is shown in Listing 7-33.

Listing 7-33. *Simple Field Validation in the Register Page Specification*

```
<!-- First Name -->
<component id="firstName" type="TextField">
    <binding name="value" value="ognl:user.firstName"/>
    <binding name="validators" value="validators:required"/>
    <binding name="displayName" value="literal:First Name"/>
</component>

<component id="firstNameLabel" type="FieldLabel">
    <binding name="field" value="component:firstName"/>
</component>
```

Tapestry includes other specific validators such an email validator. Listing 7-34 shows the component definition for the email field of the form. The email validator takes as a parameter a message that will be displayed (by the validation delegate). Validator messages are enclosed in square brackets.

Listing 7-34. *Format and Length Field Validation in the Register Page Specification*

```
<!-- Email -->
<component id="email" type="TextField">
    <binding name="value" value="ognl:user.email"/>
    <binding name="validators"
            value="validators:required,email[You must enter a valid email]"/>
    <binding name="displayName" value="literal:Email"/>
</component>
...
<!-- Password -->
<component id="password" type="TextField">
    <binding name="value" value="ognl:user.password"/>
    <binding name="validators"
            value="validators:required,maxLength=16[You must enter a password no
longer than 16 characters]"/>
    <binding name="displayName" value="literal:Password"/>
    <binding name="hidden" value="true"/>
</component>
```

Finally, in the page specification we need to declare the bean with id `delegate` used in the AjaxForm delegate attribute. The default validation delegate class is `org.apache.tapestry.valid.ValidationDelegate`. See Listing 7-35.

Listing 7-35. *Format and Length Field Validation in the Register Page Specification*

```
<!-- Delegate to do the validation -->
<bean name="delegate"
      class="org.apache.tapestry.valid.ValidationDelegate" property="delegate"/>
```

Figure 7-24 shows the result of pressing Enter in the First Name input field. In this case the form gets submitted using an AJAX request, and the error message is displayed dynamically using the "yellow fade effect", which is a popular technique for letting users know that something has changed on a page.

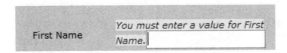

Figure 7-24. *AJAX field validation in action*

The field validation messages appear from top to bottom, one at a time. As you correct an error, the error disappears with a fade effect, and the next error from top to bottom is displayed (if there are any errors remaining on the form).

Submitting the form by clicking the Submit button uses the `ErrorDisplay` component to display the error messages. The validation delegate also decorates the fields in error by changing the color of the field labels and adding two asterisks next to the field. Figure 7-25 shows the result of submitting the form with only the First Name and Last Name fields completed and an error in the syntax of the email field (two @ signs back).

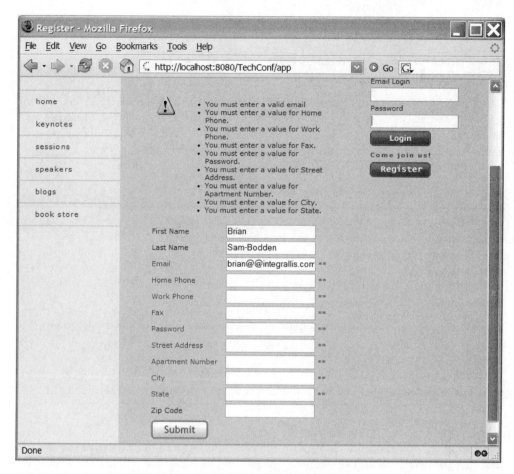

Figure 7-25. *Tapestry validation and ErrorDisplay component*

ZIP Code, City, and State Auto-completion

The next AJAX function we'll tackle is the auto-complete function, popular for decades with fat, rich-client applications and made popular on the Web by Google. In the case of the Register page, we want to show a drop-down of possible matches for a ZIP code as the user enters information. After the user selects a particular ZIP code we want to drop the values for the city and the state in their respective fields.

On the server side, we'll use the EJB3 service location lookup service that can retrieve a list of locations given a partial ZIP code, as shown in Listing 7-36.

Listing 7-36. *LocationLookupService Interface*

```
public interface LocationLookupService {
    List<Location> searchLocations(String zipCode);
    ...
}
```

To get started, we need to inject the location lookup service to the Service page configuration as shown here:

```
<inject property="locationLookupService"
        object="service:app.LocationLookupService"/>
```

To implement auto-completion on the ZIP code, we use the Tacos Autocompleter component. Behind the scenes, the Autocompleter component uses the script.aculo.us library Autocompleter functionality, which is a class that allows for auto-complete pull-down behavior driven by a remote request. Table 7-4 shows the parameters of the Autocompleter component.

Table 7-4. *Tacos Autocompleter Parameters*

Parameter	Description
displayName	The text for the associated field label
value	The object property this value is bound to
listSource	The list that provides the values for the drop-down
listener	The method that will respond to user input
listItemRenderer	The class responsible of rendering the elements of the drop-down
direct	Whether or not to do a direct service call for component
frequency	Time lapse in milliseconds before the component will submit
afterUpdateElement	Hook for the function called after the element has been updated

Listing 7-37 shows the definition of the `zipCode` component using Tacos Autocompleter in the page specification of the Register page. Since I don't want to make another round trip to the server to retrieve the values of the City and State for the selected ZIP code, the value of the `afterUpdateElement` is a JavaScript function that will parse the HTML (see Listing 7-38) for the selected element and extract the values. For this I used the Dojo JavaScript library (available with Tacos) for HTML parsing and effects as well as some fairly rudimentary JavaScript techniques (which will work only for a single-form page).

Listing 7-37. *Using the Tacos Autocompleter Component*

```
<!-- Zip Code -->
<component id="zipCode" type="tacos:Autocompleter" >
    <binding name="displayName" value="literal:Zip Code" />
    <binding name="value" value="ognl:user.address.zipCode" />
    <binding name="listSource" value="ognl:zipCodeList" />
    <binding name="listener" value="listener:searchZipCodes" />
    <binding name="listItemRenderer" value="ognl:listRenderer" />
    <binding name="direct" value="ognl:true" />
    <binding name="frequency" value="literal:0.4" />
```

```
<binding name="afterUpdateElement">
  literal:<![CDATA[
    function handleAutoComplete(field, htmlElement) {
      var span = dojo.dom.collectionToArray(
                   htmlElement.getElementsByTagName("SPAN"))[0];
      var spanBody = dojo.dom.textContent(span);
      var values = spanBody.split(",");
      var city = dojo.string.trim(values[0]);
      var state = dojo.string.trim(values[1]);
      document.getElementById("city").value=city;
      document.getElementById("state").value=state;
      dojo.graphics.htmlEffects.highlight(
        document.getElementById("city"), [255,255,184], 500, 500
      );
      dojo.graphics.htmlEffects.highlight(
        document.getElementById("state"), [255,255,184], 500, 500
      );
    }
  ]]>
</binding>
</component>
```

The optional `listItemRenderer` parameter points to a class that implements the `net.sf.tacos.ajax.components.ListItemRenderer` interface. Listing 7-38 shows the implementation used for the `zipCode` component. The `renderList` method takes an `Iterator` of the objects to be rendered. In this case we know that the type of the object returned by the server is `Location`. The location element provides getters for the ZIP code, City, and State values. The list elements should look like the following:

```
<ul>
  <li>ZipCode</li>
  <li>City, State</li>
</ul>
```

Since we are displaying additional information in the auto-complete dropdown that we don't want inserted into the field when an item is chosen, we need to surround it in a span element with the class attribute set to "informal".

Listing 7-38. *ListItemRenderer for ZIP Code Autocompleter*

```
package com.integrallis.techconf.web.tapestry.common;

import java.util.Iterator;
import net.sf.tacos.ajax.components.ListItemRenderer;
import org.apache.tapestry.IMarkupWriter;
import org.apache.tapestry.IRequestCycle;
import com.integrallis.techconf.dto.Location;
```

```java
public class LocationRenderer implements ListItemRenderer {

    public void renderList(IMarkupWriter writer, IRequestCycle cycle,
                           Iterator values) {
        if (cycle.isRewinding()) return;

        writer.begin("ul");
        writer.attribute("class", "locations");

        while (values.hasNext()) {
            Location value = (Location)values.next();
            if (value == null) continue;

            writer.begin("li");
            writer.attribute("class", "location");
            writer.begin("div");
            writer.attribute("class", "zip");
            writer.print(value.getZip());
            writer.end("div");
            writer.begin("div");
            writer.attribute("class", "description");
            writer.begin("span");
            writer.attribute("class", "informal");
            writer.print(value.getCity() + ", " + value.getState());
            writer.end("span");
            writer.end("div");
            writer.end("li");
        }
        writer.end();
    }
}
```

In the Java code the changes needed include providing an instance of the LocationRenderer and a Collection object to hold the results of the server call to retrieve the Location object matching a partial ZIP Code. The searchZipCodes method uses the LocationService to invoke the searchLocations method as shown in Listing 7-39.

Listing 7-39. *Java Changes Required for ZipCode Autocompleter*

```java
public abstract class Register extends ActiveConferencePage {
    /** List html renderer */
    private static final ListItemRenderer LOCATION_RENDERER
        = new LocationRenderer();

    ...
```

```
public ListItemRenderer getListRenderer() {
    return LOCATION_RENDERER;
}

public void searchZipCodes(String searchString) {
    List<Location> locations =
        getLocationLookupService().searchLocations(searchString);
    setZipCodeList(locations);
}

public abstract Collection getZipCodeList();
public abstract void setZipCodeList(Collection values);
}
```

Figure 7-26 shows the results of applying the Autocompleter changes to the Register page. As the user enter the digits of a ZIP Code, the values in the drop-down change; the more digits that are entered, the smaller the search set becomes. Selecting an entry drops the selected values for the city and state.

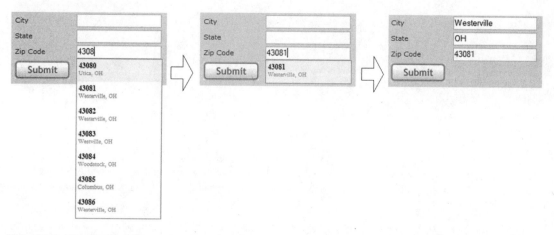

Figure 7-26. *The ZipCode Autocompleter in action*

Summary

In this chapter you've learned how to work with the Web frameworks better positioned to become the prevalent technologies to build Web applications in Java. Tapestry, along with JSF and Wicket (http://wicket.sourceforge.net), represent the new breed of Web frameworks that bring back the power of objects to the Web tier. The ability to use powerful features like annotations, inversion of control, and AJAX can make your Web applications reach the next level of evolution and be ready for the Web 2.0.

CHAPTER 8

■■■

Testing

When a piece of software grows beyond a few hundred lines, how do you know if it is broken? How do you know if it is doing what it is supposed to do? How do you know if there is a case, maybe driven by user input, that will cause the whole application to crash? Common sense will tell us that you need to develop a set of tests to test all the individual pieces, components, or modules of the application as well as tests to cover all the scenarios of possible interactions between those components and external entities such as users and other systems.

Let's illustrate some points about testing by using the perhaps most overused analogy in software engineering, the building of a house. A house can be seen from many different perspectives by the different people involved in its construction and use. The house can be seen as a collection of individual components (like bricks, wood beams, doors, nails, etc.). This is the most simplistic component view of a house. From this perspective we draw the conclusion that if each one of those components has passed some sort of quality control by the manufacturer, all that is left to test is the interaction between those components.

Today in software development the term "unit testing" is commonly used to refer to the type of testing that isolates a unit and tests its internal functionality as well as its external contracts. If you approach testing as the first stage of development, unit testing becomes testing of code that you are yet to write. The test-first philosophy is at the core of test-driven development (TDD) and has been proven to improve code quality and control the scope of a project. In the house example, the manufacturer testing would be considered unit testing. Unit testing in Java treats a Java class as the atomic unit of functionality and mixes white-box and black-box testing. For example, if a class MyClass has a public method called doSomething that depends on a private method performCommonOperation, then as part of the tests for MyClass, let's say in class MyClassTest, we will have a method performCommonOperationTest (a white-box test) and a doSomethingTest (black-box test). A software test has certain preconditions, and the actual test is checking the post-conditions against the expected state for the given preconditions.

Unit Test or Functional Test?

I mentioned previously that unit testing in Java is composed of white-box testing and black-box testing. White-box testing is testing the internals of the class, like private and protected methods, and accounting for their implementation. Black-box testing is testing the different ways the public methods might be used by other classes, including usage that might be considered erroneous. Black-box testing is sometimes referred to as functional or concrete testing, and in certain circles unit testing in Java that requires any resource outside of the class itself is not considered unit testing. Particularly, the purist definition of a unit test making its rounds in the Java community is that any test that talks to another system (such as a database, the file system, or a web service) or a test that depends on other tests executing or that can't be executed concurrently with other tests is not considered a unit test but a functional test.

The radical definition of a unit test is good for productivity since it ensures that tests can be executed in any environment, in any order, and that they execute fast. These characteristics make automation and the practice of continuous integration (see Chapter 9) more viable. Given that most testing frameworks for Java are labeled "unit testing" frameworks (including JUnit, the testing framework with the most influence in the Java world), it is easy to see where one could take the previous definition of a unit test to heart and end with a fairly fast but fairly shallow test harness. Unit testing will not address integration errors or any other systemwide issues. Cedric Beust, creator of the TestNG framework, accurately points that most tests written under a unit testing framework are not unit tests by the previous definition but are functional tests and that the line between what is considered a unit test and what is not is not clearly marked. Going back to our house analogy, restricting your test harness by the narrow definition of a unit test is like assuming that because all components of a house are tested by their respective manufacturers, they will work together appropriately and that they will be used as intended. Anyone who has built a home can attest that regardless of the quality of the materials and the amount of quality control from the manufacturer, most problems in a house are caused by how certain materials are used.

In the house analogy, other views of the house emerge. For example, to the home owners the house might be viewed as a collection of rooms, and a test from their point of view might entail criteria like how much natural light is allowed in and whether the rooms fit the typical traffic pattern of the family. The point is that a house is built in layers just like software, with cross-cutting concerns such as load-bearing walls, electrical circuits, and plumbing. Successfully testing an application is about organizing the tests based on the different levels of abstraction of an application and concentrating on covering the units and interactions between the units involved in a layer.

In this chapter we will create a test harness for the TechConf sample application by creating groups of tests that tackle the different levels of abstraction in the application, from the low-level details of the ORM layer to the high-level testing of services and the interplay of design and implementation patterns used to fulfill those services goals. In the spirit of the book, we will use the TestNG framework, which represents the next step in the evolution of testing frameworks in Java.

Testing in the Development Cycle

Software development and management methodologies have greatly evolved in the last 10 years to cope with ever-increasing turnaround times and quality levels required of enterprise Web applications. From Extreme Programming (XP), Feature-Driven Development (FDD), and Scrum we have learned that incremental, cyclical techniques are best suited to deal with the malleability of software.

In the last five years there has been a rebirth in the area of testing. Development teams have learned that they can no longer rely on just a QA team to test an application. Testing is everybody's job. We also have learned that leaving the testing of an application for the end of the project is a bad idea. Why? One reason has to do with the question of what to test. Incrementally creating tests as the code is being built (or as the driving force behind what to build) results in better test coverage, but more importantly, incremental test creation shapes the software being built by validating, repudiating, or simply questioning the assumptions made during design and development. Incremental testing leads not only to better software but also to better productivity when combined with the practice of continuous integration, which automates the testing to discover almost immediately any unwanted side effect introduced by changes in a project's code base. So instead of dealing with a convoluted set of problems which have accumulated over time and which might have effects that are now intertwined, your team instead deals with the (hopefully localized) effects of fine-grained changes.

This of course makes sense to most of us, but we do not always do the things that make sense in software development. When pressure to finish a project increases, the first thing that tends to go is testing. Why? Because sometimes testing can be tedious. Therefore we need to make testing not a side effect of development but a primary force behind it by first making it pervasive throughout the development process and by making it the path of least resistance. To date, many applications, tools, and frameworks have been developed to standardize, automate, and simplify the processes of unit and functional testing. Regardless of what tool you use, I have found that the simple practices shown in the next section can place software testing in a place of paramount importance, where it should be. Your software will do more accurately what it was meant to do.

Testing Best Practices

TDD advocates the practice of programming by writing tests first, writing the code to make the tests pass, then refactoring to optimize the code and the overall design of the application without breaking the tests. Obviously this leads to a comprehensive test suite that covers what your code does, because it was the contract of what was to be built. The following list reflects my philosophy about testing:

1. **Write tests first:** Write tests that show the typical usage of a given class first (plus some boundary or edge cases). Then write enough code to pass the tests. Coding to interfaces as seen throughout the book can help make the test-first approach attainable.

2. **Write code with clear intentions:** Follow good object-oriented practices by creating code that makes its purpose obvious to others. Keep classes small and use good naming conventions. It is easier to write a test for a component for which the intent is known, especially since it is possible that somebody else might be writing the tests or enhancing them in the future. This practice becomes easier if you choose to use practice 1.

3. **Test everything:** If it can break, test it. If it can produce effects or output that's not clear from its interface, test it. Even simple components can produce errors in other components if their intent or function is not clear. I equate tests in software to formal proofs in mathematics. Unless there is a comprehensive set of tests, any assurance of a component quality is just an illusion.

4. **Establish a test harness early in the development:** Set up testing as part of the build and if possible, use a test framework that integrates well with your development tools; doing this early in a project will ensure that the whole team embraces testing and that it becomes the path of least resistance.

5. **Code enough to pass the unit tests:** The task is complete when the unit test is complete. Just like code shouldn't be checked into a version control system without compiling, code shouldn't be checked in unless it has a comprehensive set of unit tests and those tests pass.

6. **Map tests to use cases, user stories, or features:** Regardless of what requirement gathering techniques you use, map those requirements to a clearly defined set of tests.

7. **Enable continuous integration:** As you'll learn in Chapter 9, continuous integration hinges on developers running the unit tests before the code is checked in. In addition, all unit tests should be executed in a build server at least once a day (hourly seems to work well as a build interval) or after any code has been checked in.

8. **Don't overtest:** Test enough to cover functionality. Add new tests as defects appear. Use techniques such as equivalence partitioning and boundary value analysis to minimize the number of tests needed. Grouping, categorizing, and organizing your tests can ensure that you don't write redundant tests and that the tests cover the range of features and scenarios for a given component.

Tools

The best practices mentioned in the preceding section are possible in practice thanks to the tools created by the open source community. In this chapter we will cover some of the tools, but before we jump into the code, it is important to understand the different categories of testing tools available:

- **Test Frameworks:** Frameworks such as JUnit and TestNG are inspired by the xUnit family of unit/regression testing frameworks, which provide basic capabilities for creating, running, and reporting the results of tests.

- **In-Container Testing Tools:** These tools enable you to test the functionality of container-dependent components, usually making them appear as if they are simple Java objects.

- **Web Testing Tools:** These tools usually extend an existing test framework to enable tests based on the HTTP protocol and are a subset of in-container testing tools.

- **Test Coverage Tools:** These tools enable you to determine how much of an application is covered by tests.

- **Mock Object Frameworks:** Mock object frameworks provide the ability to dynamically create objects that can be used to mock up collaborating objects required in a functional test.

JUnit

For many years, unit testing has consisted of `System.out.println()` functions or testing code in a class's main method. Though this form of testing can be effective, it is a reactive measure that has some drawbacks: it requires human intervention and interpretation, it taints production code and deploys testing code, and the results aren't very repeatable. The most notable of the testing frameworks is JUnit, which is as of this date the 400-pound gorilla of testing and has been extended by other projects to provide testing on many areas of software development. JUnit is the pioneering framework that brought testing back into the limelight. JUnit, hosted at `www.junit.org`, is a simple framework based on Java introspection and the concepts of test methods, test classes, and test suites. The framework includes extendable classes used to create tests and test runners that run the tests and present the results.

The `junit.framework` package contains the interface and classes used to develop unit tests. The Test interface is a simple interface used to define a test. Rather than implement the Test interface directly, most users extend the abstract base class `junit.framework.TestCase` or the concrete class `junit.framework.TestSuite`. A TestCase contains the tests for a single unit, while a TestSuite is a collection of Test classes.

In Java, a unit is a class. Therefore, a TestCase typically contains all the tests for a single class. A test tests a single method of a class or a single unit of work. Tests have one of three outcomes: pass, fail, or error. If a test passes, the method or unit of work implements all the functionality as expected. A failure occurs when an expected value doesn't equal an actual value. For example, a test might be written to check that the size is incremented when an object is added to a collection. Assertions are used to compare the actual value to the expected value. Uncaught Exceptions are the cause of errors. A test runner can be used to execute a TestCase and report the results. There are many test runners available.

To define a test, extend the `junit.framework.TestCase` class and add the appropriate test methods similar to those shown in Listing 8-2. A test is a method with no return value, no parameter, and the name testXXXX. In the test method, the Assert class static methods are used to determine if actual result values of a test equal the expected values. The Assert class contains many static assert methods. Aside from the expected and actual parameters, most of the methods have an optional message parameter for describing the failure. An example is the overloaded assertEquals method for comparing just about every defined data type. In addition to the assertEquals there are assertNotNull, assertFalse, assertNotSame, assertNull, and assertTrue. The Assert class also contains a fail method for explain failures. The TestCase class extends Assert so it isn't necessary to directly use the Assert class in the TestCase. A Test class can also optionally override the setUp and tearDown methods to prepare and clean up the state of a test. The setUp method is called prior to every execution of a test method, and the tearDown is called immediately afterward.

Listing 8-1 shows a simple Java class with two methods. The class Greeter contains the methods greet and greet(String).

Listing 8-1. *A Simple Java Class*

```java
public class Greeter {

    public String greet() {
        return "Hello World";
    }

    public String greet(String name) {
        return "Hello " + name;
    }
}
```

Listing 8-2 shows a simple JUnit test class for the Greeter class shown in Listing 8-1.

Listing 8-2. *A Simple JUnit TestCase*

```java
import junit.framework.TestCase;

public class GreeterTest extends TestCase {

    public void testGreet() {
        Greeter greeter = new Greeter();
        assertEquals("Hello World", greeter.greet());
    }

    public void testGreetString() {
        Greeter greeter = new Greeter();
        String name = "Michael";
        assertEquals("Hello " + name, greeter.greet(name));
    }

    public static void main(String[] args) {
        //junit.swingui.TestRunner.run(GreeterTest.class);
        junit.textui.TestRunner.run(GreeterTest.class);
    }

}
```

As you can see, the GreeterTest case tests the two public methods in the Greeter class. Executing the test case results in output similar to:

```
..
Time: 0.016

OK (2 tests)
```

If we change the `testGreet` method by replacing the expected output to "Hola", it should result in the output changing to:

```
..F
Time: 0.015
There was 1 failure:
1) testGreetString(GreeterTest)junit.framework.ComparisonFailure:
 expected:<...ola...> but was:<...ello...>
    at GreeterTest.testGreetString(GreeterTest.java:20)
    ...
    at GreeterTest.main(GreeterTest.java:25)

FAILURES!!!
Tests run: 2,  Failures: 1,  Errors: 0
```

JUnit also comes with several runners as shown in Figure 8-1, which shows the Swing runner.

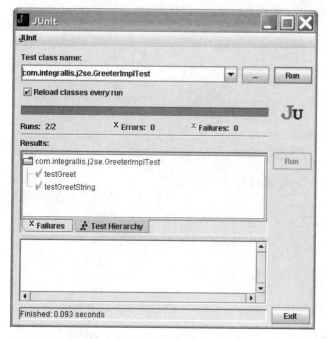

Figure 8-1. *JUnit Swing*

JUnit integration is also offered in Eclipse as a view. Figure 8-2 shows the embedded Eclipse JUnit view.

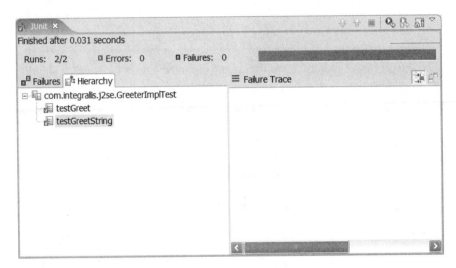

Figure 8-2. *JUnit Eclipse view*

Even though a TestCase may be run individually, it's often advantageous to run a complete set of tests at one time. JUnit supports grouping a collection of test cases with the TestSuite class. A test suite helps in organizing tests so that they can be executed as a group. Listing 8-3 shows how to create a test suite. The AllTests class creates a TestSuite in the static method suite and adds test cases to it using the addTestSuite() method.

Listing 8-3. *JUnit* TestSuite

```
public class AllTests {

    public static Test suite() {
        TestSuite suite = new TestSuite("All Tests");

        // add tests
        suite.addTestSuite(GreeterTest.class);
        ...

        return suite;
    }
}
```

TestNG

JUnit is a great framework that completely changed the way we approached testing, but like all pioneering technologies, it is not without its flaws. TestNG is a new framework created by

Cedric Beust to address some of the shortcomings of JUnit and to take advantage of the new features and trends in Java development.

TestNG uses JSE 5.0 annotations or Javadoc comments to enable simple POJOs to act as a testing class, as opposed to JUnit's more traditional approach of using inheritance and abstract classes. TestNG supports data-driven testing, acknowledging the fact that a large percentage of tests performed functional and integration tests while only a small percentage are pure unit tests. TestNG also provides an XML-based runtime configuration which, mixed with the ability to classify tests using groups, provides a powerful execution model which eliminates the need to use constructs like JUnit's TestSuite.

TestNG is hosted at www.testng.org and is distributed as a single ZIP file. At the time of this writing, version 4.3 is available (testng-4.3.zip). At the root of the archive you'll find JAR files for JDK 1.4 and JDK 1.5. For the TechConf application and the purposes of this chapter, we will use the JDK 1.5 version (testng-4.3-jdk15.jar). This JAR needs to be in your classpath for the exercises in this chapter to work.

Let's start first with a simple class to test the Greeter class previously created. In TestNG any simple Java class can become a test class by using metadata annotations. Listing 8-4 shows the TestNG version of the GreeterTest class.

Listing 8-4. *TestNG Annotated POJO*

```
import org.testng.Assert;
import org.testng.annotations.Configuration;
import org.testng.annotations.Test;

public class GreeterTest {

    private Greeter greeter;

    @Configuration(beforeTestClass = true)
    private void init() {
        greeter = new Greeter();
    }

    @Test
    public void testGreet() {
        assert "Hello World".equals(greeter.greet());
    }

    @Test
    public void testGreetString() {
        String name = "Michael";
        Assert.assertEquals("Hello " + name, greeter.greet(name));
    }

}
```

The first thing to notice is that our test class doesn't have to extend any base class or implement any interfaces. The two test methods are annotated with the org.testng.annotations.Test, and instead of having the Greeter class instantiate in each method we now have a private instance which is initialized in the init method. The init method is annotated with the org.testng.annotations.Configuration annotation, which enables us to control what happens before and after a test method, class, test, or suite. In the case of the init method we are instructing TestNG to execute that method once before it executes the test methods. This is in contrast to JUnit's behavior in which the class is instantiated for each execution of a test method, therefore making it hard to keep any state between method invocations. Equally inconvenient is the behavior of JUnit setup and teardown methods which are invoked before and after each test method.

In the testGreet method we use the Java assert keyword while in the testGreetString we use one of the assertion static methods provided in the org.testng.Assert class. To execute the test on the command line, you'll need to specify the location of your compiled test classes and the TestNG library as shown next (in the following case the compiled classes are in the bin directory and the TestNG library is located in lib/testng directory):

```
java -ea -cp bin;lib/testng/testng-4.3-jdk15.jar org.testng.TestNG -testclass
GreeterTest
```

Also notice that we have enabled assertions by using the –ea flag. The output should resemble:

```
===================================================
Suite for Command line test
Total tests run: 2, Failures: 0, Skips: 0
===================================================
```

If we change the testGreet method by replacing the expected output to "Hola" as done previously with the JUnit example, it should result in the output changing to:

```
===================================================
Suite for Command line test
Total tests run: 2, Failures: 1, Skips: 0
===================================================
```

So, far you can see that TestNG provides the same support for simple testing as does JUnit but with simpler constructs, which make for cleaner and more-compact code. The real power of TestNG lies in the powerful XML configuration mechanism. TestNG is configured via an XML file typically named testng.xml. The XML defines a test suite and enables the specification of tests. In this file you can define which classes and methods are to be included or excluded in a test run, as well as other execution parameters such as the number of threads to be used in the test run.

Figure 8-3 shows a depiction of the structure of the XML file as dictated by the DTD located at `http://beust.com/testng/testng-1.0.dtd`.

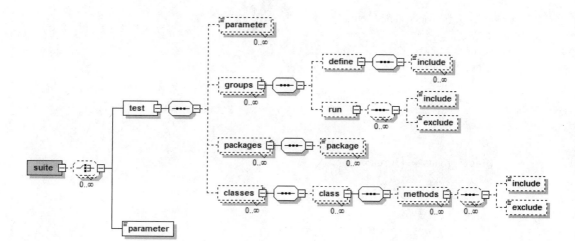

Figure 8-3. *TestNG DTD*

The simplest testng.xml for the previous test is shown in Listing 8-5. The XML file defines the suite "My Suite", which contains one test named "Simple Test", which in turn contains a single class to be tested. TestNG will scan the classes listed for annotations.

Listing 8-5. *TestNG XML Configuration*

```
<!DOCTYPE suite SYSTEM "http://beust.com/testng/testng-1.0.dtd" >

<suite name="My Suite">
  <test name="Simple Test">
    <classes>
      <class name="GreeterTest" />
    </classes>
  </test>
</suite>
```

To run the tests using the testng.xml, use the simple command line shown next:

```
java -ea -cp bin;lib/testng/testng-4.3-jdk15.jar org.testng.TestNG testng.xml
```

Groups

The power of the TestNG configuration lies in the concept of groups. A test method can be declared to belong to one or more groups. Let's look at an example involving three classes shown in Listings 8-6, 8-7, and 8-8.

Listing 8-6. *TestA TestNG Class*

```java
package package1;

import org.testng.annotations.Test;

public class TestA {
    @Test(groups = {"GroupX"})
    public void testA1() {
        System.out.println("testA1");
        assert true;
    }

    @Test(groups = {"GroupY"})
    public void testA2() {
        System.out.println("testA2");
        assert true;
    }
}
```

TestA belongs to package1 and contains the test methods testA1 and testA2. The method testA1 belongs to the test group GroupX, and testA2 belongs to GroupY as reflected in the parameters to the Test annotation.

Listing 8-7. *TestB TestNG Class*

```java
package package2;

import org.testng.annotations.Test;

public class TestB {
    @Test(groups = {"GroupX","GroupY"})
    public void testB1() {
        System.out.println("testB1");
        assert true;
    }

    @Test(groups = {"GroupZ"})
    public void testB2() {
        System.out.println("testB2");
        assert true;
    }
}
```

TestB belongs to package2 and contains the test methods testB1 and testB2. The method testB1 belongs to the test group GroupY, and testB2 belongs to both GroupX and GroupY (the groups parameter takes a comma-delimited list of groups).

Listing 8-8. *TestC TestNG Class*

```java
package package3;

import org.testng.annotations.Test;

public class TestC {
    @Test(groups = {"GroupY"})
    public void testC1() {
        System.out.println("testC1");
        assert true;
    }

    @Test(groups = {"GroupX","GroupZ"})
    public void testC2() {
        System.out.println("testC2");
        assert true;
    }
}
```

Finally, the class TestC belongs to package3 and contains the test methods testC1 and testC2. The method testC1 belongs to the test group GroupY, and testC2 belongs to both GroupX and GroupZ.

If we wanted, for example, to run all tests belonging to GroupX, we could use a testng.xml file like that shown in Listing 8-9.

Listing 8-9. *TestNG Configuration for Running Tests in GroupX*

```xml
<!DOCTYPE suite SYSTEM "http://beust.com/testng/testng-1.0.dtd" >

<suite name="Some Tests" verbose="1">
  <test name="Group Test">
    <groups>
      <run>
        <include name="GroupX"/>
      </run>
    </groups>
    <classes>
      <class name="package1.TestA"/>
      <class name="package2.TestB"/>
      <class name="package3.TestC"/>
    </classes>
  </test>
</suite>
```

The testng.xml file also specified the classes to be included in the test. Running the test will produce output similar to:

```
testA1
testB1
testC2


=================================================
Some Tests
Total tests run: 3, Failures: 0, Skips: 0
=================================================
```

TestNG not only enables you to group test methods under one or more groups but also to create a group of groups. Powerful filtering capabilities enable you to include and exclude groups using regular expressions. For example, to run the tests in GroupX and GroupY, we can use the regular expression "Group[XY]" as shown in Listing 8-10.

Listing 8-10. *TestNG Configuration for Running Tests in GroupX and GroupY*

```
<!DOCTYPE suite SYSTEM "http://beust.com/testng/testng-1.0.dtd" >

<suite name="Some Tests" verbose="1">
  <test name="Group Test">
    <groups>
      <run>
        <include name="Group[XY]"/>
      </run>
    </groups>
    <packages>
      <package name="package1"/>
      <package name="package2"/>
      <package name="package3"/>
    </packages>
  </test>
</suite>
```

Also notice that instead of declaring which classes for TestNG to look for tests, we instead are declaring the packages. Running the example in Listing 8-10 should produce output similar to:

```
testA2
testA1
testB1
testC2
testC1


=================================================
Some Tests
Total tests run: 5, Failures: 0, Skips: 0
=================================================
```

TestNG grouping provides much more flexibility than JUnit since there is no need to recompile any code. TestNG also provides the ability to create groups of methods and, as mentioned previously, groups of groups.

Dependent Methods

TestNG also provides a mechanism for declaring dependencies amongst test methods and avoiding being overwhelmed by what Beust refers to as the "failure cascade trauma" in JUnit when it reports all the failures of dependent tests as well as the root failure. The Test annotation can take a parameter of dependsOnMethods, which takes a comma-separated list of methods. Similarly, you can declare method dependencies on a group via the dependsOnGroups parameter, which takes a comma-separated list of groups. TestNG will guarantee that all of the methods in a dependent group are executed before the method.

Parameters

TestNG allows test parameters to be passed from the testng.xml file or via the Parameters and DataProvider annotations. The org.testng.annotations.Parameters annotation applies to the org.testng.annotations.Test and org.testng.annotations.Configuration parameters.

For example, if you wanted to have a set of database-specific tests, you could define the database parameters in the textng.xml file as shown in Listing 8-11.

Listing 8-11. *TestNG Parameterized Configuration*

```
<!DOCTYPE suite SYSTEM "http://beust.com/testng/testng-1.0.dtd" >

<suite name="Test Suite"
  <parameter name="url" value="jdbc:mysql://localhost/test" />
  <parameter name="driver" value="com.mysql.jdbc.Driver" />
  <parameter name="username" value="user" />
  <parameter name="password" value="pass" />

  <test name="DBTest">
    ...
  </test>
</suite>
```

To use the parameters in your test code simply use the parameters annotation as shown in Listing 8-12.

Listing 8-12. *Using TestNG Parameters in Code*

```
Connection connection = null;

@Parameters({ "url", "driver", "username", "password" })
@Configuration(beforeTestClass = true)
private void initializeDB(String url, String driver,
                          String username, String password) {
```

```
    try {
        // Load the JDBC driver
        Class.forName(driver);
        connection = DriverManager.getConnection(url, username, password);
    } catch (ClassNotFoundException e) {
        // Could not find the driver
    } catch (SQLException e) {
        // Could not connect to the database
    }
}

@Test
public void testXXX() {
    // do something with the connection
}
```

TestNG Eclipse Plug-in

TestNG provides a powerful Eclipse plug-in (there is also an IntelliJ IDEA plug-in available) that enables you to run test classes and methods similarly to the native JUnit Eclipse plug-in (with a similar streetlight analogy). The Eclipse plug-in enables easy selection of groups and test suite files for a TestNG test run. Like the built-in JUnit plug-in, the TestNG plug-in is tightly integrated with the Java Development Tools (JDT). Also, if you are migrating from JUnit, the plug-in offers a wizard to convert JUnit tests into TestNG tests which use the class JUnitConverter, which converts JUnit test classes into TestNG by annotating them.

To install the plug-in in Eclipse select Help ➤ Software Updates ➤ Find and Install. Select "Search for new features to install" and then Next. Add a new remote update site by selecting New Remote Site. In the dialog, enter "TestNG" for the name and http://beust.com/eclipse as shown in Figure 8-4.

Figure 8-4. *Adding a new update site for TestNG*

Next, click OK, then check the TestNG update site, and uncheck all others and click Finish. In the Search Results dialog, select the TestNG version as shown in Figure 8-5.

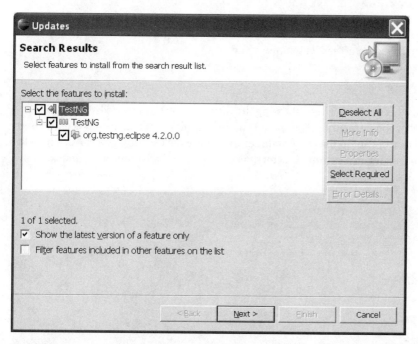

Figure 8-5. *Installing the TestNG Eclipse plug-in*

Select Next, accept the license agreement, and the download and installation should begin. After it is completed Eclipse will be restarted, and you should be ready to use the TestNG plug-in.

To open the TestNG view, select Window ➤ Show View ➤ Other and select the TestNG view. You can now right-click any TestNG annotated class and select Run As ➤ TestNG Test. This will create a TestNG Eclipse launch configuration and automatically run it. The TestNG results view is nearly identical to the JUnit results view as shown in Figure 8-6.

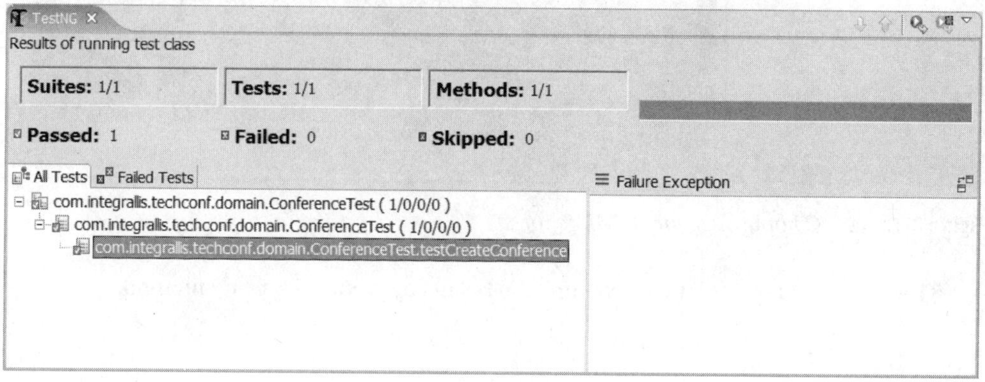

Figure 8-6. *TestNG Eclipse plug-in results view*

For complete control of the execution of your TestNG tests, you can configure the launch configuration by selecting Run ➤ Run or Run ➤ Debug and configure TestNG to run a specific class, group, or run based on a TestNG definition file.

TestNG Reports

TestNG generated a set of HTML pages showing the result of a test run as well as an XML file which can be used to generate other types of output. By default the HTML report is generated in a folder named test-output in the current directory. (In the next section you can see how to use Ant to create the reports in a custom directory.) Figure 8-7 shows the home page (index.html) for a typical TestNG test run.

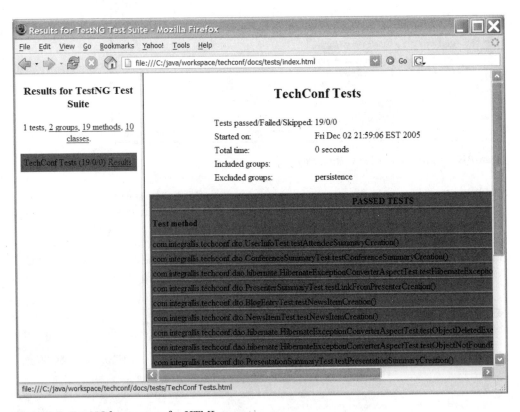

Figure 8-7. *TestNG home page for HTML reports*

The generated reports let you examine the results by group, class, and method.

TestNG and Ant

To run the TestNG tests from the exiting TechConf Ant buildfile, I've added the "test-run" Ant macrodef to the macros.xml file created in Chapter 3. Listing 8-13 shows the macrodef definition, which uses the testng task. Assuming that the TestNG JAR is in the lib/testng directory, we create the Ant path testng, which is used as the classpath for loading the task via the taskdef.

Listing 8-13. *TestNG Ant Macrodef*

```xml
<!-- ================================================================== -->
<!-- TestNG                                                             -->
<!-- ================================================================== -->
<path id="testng.class.path">
    <fileset dir="lib/testng">
        <include name="*.jar"/>
    </fileset>
</path>

<!-- TestNG - testng.org -->
<taskdef
    resource="testngtasks"
    classpathref="testng.class.path"
/>

<macrodef name="test-run">
    <attribute name="classpathref" />
    <attribute name="output" />
    <sequential>
        <testng
            classpathref="@{classpathref}"
            outputDir="@{output}"
            target="1.5"
            >
            <sysproperty key="ant.basedir" value="${basedir}"/>
            <xmlfileset dir="${basedir}" includes="testng.xml"/>
        </testng>
    </sequential>
</macrodef>
```

To use the test-run TestNG macrodef, we simply provide the classpath containing the test classes and an output directory to store the generated reports as shown in Listing 8-14.

Listing 8-14. *Using the TestNG Ant Macrodef in the TechConf Build*

```xml
<!-- ================================================================== -->
<!-- Target: test                                                       -->
<!-- Runs all tests                                                     -->
<!-- ================================================================== -->
<target name="test" depends="compile,test-clean"
        description="Runs all tests">
    <target-banner target="tests"/>
    <test-run
        classpathref="app.class.path"
        output="${docs-test}"
    />
</target>
```

Testing Against the Database

In the TechConf application the first layer of code that interacts with the database is that consisting of the Hibernate-mapped POJOs in the domain package. In Chapter 4 we learned how to map the TechConf POJOs to the database.

In this section we will look at ways to test the Hibernate ORM mappings by performing simple CRUD tests on the mapped POJOs using TestNG. There are several ways we can go about testing the Hibernate-mapped POJOs (or any other database code), but most techniques for this type of integration test have to account for the following:

- **Database Instance:** Do you use a per-developer instance of a database that matches the target database? Do you use an in-memory embedded database?

- **Testing Data:** How do you provide the testing data? In the Java code? Or via some sort of external configuration?

- **Set Up/Tear Down:** How do you set up data that is a precondition for a test, and how do you clean up afterwards?

The simplest scenario is to have a base class for the Hibernate tests that can provide the ability to create a Hibernate SessionFactory from configuration data (hibernate.cfg.xml) and the properties for the current user's test database. Listing 8-15 shows the class BaseHibernateTestCase, which serves as the parent class for all Hibernate tests:

Listing 8-15. *BaseHibernateTestCase*

```
package com.integrallis.techconf.domain;

...

import org.apache.commons.logging.Log;
import org.apache.commons.logging.LogFactory;
import org.hibernate.Criteria;
import org.hibernate.HibernateException;
import org.hibernate.Session;
import org.hibernate.SessionFactory;
import org.hibernate.Transaction;
import org.hibernate.cfg.Configuration;

import com.integrallis.techconf.test.util.Paths;

public abstract class BaseHibernateTestCase {
    // logger
    protected static Log logger = LogFactory.getLog(BaseHibernateTestCase.class);

    // hibernate session factory
    protected SessionFactory factory;
```

```
// persistent classes to be used in the test(s)
protected List<Class> persistentClasses = new ArrayList<Class>();

@org.testng.annotations.Configuration(beforeTestClass = true)
protected void setUp() throws FileNotFoundException, IOException {
    logger.info("[BaseHibernateTestCase] hibernate initializing...");

    // load build properties
    Properties properties = new Properties();
    properties.load(new FileInputStream(Paths.BASEDIR + "/build.properties"));

    // load hibernate cfg
    File configFile = new File(Paths.BASEDIR
                                +"/dd/hibernate/hibernate.cfg.xml");

    // configure via a Hibernate.cfg.xml or via properties only
    Configuration configuration = null;
    if (configFile.exists()) {
        configuration = new Configuration().configure(configFile);
    }
    else {
        configuration = new Configuration();
    }

    String dialect = properties.getProperty("test.db.hibernate.dialect");
    String driver = properties.getProperty("test.db.driver");
    String url = properties.getProperty("test.db.url");
    String user = properties.getProperty("test.db.username");
    String password = properties.getProperty("test.db.password");

    configuration.setProperty("hibernate.dialect", dialect);
    configuration.setProperty("hibernate.connection.driver_class", driver);
    configuration.setProperty("hibernate.connection.url", url);
    configuration.setProperty("hibernate.connection.username", user);
    configuration.setProperty("hibernate.connection.password", password);

    addPersistentClasses();

    for (Iterator i = persistentClasses.iterator(); i.hasNext();) {
        Class clazz = (Class) i.next();
        configuration.addClass(clazz);
    }

    factory = configuration.buildSessionFactory();
    logger.info("[BaseHibernateTestCase] hibernate initialized");
}
```

```
protected void addPersistentClasses() {};

    ...


}
```

This simple base class provides a setUp method, which is annotated with the TestNG annotation Configuration(beforeTestClass = true), which will execute the method before any test method in a child class. The setUp method loads any properties contained in the build.properties file for the project. It is in this property file where the individual developers can specify their test database properties as shown next:

```
// test db
test.db.url=jdbc:mysql://localhost/test
test.db.driver=com.mysql.jdbc.Driver
test.db.username=user
test.db.password=pass
test.db.hibernate.dialect=org.hibernate.dialect.MySQLDialect
```

The BaseHibernateTestCase can read the mappings via a Hibernate configuration file (hibernate.cfg.xml) as shown in Chapter 4, or alternatively, persistent classes can be made available to a child class by implementing the addPersistentClasses method. This enables you to load only the mappings that you are testing, while the approach using the XML configuration file assumes that you want to load all the mappings. For example, if we were testing the Address class, we would implement the addPersistentClasses method as follows:

```
public void addPersistentClasses() {
    persistentClasses.add(Address.class);
};
```

That mode of operation will make the initial time to configure the Hibernate SessionFactory not much of a concern.

In the BaseHibernateTestCase we are also providing several DAO-like utility methods to simplify the testing code. These methods are shown in Listing 8-16.

Listing 8-16. *BaseHibernateTestCase DAO-like Utility Methods*

```
    ...
    protected Object persist(Object object) {
        Session session = null;
        Transaction tx = null;
        try {
            session = factory.openSession();
            tx = session.beginTransaction();
            session.persist(object);
            tx.commit();
```

```
        } catch (Exception ex) {
            if (tx != null) {
                tx.rollback();
            }
        } finally {
            session.close();
        }
        return object;
    }

    protected void delete(Object object) {
        Session session = null;
        Transaction tx = null;
        try {
            session = factory.openSession();
            tx = session.beginTransaction();
            session.delete(object);
            tx.commit();
        } catch (Exception ex) {
            if (tx != null) {
                tx.rollback();
            }
        } finally {
            session.close();
        }
    }

    protected void delete(Class c, Serializable pk) {
        Object o = getByPk(c, pk);
        delete(o);
    }

    protected Object getByPk(Class c, Serializable pk) {
        Object result = null;
        Session session = null;
        try {
            session = factory.openSession();
            result = session.get(c, pk);
        } finally {
            session.close();
        }
        return result;
    }
```

```
    protected List findAll(Class clazz) {
        List result = Collections.EMPTY_LIST;
        Session session = null;
        try {
            session = factory.openSession();
            result = createCriteria(clazz, session).list();
        } finally {
            session.close();
        }
        return result;
    }

  protected Criteria createCriteria(Class c, Session s) {
      return s.createCriteria(c);
  }

  protected Session getSession() {
      return factory.openSession();
  }
...
```

In this implementation of the Hibernate tests I've chosen to provide the test data in the Java code and to perform all clean up as part of the test. Let's create a test case for the Conference class. The Conference class is related to the CONFERENCE table, which has some not-null foreign constrains to the tables ADDRESS and VENUE. In this test shown in Listing 8-17 we are testing basic CRUD functionality. The private method createConference creates a Venue and an Address object and attaches them to a newly created Conference object.

Listing 8-17. *A Hibernate Integration Test*

```
private Conference createConference() {
    Conference conference = new Conference();

    // utility objects
    Date today = new Date();

    String confDesc = "A Test Conference";
    String confName = "TestConf 2005";
    String fax = "555.867.5309";
    String venueName = "Steve's House";
    String venuePhone = "555.888.8888";
    String appNumber = "n/a";
    String city = "Woodside";
    String state = "CA";
    String streetAddress = "460 Mountain Home Road";
    String zipCode = "94062";
```

```
conference.setAbstractSubmissionEndDate(today);
conference.setAbstractSubmissionStartDate(today);
conference.setDescription(confDesc);
conference.setEndDate(today);
conference.setName(confName);
conference.setStartDate(today);

// venue
Venue venue = new Venue();
venue.setFax(fax);
venue.setName(venueName);
venue.setPhone(venuePhone);

// venue-->address
Address address = new Address();
address.setAptNumber(appNumber);
address.setCity(city);
address.setState(state);
address.setStreetAddress(streetAddress);
address.setZipCode(zipCode);

venue.setAddress(address);

conference.setVenue(venue);

return conference;
}
```

The testCreateConference method shown in Listing 8-18 tests several aspects of the persistence and OR layers as they apply to the Conference POJO, including

- Testing that a primary ID was assigned after a save operation

- Comparing the values before and after a save operation

- Testing cascading behavior in Save/Update/Delete operations

Listing 8-18. *Hibernate Test Case for the Conference POJO*

```
package com.integrallis.techconf.domain;

...
import org.testng.Assert;
import org.testng.annotations.Test;

public class ConferenceTest extends BaseHibernateTestCase {
```

```
@Test(groups = {"persistence"})
public void testCreateConference() {
    Conference conference = createConference();

    // save the user to the database
    Conference savedConference = (Conference) persist(conference);

    // get the id of the newly created entry
    Integer id = savedConference.getId();

    // did the db assign an id?
    Assert.assertNotNull(id);

    // load the user from the database using the id
    Conference retrievedConference = (Conference)
        getByPk(Conference.class, id);

    // test that it was saved
    Assert.assertNotNull(retrievedConference);

    // test that the values are the same
    Assert.assertTrue(checkValues(savedConference,retrievedConference));

    Venue venue = retrievedConference.getVenue();

    Integer venueId = venue.getId();

    Assert.assertNotNull(venue);

    Address address = venue.getAddress();

    Integer addressId = address.getId();

    Assert.assertNotNull(address);

    //clean up
    delete(retrievedConference);

    // test cascading delete - should not delete venue

    // load the address from the database using the id
    Venue retrievedVenue = (Venue) getByPk(Venue.class, venueId);

    // did it get deleted?
    Assert.assertNotNull(retrievedVenue);
```

```
        // load the address from the database using the id
        Assert.assertNotNull(getByPk(Address.class, addressId));

        // now delete the venue
        delete(retrievedVenue);

        // test the cascading delete

        // load the address from the database using the id
        Assert.assertNull(getByPk(Address.class, addressId));
    }

    //
    // private methods
    //


    ...

}
```

Executing the tests should produce output similar to that shown next:

```
Dec 4, 2005 1:28:29 PM com.integrallis.techconf.domain.BaseHibernateTestCase setUp
INFO: [BaseHibernateTestCase] hibernate initializing...
...
Hibernate: insert into address (StreetAddress, State, ZipCode, City, AptNumber)
values (?, ?, ?, ?, ?)
Dec 4, 2005 1:28:33 PM com.integrallis.techconf.domain.BaseHibernateTestCase setUp
INFO: [BaseHibernateTestCase] hibernate initialized
Hibernate: insert into venue (FAX, NAME, PHONE, FK_ADDRESS_ID) values (?, ?, ?, ?)
Hibernate: insert into conference (AbstractSubmissionStartDate, Name, Description,
 AbstractSubmissionEndDate, EndDate, StartDate, FK_VENUE_ID) values (?, ?, ?, ?, ?,
 ?, ?)
...
Hibernate: delete from conference where PK_ID=?
...
Hibernate: delete from venue where PK_ID=?
Hibernate: delete from address where PK_ID=?
Hibernate: select address0_.PK_ID as PK1_0_, address0_.StreetAddress as
 StreetAd2_2_0_, address0_.State as State2_0_, address0_.ZipCode as ZipCode2_0_,
 address0_.City as City2_0_, address0_.AptNumber as AptNumber2_0_ from address
 address0_ where address0_.PK_ID=?
PASSED: testCreateConference


===============================================
    com.integrallis.techconf.domain.ConferenceTest
    Tests run: 1, Failures: 0, Skips: 0
===============================================
```

The previously shown technique works well for tests using a small number of tables. If your domain objects are fairly intertwined, then it becomes difficult to load only a few mappings since Hibernate will require that you load all associated mappings. This will result in increasing initialization times for the setUp method. In such cases, I recommend that you load all the mappings at once from the hibernate.cfg.xml and keep the SessionFactory in a static singleton to be used by all the test classes.

DbUnit

The other glaring problem with the previous approach is the amount of redundant code needed to populate the database with test data. Although you could use a SQL script to set up the test data, you would still be faced with the task of testing the state of the database after the test. In the previous approach we tested the database results indirectly via the Hibernate-mapped POJOs. Another approach would be to load some test data, perform tests on that data, check the state of the database before and after, and then clean up.

The DbUnit project, created by Manuel Laflamme, can be found at www.dbunit.org. DbUnit provides the functionality to load test data and verify the state of the database after a test. DbUnit uses XML files to provide test data. To load the data, you must initially format the data into DbUnit's specific XML dataset format. The easiest way is to export the data from an existing database in the desired state. DbUnit includes an export utility and Ant task for performing this activity. Listing 8-19 shows an Ant macrodef that uses the DbUnit export subtask to export the data in a database to a file named dataExport.xml in the setup/data/dbunit directory (the name and the location can be overridden). This macrodef is to be added to the macros.xml file created in Chapter 3 and provides a good starting point to create data sets for your DbUnit tests. The generated XML file can be renamed and edited for a specific state. I like to use names that tie the file to a specific test like beforeAddressTest.xml and afterAddressTest.xml, for example. The macrodef takes as parameters the JDBC information and the destination and name of the DbUnit XML file to be generated.

Listing 8-19. *DbUnit Ant Macrodef for Data Export*

```
<path id="dbunit.class.path">
    <fileset dir="lib/dbunit">
        <include name="*.jar"/>
    </fileset>
</path>


<!-- DBUnit - dbunit.sourceforge.net -->
<taskdef
    name="dbunit"
    classname="org.dbunit.ant.DbUnitTask"
    classpathref="dbunit.class.path"
/>


<!-- ================================================================= -->
<!-- DB Unit Data Export                                               -->
<!-- ================================================================= -->
```

```
<macrodef name="export-data">
    <attribute name="driver" />
    <attribute name="url" />
    <attribute name="username" />
    <attribute name="password" />
    <attribute name="target-dest" default="setup/data/dbunit" />
    <attribute name="filename" default="dataExport" />
    <sequential>
        <dbunit
            driver="@{driver}"
            url="@{url}"
            userid="@{username}"
            password="@{password}">
            <export dest="@{target-dest}/@{filename}.xml" format="xml" />
            <classpath>
                <path refid="dbunit.class.path" />
            </classpath>
        </dbunit>
    </sequential>
</macrodef>
```

To create a sample dataset you can either populate the database by hand (by writing SQL INSERT statements), or you can use the Hibernate-mapped POJOs to set the database's initial state. Once you have the database in the desired state, execute the macro, and the XML file will capture the state of the database. Listing 8-20 shows a target using the macrodef previously defined.

Listing 8-20. *Ant Target Using the DbUnit Macrodef*

```
<!-- ===================================================================== -->
<!-- Target: export-db                                                   -->
<!-- Exports the contents of the test database                           -->
<!-- ===================================================================== -->
<target name="export-db" description="Exports the content of the test database">
    <target-banner target="export-db"/>
    <export-data
        driver="${test.db.driver}"
        url="${test.db.url}"
        username="${test.db.username}"
        password="${test.db.password}"
    />
</target>
```

For example, if we load some data in the address table and run the Ant target, the resulting DbUnit XML data set will resemble the output shown in Listing 8-21.

Listing 8-21. *DbUnit XML Data Set for Table ADDRESS*

```xml
<?xml version='1.0' encoding='UTF-8'?>
<dataset>
  <table name="address">
    <column>PK_ID</column>
    <column>STREETADDRESS</column>
    <column>APTNUMBER</column>
    <column>CITY</column>
    <column>STATE</column>
    <column>ZIPCODE</column>
    <row>
      <value>2</value>
      <value><![CDATA[204 Bluestone Court]]></value>
      <value>N/A</value>
      <value>Westerville</value>
      <value>OH</value>
      <value>43081</value>
    </row>
  </table>
</dataset>
```

Since DbUnit is a JUnit extension, most examples show how to use DbUnit in the context of a JUnit test. The DbUnitUtils class provides static methods to use DbUnit functionality from any POJO as shown in Listing 8-22.

Listing 8-22. DbUnitUtils

```java
package com.integrallis.techconf.test.util;

import java.io.FileInputStream;
import java.sql.Connection;
import java.sql.DriverManager;
import java.util.Properties;

import org.dbunit.database.DatabaseConnection;
import org.dbunit.database.IDatabaseConnection;
import org.dbunit.dataset.IDataSet;
import org.dbunit.dataset.xml.XmlDataSet;

public class DbUnitUtils {
```

```
/**
 * Creates a DbUnit database connection.
 * @return test database connection
 */
public static IDatabaseConnection createConnection()
        throws Exception {
    Properties properties = new Properties();
    properties.load(new FileInputStream(Paths.BASEDIR + "/build.properties"));

    String driver = properties.getProperty("test.db.driver");
    String url = properties.getProperty("test.db.url");
    String user = properties.getProperty("test.db.username");
    String password = properties.getProperty("test.db.password");

    Class.forName(driver);
    Connection connection = DriverManager.getConnection(url, user, password);

    return new DatabaseConnection(connection);
}

/**
 * Creates a DbUnit dataset based on an XML file.
 * @param xmlFile path to an XML file containing the dataset
 * @return requested dataset
 */
public static IDataSet createDataSet(String file) throws Exception {
    return new XmlDataSet(new FileInputStream(Paths.BASEDIR +
                                        "/setup/data/dbunit/" + file));
}
}
```

To use DbUnit in your tests you interact with the DatabaseOperation class, which provides methods for operations performed against the database. The DbUnitUtils class provides methods to create a connection and create a DbUnit data set. Listing 8-23 shows the usage of the DbUnitUtils class in a TestNG class. In the init method, annotated to execute once before any test method in the test class, the DbUnitUtils class method createConnection is used to get a database connection and to load a dataset. The DatabaseOperation DbUnit class is then used to perform a CLEAN_INSERT operation using the connection and the loaded dataset.

DbUnit supports several combinations of operations for inserting, updating, and deleting data from the database using a data set. The CLEAN_INSERT operation deletes all rows from tables in the data set and inserts the data contained in the data set. If you don't want to clear the database before the test but only want to modify the data, use the REFRESH operation, which only performs updates and inserts against the database.

Listing 8-23. *Using* DbUnitUtils *in a TestNG Test*

```
import org.dbunit.operation.DatabaseOperation;

public class MyDbTest {

    @Configuration(beforeTestClass = true)
    protected void init() {
        IDatabaseConnection connection = DbUnitUtils.createConnection();
        try {
            DatabaseOperation.CLEAN_INSERT.execute(
                connection,
                DbUnitUtils.createDataSet(myDataSet));
        } finally {
            connection.close();
        }
    }
    ...
}
```

Finally, in your test methods DbUnit can also be used to compare changes to the database.
Listing 8-24 shows an example of what the DbUnit code will look like for comparing the state
of the database after a database insert of a record into a table with a database-generated
primary key. DbUnit is used to verify that the insert is successful by comparing the contents of
the database with an XML data set file named AfterDataSubmitted.xml, using the DbUnit
Assertion class.

Listing 8-24. *A Typical DbUnit/TestNG Test*

```
import org.dbunit.Assertion;
import org.dbunit.database.IDatabaseConnection;
import org.dbunit.dataset.IDataSet;
import org.dbunit.dataset.ITable;
import org.dbunit.operation.DatabaseOperation;

public class MyDbTest {
    ...

    @Test(groups = {"db"})
    public void testCreateData() {
        // do something that causes a SQL insert
        ...

        // compare contents of database
        // ignore primary key since it is auto generated
        IDatabaseConnection connection =
            DatabaseConnectionFactory.createConnection();
```

```
    // load the contents of the table, since we want to ignore the PK it is not
    // part of the select statement
    ITable actualTable = connection
        .createQueryTable("MYTABLE", "select COLUMN1,COLUMN2,… from MYTABLE");

    // load the expected data set from the XML DbUnit file
    IDataSet expectedDataSet = DatabaseConnectionFactory
        .createDataSet("AfterDataSubmitted.xml");

    // create a virtual table out of the loaded data for the comparison
    ITable expectedTable = expectedDataSet.getTable("MYTABLE");

    // using the DbUnit Assertion class compare the tables
    Assertion.assertEquals(expectedTable, actualTable);
  }

  ...

}
```

Testing the DTO Layer

Testing the DTO layer implemented with DynaDTO in Chapter 5 becomes very simple with
TestNG. Listing 8-25 shows a TestNG class with two methods. In the setUp method the DynaDTO
configuration is loaded using the DynaDTO ConfigurationLoader class.

In the testNewsItemCreation method a News domain object is created, and then, using the
DynaDTO Builder, a dynamic DTO is created. The rest of the method uses the TestNG Assert
class to compare every field of the domain object against the DTO. (In this case the DTO is a
mirror image of the domain object.)

Listing 8-25. *A TestNG Test for a DynaDTO DTO*

```
package com.integrallis.techconf.dto;

import java.io.File;
import java.util.Date;

import org.dynadto.Builder;
import org.dynadto.BuilderFactory;
import org.dynadto.ConfigurationLoader;
import org.dynadto.exception.ConfigurationException;
import org.testng.Assert;
import org.testng.annotations.Configuration;
import org.testng.annotations.Test;

import com.integrallis.techconf.domain.News;
import com.integrallis.techconf.test.util.Paths;
```

```java
public class NewsItemTest {

    @Configuration(beforeTestClass = true)
    protected void setUp() throws ConfigurationException {
        ConfigurationLoader.loadMapping(
            new File(Paths.BASEDIR + "/dd/dynadto/NewsItem.dto.xml"));
    }

    @SuppressWarnings("unchecked")
    @Test(groups = {"dto"})
    public void testNewsItemCreation() {
        // utility objects
        Date today = new Date();

        // create a News domain object
        News news = new News();
        news.setId(1);
        news.setUserId(4);
        news.setTitle("this is the title");
        news.setBody("this body");
        news.setConferenceId(1);
        news.setCreatedOn(today);
        news.setDate(today);
        news.setIsGlobal(false);
        news.setIsPublished(true);
        news.setRemoveOn(today);

        Builder builder = BuilderFactory.getInstance().getBuilder(NewsItem.class);
        NewsItem newsItem = (NewsItem) builder.build(news);

        Assert.assertEquals(news.getId(), newsItem.getId());
        Assert.assertEquals(news.getTitle(), newsItem.getTitle());
        Assert.assertEquals(news.getBody(), newsItem.getBody());
        Assert.assertEquals(news.getConferenceId().intValue(),
                            newsItem.getConferenceId());
        Assert.assertEquals(news.getCreatedOn(), newsItem.getCreatedOn());
        Assert.assertEquals(news.getDate(), newsItem.getDate());
        Assert.assertEquals(news.getUserId().intValue(), newsItem.getUserId());
        Assert.assertEquals(news.getIsGlobal(), newsItem.getIsGlobal());
        Assert.assertEquals(news.getIsPublished().booleanValue(),
                            newsItem.getIsPublished());
        Assert.assertEquals(news.getRemoveOn(), newsItem.getRemoveOn());
    }
}
```

Testing EJB3 Stateless Session Beans

One of the advantages of EJB3 being POJOs is that it makes testing them almost as easy as it is to test any other Java class. To demonstrate how to test a EJB3 SLSB we'll make use of mock objects.

Mock objects are test-oriented objects that serve as stand-ins for the collaborating objects or the unit being tested. The technique has been around for a while, but it was formalized by Tim Mackinnon, Steve Freeman, and Philip Craig in a paper presented at an Extreme Programming conference in 2000.

Mock objects are more than stubs in that they are more than a simple holder of data. Mock objects simulate part of the behavior of a collaborator and also provide for a way to verify the behavior. Mock objects can be used as stubs, but their real power lies in testing the interactions between a class and its collaborators. Unit testing is about testing the units of a system in isolation, but in most cases a unit's behavior can be tested only in the context of its interactions with collaborating objects. Mock objects provide a way to provide a testing-time replacement for a facet of the behavior provided by a collaborating object.

Most of the EJB services in the TechConf system depend on DAOs to retrieve data from the database. In order to mock these DAO collaborators we'll use the EasyMock 2 library, which is a mock-objects library that can dynamically generate a mock object for a given interface. EasyMock 2 can be downloaded from www.easymock.org. To use EasyMock, simply add the easymock.jar file to your classpath.

As an example of how to test an EJB3 SLSB, we'll use the LocationLookupServiceBean, which uses an instance of the ZipcodeDAO interface as a collaborator to retrieve data from the database. The EJB also uses the DynaDTO library to create DTOs to be returned to the EJB clients. Listing 8-26 shows the LocationLookupServiceBean.

Listing 8-26. *The LocationLookupServiceBean EJB*

```
package com.integrallis.techconf.ejb;

import java.util.List;
import javax.annotation.EJB;
import javax.annotation.Resource;
import javax.ejb.PostConstruct;
import javax.ejb.Stateless;
import org.dynadto.Builder;
import org.dynadto.BuilderFactory;
import com.integrallis.techconf.dao.ZipcodeDAO;
import com.integrallis.techconf.domain.Zipcode;
import com.integrallis.techconf.dto.Location;
import com.integrallis.techconf.service.LocationLookupService;

@Stateless
public class LocationLookupServiceBean implements LocationLookupService {
```

```
@Resource(name = "java:/dynadto/BuilderFactory")
protected BuilderFactory builderFactory;

// DAOs
@EJB protected ZipcodeDAO zipcodeDAO;

// DynaDTO Builders
protected Builder locationBuilder;

@PostConstruct
public void initialization() {
    locationBuilder = builderFactory.getBuilder(Location.class);
}

@SuppressWarnings("unchecked")
public List<Location> searchLocations(String zipCode) {
    List<Zipcode> entities = zipcodeDAO.find(zipCode);
    return locationBuilder.buildList(entities);
}

public Location getLocationByZipCode(String zipCode) {
    Integer id = Integer.parseInt(zipCode);
    Zipcode zip = zipcodeDAO.getById(id);

    Location location = null;
    if (zip != null) {
        location = (Location) locationBuilder.build(zip);
    }
    return location;
}

public void setZipcodeDAO(ZipcodeDAO zipcodeDAO) {
    this.zipcodeDAO = zipcodeDAO;
}

public void setBuilderFactory(BuilderFactory builderFactory) {
    this.builderFactory = builderFactory;
}
}
```

Without a database present, we need to create a mock for the ZipcodeDAO collaborator. To create a proxy class that can be treated as the required DAO, we can use the following snippet of code:

```
ZipcodeDAO mock = createMock(ZipcodeDAO.class);
```

To make the createMock static method available to your test class, you need to use a static import (which allows unqualified access to static members) as shown next:

```
import static org.easymock.EasyMock.createMock;
```

The created instance of ZipcodeDAO possesses no behavior. If we attempt to invoke any of the methods in the ZipcodeDAO interface, the mock will throw an exception. The power of the mock object comes in the way we can programmatically "record" expectations. The recording of expectations entails specifying the sequence of events and responses that the mock object will respond to in the context of the test at hand.

For example, if we examine the searchLocations method in Listing 8-26 we can see that the DAO instance is used to invoke the find method as zipcodeDAO.find(zipCode), which is expected to return a typed list of Zipcode domain objects. To train our mock object to respond correctly for the purposes of testing the searchLocation method, we can create some stub data objects to be used to set the expected response for our mock. The snippet of code that follows creates a Zipcode domain object and a List to contain the object.

```
// data stub
Zipcode stub = new Zipcode();
stub.setZip(43081);
stub.setCity("Westerville");
stub.setState("OH");

List<Zipcode> stubList = new ArrayList<Zipcode>();
stubList.add(stub);
```

With the sample data we can now proceed to set the expectations of the mock object. Easy-Mock provides static methods that allow you to record the expected method call on the mock object and the return value of the call. In the code shown next we train the mock object to expect a call to the method find with the parameter "43081" and to return the list containing the stub Zipcode object previously created.

```
expect(mock.find("43081")).andReturn(stubList);
replay(mock);
```

The call to replay the mock object activates it by stopping the recording phase. After the call to replay, the object will now behave like an instance of ZipcodeDAO in the context of the find method.

Now we can use the mock object just as if it were a real implementation of ZipCodeDAO. Listing 8-27 shows the complete implementation of the test using TestNG and also passing an instance of the DynaDTO builder factory dynamically to replace the one that is injected dynamically from JNDI by the EJB container.

Listing 8-27. *Testing an EJB3 Without a Container* (LocationLookupServiceBeanTest)

```
package com.integrallis.techconf.ejb;

import static org.easymock.EasyMock.createMock;
import static org.easymock.EasyMock.expect;
import static org.easymock.EasyMock.replay;
import static org.easymock.EasyMock.verify;
```

```java
import java.io.File;
import java.util.ArrayList;
import java.util.List;

import org.dynadto.BuilderFactory;
import org.dynadto.ConfigurationLoader;
import org.dynadto.exception.ConfigurationException;
import org.testng.Assert;
import org.testng.annotations.Configuration;
import org.testng.annotations.Test;

import com.integrallis.techconf.dao.ZipcodeDAO;
import com.integrallis.techconf.domain.Zipcode;
import com.integrallis.techconf.dto.Location;
import com.integrallis.techconf.test.util.Paths;

public class LocationLookupServiceBeanTest {

    private LocationLookupServiceBean service;
    private ZipcodeDAO mock;

    @Configuration(beforeTestClass = true)
    protected void setUp() throws ConfigurationException {
        ConfigurationLoader.loadMapping(new File(Paths.BASEDIR
            + "/dd/dynadto/Location.dto.xml"));

        mock = createMock(ZipcodeDAO.class);
        service = new LocationLookupServiceBean();
        service.setZipcodeDAO(mock);
        service.setBuilderFactory(BuilderFactory.getInstance());
        service.initialization();
    }

    @Test(groups = {"services"})
    public void testSearchLocations() {
        // data stub
        Zipcode stub = new Zipcode();
        stub.setZip(43081);
        stub.setCity("Westerville");
        stub.setState("OH");

        List<Zipcode> stubList = new ArrayList<Zipcode>();
        stubList.add(stub);
```

```
    // set expectations
    expect(mock.find("43081")).andReturn(stubList);
    replay(mock);

    // execute the test
    List<Location> locations = service.searchLocations("43081");
    verify(mock);

    // check results
    Assert.assertEquals(locations.size(), 1);
    Location location = locations.get(0);
    Assert.assertEquals(location.getZip(), stub.getZip().toString());
    Assert.assertEquals(location.getCity(), stub.getCity());
    Assert.assertEquals(location.getState(), stub.getState());
  }
}
```

Using mock objects is not rocket science, but with powerful framework like EasyMock we can use mock objects to truly isolate a class under test by creating an environment of simulated collaborators with predetermined behaviors for the context of a test. The same techniques applied to testing an EJB can be applied to any object that depends on another object to perform its work. Frameworks that promote coding to interfaces such as the Spring framework are the perfect candidates for mock object testing with a tool such as EasyMock.

Summary

In this chapter you've learned the importance of setting a test harness for your Web application early in the development process. By taking a layered approach to testing, you can make sure that your application testing needs are covered. Using testing frameworks like JUnit and TestNG and the myriad of supporting tools and frameworks, testing is no longer a dreadful process left for the end of your projects but an active and primary part of the iterative development process.

CHAPTER 9

■ ■ ■

Continuous Integration

We have all heard the figures of how many software projects fail. The statistics tell us that the larger the project, the more likely it is to fail. In my own experience, I've seen projects that on the surface appear to be marching along until that dreaded day when you have to give your customers a demo. As you check down the features list and talk to the developers responsible, you learn that some of the features are working but have not yet been integrated. Everybody checked their code in, and one poor soul, probably the one labeled QA engineer, attempts to build the application. The anticipation fills the air as you see a barrage of errors on the QA machine. What happened? It worked for every developer individually. So, who do you blame?

From these lessons, we arrived at the nightly build, which typically creates a deliverable of some sort that a QA person can test in the morning. This practice, although good, still doesn't solve the problem. At the root of the problem there's an issue of culture. Programmers grew accustomed to getting a copy of the source code that they would work on until they deemed it worthy of being integrated into the main code base.

One modern software development practice that's been embraced and promoted by many methodologies, particularly by the Extreme Programming (XP) movement, is the practice of continuous integration (CI). This practice might be one the most important lessons you'll ever learn from the XP and agile movements (although it's not a new concept, it has now been formalized and championed by these movements). The main idea is that developers working on a project should integrate changes to their code at least on a daily basis. With a powerful set of unit tests and a system that enables those tests to be performed in a continuous and automated fashion, you can ensure that any problem introduced into the system will be discovered in the next build. So, CI is about developer discipline and tools that make the desired behaviors the path of least resistance.

Continuous integration, coupled with a strong set of tests, prevents problems from going unnoticed. It localizes in time problems introduced into the code base and the knowledge of the existence of those problems, enabling you to react as they occur. A well-configured CI system is like having a heart monitor on the pulse of your application that makes developers accountable for the code they check into the project.

CI is more that just building the code often. Its success depends on many factors. Some of them are fortunately common practice nowadays, but others require a bit of forethought, including the following:

- **Version Control:** There should be a single, versioned repository where all developers can get access to the latest version of the application code as well as previous versions.

- **Build Automation:** It should be relatively simple for developers to build the application. Typically, a single command and a minimum amount of configuration should be required.

- **Test Automation:** The application's test suite should be easy to execute, and adding new tests should be very simple.

In Chapter 8, you learned how to create unit tests for your applications. The build created in Chapter 3 and enhanced throughout the book should set the stage for making CI a reality in your next project and keep your project's health in check. With the foundations in place, the basic steps to accomplish continuous integration are simple:

- **Integrate:** Changes are checked into a central repository. (Code that adds new features requires new test cases that must also be checked in.)

- **Test:** All tests are performed. A successful integration is bound by a 100 percent success rate of the testing stage. If any tests fail, the offending code is rolled back, and code is refactored until it passes the tests.

- **Repeat:** With the help of automation, you can run this process at well-defined intervals (ideally a minimum of once a day) and every time a change is introduced into the code base. This ensures that the system code base remains fully tested at all times and that bugs and missing features are addressed as soon as possible.

CI as championed by XP and agile-methodology proponents is one of those concepts that most developers agree with but few teams ever implement. You should build only what's necessary, and it should be tested for compliance with the requirements as often as possible and as soon as it is introduced into the code base. You also should understand that making lots of changes at once leads to hours of "big-bang" integration testing later on.

By never holding on to changes in the code for more than a day, a team can minimize the chances that the code will become fragmented. What can produce hard-to-find bugs and countless hours of integration effort are these "unofficial forks" to a code base that occur when a developer never integrates changes to the code base and is effectively working on an older version in their development environment.

By adopting a test-driven approach to development in combination with build-process automation, a team can achieve continuous integration and build only what's needed when it's needed, and build it right. CI increases the team's knowledge about the system being built, thereby boosting its reaction time to feedback from the system and the system's stakeholders. CI reduces the overall cost of developing software by making it easier to find, diagnose, and fix problems.

CI takes some preparation, coordination, and buy-in from your team. In my experience, CI works best in conjunction with test-driven development on newer code bases. If you have inherited a code base with little or no tests, the first step is to understand the code by writing tests before you can implement a CI solution.

■**Tip** One of the best essays on CI was written by Martin Fowler and can be read on his website at www.martinfowler.com/articles/continuousIntegration.html.

Cruise Control

To enable CI for the TechConf system, we will use the CruiseControl continuous integration framework which is hosted at the SourceForge under http://cruisecontrol.sourceforge.net. CruiseControl encompasses a free Java open source build scheduler and several utilities for notification and reporting. You can think of CruiseControl as Cron for Ant. CruiseControl integrates seamlessly with build tools like Ant, Maven, or any tool that can be invoked from a command line. CruiseControl works with many of the most popular version control systems like CVS, Subversion, Visual SourceSafe, PVCS, and ClearCase among many.

CruiseControl is distributed in both a binary and source distribution. (At the time of this writing the latest version is 2.3.1.)

CruiseControl consists of two subsystems:

- **Build Loop:** An application designed to run as a daemon that watches your source control repository for changes. If it encounters any changes, it runs the build and sends reports about the status of the build.

- **Build Results JSP:** A Web application that formats and displays the results and status of the CruiseControl build loop as well as results from previous builds. It displays information such as compilation errors, test results, and source repository changes.

Typically you'll setup CruiseControl on your "build server," which should be a high-availability machine. The build server is also referred to as the Continuous Integration server. Figure 9-1 shows a typical setup.

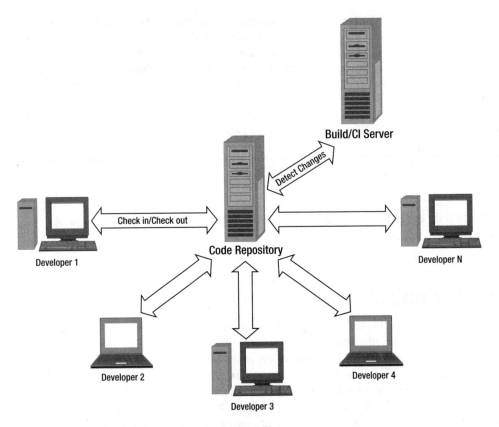

Figure 9-1. *Typical setup for Continuous Integration*

Configuring the Build Server

To setup the TechConf build server we'll need a machine configured with Java, CruiseControl, a Web container (such as Tomcat or Jetty), and the Ant build tool.

For this chapter I'm working with a machine configured with Fedora Linux Core 4. The installation instructions are tailored for that platform but should be similar for other platforms. The first step is to download the binary distribution of CruiseControl and unzip the file to a suitable location. For a Linux system, I recommend that you keep CruiseControl under the opt directory. For version 2.3.1 this would be /opt/cruisecontrol-2.3.1. I find it convenient to create a symbolic link to that directory and name it /opt/cruisecontrol. This is typically done if you have multiple versions of one product, therefore making the symbolic link point to the latest or default version that you want to use in your system.

CruiseControl Working Directory

The next step is to create the CruiseControl working directory. For the sample Linux system I used /opt/cc-working-dir. Under the working directory create the following directories:

- **checkout:** This directory will contain the source code of the projects being built (the source to build)

- **logs:** This directory is where CruiseControl will store logs and reports about the applications being built (the details about each build)

- **artifacts:** This directory is where any output files resulting from the builds are kept (build products like JARs, WARs, and EARs)

At the root of the working directory, create a file name config.xml with the following contents:

```
<cruisecontrol></cruisecontrol>
```

To get CruiseControl running successfully under Linux follow these steps:

1. In the working directory, create a symbolic link of the webapps directory located in the CruiseControl directory.

2. Edit the shell script cruisecontrol.sh under the CruiseControl directory and change the value of the variable CC_DIR=/opt/cruisecontrol (or the location where you unzipped the CruiseControl archive).

3. Add the CruiseControl directory to the system's execution path. You can accomplish this by running the shell commands `export PATH=/opt/cruisecontrol:$PATH`.

4. Make sure that your system's JAVA_HOME environment variable is defined and that the Java executables are in the system's execution path.

5. Set executable permissions on the shell script cruisecontrol.sh.

The CruiseControl working directory should look like Figure 9-2.

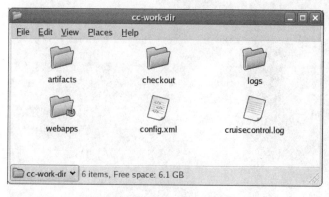

Figure 9-2. *CruiseControl working directory*

To test the installation, change directories to the working directory and execute the cruisecontrol.sh script. The output should resemble the following:

```
[cc]Dec-05 23:14:04 Main          - CruiseControl Version 2.3.1 Compiled on October
10 2005 0917
[cc]Dec-05 23:14:06 HttpServer    - Version Jetty/5.1.3
[cc]Dec-05 23:14:07 Credential    - Checking Resource aliases
[cc]Dec-05 23:14:07 trolController- no projects found in config file
[cc]Dec-05 23:14:08 BuildQueue    - BuildQueue started
[cc]Dec-05 23:14:12 Container     - Started
org.mortbay.jetty.servlet.WebApplicationHandler@1b09468
[cc]Dec-05 23:14:13 Container     - Started
WebApplicationContext[/cruisecontrol,CruiseControl Reporting App]
[cc]Dec-05 23:14:13 SocketListener- Started SocketListener on 0.0.0.0:8080
[cc]Dec-05 23:14:13 Container     - Started org.mortbay.jetty.Server@dd87b2
```

The build queue should be started now, and the build results Web application should be running under the embedded Jetty Web container running by default on port 8080. Point your browser to the build server machine at the URL http://ccserver:8080/cruisecontrol (where "ccserver" is the name or IP of your machine). You should see the CruiseControl status page of the reporting Web application as shown in Figure 9-3.

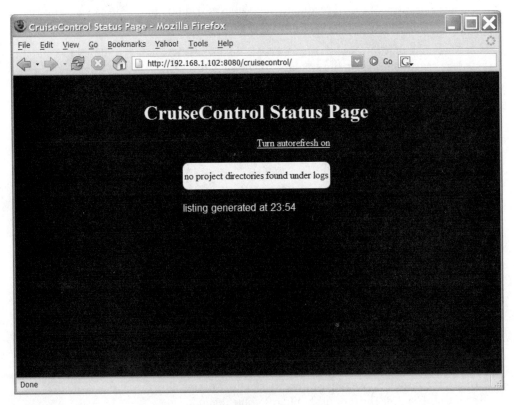

Figure 9-3. *Testing the CruiseControl installation*

Setting Up a Project for Continuous Integration

Now that we have the infrastructure to set up CI, we can check out projects to be built into the checkout directory. Let's start our exploration of CruiseControl by simply checking out a well-known project from a publicly available CVS repository and configuring CruiseControl to build it.

For the example, I have chosen the popular project Lucene hosted by the Apache foundation at http://lucene.apache.org. I've chosen Lucene since it is a pretty active project and has a comprehensive test suite. To check out a copy of Lucene change directory to the cc-work-dir/ checkout and type:

```
cvs -d :pserver:anoncvs@cvs.apache.org:/home/cvspublic login
```

This is the CVS client command to log in anonymously to the java.net CVS server. The console will prompt you for a password as shown next. The password for anonymous login is anonymous.

```
Logging in to :pserver:anoncvs@cvs.apache.org:2401/home/cvspublic
CVS password:
```

To checkout the project now type:

```
cvs -d :pserver:anoncvs@cvs.apache.org:/home/cvspublic checkout jakarta-lucene
```

You should now see a lot of output on the console as the CVS client checks out a copy of the Lucene project under the checkout directory. After the checkout is complete, we can explore and test the build by changing directories to the newly created jakarta-lucene directory under the checkout directory and type:

```
ant -p
```

This should reveal the targets available in the Lucene buildfile as shown next.

```
Buildfile: build.xml

Main targets:

 clean                   Removes contents of build and dist directories
 compile-core            Compiles core classes
 generate-test-reports   Generates test reports
 jar-core                Generates the Jar file
 package-all-binary      --> Generates the .tar.gz and .zip distributions
 package-all-src         --> Generates the .tar.gz and .zip source distributions
 package-tgz             --> Generates the lucene distribution as .tar.gz
 package-tgz-src         --> Generates the Lucene distribution as .tar.gz
 package-zip             --> Generates the Lucene distribution as .zip
 package-zip-src         --> Generates the Lucene sources as .zip
 test                    Runs unit tests
 test-deprecated         Runs deprecated unit tests
Default target: default
```

As you can see, the Lucene project provides targets for compiling and for testing the application. Test the build manually by typing `ant test`. If the build works correctly from the command line, it should also work when invoked by the CruiseControl build loop.

Next we will create a small Ant build script that CruiseControl will use. This delegating build script shown in Listing 9-1 will invoke the Lucene project's build after it obtains the latest copy of the code base from the CVS repository. Notice that the basedir property is set to the directory of the project we are trying to build. Name this buildfile build-jakarta-lucene and place it in the cc-work-dir directory. In this example buildfile, I've chosen to update only the existing code base from CVS rather than deleting the jakarta-lucene directory and checking out the project from scratch. Many experts recommend that you do so, since otherwise you are depending on the build having the ability to reset or clean any artifacts of a previous build run. See Chapter 3 regarding the importance of a good Ant clean target.

Listing 9-1. *Delegate Buildfile for CruiseControl Automation*

```
<project name="cc-lucene-build" default="test" basedir="checkout/jakarta-lucene">
    <!-- ================================================================= -->
    <!-- Target: cvs                                                       -->
    <!-- Retrieves the latest changes from the CVS repository              -->
    <!-- ================================================================= -->
    <target name="cvs">
        <!-- get latest changes from CVS -->
        <cvs command="up -d -P"/>
        <!-- clean any build artifacts -->
        <ant antfile="build.xml" target="clean" />
    </target>

    <!-- ================================================================= -->
    <!-- Target: test                                                      -->
    <!-- Invokes the test target in the Lucene project buildfile           -->
    <!-- ================================================================= -->
    <target name="test" depends="cvs">
        <ant antfile="build.xml" target="test" />
    </target>
</project>
```

You can test the script by changing directories to the cc-work-dir and typing

```
ant -f build-jakarta-lucene
```

With the delegate build script in place, we can proceed to enhance the empty XML configuration we previously created. CruiseControl uses the XML configuration to determine what projects to build and what reporting and alerting features to enable for any given project.

The configuration file is named config.xml by default, although you can use any other name and use the `configfile` command-line argument when running the CruiseControl script (cruisecontrol.sh or cruisecontrol.bat). The config XML file is shown in Listing 9-2 and its format is formally documented at http://cruisecontrol.sourceforge.net/main/configxml.html.

Listing 9-2. *CruiseControl XML Configuration File*

```
<cruisecontrol>
    <!-- ================================================================= -->
    <!-- Project                                                           -->
    <!-- ================================================================= -->
    <project name="jakarta-lucene" buildafterfailed="true">
        <!-- ========================================================= -->
        <!-- Listeners                                                 -->
        <!-- ========================================================= -->
        <listeners>
            <currentbuildstatuslistener file="logs/jakarta-lucene/status.txt"/>
        </listeners>

        <!-- ========================================================= -->
        <!-- Modification Set                                          -->
        <!-- ========================================================= -->
        <modificationset quietperiod="60">
            <cvs localworkingcopy="checkout/jakarta-lucene"/>
        </modificationset>

        <!-- ========================================================= -->
        <!-- Schedule                                                  -->
        <!-- ========================================================= -->
        <schedule interval="60" >
            <ant
                buildfile="build-jakarta-lucene.xml"
                target="test"
                uselogger="true"
                usedebug="false"
            />
        </schedule>

        <!-- ========================================================= -->
        <!-- Logs                                                      -->
        <!-- ========================================================= -->
        <log dir="logs/jakarta-lucene">
            <merge dir="checkout/jakarta-lucene/build/test/" />
        </log>

    </project>

</cruisecontrol>
```

The CruiseControl file can contain zero or more projects. In each project element you can define the delegate build script to execute, how often to check the repository for changes and how to report the results of a build attempt.

Let's walk through the elements of the config.xml file. In the case of the example for Lucene, the listeners element contains one listener that logs the current build status to the file status.txt.

```
<listeners>
    <currentbuildstatuslistener file="logs/jakarta-lucene/status.txt"/>
</listeners>
```

Next, the modificationset element specifies where CruiseControl should check to determine if a build should be triggered. In the case of the example, CruiseControl will check the local working copy of the project for changes. The attribute quietperiod determines the time in seconds that CruiseControl will wait for it to determine that there are no check-ins occurring on the project. Set this parameter based on the habits of your team. For example I like to set this parameter to about 120 seconds, since I like to take my time with the check-in comments.

```
<modificationset quietperiod="60">
    <cvs localworkingcopy="checkout/jakarta-lucene"/>
</modificationset>
```

The interval attribute of the schedule element determines how often CruiseControl will check the modification set to determine whether to run the build. Set this attribute based on the number of projects on your build machine and the priority and frequency of change of those projects.

The ant element is one of the possible actions to perform when a build is deemed necessary. In here we are invoking the delegate buildfile created for the Lucene project.

```
<schedule interval="60" >
    <ant
        buildfile="build-jakarta-lucene.xml"
        target="test"
        uselogger="true"
        usedebug="false"
    />
</schedule>
```

Finally, the log element determines the directory for the CruiseControl logs. The merge element tells CruiseControl to "merge" the JUnitReport XML files produced during the build of the Lucene project. In the case of the Lucene project those files are located in the build/test directory. You'll determine this by examining the build.xml or simply running the build and searching for the reports.

```
<log dir="logs/jakarta-lucene">
    <merge dir="checkout/jakarta-lucene/build/test/" />
</log>
```

With everything now set, let's fire up CruiseControl and watch it build the Lucene project. As done previously, change directories to the CruiseControl working directory and execute the cruisecontrol.sh script. In the output, you should see the project sources being retrieved from CVS and the build executing.

Refreshing the CruiseControl reporting Web application should reveal the Lucene project as shown in Figure 9-4.

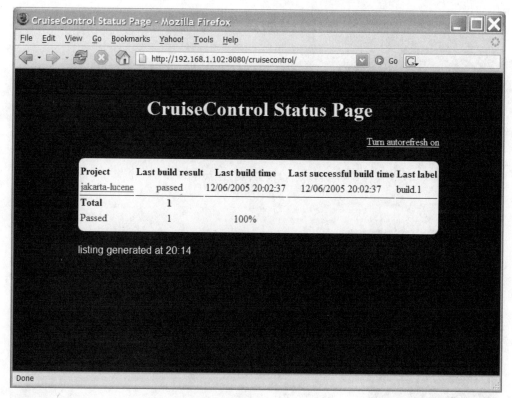

Figure 9-4. *A project under CruiseControl*

The CruiseControl reporting application provides information about the time of the last build and whether it was successful or not. If we drill down further by clicking on the project's name link, we are presented with a page that provides five tabs: Build Results, Test Results, XML Log File, Metrics, and a JMX Control Panel.

In the Build Results page you will find information about errors and warnings produced during the build, general information about the result of running the test suite, and a summary of any modifications since the last successful build. Figure 9-5 shows the Unit Tests summary for the Lucene project.

Figure 9-5. *Unit Tests summary under the Build Results page*

The Test Results page gives you a more detailed view of each test executed, including timings. Figure 9-6 shows the Test Results page for the Lucene project.

The metrics page provides a historical graph showing the distribution in time of good versus bad builds as well as a pie chart showing the percentage of good and bad builds. This view is a favorite of programming managers.

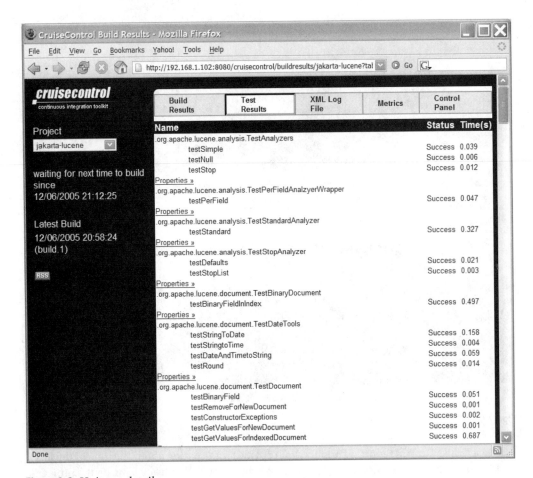

Figure 9-6. *Unit test details*

Notification Mechanisms

CruiseControl provides several publishers that can generate specific types of output after a build has been performed. The listener used in the sample config.xml notifies the CruiseControl reporting Web application about the latest build results. Typically in most development teams, developers use the Web application for problem resolution after they have been notified of the build failure via a more direct way such as email.

Email is one of the typical channels used for publishing the results of a build. CruiseControl provides two types of email publishers. The simple email publisher can generate a plain text email, while the more popular htmlemail can generate an email with hyperlinks to the reporting Web application. The HTML email is generated via a set of XSLT templates. The generated HTML email can be customized by providing your own XSLT files to transform the raw XML.

Listing 9-3 shows a typical configuration of the HTML email publisher.

Listing 9-3. *HTML Email Publisher Configuration*

```
<publishers>
    <htmlemail
        mailhost="localhost"
        skipusers="true"
        reportsuccess="fixes"
        subjectprefix="[build notification]"
        returnaddress="cc@integrallis.com"
        defaultsuffix="@integrallis.com"
        css="/opt/cruisecontrol/webapps/cruisecontrol/css/cruisecontrol.css"
        xsldir="/opt/cruisecontrol/webapps/cruisecontrol/xsl"
        logdir="logs/jakarta-lucene"
        >
        <always address="bigboss@integrallis.com"/>
        <failure address="group1@integrallis.com" />
        <success address="group2@integrallis.com" />
    </htmlemail>
</publishers>
```

Most of the attributes in the `htmlemail` element are related to the SMTP configuration or to the formatting of the outgoing email. The elements of interest are the three sub-elements `always`, `failure`, and `success`. The `always` element specifies that bigboss@integrallis.com will always get an email regardless of whether the build was a success or a failure, while the `failure` and `success` elements determine who gets an email in the case of a successful build or a failed one respectively.

The `skipusers` attribute can be set to false to enable individual developers to receive emails for all of the builds where they have made changes. You'll need to create a mapping of the CVS users to their respective email addresses. This is accomplished by adding map elements under the email element as shown here:

```
<map alias="cvsuser1" address="cvsuser1@integrallis.com" />
<map alias="cvsuser2" address="cvsuser2@integrallis.com" />
```

CruiseControl provides many other publishers including FTP, instant messaging via Jabbers XMPP protocol, and RSS. There are also a variety of applications to monitor your CruiseControl builds. As a user of the Firefox browser, I've found the CruiseControl extension created by Dmitri Maximovich very useful (Firefox extensions can be found at `https://addons.mozilla.org`). Figure 9-7 shows the Firefox CruiseControl extension.

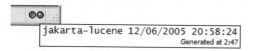

Figure 9-7. *Monitoring your CruiseControl builds in the Firefox browser*

TechConf on CruiseControl

In the previous section you learned how to configure a Java application which used JUnit for testing under CruiseControl. On the other hand, the TechConf project uses TestNG as its testing framework. The steps to setup the TechConf application are similar. First we check out the TechConf application under the directory checkout/techconf. In the cc-work-dir we have the delegate Ant script called build-techconf.xml as shown in Listing 9-4.

Listing 9-4. *Delegate Buildfile for TechConf Project*

```
<project name="cc-techconf-build" default="test" basedir="checkout/techconf">
    <!-- ================================================================ -->
    <!-- Target: cvs                                                      -->
    <!-- Retrieves the latest changes from the CVS repository             -->
    <!-- ================================================================ -->
    <target name="cvs">
        <cvs command="up -d -P"/>
    </target>


    <!-- ================================================================ -->
    <!-- Target: test                                                     -->
    <!-- Invokes the test target in the TechConf project buildfile        -->
    <!-- ================================================================ -->
    <target name="test" depends="cvs">
        <ant antfile="build.xml" target="all-clean-first" />
    </target>
</project>
```

In the CruiseControl config.xml file we incorporate the project by adding a new project element as shown in Listing 9-5.

Listing 9-5. *Project Element for the TechConf Application*

```
<!-- ================================================================ -->
<!-- Project                                                          -->
<!-- ================================================================ -->
<project name="techconf" buildafterfailed="true">

    <!-- ================================================================ -->
    <!-- Listeners                                                        -->
    <!-- ================================================================ -->
    <listeners>
        <currentbuildstatuslistener file="logs/techconf/status.txt"/>
    </listeners>
```

```
<!-- ================================================================ -->
<!-- Modification Set                                                 -->
<!-- ================================================================ -->
<modificationset quietperiod="25">
    <cvs localworkingcopy="checkout/techconf"/>
</modificationset>


<!-- ================================================================ -->
<!-- Schedule                                                         -->
<!-- ================================================================ -->
<schedule interval="60" >
    <ant
        antscript="/opt/cruisecontrol/apache-ant-1.6.3/bin/ant"
        buildfile="build-techconf.xml"
        target="test"
        uselogger="true"
        usedebug="false"
    />
</schedule>


<!-- ================================================================ -->
<!-- Logs                                                             -->
<!-- ================================================================ -->
<log dir="logs/techconf">
    <merge dir="checkout/techconf/docs/tests/" />
</log>

</project>
```

The crucial element for CruiseControl to work with TestNG is to correctly specify the location where the TestNG-generated XML files reside, which corresponds to the value of the attribute outputDir in the TestNG Ant task. In Chapter 8 we set that value to the docs/tests directory. In the log element in Listing 9-5 we set the merge directory property to the value of the outputDir relative to the root of the cc-work-dir.

Since we own the TechConf project, we can purposely introduce an error and check the CruiseControl results. In one of the TechConf methods, we can add an assertion that will fail such as Assert.assertEquals(true, false). Figure 9-8 shows the result of the build in the CruiseControl Web application.

In Figure 9-8 we added the failed assertion to the method testNewsItemsCreation in the class BlogEntryTest. CruiseControl will show you the errors in the build (with a full stack trace) as well as the changes introduced in the last check-in.

BUILD COMPLETE - build.28

Date of build:	01/28/2006 13:06:40
Time to build:	2 minutes 23 seconds
Last changed:	01/28/2006 11:36:40
Last log entry:	Failed test to trigger CruiseControl notification

Build Artifacts

Errors/Warnings: (235)

...

Unit Tests: (20)

failure   testNewsItemCreation   TechConf Tests

Unit Test Error Details: (1)

Test: testNewsItemCreation

Class: TechConf Tests

Type: java.lang.AssertionError

Message: expected:<false> but was:<true>

```
java.lang.AssertionError: expected:<false> but was:<true>
        at org.testng.Assert.fail(Assert.java:73)
        at org.testng.Assert.failNotEquals(Assert.java:345)
        at org.testng.Assert.assertEquals(Assert.java:94)
        at org.testng.Assert.assertEquals(Assert.java:191)
        at org.testng.Assert.assertEquals(Assert.java:198)
        at com.integrallis.techconf.dto.BlogEntryTest.testNewsItemCreation(BlogEntryTest.java:59)
        at sun.reflect.NativeMethodAccessorImpl.invoke0(Native Method)
        at sun.reflect.NativeMethodAccessorImpl.invoke(NativeMethodAccessorImpl.java:39)
        at sun.reflect.DelegatingMethodAccessorImpl.invoke(DelegatingMethodAccessorImpl.java:25)
        at java.lang.reflect.Method.invoke(Method.java:585)
        at org.testng.internal.MethodHelper.invokeMethod(MethodHelper.java:435)
        at org.testng.internal.Invoker.invokeMethod(Invoker.java:356)
        at org.testng.internal.Invoker.invokeTestMethods(Invoker.java:523)
        at org.testng.internal.TestMethodWorker.run(TestMethodWorker.java:89)
        at org.testng.TestRunner.privateRun(TestRunner.java:622)
        at org.testng.TestRunner.run(TestRunner.java:505)
        at org.testng.SuiteRunner.privateRun(SuiteRunner.java:200)
        at org.testng.SuiteRunner.run(SuiteRunner.java:126)
        at org.testng.TestNG.run(TestNG.java:285)
        at org.testng.TestNG.privateMain(TestNG.java:372)
        at org.testng.TestNG.main(TestNG.java:321)
```

Modifications since last successful build: (1)

modified   bsbodden   src/test/com/integrallis/techconf/dto/BlogEntryTest.java   Failed test to trigger CruiseControl notification

Figure 9-8. *Breaking the TechConf build*

Metrics

A view that can communicate a lot about the state and history of a project is the metrics view in the CruiseControl Web application. Figure 9-9 shows the metrics for the TechConf application (before we introduced the error in the previous section).

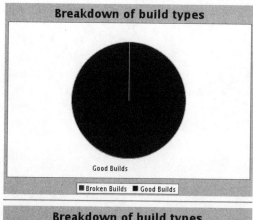

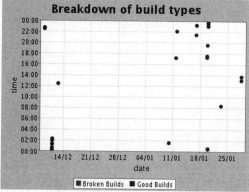

Figure 9-9. *CruiseControl Metrics view*

Summary

In this chapter you've learned the value of Continuous Integration. If one thing is clear, it is that the success of CI depends heavily on making developers embrace the concept of not holding on to changes for longer than a day and that a test-first approach is the easiest way to have a measurement of when to check code back in. Tools like CruiseControl replace the hodgepodge of ad hoc tools and shell scripts that developers cobbled together in the past to accomplish CI. Automation in the case of CI is the key to adoption. The hours spent setting up a build server will save you and your team countless hours of productivity loss in the future.

CHAPTER 10

■■■

Additional Topics

To build a feature complete J2EE Web application, you'll need more than what an application server or any framework can provide by itself, including technologies that enable you to write less and cleaner code to tools that provide searching capabilities and RSS feeds to your Web application.

In this chapter we'll explore some of the tools and technologies that fill in the gaps when developing Java Web applications. Although we won't cover all the details of each technology, this chapter should help you get started with some of the many tools available in the open source ecosystem and what you need to do to integrate them into your development.

AOP with AspectJ

One technology that has greatly simplified the way we develop software is aspect-oriented programming (AOP), which offers extension mechanisms to OOP for decomposing a solution to a problem domain into encapsulated entities. AOP techniques allow us to apply certain behaviors to several parts of an application or completely change or enhance the behavior of certain parts of an application in a declarative and unobtrusive way.

The principles of procedural and object-oriented programming all hinge on the concept of modularization. But there are aspects of a software system that are inherently hard to modularize. This is especially true of aspects that touch many areas of a system. For example, logging and tracing is the quintessential example of an aspect of a software application that crosses many boundaries, a cross-cutting aspect. Although we can somewhat modularize logging by encapsulating all logging functionality in logging libraries, the usage of the logging libraries itself is dispersed all over the code base. AOP techniques can help us cope with the cost of redundant and tangled code. In the case of logging we see the same fragment of code in many places, which causes many problems. The biggest problem is that the logging statements, although they help us diagnose problems, make the code less legible than it could be. Logging is a non-business requirement of the application that ends up obscuring the business-related code, making it harder to understand. The next problem is maintenance; with the code dispersed all over the code base it becomes difficult to apply changes consistently to the way the logging is being used.

AOP is about creating recipes that can be applied to a code base without changing the code itself at development time. In the logging and tracing scenario, this might equate to a rule like, "for all methods in packages A and B, execute this code before any method call," or "for any exception thrown in any method with a name that starts with save, output a logging statement."

In AOP parlance an aspect is the implementation of a cross-cutting concern encapsulated into a unit of functionality. An aspect is the code that implements the functionality you want to be applied to one or more places in your code. How an aspect interacts with your code is defined by the join point model (JPM). In AOP a join point defines the places or events in your code where an aspect can be applied such as the constructor of a class, before, around, or after the execution of a method, before the value of a class member is modified or when an exception is thrown or handled. In an aspect definition, you declare which join points to apply the aspect. These join point declarations are called pointcuts which are a way to express one or more join points using patterns or regular expressions. The actual code that is applied to a join point is called an advice. The act of applying an advice to a join point is called weaving. Weaving can occur statically at compile time, or it can happen dynamically at runtime.

■**Note** While an AOP advice provides for a dynamic way to apply an aspect in a systemwide manner, an introduction offers a way to modify or augment a class statically. I will not cover introductions in this chapter, but it is a feature that you will most likely use as you delve deeper into the capabilities of AspectJ.

AOP-like techniques have been used for years, but not until recently have extensions to a language been created to support AOP. Most open source implementations are based on dynamic proxies and reflection. AspectJ is the pioneering aspect-oriented extension to the Java programming language, and it's partially the brainchild of Gregor Kiczales and colleagues, who produced some of the earliest works on AOP in the mid-'90s. AspectJ began life as a Xerox PARC project partially funded by NIST ATP (National Institute of Standards and Technology Advanced Technology Program) and DARPA (Defense Advanced Research Projects Agency). The framework originated from the ideas and conclusions of research into several areas of software engineering, particularly meta-object protocols and reflective and adaptive programming. The AspectJ project was donated to the Eclipse Foundation's project in December 2002. AspectJ's home on the Web can be found at http://eclipse.org/aspectj.

AspectJ is a collection of tools to extend the Java language with support for AOP constructs. At the heart of the system is the AspectJ compiler (ajc), which extends the functionality of the javac compiler with the ability to compile aspects and weave them statically into the code. AspectJ-enhanced bytecode can run on any compliant standard Java VM.

Obtaining and Installing AspectJ

AspectJ is distributed as a JAR-based installer. At the time of this writing the file is aspectj-1.5.0.jar. To run the installer simply type

```
java -jar aspectj-1.5.0.jar
```

The Java-based installer will attempt to determine the location of the JDK on your machine, and then it will create the installation for the AspectJ tools and documentation as shown in Figure 10-1.

Follow the prompts and select a location for the AspectJ installation. After the installation is complete, a directory like that shown in Figure 10-2 will be created in the location of your choice.

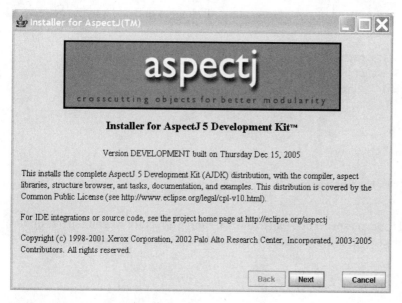

Figure 10-1. *AspectJ graphical installer*

Figure 10-2. *AspectJ installation directory*

The lib directory contains the JAR files needed to use AspectJ. Add the aspectjrt.jar file located in the lib directory to your Java classpath. The bin directory contains convenient UNIX shell and Windows batch scripts. To simplify running the AspectJ tools add the bin directory to your system's executable path.

AspectJ provides a graphical tool called the AspectJ browser that enables you to build and run AspectJ-enhanced Java programs. Although useful, we will not cover it here and instead will cover the usage of AspectJ from within an Ant buildfile and also from within the Eclipse IDE via the AJDT plug-in. For more information on using the AspectJ browser, see `http://www.eclipse.org/aspectj/doc/released/devguide/ajbrowser.html`.

AspectJ and Ant

Let's start by modifying the Ant build script created in Chapter 3 to use the AspectJ ajc compiler rather than javac. First we'll add the JAR files contained in the AspectJ lib directory under the directory lib/aspectj of the TechConf application. The required JARs are

- aspectjlib.jar

- aspectjrt.jar

- aspectjtools.jar

- aspectjweaver.jar

To add the JARs to the classpath we can create a path element and add it to the project's classpath as shown next:

```
<path id="aspectj.class.path">
    <fileset dir="${aspectj-lib}">
        <include name="*.jar"/>
    </fileset>
</path>

<path id="class.path">
    ...
    <path refid="aspectj.class.path"/>
</path>
```

We will keep all AspectJ aspect code (.aj) in its own source directory named aspects under the src directory and add it to the global path of code to be compiled as shown next:

```
...
<property name="src-aspects" location="${src}/aspects" />

<path id="all.source.path">
    ...
    <pathelement path="${src-aspects}"/>
</path>
```

To use the AspectJ ajc compiler, we use a taskdef element to import the tasks as shown next:

```
<!-- AspectJ - eclipse.org -->
<taskdef
    resource="org/aspectj/tools/ant/taskdefs/aspectjTaskdefs.properties"
    classpathref="aspectj.class.path"
/>
```

Finally we can modify the compile target to use the iajc task as shown:

```
<!-- =================================================================== -->
<!-- Target: compile                                                     -->
<!-- Compiles all classes                                                -->
<!-- =================================================================== -->
<target name="compile" depends="compile-init"
        description="Compiles all classes (JDK1.5)">
    <iajc source="1.5"
        destdir="${classes}"
        classpathref="class.path"
        debug="on"
        showWeaveInfo="${aspectj.showWeaveInfo}">
```

```
    <sourceroots>
        <path refid="all.source.path" />
    </sourceroots>
  </iajc>
</target>
```

The only new property used in this target is the `aspectj.showWeaveInfo` which you can define in the build.properties file with an initial value of "false". Now that the buildfile has been modified to use AspectJ we can move to create our first AspectJ aspect. At this point the build should work in exactly the same way it did previously. Since there are no aspects defined, the compiled bytecode will be equivalent to that produced with the javac compiler.

In order to run the AspectJ-enhanced code you'll also need to include the aspectjrt.jar file in your deployable archive on JBoss or Tomcat.

In the next section we will learn how to use AspectJ to fulfill several cross-cutting concerns in the TechConf Web application. This section is by no means an exhaustive coverage of AOP or AspectJ but a pragmatic introduction in the context of a real application.

Logging and Tracing with AspectJ

The logging and tracing aspect will allow us to trap method calls from specific packages and cause log statements to be issued without polluting the application code with logging statements. For the actual logging we will use the Jakarta Commons Logging package (http://jakarta.apache.org/commons/logging/), which provides a useful abstraction over the most common logging packages including Log4J and the JSE Logging.

In AspectJ an aspect is defined using syntax that is an extension of the Java language. Beside the special constructs provided by AspectJ, any other valid Java code is by definition valid code in an AspectJ file. The simplest, empty aspect we can create in AspectJ is

```
public aspect LoggingAndTracingAspect {}
```

As you can see, the keyword aspect is an extension to the Java language. Of course, the aspect previously defined doesn't do anything at all. First, let us add code to determine where our aspect will be applied. In AOP lingo, we are going to define pointcuts that will be used by the AspectJ compiler to decide at which join points the aspect will be applied. Join points are points in the dynamic call graph. In AspectJ there are several kinds of join points:

- Method and constructor call

- Method and constructor execution

- Field get and set

- Exception handler execution

- Static and dynamic initialization

- Advice execution

The definition of the aspect's pointcuts is the criteria for when to use the aspect and it is provided via a rich pointcut expression language (as well as Java 1.5 annotations and XML-based syntax). Let's start with defining a pointcut called `traceMethods` that

- Includes the execution of any methods in any class with a name ending in DAO

- Includes the execution of any methods in the service package

- Excludes the current aspect

- Excludes any call to the toString, equals, and hashCode methods

Using the AspectJ pointcut expression language, we can define the desired pointcut as follows:

```
pointcut traceMethods() :
    execution(* com.integrallis.techconf.dao.*DAO.*(..))
    || execution(* com.integrallis.techconf.service.*.*(..))
    && !within(LoggingAndTracingAspect)
    && !cflow(execution(int *.hashCode()))
    && !cflow(execution(boolean *.equals(..)))
    && !cflow(execution(String *.toString()));
```

Pointcuts in AspectJ are declared using the pointcut keyword. I like to think of join points as data and pointcuts as queries. As you can see, the AspectJ pointcut expression language allows you to use wildcards as shown in the first two execution elements. Notice that the wildcards can be used to indicate a method return value, package names, and formal parameters in a syntactical way. Expressions can be combined logically with and && or || and negation ! operators.

Pointcuts can be named (as in the example) or they can be anonymous. By naming a pointcut, you have the ability to reuse the pointcut in several advices, while an anonymous pointcut is used inline in the advice itself.

The execution operator used in the first two elements of the pointcut captures the body of a method. A similar operator, the call operator, can also be used, which captures the execution point of a method before the call to method but after its arguments are evaluated.

The within operator is used here to exclude the actual aspect from being adviced. This brings to attention two important concepts in an AOP implementation: advice precedence and the application of aspects against other aspects. These concepts are out of the scope of this chapter but should be kept in mind when developing more-advanced aspects.

Finally the three cflow operators are used to exclude any code in the control flow of the execution of any hashCode, equals, and toString methods. The cflow operator is a control flow–based pointcut operator that is used to match join points in the execution flow or dynamic context of another join point, including the join point itself (to exclude the join point, use cflowbelow). The control flow operators are powerful since they give you the ability to follow the code as if you had control over a dynamic sequence diagram.

With the pointcut defined, we can move to the implementation of the advice. AspectJ provides three kinds of advice: before advice, after advice, and around advice. The before and after advice types allow you to insert functionality before and after the execution of a join point. In the case of the LoggingAndTracing aspect advice, we'll use the before and after advices to log statements reporting the beginning and end of a method's execution. The code for the before and after advice is shown next:

```
before() : traceMethods() {
    Signature signature = thisJoinPointStaticPart.getSignature();
    traceMethodWithMessage(signature, "Entering");
}

after() returning : traceMethods() {
    Signature signature = thisJoinPointStaticPart.getSignature();
    traceMethodWithMessage(signature, "Exiting");
}
```

Notice that the advice type is followed, after the semicolon, by the pointcut to which it applies. The before advice on traceMethods is pretty straightforward; in the body of the advice we are using the field thisJoinPointStaticPart, which gives us access to the signature of the method being advised. AspectJ provides several ways to access the context of the current advice. The signature of the method is then passed to the custom method traceMethodWithMessage alongside the message string parameter "Entering".

The after advice can be defined for the different outcomes of a method call. It can either apply after the successful return from the method call, after an exception, or in both cases. In our case we want the advice to apply after a successful method call as signified by the keyword "returning".

If we want to log methods which throw an exception, we can use an after advice as follows:

```
after() throwing(Throwable t) : traceMethods() {
    Signature signature = thisJoinPointStaticPart.getSignature();
    traceMethodWithMessage(signature, "Exception", t);
}
```

The traceMethodWithMessage methods make use of the Jakarta Commons Logging package to perform the actual logging as shown next:

```
private void traceMethodWithMessage(Signature signature, String message) {
    traceMethodWithMessage(signature, message, null);
}

private void traceMethodWithMessage(Signature signature,
                                    String message, Throwable t) {
    Log log = LogFactory.getLog(signature.getDeclaringType());
    if (log.isTraceEnabled()) {
        String logMessage = message + " [" + getMethodName(signature) +
                            "]" + (t != null ? t : "");
        log.trace(logMessage);
    }
}

private String getMethodName(Signature signature) {
    return signature.getDeclaringType().getName() + "." + signature.getName();
}
```

The method getMethodName is used to extract and format the name of the method being adviced so that it can be used as part of the logging message.

Listing 10-1 shows the LoggingAndTracing aspect in its entirety. Notice that I have also declared this aspect as preceding any other aspects explicitly using declare precedence.

Listing 10-1. *The LoggingAndTracing Aspect for the TechConf Application*

```
package com.integrallis.techconf.logging;

import org.aspectj.lang.*;
import org.apache.commons.logging.Log;
import org.apache.commons.logging.LogFactory;

/**
 * Basic Aspect for Logging and Tracing
 * It traces entering, exiting and exceptions for
 * methods implementing the interfaces in the DAO and
 * Services packages
 */
public aspect LoggingAndTracingAspect {

    declare precedence : LoggingAndTracingAspect, *;

    pointcut traceMethods() :
        execution(* com.integrallis.techconf.dao.*DAO.*(..))
        || execution(* com.integrallis.techconf.service.*.*(..))
        && !within(LoggingAndTracingAspect)
        && !cflow(execution(boolean *.equals(..)))
        && !cflow(execution(int *.hashCode()))
        && !cflow(execution(String *.toString()));

    before() : traceMethods() {
        Signature signature = thisJoinPointStaticPart.getSignature();
        traceMethodWithMessage(signature, "Entering");
    }

    after() returning : traceMethods() {
        Signature signature = thisJoinPointStaticPart.getSignature();
        traceMethodWithMessage(signature, "Exiting");
    }

    after() throwing(Throwable t) : traceMethods() {
        Signature signature = thisJoinPointStaticPart.getSignature();
        traceMethodWithMessage(signature, "Exception", t);
    }

    //
```

```
// private methods
//

private void traceMethodWithMessage(Signature signature, String message) {
    traceMethodWithMessage(signature, message, null);
}

private void traceMethodWithMessage(Signature signature,
                                String message, Throwable t) {
    Log log = LogFactory.getLog(signature.getDeclaringType());
    if (log.isTraceEnabled()) {
        String logMessage = message + " [" + getMethodName(signature) +
                        "]" + (t != null ? t : "");
        log.trace(logMessage);
    }
}

private String getMethodName(Signature signature) {
    return signature.getDeclaringType().getName() + "." + signature.getName();
}
}
```

Using the LoggingAndTracing Aspect

To see the effects of the LoggingAndTracing aspect in the JBoss-based implementation of the
TechConf application, we need to configure the logging subsystem, which is Log4J. Commons
Logging is a thin API that can detect and wrap the underlying logging mechanism, therefore
our logging statements in the aspect should cascade down to the Log4J logger. To configure
log4j, edit the file log4j.xml located in the JBOSS_HOME/server/conf directory and add a Log4J
appender and a category as shown in Listing 10-2.

Listing 10-2. *Configuring Log4J Under JBoss*

```
<?xml version="1.0" encoding="UTF-8"?>
<!DOCTYPE log4j:configuration SYSTEM "log4j.dtd">
<log4j:configuration xmlns:log4j="http://jakarta.apache.org/log4j/" debug="false">
    <appender name="TechConfLog" class="org.apache.log4j.FileAppender">
        <errorHandler class="org.jboss.logging.util.OnlyOnceErrorHandler"/>
        <param name="Append" value="false"/>
        <param name="File" value="${jboss.server.home.dir}/log/techconf.log"/>
        <layout class="org.apache.log4j.PatternLayout">
            <param name="ConversionPattern" value="%d %-5p [%c] %m%n"/>
        </layout>
    </appender>
    <category name="com.integrallis">
        <priority value="TRACE"/>
        <appender-ref ref="TechConfLog"/>
    </category>
```

...

The appender is a file appender to log statements to a log file in the log directory of the JBoss server configuration directory. The level of logging can be increased and decreased by changing the `priority` element under any `category` element such as the com.integrallis logging category shown in Listing 10-2.

Building and deploying the application should result in output in the techconf.log file similar to that shown next:

```
2005-12-17 20:51:33,546 DEBUG [com.integrallis.techconf.ejb.ConferenceServiceBean]
 Entering [com.integrallis.techconf.ejb.ConferenceServiceBean.getConferenceSummary]
2005-12-17 20:51:33,546 DEBUG
[com.integrallis.techconf.ejb.dao.hibernate.ConferenceDAOBean] Entering
[com.integrallis.techconf.ejb.dao.hibernate.ConferenceDAOBean.getConference]
2005-12-17 20:51:33,578 DEBUG
[com.integrallis.techconf.ejb.dao.hibernate.ConferenceDAOBean] Exiting
[com.integrallis.techconf.ejb.dao.hibernate.ConferenceDAOBean.getConference]
2005-12-17 20:51:33,593 DEBUG [com.integrallis.techconf.ejb.ConferenceServiceBean]
 Exiting [com.integrallis.techconf.ejb.ConferenceServiceBean.getConferenceSummary]
```

AJDT

The `LoggingAndTracing` aspect shows the basic functionality that can be achieved with AspectJ by modularizing a concern. But to do anything complex with AOP, you need good tool support. Understanding the effects of aspects on your program is indispensable when working with AOP. The AspectJ Development Tools (AJDT) are a collection of Eclipse plug-ins that provides tool support for editing, building, and debugging AspectJ applications.

The easiest way to install the AJDT plug-in is to use the Eclipse software updates feature. To do this select Help ➤ Software Updates ➤ Find and Install. Select "Search for new features to install" and click Next. Add a new remote update site by selecting New Remote Site. In the dialog enter "AJDT" for the name and `http://download.eclipse.org/technology/ajdt/31/update` for the location.

AJDT adds decorations related to AspectJ to the Eclipse gutter. For example, in Figure 10-3 we can see the decoration (a curved arrow pointing to the left) related to the before advice of the `LoggingAndTracing` aspect. If you hover over the decoration you can see a pop-up balloon indicating the number of AspectJ markers.

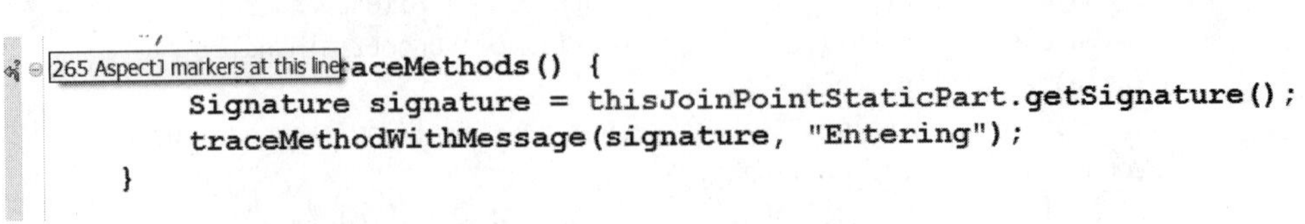

```
265 AspectJ markers at this line  raceMethods() {
            Signature signature = thisJoinPointStaticPart.getSignature();
            traceMethodWithMessage(signature, "Entering");
    }
```

Figure 10-3. *AJDT gutter decorations*

Right-clicking on the gutter decoration will reveal a context menu from which you can see the methods being advised by this particular advice as shown on Figure 10-4.

Figure 10-4. *Viewing adviced methods*

On a method in an advised class, the gutter decoration is a straight arrow pointing to the right. Hovering over the decoration reveals once again the number of AspectJ markers, as shown in Figure 10-5.

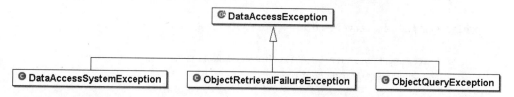

Figure 10-5. *Gutter decorations on an adviced method*

Right-clicking on the gutter decoration reveals the Advised By context menu choice, which reveals that the method is being advised by the three advices provided by the LoggingAndTracing aspect.

Translating Exceptions

The second aspect that we will explore is an aspect used in the implementation of the DAO pattern in Chapter 5. The premise is that the methods can throw one of the many child classes of the Hibernate exception. In our design of the DAO layer will throw customized exceptions. The idea is to map the one or more fine-grained Hibernate exceptions to our simpler custom DAO exceptions. The custom DAO exception hierarchy is shown in Figure 10-6.

```
                    DataAccessException
                           △
          ┌────────────────┼────────────────┐
DataAccessSystemException  ObjectRetrievalFailureException  ObjectQueryException
```

Figure 10-6. *Custom DAO exceptions*

To accomplish this without AOP, you would wrap each method call to Hibernate that could result in a Hibernate Exception in order to catch the thrown exception and throw one of the custom DAO exceptions. It is easy to see how this can result in a great amount of redundant code that would pollute the DAO code. Instead, the code shown in Listing 10-3 shows an aspect that can accomplish this transformation.

Listing 10-3. *HibernateExceptionConverter Aspect*

```java
package com.integrallis.techconf.dao;

import org.hibernate.HibernateException;
import org.hibernate.ObjectDeletedException;
import org.hibernate.ObjectNotFoundException;
import org.hibernate.UnresolvableObjectException;
import org.hibernate.WrongClassException;
import org.hibernate.QueryException;

import com.integrallis.techconf.dao.exception.*;

public aspect HibernateExceptionConverterAspect {
    pointcut daoClasses() :
        call(* com.integrallis.techconf.ejb.dao.hibernate.*DAO*.*(..));
    pointcut testClasses() :
        call(* com.integrallis.techconf.dao.hibernate.*Test.*(..));

    Object around() : daoClasses() || testClasses() {
        try {
            return proceed();
        }
        catch (Throwable t) {
            convertAndThrow(t);
        }
        return null;
    }

    /**
     * Converts a HibernateException to a custom DAO exception
     * @param t
     */
    public static void convertAndThrow(Throwable t) {
        /**
         * Catch any Hibernate QueryExceptions and retrow
         * the as ObjectQueryException
         */
        if (t instanceof QueryException) {
            QueryException ex = (QueryException)t;
            ObjectQueryException oqe = new ObjectQueryException(t);
            oqe.setQueryString(ex.getQueryString());
            throw oqe;
        }
        /**
         * Catch Hibernate's Object retrieval exceptions and retrow
         * as ObjectRetrievalException
         */
```

```
        else if (t instanceof UnresolvableObjectException) {
            UnresolvableObjectException ex = (UnresolvableObjectException)t;
            throw new ObjectRetrievalFailureException(ex.getEntityName(),
                ex.getIdentifier(), ex.getMessage(), ex);
        }
        else if (t instanceof ObjectNotFoundException) {
            ObjectNotFoundException ex = (ObjectNotFoundException)t;
            throw new ObjectRetrievalFailureException(ex.getEntityName(),
                ex.getIdentifier(), ex.getMessage(), ex);
        }
        else if (t instanceof ObjectDeletedException) {
            ObjectDeletedException ex = (ObjectDeletedException)t;
            throw new ObjectRetrievalFailureException(ex.getEntityName(),
                ex.getIdentifier(), ex.getMessage(), ex);
        }
        else if (t instanceof WrongClassException) {
            WrongClassException ex = (WrongClassException)t;
            throw new ObjectRetrievalFailureException(ex.getEntityName(),
                ex.getIdentifier(), ex.getMessage(), ex);
        }
        /**
         * Catch any HibernateException
         */
        else if (t instanceof HibernateException) {
            throw new DataAccessSystemException(t);
        }
        /**
         * If hibernate throws anything else that is not a HibernateException
         * or a child of it, then retrow it as a RuntimeException
         */
        else {
            throw new RuntimeException(t);
        }
    }
}
}
```

The aspect defines two pointcuts, the daoClasses and the testClasses pointcuts. The daoClasses pointcut defines all the classes in the DAO packages, while the testClasses pointcut is used to cover testing classes. In this aspect we use the around advice, which is used to wrap the implementation of the advised methods in a try-catch block used to trap the Hibernate Exceptions and throw the equivalent DAO custom exception as determined by the convertAndThrow method.

Other Applications of AOP

In this chapter we explored some very basic applications of AOP in the context of the TechConf application. Both of the problems tackled involved non-business system concerns, logging, and exception mapping. AOP techniques can also be used to enhance and improve the design of business concerns in an application.

RSS with Informa

Today, one of the features that seem prevalent in most websites is the addition of syndicated materials from blogs, news sites, and any other newslike feed. The RSS (Rich Site Summary/RDF Site Summary) and Atom protocols specify how to format XML documents for syndicating and aggregating list-oriented information. Using RSS you can create a data feed of headline, article, or blog entries summaries for a website, and you can also consume other sites' feeds to enhance the content of your website or application. The XML syndication protocols allow systems to process, transform, or format the information from a feed in a consistent manner. (Remember the old days of HTML screen scrapping?)

A website feed or channel is available via HTTP just like any other resource on a Web server. The feed provides metadata about several aspects of the data such as update frequency. The Informa RSS library is a pure Java open source API for producing and handling RSS and Atom feeds. Informa emerged as the result of the merging of the underlying libraries of two Java RSS aggregator programs.

One of the problems posed by feed producers and consumers is the different protocols available. With RSS we have three different flavors: RSS 0.9x, RSS 1.0, and RSS 2.0. Informa aims at providing a unified object model for a feed channel object model regardless of the format of the feed. Informa can be used to create a feed in any of the supported formats by using the Informa object model. Informa can also be used to aggregate feeds from different sources efficiently. Informa's object model can be persisted via Hibernate, and integration with the Lucene search engine is provided for efficient full-text searching of a feed's content.

Figure 10-7 shows a partial view of Informa's object model showing the FeedManager, which is used to serve instances of the FeedIF interface, which in turn is used to create instances of ChannelIF interface. From a ChannelIF, you can get the objects representing the feed items that are instances of the interface ItemIF. Figure 10-7 also shows some of the classes involved in the caching and refreshing of a feed.

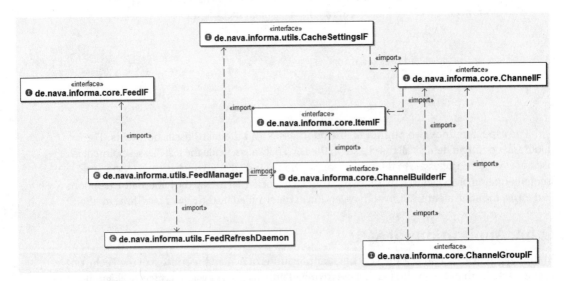

Figure 10-7. *Partial view of Informa's object model*

In the TechConf system, conference presenters can have their blog entries displayed on the conference website. To accomplish this, we are using a simple utility class in the TechConf application that uses the Informa API. The RSSFeedManager class keeps a static singleton FeedManager instance. The FeedManager is used to manage the feeds. Feeds are added to the manager using the addFeed method. Requests to retrieve a feed using getFeed or addFeed will return a cached copy if the feed is up to date, or it will be retrieved directly from the source. Listing 10-4 shows the complete code for the RSSFeedManager class.

Listing 10-4. *Informa-based* RSSFeedManager

```
package com.integrallis.techconf.rss;

import java.util.ArrayList;
import java.util.Collection;
import java.util.Collections;
import java.util.Iterator;
import java.util.List;

import de.nava.informa.core.ChannelIF;
import de.nava.informa.core.FeedIF;
import de.nava.informa.core.ItemIF;
import de.nava.informa.utils.FeedManager;
import de.nava.informa.utils.FeedManagerException;

public class RSSFeedManager {

    // singleton - temporary in-memory until informa updates their
    // persistence manager to use Hibernate 3.X
    private static FeedManager feedManager = new FeedManager();

    public ChannelIF getChannelForFeed(String feedUri) {
        FeedIF feed = null;
        try {
            feed = feedManager.addFeed(feedUri);
        } catch (FeedManagerException fme) {
            throw ServiceException("Could not retrieved the feed for : "
                                + feedUri, fme);
        }

        ChannelIF result = null;
        if (feed != null) {
            result = feed.getChannel();
        }

        return result;
    }
```

```
@SuppressWarnings("unchecked")
public List<ItemIF> getChannelItems(String feedUri) {
    return new ArrayList<ItemIF>(getChannelForFeed(feedUri).getItems());
}

@SuppressWarnings("unchecked")
public List<ItemIF> getChannelItems(String feedUri, int numberOfItems) {
    Collection items = getChannelForFeed(feedUri).getItems();
    Collection<ItemIF> selected = Collections.EMPTY_LIST;
    if (items.size() <= numberOfItems) {
        selected = items;
    }
    else {
        selected = new ArrayList(numberOfItems);

        for (Iterator<ItemIF> i = items.iterator();
             i.hasNext() && (selected.size() < numberOfItems);) {
            selected.add(i.next());
        }
    }
    return new ArrayList<ItemIF>(selected);
}
}
```

The RSSFeedManager class is used in the ConferenceServiceBean to retrieve blog entries for an entire conference (all blog entries for all presenters) or for a particular presenter. Following the pattern for developing services shown in Chapter 5, a presenter blog's URI is retrieved using the BlogDAO instance, then the RSSFeedManager is used to get all items (ItemIF) for the feed, and then those items are converted to the BlogEntry DTO using DynaDTO as shown in Listing 10-5.

Listing 10-5. *Usage of RSSFeedManager in the ConferenceServiceBean*

```
@Stateless
public class ConferenceServiceBean implements ConferenceService {

    ...

    // DAOs
    @EJB protected BlogDAO blogDAO;

    // DynaDTO Builders
    protected Builder blogEntryBuilder;

    ...
```

```
public List<BlogEntry> getBlogEntries(int conferenceId) {
    List<BlogLink> links = blogDAO.getAllBlogLinks(conferenceId);
    List<ItemIF> items = new ArrayList<ItemIF>();
    for (Iterator<BlogLink> i = links.iterator(); i.hasNext();) {
        BlogLink link = i.next();
        RSSFeedManager feedManager = new RSSFeedManager();
        items.addAll(feedManager.getChannelItems(link.getFeedURL()));
    }
    return blogEntryBuilder.buildList(items);
}
...
```

Summary

In this chapter you learned about AOP and how it can simplify and reduce the non-functional aspects from obscuring into the business logic of your applications. Although a simple introduction, I showed two uses of AOP that allow you to apply in a non-intrusive way systemwide policies to the system. AOP can also be used to solve functional or business requirements, and as you work more with an AOP framework you'll start finding new ways to apply this powerful technology to your applications.

In the second half of the chapter we explored the world of RSS feeds in Java by using the Informa library to add author feeds to the TechConf website. RSS feeds are a common feature of many of today's successful websites, and Informa provides a flexible solution to handle the multitude of available formats.

Index

Find it faster at http://superindex.apress.com

You Need the Companion eBook

Your purchase of this book entitles you to its companion eBook for only $10.

We believe this Apress title will prove so indispensable that you'll want to carry it with you everywhere, which is why we are offering the companion eBook for $10 to customers who purchase this book now. Convenient and fully searchable, the eBook version of any content-rich, page-heavy Apress book makes a valuable addition to your programming library. You can easily find, copy, and apply code—and then perform examples by quickly toggling between instructions and the application. Even simultaneously tackling a donut, diet soda, and complex code becomes simplified with hands-free eBooks!

Once you purchase this book, getting the $10 companion eBook is simple:

❶ Visit **www.apress.com/promo/tendollars/**.

❷ Complete a basic registration form to receive a randomly generated question about this title.

❸ Answer the question correctly in 60 seconds and you will receive a promotional code to redeem for the $10 eBook.

2560 Ninth Street • Suite 219 • Berkeley, CA 94710

Offer valid through 9/27/06.